George Adam Smith

The book of Isaiah

Vol. I

George Adam Smith

The book of Isaiah
Vol. I

ISBN/EAN: 9783743329362

Manufactured in Europe, USA, Canada, Australia, Japa

Cover: Foto ©Lupo / pixelio.de

Manufactured and distributed by brebook publishing software (www.brebook.com)

George Adam Smith

The book of Isaiah

THE
BOOK OF ISAIAH.

BY THE REV.
GEORGE ADAM SMITH, M.A.,
QUEEN'S CROSS, ABERDEEN.

IN TWO VOLUMES.
VOL. I.—ISAIAH I.–XXXIX.

FIFTH EDITION.

London:
HODDER AND STOUGHTON,
27, PATERNOSTER ROW.
MDCCCXC.

[All rights reserved.]

Printed by Hazell, Watson, & Viney, Ld., London and Aylesbury.

CONTENTS.

	PAGE
INTRODUCTION	ix
TABLE OF DATES	xvi

BOOK I.

ISAIAH'S PREFACE AND PROPHECIES TO THE DEATH OF AHAZ, 727 B.C.

CHAP.

I. ISAIAH'S PREFACE—THE ARGUMENT OF THE LORD . 3
    ISAIAH i.

II. THE THREE JERUSALEMS 19
    ISAIAH ii.—iv. 740—735 B.C.

III. THE VINEYARD OF THE LORD 35
    ISAIAH v.; ix. 8—x. 4. 735 B.C.

IV. ISAIAH'S CALL AND CONSECRATION 57
    ISAIAH vi. 740. WRITTEN 735 OR 727 B.C. (?).

V. THE WORLD IN ISAIAH'S DAY AND ISRAEL'S GOD . 91
    WITH A MAP.

VI. KING AND MESSIAH; PEOPLE AND CHURCH . . 103
    ISAIAH vii.—ix. 1—8. 735—732 B.C.

VII. THE MESSIAH 131

BOOK II.

PROPHECIES FROM THE ACCESSION OF HEZEKIAH TO THE DEATH OF SARGON,
727—705 B.C.

CHAP.		PAGE
VIII.	GOD'S COMMONPLACE	151
	Isaiah xxviii. About 725 B.C.	
IX.	ATHEISM OF FORCE AND ATHEISM OF FEAR	168
	Isaiah x. 5—34. About 721 B.C.	
X.	THE SPIRIT OF GOD IN MAN AND THE ANIMALS	179
	Isaiah xi.; xii. About 720 B.C. (?).	
XI.	DRIFTING TO EGYPT, 720—705 B.C.	196
	Isaiah xx. (711 B.C.); xxi. 1—10 (710 B.C.); xxxviii.; xxxix.	

BOOK III.

ORATIONS ON INTRIGUES WITH EGYPT, AND ORACLES ON FOREIGN NATIONS,
705—702 B.C.

XII.	ARIEL, ARIEL	209
	Isaiah xxix. About 703 B.C.	
XIII.	POLITICS AND FAITH	221
	Isaiah xxx. About 702 B.C.	
XIV.	THREE TRUTHS ABOUT GOD	238
	Isaiah xxxi. About 702 B.C.	
XV.	A MAN; OR, CHARACTER AND THE CAPACITY TO DISCRIMINATE CHARACTER	248
	Isaiah xxxii. 1—8. About 702 B.C. (?).	
XVI.	ISAIAH TO WOMEN	262
	Isaiah xxxii. 9—20. Date Uncertain.	
XVII.	ISAIAH TO THE FOREIGN NATIONS	271
	Isaiah xiv. 24—xxi.; xxiii. Various Dates.	
XVIII.	TYRE; OR, THE MERCENARY SPIRIT	288
	Isaiah xxiii. 702 B.C.	

BOOK IV.

JERUSALEM AND SENNACHERIB, 701 B.C.

CHAP.		PAGE
XIX.	AT THE LOWEST EBB	306
	ISAIAH i.; xxii. EARLY IN 701 B.C.	
XX.	THE TURN OF THE TIDE: MORAL EFFECTS OF FORGIVENESS	320
	ISAIAH xxii.; xxxiii. LATER IN 701 B.C.	
XXI.	OUR GOD A CONSUMING FIRE	331
	ISAIAH xxxiii.	
XXII.	THE RABSHAKEH; OR, LAST TRIALS OF FAITH	343
	ISAIAH xxxvi. 701 B.C.	
XXIII.	THIS IS THE VICTORY . . . . OUR FAITH	352
	ISAIAH xxxvii. 701 B.C.	
XXIV.	A REVIEW OF ISAIAH'S PREDICTIONS CONCERNING THE DELIVERANCE OF JERUSALEM .	363
XXV.	AN OLD TESTAMENT BELIEVER'S SICK-BED; OR, THE DIFFERENCE CHRIST HAS MADE . . .	375
	ISAIAH xxxviii.; xxxix. DATE UNCERTAIN.	
XXVI.	HAD ISAIAH A GOSPEL FOR THE INDIVIDUAL? .	389

BOOK V.

PROPHECIES NOT RELATING TO ISAIAH'S TIME.

XXVII.	BABYLON AND LUCIFER	405
	ISAIAH xii. 12–xiv. 23. DATE UNKNOWN.	
XXVIII.	THE EFFECT OF SIN ON OUR MATERIAL SURROUNDINGS	416
	ISAIAH xxiv. DATE UNKNOWN.	
XXIX.	GOD'S POOR	428
	ISAIAH xxv.—xxvii.; xxxiv.; xxxv. DATES UNKNOWN.	
XXX.	THE RESURRECTION	444
	ISAIAH xxvi.; xxvii.	
INDEX OF CHAPTERS . . .		453
INDEX OF SUBJECTS		455

INTRODUCTION.

AS the following Exposition of the Book of Isaiah does not observe the canonical arrangement of the chapters, a short introduction is necessary upon the plan which has been adopted.

The size and the many obscurities of the Book of Isaiah have limited the common use of it in the English tongue to single conspicuous passages, the very brilliance of which has cast their context and original circumstance into deeper shade. The intensity of the gratitude with which men have seized upon the more evangelical passages of Isaiah, as well as the attention which apologists for Christianity have too partially paid to his intimations of the Messiah, has confirmed the neglect of the rest of the Book. But we might as well expect to receive an adequate conception of a great statesman's policy from the epigrams and perorations of his speeches as to appreciate the message, which God has sent to the world through the Book of Isaiah, from a few lectures on isolated, and often dislocated, texts. No book of the Bible is less susceptible of treatment apart from the history out of which it sprang than the Book of Isaiah; and it may be added, that in the Old Testament at least there is none which, when set in its original circumstance and methodically considered as a whole, appeals with greater power to the modern conscience. Patiently to learn how these great prophecies were suggested by, and first met, the actual occasions of human life, is vividly to hear them speaking home to life still.

I have, therefore, designed an arrangement which embraces all the prophecies, but treats them in chronological order. I will endeavour to render their contents in terms which appeal to the modern conscience; but, in order to be successful, such an endeavour presupposes the exposition of them in relation to the history which gave them birth. In these volumes, therefore, narrative and historical exposition will take precedence of practical application.

Every one knows that the Book of Isaiah breaks into two parts between chaps. xxxix. and xl. Vol. I. of this Exposition covers chaps. i.—xxxix. Vol. II. will treat of chaps. xl.—lxvi. Again, within chaps. i.—xxxix. another division is apparent. The most of these chapters evidently bear upon events within Isaiah's own career, but some imply historical circumstances that did not arise till long after he had passed away. Of the five books into which I have divided Vol. I., the first four contain the prophecies relating to Isaiah's time (740—701 B.C.), and the fifth the prophecies which refer to later events (chaps. xiii. – xiv. 23; xxiv.—xxvii.; xxxiv.; xxxv.).

The prophecies, whose subjects fall within Isaiah's times, I have taken in chronological order, with one exception. This exception is chap. i., which, although it was published near the end of the prophet's life, I treat of first, because, from its position as well as its character, it is evidently intended as a preface to the whole book. The difficulty of grouping the rest of Isaiah's oracles and orations is great. The plan I have adopted is not perfect, but convenient. Isaiah's prophesying was determined chiefly by *four* Assyrian invasions of Palestine: the first, in 734—732 B.C., by Tiglath-pileser II., while Ahaz was on the throne; the second by Salmanassar and Sargon in 725—720, during which Samaria fell in 721; the third by Sargon, 712—710; the fourth by Sennacherib in 701, which last three occurred while Hezekiah was king of Judah. But outside the Assyrian invasions there were three other cardinal dates in Isaiah's life: 740, his call to be a prophet; 727, the death of Ahaz, his enemy, and the accession of his pupil, Hezekiah; and 705, the death of Sargon, for Sargon's death led to the rebellion of the Syrian States, and it was this rebellion which brought on Sennacherib's invasion. Taking all these dates into consideration, I have placed in Book I. all the prophecies of Isaiah from his call in 740 to the death of Ahaz in 727; they lead up to and illustrate Tiglath-pileser's invasion; they cover what I have ventured to call the prophet's apprenticeship, during which the theatre of his vision was mainly the internal life of his people, but he gained also his first outlook upon the world beyond. Book II. deals with the prophecies from the accession of Hezekiah in 727 to the death of Sargon in 705—a long period, but few prophecies, covering both Salmanassar's and Sargon's campaigns. Book III. is filled with the prophecies from 705 to 702, a numerous group, called forth from Isaiah by the rebellion and political activity in

Palestine consequent on Sargon's death and preliminary to Sennacherib's arrival. Book IV. contains the prophecies which refer to Sennacherib's actual invasion of Judah and siege of Jerusalem, in 701.

Of course, any chronological arrangement of Isaiah's prophecies must be largely provisional. Only some of the chapters are fixed to dates past possibility of doubt. The Assyriology which has helped us with these must yield further results before the controversies can be settled that exist with regard to the rest. I have explained in the course of the Exposition my reasons for the order which I have followed, and need only say here that I am still more uncertain about the generally received dates of chaps. x. 5—xi., xvii. 12—14 and xxxii. The religious problems, however, were so much the same during the whole of Isaiah's career that uncertainties of date, *if they are confined to the limits of that career*, make little difference to the exposition of the book.

Isaiah's doctrines, being so closely connected with the life of his day, come up for statement at many points of the narrative, in which this Exposition chiefly consists. But here and there I have inserted chapters dealing summarily with more important topics, such as The World in Isaiah's Day ; The Messiah ; Isaiah's Power of Prediction, with its evidence on the character of Inspiration ; and the question, Had Isaiah a Gospel for the Individual ? A short index will guide the student to Isaiah's teaching on other important points of theology and life, such as holiness, forgiveness, monotheism, immortality, the Holy Spirit, etc.

Treating Isaiah's prophecies chronologically as I

have done, I have followed a method which put me on the look-out for any traces of development that his doctrine might exhibit. I have recorded these as they occur, but it may be useful to collect them here. In chaps. ii.—iv. we have the struggle of the apprentice prophet's thoughts from the easy religious optimism of his generation, through unrelieved convictions of judgement for the whole people, to his final vision of the Divine salvation of a remnant. Again, chap. vii. following on chaps. ii.—vi. proves that Isaiah's belief in the Divine righteousness preceded, and was the parent of, his belief in the Divine sovereignty. Again, his successive pictures of the Messiah grow in contents, and become more spiritual. And again, he only gradually arrived at a clear view of the siege and deliverance of Jerusalem. One other fact of the same kind has impressed me since I wrote the exposition of chap. i. I have there stated that it is plain that Isaiah's conscience was perfect just because it consisted of two complementary parts: one of God the infinitely High, exalted in righteousness, far above the thoughts of His people, and the other of God the infinitely Near, concerned and jealous for all the practical details of their life. I ought to have added that Isaiah was more under the influence of the former in his earlier years, but that as he grew older and took a larger share in the politics of Judah it was the latter view of God, to which he most frequently gave expression. Signs of a development like these may be fairly used to correct or support the evidence which Assyriology affords for determining the chronological order of the chapters.

But these signs of development are more valuable for the proof they give that the Book of Isaiah contains the experience and testimony of a real life: a life that learned and suffered and grew, and at last triumphed. There is not a single word about the prophet's birth, or childhood, or fortune, or personal appearance, or even of his death. But between silence on his origin and silence on his end—and perhaps all the more impressively because of these clouds by which it is bounded—there shines the record of Isaiah's spiritual life and of the unfaltering career which this sustained,—clear and whole, from his commission by God in the secret experience of his own heart to his vindication in God's supreme tribunal of history. It is not only one of the greatest, but one of the most finished and intelligible, lives in history. My main purpose in expounding the book is to enable English readers, not only to follow its course, but to feel, and to be elevated by, its Divine inspiration.

I may state that this Exposition is based upon a close study of the Hebrew text of Isaiah, and that the translations are throughout my own, except in one or two cases where I have quoted from the revised English version.

With regard to the Revised Version of Isaiah, which I have had opportunities of thoroughly testing, I would like to say that my sense of the immense service which it renders to English readers of the Bible is only exceeded by my wonder that the Revisers have not gone just a very little farther, and adopted one or two simple contrivances which are in the line of their own improvements and would have greatly increased our large debt to them. For instance, why did they not make plain by inverted commas such undoubted interruptions of the prophet's own speech as that of the drunkards in chap. xxviii. 9, 10? Not to know that these verses are spoken in mockery of Isaiah, a mockery to which he replies in vv. 10—13, is to miss the meaning of the whole passage. Again, when they printed Job and the Psalms in metrical form, as well as the Hymn of Hezekiah, why did they not do the same with other poetical passages of Isaiah, particularly the great Ode on the King of Babylon in chap. xiv.? This is utterly spoiled in the form in which the Revisers have printed it. What English reader would guess that it was as much a piece of metre as any of the Psalms? Again, why have they so consistently rendered by the misleading word "judgement" a Hebrew term that no doubt sometimes means an act of doom, but far oftener the abstract quality of justice? It is such defects, along with a frequent failure to mark the proper emphasis in a sentence, that have led me to substitute a more literal version of my own.

I have not thought it necessary to discuss the question of the chronology of the period. This has been done so often and so recently. See Robertson Smith's *Prophets of Israel*, pp. 145, 402, 413, Driver's *Isaiah*, p. 12, or any good commentary.

I append a chronological table, and an index to the canonical chapters will be found before the index of subjects. The publishers have added a map of Isaiah's world in illustration of chap. **v.**

TABLE OF DATES.

B.C.
- **745.** Tiglath-pileser II. ascends the Assyrian Throne.
- **740.** Uzziah dies. Jotham becomes sole King of Judah. Isaiah's Inaugural Vision (Isa. vi.).
- **735.** Jotham dies. Ahaz succeeds. League of Syria and Northern Israel against Judah.
- **734—732.** Syrian Campaign of Tiglath-pileser II. Siege and Capture of Damascus. Invasion of Israel. Captivity of Zebulon, Naphtali and Galilee (Isa. ix. 1). Ahaz visits Damascus.
- **727.** Salmanassar IV. succeeds Tiglath-pileser II. Hezekiah succeeds Ahaz (or in 725?).
- **725.** Salmanassar marches on Syria.
- **722 or 721.** Sargon succeeds Salmanassar. Capture of Samaria. Captivity of all Northern Israel.
- **720 or 719.** Sargon defeats Egypt at Rafia.
- **711.** Sargon invades Syria (Isa. xx.). Capture of Ashdod.
- **709.** Sargon takes Babylon from Merodach-baladan.
- **705.** Murder of Sargon. Sennacherib succeeds.
- **701.** Sennacherib invades Syria. Capture of Coast Towns. Siege of Ekron and Battle of Eltekeh. Invasion of Judah. Submission of Hezekiah. Jerusalem spared. Return of Assyrians with the Rabshakeh to Jerusalem, while Sennacherib's Army marches on Egypt. Disaster to Sennacherib's Army near Pelusium. Disappearance of Assyrians from before Jerusalem—all happening in this order.
- **697 or 696.** Death of Hezekiah. Manasseh succeeds.
- **681.** Death of Sennacherib.
- **607.** Fall of Nineveh and Assyria. Babylon supreme. Jeremiah.
- **599.** First Deportation of Jews to Babylon by Nebuchadnezzar.
- **588.** Jerusalem destroyed. Second Deportation of Jews.
- **538.** Cyrus captures Babylon. First Return of Jewish Exiles, under Zerubbabel, happens soon after.
- **458.** Second Return of Jewish Exiles, under Ezra.

BOOK I.

PREFACE AND PROPHECIES TO THE DEATH OF AHAZ,

727 B.C.

ISAIAH: i. THE PREFACE.
,, ii.—iv. 740—735 B.C.
,, v., ix. 8—x. 4. 735 B.C.
,, vi. About 735 B.C.
,, vii.—ix. 7. 734—732 B.C.

CHAPTER I.

THE ARGUMENT OF THE LORD AND ITS CONCLUSION.

Isaiah i.—His General Preface.

THE first chapter of the Book of Isaiah owes its position not to its date, but to its character. It was published late in the prophet's life. The seventh verse describes the land as overrun by foreign soldiery, and such a calamity befell Judah only in the last two of the four reigns over which the first verse extends Isaiah's prophesying. In the reign of Ahaz, Judah was invaded by Syria and Northern Israel, and some have dated chapter i. from the year of that invasion, 734 B.C. In the reign again of Hezekiah some have imagined, in order to account for the chapter, a swarming of neighbouring tribes upon Judah; and Mr. Cheyne, to whom regarding the history of Isaiah's time we ought to listen with the greatest deference, has supposed an Assyrian invasion in 711, under Sargon. But hardly of this, and certainly not of that, have we adequate evidence, and the only other invasion of Judah in Isaiah's lifetime took place under Sennacherib, in 701. For many reasons this Assyrian invasion is to be preferred to that by Syria and Ephraim in 734 as the occasion of this prophecy. But there is really no need to be determined on the point. The prophecy has been lifted out of its original circumstance and placed in the front of the book, perhaps by Isaiah himself, as a general introduction to his collected pieces. It owes its position, as we have said, to its character. It is a clear, complete statement of the points which were at issue between the Lord and His own all the time Isaiah was the Lord's prophet. It is the most representative of Isaiah's prophecies, a summary, perhaps better than any other single chapter of the Old Testament, of the substance of prophetic doctrine, and a very vivid illustration of the prophetic spirit and method. We propose to treat it here as introductory to the main subjects and lines of Isaiah's teaching, leaving its historical references till we arrive in due course at the probable year of its origin, 701 B.C.*

Isaiah's preface is in the form of a Trial or Assize. Ewald calls it "The Great Arraignment." There are all the actors in a judicial process. It is a Crown case, and God is at once Plaintiff and Judge. He delivers both the Complaint in the beginning (vv. 2, 3) and the Sentence in the end. The Assessors are Heaven and Earth, whom the Lord's herald invokes to hear the Lord's plea (ver. 2). The people of Judah are the Defendants. The charge against them is one of brutish, ingrate stupidity, breaking out into rebellion. The Witness is the prophet himself, whose evidence on the guilt of his people consists in recounting the misery that has overtaken their land (vv. 4—9), along with their civic injustice and social cruelty—sins of the upper and ruling classes (vv. 10, 17, 21—23). The people's Plea-in-defence, laborious worship and multiplied sacrifice, is repelled and exposed (vv. 10—17). And the Trial is concluded—*Come now, let us bring our reasoning*

* See p 343

to a close, saith the Lord—by God's offer of pardon to a people thoroughly convicted (ver. 18). On which follow the Conditions of the Future: happiness is sternly made dependent on repentance and righteousness (vv. 19, 20). And a supplementary oracle is given (vv. 24—31), announcing a time of affliction, through which the nation shall pass as through a furnace; rebels and sinners shall be consumed, but God will redeem Zion, and with her a remnant of the people.

That is the plan of the chapter—a Trial at Law. Though it disappears under the exceeding weight of thought the prophet builds upon it, do not let us pass hurriedly from it, as if it were only a scaffolding.

That God should argue at all is the magnificent truth on which our attention must fasten, before we inquire what the argument is about. God reasons with man—that is the first article of religion according to Isaiah. Revelation is not magical, but rational and moral. Religion is reasonable intercourse between one intelligent Being and another. God works upon man first through conscience.

Over against the prophetic view of religion sprawls and reeks in this same chapter the popular—religion as smoky sacrifice, assiduous worship, and ritual. The people to whom the chapter was addressed were not idolaters.* Hezekiah's reformation was over. Judah worshipped her own God, whom the prophet introduces not as for the first time, but by Judah's own familiar

---

* At least those to whom the first twenty-three verses were addressed. There is distinct blame of worshipping in the groves of Asherah in the appended oracle (vv. 24—31), which is proof that this oracle was given at an earlier period than the rest of the chapter—a fair instance of the very great difficulty we have in determining the dates of the various prophecies of Isaiah.

names for Him—Jehovah, Jehovah of Hosts, the Holy One of Israel, the Mighty One, or Hero, of Israel. In this hour of extreme danger the people are waiting on Jehovah with great pains and cost of sacrifice. They pray, they sacrifice, they solemnize to perfection. But they do not *know*, they do not *consider;* this is the burden of their offence. To use a better word, they do not *think*. They are God's grown-up children (ver. 2)—*children*, that is to say, like the son of the parable, with native instincts for their God; and *grown up*—that is to say, with reason and conscience developed. But they use neither, stupider than very beasts. *Israel doth not know, my people doth not consider*. In all their worship conscience is asleep, and they are drenched in wickedness. Isaiah puts their life in an epigram—*wickedness and worship: I cannot away*, saith the Lord, *with wickedness and worship* (ver. 13).

But the pressure and stimulus of the prophecy lie in this, that although the people have silenced conscience and are steeped in a stupidity worse than ox or ass, God will not leave them alone. He forces Himself upon them; He compels them to think. In the order and calmness of nature (ver. 2), apart from catastrophe nor seeking to influence by any miracle, God speaks to men by the reasonable words of His prophet. Before He will publish salvation or intimate disaster He must rouse and startle conscience. His controversy precedes alike His peace and His judgements. An awakened conscience is His prophet's first demand. Before religion can be prayer, or sacrifice, or any acceptable worship, it must be a *reasoning together* with God.

That is what mean the arrival of the Lord, and the opening of the assize, and the call to know and consider. It is the terrible necessity which comes back upon men, however engrossed or drugged they may be, to pass their lives in moral judgement before themselves; a debate to which there is never any closure, in which forgotten things will not be forgotten, but a man "is compelled to repeat to himself things he desires to be silent about, and to listen to what he does not wish to hear, . . . yielding to that mysterious power which says to him, Think. One can no more prevent the mind from returning to an idea than the sea from returning to a shore. With the sailor this is called the tide; with the guilty it is called remorse. God upheaves the soul as well as the ocean."* Upon that ever-returning and resistless tide Hebrew prophecy, with its Divine freight of truth and comfort, rides into the lives of men. This first chapter of Isaiah is just the parable of the awful compulsion to think which men call conscience. The stupidest of generations, formal and fat-hearted, are forced to consider and to reason. The Lord's court and controversy are opened, and men are whipped into them from His Temple and His altar.

For even religion and religiousness, the common man's commonest refuge from conscience—not only in Isaiah's time—cannot exempt from this writ. Would we be judged by our moments of worship, by our *temple-treading*, which is Hebrew for church-going, by the wealth of our sacrifice, by our ecclesiastical position? This chapter drags us out before the austerity and incorruptibleness of Nature. The assessors of the Lord are not the Temple nor the Law, but Heaven and Earth—not ecclesiastical conventions, but the grand moral fundamentals of the universe,

---

* *Les Misérables:* "a Tempest in a Brain."

purity, order and obedience to God. Religiousness, however, is not the only refuge from which we shall find Isaiah startling men with the trumpet of the Lord's assize. He is equally intolerant of the indulgent silence and compromises of the world, that give men courage to say, We are no worse than others. Men's lives, it is a constant truth of his, have to be argued out not with the world, but with God. If a man will be silent upon shameful and uncomfortable things, he cannot. His thoughts are not his own; God will think them for him as God thinks them here for unthinking Israel. Nor are the practical and intellectual distractions of a busy life any refuge from conscience. When the politicians of Judah seek escape from judgement by plunging into deeper intrigue and a more bustling policy, Isaiah is fond of pointing out to them that they are only forcing judgement nearer. They do but sharpen on other objects the thoughts whose edge must some day turn upon themselves.

What is this questioning nothing holds away, nothing stills, and nothing wears out? It is the voice of God Himself, and its insistence is therefore as irresistible as its effect is universal. That is not mere rhetoric which opens the Lord's controversy: *Hear, O heavens, and give ear, O earth, for the Lord hath spoken.* All the world changes to the man in whom conscience lifts up her voice, and to the guilty Nature seems attentive and aware. Conscience compels heaven and earth to act as her assessors, because she is the voice, and they the creatures, of God. This leads us to emphasize another feature of the prophecy.

We have called this chapter a trial-at-law; but it is far more a *personal* than a legal controversy; of the formally forensic there is very little about it. Some theologies and many preachers have attempted the conviction of the human conscience by the technicalities of a system of law, or by appealing to this or that historical covenant, or by the obligations of an intricate and burdensome morality. This is not Isaiah's way. His generation is here judged by no system of law or ancient covenants, but by a living Person and by His treatment of them—a Person who is a Friend and a Father. It is not Judah and the law that are confronted; it is Judah and Jehovah. There is no contrast between the life of this generation and some glorious estate from which they or their forefathers have fallen; but they are made to hear the voice of a living and present God: *I have nourished and brought up children, and they have rebelled against Me.* Isaiah begins where Saul of Tarsus began, who, though he afterwards elaborated with wealth of detail the awful indictment of the abstract law against man, had never been able to do so but for that first confronting with the Personal Deity, *Saul, Saul, why persecutest thou Me?* Isaiah's ministry started from the vision of the Lord; and it was no covenant or theory, but the Lord Himself, who remained the prophet's conscience to the end.

But though the living God is Isaiah's one explanation of conscience, it is God in two aspects, the moral effects of which are opposite, yet complementary. In conscience men are defective by forgetting either the sublime or the practical, but Isaiah's strength is to do justice to both. With him God is first the infinitely High, and then equally the infinitely Near. *The Lord is exalted in righteousness!* yes, and sublimely above the people's vulgar identifications of His will with their own safety and success, but likewise concerned with every detail of their politics and social behaviour, not to be relegated to the Temple, where they were wont to confine Him, but by His prophet descending to their markets and councils, with His own opinion of their policies, interfering in their intrigues, meeting Ahaz at the conduit of the upper pool in the highway of the fuller's field, and fastening *eyes of glory* on every pin and point of the dress of the daughters of Zion. He is no merely transcendent God. Though He be the High and Holy One, He will discuss each habit of the people, and argue upon its merits every one of their policies. His constant cry to them is *Come and let us reason together*, and to hear it is to have a conscience. Indeed, Isaiah lays more stress on this intellectual side of the moral sense than on the other, and the frequency with which in this chapter he employs the expressions *know*, and *consider*, and *reason*, is characteristic of all his prophesying. Even the most superficial reader must notice how much this prophet's doctrine of conscience and repentance harmonizes with the *metanoia* of New Testament preaching.

This doctrine, that God has an interest in every detail of practical life and will argue it out with men, led Isaiah to a revelation of God quite peculiar to himself. For the Psalmist it is enough that his soul *come to God, the living God*. It is enough for other prophets to awe the hearts of their generations by revealing *the Holy One;* but Isaiah, with his intensely practical genius, and sorely tried by the stupid inconsistency of his people, bends himself to make them understand that God is at least a *reasonable* Being. Do not, his constant cry is, and he puts it sometimes in almost as many words—do not act as if there were a Fool on the throne of the universe, which you virtually do when you take these meaningless forms of worship as your only intercourse with Him, and beside them practise your rank iniquities, as if He did not see nor care. We need not here do more than mention the passages in which, sometimes by a word, Isaiah stings and startles self-conscious politicians and sinners beetle-blind in sin, with the sense that God Himself takes an interest in their deeds and has His own working-plans for their life. On the land question in Judah (v. 9): *In mine ears, saith the Lord of hosts.* When the people were paralyzed by calamity, as if it had no meaning or term (xxviii. 29): *This also cometh forth from the Lord of hosts, which is wonderful in counsel and excellent in effectual working.* Again, when they were panic-stricken, and madly sought by foolish ways their own salvation (xxx. 18): *For the Lord is a God of judgement*—i.e., of principle, method, law, with His own way and time for doing things—*blessed are all they that wait for Him.* And again, when politicians were carried away by the cleverness and success of their own schemes (xxxi. 2): *Yet He also is wise,* or clever. It was only a personal application of this Divine attribute when Isaiah heard the word of the Lord give him the minutest directions for his own practice — as, for instance, at what exact point he was to meet Ahaz (vii. 3); or that he was to take a board and write upon it in the vulgar character (viii. 1); or that he was to strip frock and sandals, and walk without them for three years (xx). Where common men feel conscience only as something vague and inarticulate, a flavour, a sting, a foreboding, the obligation of work, the constraint of affection, Isaiah heard the word of the Lord, clear and decisive on matters of policy, and definite even to the details of method and style.

Isaiah's conscience, then, was perfect, because it was two-fold: *God is holy; God is practical.* If there be the glory, the purity as of fire, of His Presence to overawe, there is His unceasing inspection of us, there is His interest in the smallest details of our life, there are His fixed laws, from regard for all of which no amount of religious sensibility may relieve us. Neither of these halves of conscience can endure by itself. If we forget the first we may be prudent and for a time clever, but will also grow self-righteous, and in time self-righteousness means stupidity too. If we forget the second we may be very devotional, but cannot escape becoming blindly and inconsistently immoral. Hypocrisy is the result either way, whether we forget how high God is or whether we forget how near.

To these two great articles of conscience, however— God is high and God is near—the Bible adds a greater third, God is Love. This is the uniqueness and glory of the Bible's interpretation of conscience. Other writings may equal it in enforcing the sovereignty and detailing the minutely practical bearings of conscience: the Bible alone tells man how much of conscience is nothing but God's love. It is a doctrine as plainly laid down as the doctrine about chastisement, though not half so much recognised—*Whom the Lord loveth He chasteneth.* What is true of the material pains and penalties of life is equally true of the inward convictions, frets, threats and fears, which will not leave stupid man alone. To men with their obscure sense of shame, and restlessness, and servitude to sin the Bible plainly says, "You are able to sin because you have turned your back to the love of God; you are unhappy because you do not take that love to your heart; the bitterness of your remorse is that it is love against which you are ungrateful." Conscience is not the Lord's persecution, but His jealous pleading, and not the fierceness of His anger, but the reproach of His love. This is the Bible's doctrine throughout, and it is not absent from the chapter we are considering. Love gets the first word even in the indictment of this austere assize: *I have nourished and brought up children, and they have rebelled against Me.* Conscience is already a Father's voice: the recollection, as it is in the parable of the prodigal, of a Father's mercy; the reproach, as it is with Christ's lamentation over Jerusalem, of outraged love. We shall find not a few passages in Isaiah, which prove that he was in harmony with all revelation upon this point, that conscience is the reproach of the love of God.

But when that understanding of conscience breaks out in a sinner's heart forgiveness cannot be far away. Certainly penitence is at hand. And therefore, because of all books the Bible is the only one which interprets conscience as the love of God, so is it the only one that can combine His pardon with His reproach, and as Isaiah now does in a single verse, proclaim His free forgiveness as the conclusion of His bitter quarrel. *Come, let us bring our reasoning to a close, saith the* LORD. *Though your sins be as scarlet, they shall be white as snow; though they be red like crimson, they shall be as wool.* Our version, *Come, and let us reason together,* gives no meaning here. So plain an offer of pardon is not reasoning together; it is bringing reasoning to an end; it is the settlement of a dispute that has been in progress. Therefore we translate, with Mr. Cheyne, *Let us bring our reasoning to an end.* And how pardon can be the end and logical conclusion of conscience is clear to us, who have seen how much of conscience is love, and that the Lord's controversy is the reproach of His Father's heart, and His jealousy to make His own consider all His way of mercy towards them.

But the prophet does not leave conscience alone with its personal and inward results. He rouses it to its social applications. The sins with which the Jews are charged in this charge of the Lord are public sins. The whole people is indicted, but it is the judges, princes and counsellors who are denounced. Judah's disasters, which she seeks to meet by worship, are due to civic faults, bribery, corruption of justice, indifference to the rights of the poor and the friendless. Conscience with Isaiah is not what it is with so much of the religion of to-day, a *cul de sac*, into which the Lord chases a man and shuts him up to Himself, but it is a thoroughfare by which the Lord drives the man out upon the world and its manifold need of him. There is little dissection and less study of individual character with Isaiah. He has no time for it. Life is too much about him, and his God too much interested in life. What may be called the more personal sins—drunkenness, vanity, dress, thoughtlessness, want of faith in God and patience to wait for Him—are to Isaiah more social than individual symptoms, and it is for their public and political effects that he mentions them. Forgiveness is no end in itself, but the opportunity of social service; not a sanctuary in which Isaiah leaves men to sing its praises or form doctrines of it, but a gateway through which he leads God's people upon the world with the cry that rises from him here: *Seek justice, relieve the oppressed, judge the fatherless, plead for the widow.*

Before we pass from this form in which Isaiah figures religion we must deal with a suggestion it raises. No modern mind can come into this ancient court of the LORD's controversy without taking advantage of its open forms to put a question regarding the rights of man there. That God should descend to argue with men, what licence does this give to men? If religion be reasonable controversy of this kind, what is the place of doubt in it? Is not doubt man's side of the argument? Has he not also questions to put—the Almighty from his side to arraign? For God has Himself here put man on a level with Him, saying, *Come, and let us reason together.*

A temper of this kind, though not strange to the Old Testament, lies beyond the horizon of Isaiah. The only challenge of the Almighty which in any of his prophecies he reports as rising from his own countrymen is the bravado of certain drunkards (chaps. v. and xxviii.). Here and elsewhere it is the very opposite temper from honest doubt which he indicts—the temper that *does not know*, that *does not consider*. Ritualism and sensualism are to Isaiah equally false, because equally unthinking. The formalist and the fleshly he classes together, because of their stupidity. What does it matter whether a man's conscience and intellect be stifled in his own fat or under the clothes with which he dresses himself? They are stifled, and that is the main thing. To the formalist Isaiah says, *Israel doth not know, my people doth not consider;* to the fleshly (chap. v.), *My people are gone into captivity for want of knowledge.* But *knowing* and *considering* are just that of which doubt, in its modern sense, is the abundance, and not the defect. The mobility of mind, the curiosity, the moral sensitiveness, the hunger that is not satisfied with the chaff of formal and unreal answers, the spirit to find out truth for one's self, wrestling with God—this is the very temper Isaiah would have welcomed in a people whose sluggishness of reason was as justly blamed by him as the grossness of their moral sense. And if revelation be of the form in which Isaiah so prominently sets it, and the whole Bible bears him out in this—if revelation be this argumentative and reasonable process, then human doubt has its part in revelation. It is, indeed, man's side of the argument, and as history shows, has often helped to the elucidation of the points at issue.

Merely intellectual scepticism, however, is not within Isaiah's horizon. He would never have employed (nor would any other prophet) our modern habits of doubt, except as he employs these intellectual terms, *to know* and *to consider*—viz., as instruments of moral search and conviction. Had he lived now he would have been found among those few great prophets who use the resources of the human intellect to expose the moral state of humanity; who, like Shakespeare and Hugo, turn man's detective and reflective processes upon his own conduct; who make himself stand at the bar of his conscience. And truly to have doubt of everything in heaven and earth, and never to doubt one's self, is to be guilty of as stiff and stupid a piece of self-righteousness as the religious formalists whom Isaiah exposes. But the moral of the chapter is plainly what we have shown it to be, that a man cannot stifle doubt and debate about his own heart or treatment of God; whatever else he thinks about and judges, he cannot help judging himself.

Note on the Place of Nature in the Argument of the Lord.—The office which the Bible assigns to Nature in the controversy of God with man is fourfold—Assessor, Witness, Man's Fellow-Convict, and Doomster or Executioner. Taking these backward :—1. Scripture frequently exhibits Nature as the *doomster of the Lord.* Nature has a terrible power of flashing back from her vaster surfaces the guilty impressions of man's heart; at the last day her thunders shall peal the doom of the wicked, and her fire devour them. In those prophecies of the book of Isaiah which relate to his own time this use is not made of Nature, unless it be in his very earliest prophecy in chap. ii., and in his references to the earthquake (v. 25). To Isaiah the sentences and scourges of God are political and historical, the threats and arms of Assyria. He employs the violences of Nature only as metaphors for Assyrian rage and force. But he often promises fertility as the effect of the Lord's pardon, and when the prophets are writing about Nature, it is difficult to say whether they are to be understood literally or poetically. But, at any rate, there is much larger use made of physical catastrophes and convulsions in those other prophecies which do not relate to Isaiah's own time, and are now generally thought not to be his. Compare chaps. xiii. and xiv. 2. The representation of the earth as the *fellow-convict* of guilty man, sharing his curse, is very vivid in Isaiah xxiv.—xxvii. In the prophecies relating to his own time Isaiah, of course, identifies the troubles that afflict the land with the sin of the people, of Judah. But these are due to political causes—viz., the Assyrian invasion. 3. In the LORD's court of judgement the prophets sometimes employ Nature as *a witness* against man, as, for instance, the prophet Micah (vi. 1, *ff*). Nature is full of associations; the enduring mountains have memories from old, they have been constant witnesses of the dealing of God with His people. 4. Or lastly, Nature may be used as the great *assessor* of the conscience, sitting to expound the principles on which God governs life.

This is Isaiah's favourite use of Nature. He employs her to corroborate his statement of the Divine law and illustrate the ways of God to men, as in the end of chap. xxviii., and no doubt in the opening verse of this chapter.

CHAPTER II.

THE THREE JERUSALEMS.

Isaiah ii.--iv. (740—735 b.c.).

AFTER the general introduction, in chap. i., to the prophecies of Isaiah, there comes another portion of the book, of greater length, but nearly as distinct as the first. It covers four chapters, the second to the sixth, all of them dating from the same earliest period of Isaiah's ministry, before 735 b.c. They deal with exactly the same subjects, but they differ greatly in form. One section (chaps. ii.—iv.) consists of a number of short utterances—evidently not all spoken at the same time, for they conflict with one another—a series of consecutive prophecies, that probably represent the stages of conviction through which Isaiah passed in his prophetic apprenticeship; a second section (chap. v.) is a careful and artistic restatement, in parable and oration, of the truths he has thus attained; while a third section (chap. vi.) is narrative, probably written subsequently to the first two, but describing an inspiration and official call, which must have preceded them both. The more one examines chaps. ii.—vi., and finds that they but express the same truths in different forms, the more one is confirmed in some such view of them as this, which, it is believed, the following exposition will justify. Chaps. v. and vi.

are twin appendices to the long summary in ii.—iv.: chap. v. a public vindication and enforcement of the results of that summary, chap. vi. a private vindication to the prophet's heart of the very same truths, by a return to the secret moment of their original inspiration. We may assign 735 B.C., just before or just after the accession of Ahaz, as the date of the latest of these prophecies. The following is their historical setting.

For more than half a century the kingdom of Judah, under two powerful and righteous monarchs, had enjoyed the greatest prosperity. Uzziah strengthened the borders, extended the supremacy and vastly increased the resources of his little State, which, it is well to remember, was in its own size not larger than three average Scottish counties. He won back for Judah the port of Elath on the Red Sea, built a navy, and restored the commerce with the far East, which Solomon began. He overcame, in battle or by the mere terror of his name, the neighbouring nations—the Philistines that dwelt in cities, and the wandering tribes of desert Arabs. The Ammonites brought him gifts. With the wealth, which the East by tribute or by commerce poured into his little principality, Uzziah fortified his borders and his capital, undertook large works of husbandry and irrigation, organized a powerful standing army, and supplied it with a siege artillery capable of slinging arrows and stones. *His name spread far abroad, for he was marvellously helped till he was strong.* His son Jotham (740—735 B.C.) continued his father's policy with nearly all his father's success. He built cities and castles, quelled a rebellion among his tributaries, and caused their riches to flow faster still into Jerusalem. But while Jotham bequeathed to his country a sure defence and great wealth, and to his people a strong spirit and prestige among the nations, he left another bequest, which robbed these of their value—the son who succeeded him. In 735 Jotham died and ³Ahaz became king. He was very young, and stepped to the throne from the hareem. He brought to the direction of the government the petulant will of a spoiled child, the mind of an intriguing and superstitious woman. It was when the national policy felt the paralysis consequent on these that Isaiah published at least the later part of the prophecies now marked off as chaps. ii.—iv. of his book. *My people*, he cries—*my people! children are their oppressors, and women rule over them. O my people, they which lead thee cause thee to err, and destroy the way of thy paths.*

Isaiah had been born into the flourishing nation while Uzziah was king. The great events of that monarch's reign were his education, the still grander hopes they prompted the passion of his virgin fancy. He must have absorbed as the very temper of his youth this national consciousness which swelled so proudly in Judah under Uzziah. But the accession of such a king as Ahaz, while it was sure to let loose the passions and follies fostered by a period of rapid increase in luxury, could not fail to afford to Judah's enemies the long-deferred opportunity of attacking her. It was an hour both of the manifestation of sin and of the judgement of sin—an hour in which, while the majesty of Judah, sustained through two great reigns, was about to disappear in the follies of a third, the majesty of Judah's God should become more conspicuous than ever. Of this Isaiah had been privately conscious, as we shall see, for five years. *In the year that king*

Uzziah died (740), the young Jew *saw the Lord sitting upon a throne, high and lifted up.* Startled into prophetic consciousness by the awful contrast between an earthly majesty that had so long fascinated men, but now sank into a leper's grave, and the heavenly, which rose sovereign and everlasting above it, Isaiah had gone on to receive conviction of his people's sin and certain punishment. With the accession of Ahaz, five years later, his own political experience was so far developed as to permit of his expressing in their exact historical effects the awful principles of which he had received foreboding when Uzziah died. What we find in chaps. ii.—iv. is a record of the struggle of his mind towards this expression; it is the summary, as we have already said, of Isaiah's apprenticeship.

The word that Isaiah, the son of Amoz, saw concerning Judah and Jerusalem. We do not know anything of Isaiah's family or of the details of his upbringing. He was a member of some family of Jerusalem, and in intimate relations with the Court. It has been believed that he was of royal blood, but it matters little whether this be true or not. A spirit so wise and masterful as his did not need social rank to fit it for that intimacy with princes which has doubtless suggested the legend of his royal descent. What does matter is Isaiah's citizenship in Jerusalem, for this colours all his prophecy. More than Athens to Demosthenes, Rome to Juvenal, Florence to Dante, is Jerusalem to Isaiah. She is his immediate and ultimate regard, the centre and return of all his thoughts, the hinge of the history of his time, the one thing worth preserving amidst its disasters, the summit of those brilliant hopes with which he fills the future. He has traced for us the main features of her position and some of the lines of her construction, many

of the great figures of her streets, the fashions of her
women, the arrival of embassies, the effect of rumours.
He has painted her aspect in triumph, in siege, in famine
and in earthquake; war filling her valleys with chariots,
and again nature rolling tides of fruitfulness up to her
gates; her moods of worship and panic and profligacy
till we see them all as clearly as the shadow following
the sunshine and the breeze the breeze across the corn-
fields of our own summers.

If he takes wider observation of mankind, Jerusalem
is his watch-tower. It is for her defence he battles
through fifty years of statesmanship, and all his
prophecy may be said to travail in anguish for her
new birth. He was never away from her walls, but
not even the psalms of the captives by the rivers of
Babylon, with the desire of exile upon them, exhibit
more beauty and pathos than the lamentations which
Isaiah poured upon Jerusalem's sufferings or the visions
in which he described her future solemnity and peace.

It is not with surprise, therefore, that we find the
first prophecies of Isaiah directed upon his mother city:
*The word that Isaiah the son of Amoz saw concerning
Judah and Jerusalem.* There is little about Judah
in these chapters: the country forms but a fringe to
the capital.

Before we look into the subject of the prophecy,
however, a short digression is necessary on the manner
in which it is presented to us. It is not a reasoned
composition or argument we have here; it is a vision,
it is the word which Isaiah *saw*. The expression is
vague, often abused and in need of defining. Vision is
not employed here to express any magical display before
the eyes of the prophet of the very words which he
was to speak to the people, or any communication to

his thoughts by dream or ecstasy. They are higher qualities of "vision" which these chapters unfold. There is, first of all, the power of forming an ideal, of seeing and describing a thing in the fulfilment of all the promise that is in it. But these prophecies are much more remarkable for two other powers of inward vision, to which we give the names of insight and intuition —insight into human character, intuition of Divine principles—*clear knowledge of what man is and how God will act*—a keen discrimination of the present state of affairs in Judah, and unreasoned conviction of moral truth and the Divine will. The original meaning of the Hebrew word *saw*, which is used in the title to this series, is to cleave, or split; then to see into, to see through, to get down beneath the surface of things and discover their real nature. And what characterizes the bulk of these visions is *penetrativeness*, the keenness of a man who will not be deceived by an outward show that he delights to hold up to our scorn, but who has a conscience for the inner worth of things and for their future consequences. To lay stress on the moral meaning of the prophet's vision is not to grudge, but to emphasize its inspiration by God. Of that inspiration Isaiah was himself assured. It was God's Spirit that enabled him to see thus keenly; for he saw things keenly, not only as men count moral keenness, but as God Himself sees them, in their value in His sight and in their attractiveness for His love and pity. In this prophecy there occurs a striking expression—*the eyes of the glory of God*. It was the vision of the Almighty Searcher and Judge, burning through man's pretence, with which the prophet felt himself endowed. This then was the second element in his vision—to penetrate men's hearts as God Himself penetrated them, and constantly, without squint or blur, to see right from wrong in their eternal difference. And the third element is the intuition of God's will, the perception of what line of action He will take. This last, of course, forms the distinct prerogative of Hebrew prophecy, that power of vision which is its climax; the moral situation being clear, to see then how God will act upon it.

Under these three powers of vision Jerusalem, the prophet's city, is presented to us—Jerusalem in three lights, really three Jerusalems. First, there is flashed out (chap. ii. 2—5) a vision of the ideal city, Jerusalem idealized and glorified. Then comes (ii. 6—iv. 1) a very realistic picture, a picture of the actual Jerusalem. And lastly at the close of the prophecy (iv. 2—6) we have a vision of Jerusalem as she shall be after God has taken her in hand—very different indeed from the ideal with which the prophet began. Here are three successive motives or phases of prophecy, which, as we have said, in all probability summarize the early ministry of Isaiah, and present him to us *first* as the idealist or visionary, *second* as the realist or critic, and *third* as the prophet proper or revealer of God's actual will.

I. THE IDEALIST (ii. 1—5).

All men who have shown our race how great things are possible have had their inspiration in dreaming of the impossible. Reformers, who at death were content to have lived for the moving forward but one inch of some of their fellow-men, began by believing themselves able to lift the whole world at once. Isaiah was no exception to this human fashion. His first vision was that of a Utopia, and his first belief that his countrymen would immediately realize it. He lifts up to us a very grand picture of a vast commonwealth centred in Jerusalem. Some think he borrowed it from an older prophet; Micah has it also; it may have been the ideal of the age. But, at any rate, if we are not to take verse 5 in scorn, Isaiah accepted this as his own. *And it shall come to pass in the last days, that the mountain of the Lord's house shall be established in the top of the mountains, and exalted above the hills, and all nations shall flow unto it.* The prophet's own Jerusalem shall be the light of the world, the school and temple of the earth, the seat of the judgement of the Lord, when He shall reign over the nations, and all mankind shall dwell in peace beneath Him. It is a glorious destiny, and as its light shines from the far-off horizon, *the latter days,* in which the prophet sees it, what wonder that he is possessed and cries aloud, *O house of Jacob, come ye, and let us walk in the light of the* LORD *!* It seems to the young prophet's hopeful heart as if at once that ideal would be realized, as if by his own word he could lift his people to its fulfilment.

But that is impossible, and Isaiah perceives so as soon as he turns from the far-off horizon to the city at his feet, as soon as he leaves to-morrow alone and deals with to-day. The next verses of the chapter—from verse 6 onwards—stand in strong contrast to those which have described Israel's ideal. There Zion is full of the law and Jerusalem of the word of the Lord, the one religion flowing over from this centre upon the world. Here into the actual Jerusalem they have brought all sorts of foreign worship and heathen prophets; *they are replenished from the East, and are soothsayers like the Philistines, and strike hands with the children of strangers.* There all nations come to worship at

Jerusalem; here her thought and faith are scattered over the idolatries of all nations. The ideal Jerusalem is full of spiritual blessings, the actual of the spoils of trade. There the swords are beat into ploughshares and the spears into pruning-hooks; here are vast and novel armaments, horses and chariots. There the Lord alone is worshipped; here the city is crowded with idols. The real Jerusalem could not possibly be more different from the ideal, nor its inhabitants as they are from what their prophet had confidently called on them to be.

II. THE REALIST (ii. 6—iv. 1).

Therefore Isaiah's attitude and tone suddenly change. The visionary becomes a realist, the enthusiast a cynic, the seer of the glorious city of God the prophet of God's judgement. The recoil is absolute in style, temper and thought, down to the very figures of speech which he uses. Before, Isaiah had seen, as it were, a lifting process at work, *Jerusalem in the top of the mountains, and exalted above the hills.* Now he beholds nothing but depression. *For the day of the LORD of hosts shall be upon every one that is proud and haughty, upon all that is lifted up, and it shall be brought low, and the Lord alone shall be exalted in that day.* Nothing in the great civilization, which he had formerly glorified, is worth preserving. The high towers, fenced walls, ships of Tarshish, treasures and armour must all perish; even the hills lifted by his imagination shall be bowed down, and *the LORD alone be exalted in that day.* This recoil reaches its extreme in the last verse of the chapter. The prophet, who had believed so much in man as to think possible an immediate commonwealth of nations, believes in man now so little that he does not hold him worth preserving: *Cease ye from man, whose breath is in his nostrils; for wherein is he to be accounted of?*

Attached to this general denunciation are some satiric descriptions, in the third chapter, of the anarchy, to which society in Jerusalem is fast being reduced under its childish and effeminate king. The scorn of these passages is scathing; *the eyes of the glory of God* burn through every rank, fashion and ornament in the town. King and court are not spared; the elders and princes are rigorously denounced. But by far the most striking effort of the prophet's boldness is his prediction of the overthrow of Jerusalem itself (ver. 8). What it cost Isaiah to utter and the people to hear we can only partly measure. To his own passionate patriotism it must have felt like treason, to the blind optimism of the popular religion it doubtless appeared the rankest heresy—to aver that the holy city, inviolate and almost unthreatened since the day David brought to her the ark of the Lord, and destined by the voice of her prophets, including Isaiah himself, to be established upon the tops of the mountains, was now to fall into ruin. But Isaiah's conscience overcomes his sense of consistency, and he who has just proclaimed the eternal glory of Jerusalem is provoked by his knowledge of her citizens' sins to recall his words and intimate her destruction. It may have been, that Isaiah was partly emboldened to so novel a threat, by his knowledge of the preparations which Syria and Israel were already making for the invasion of Judah. The prospect of Jerusalem, as the centre of a vast empire subject to Jehovah, however natural it was under a successful ruler like Uzziah, became, of course, unreal when every one of Uzziah's and Jotham's tributaries had risen in revolt against their successor, Ahaz. But of these outward movements Isaiah tells us nothing. He is wholly engrossed with Judah's sin. It is his growing acquaintance with the corruption of his fellow-countrymen that has turned his back on the ideal city of his opening ministry, and changed him into a prophet of Jerusalem's ruin. *Their tongue and their doings are against the Lord, to provoke the eyes of His glory.* Judge, prophet and elder, all the upper ranks and useful guides of the people, must perish. It is a sign of the degradation to which society shall be reduced, when Isaiah with keen sarcasm pictures the despairing people choosing a certain man to be their ruler because he alone has a coat to his back! (iii. 6).

With increased scorn Isaiah turns lastly upon the women of Jerusalem (iii. 16—iv. 2), and here perhaps the change which has passed over him since his opening prophecy is most striking. One likes to think of how the citizens of Jerusalem took this alteration in their prophet's temper. We know how popular so optimist a prophecy as that of the mountain of the Lord's house must have been, and can imagine how men and women loved the young face, bright with a far-off light, and the dream of an ideal that had no quarrel with the present. "But what a change is this that has come over him, who speaks not of to-morrow, but of to-day, who has brought his gaze from those distant horizons to our streets, who stares every man in the face (iii. 9), and makes the women feel that no pin and trimming, no ring and bracelet, escape his notice! Our loved prophet has become an impudent scorner!" Ah, men and women of Jerusalem, beware of those eyes! *The glory of God* is burning in them; they see you through and through, and they tell us that all your armour and the *show of your countenance*, and your foreign fashions are as nothing, for there are corrupt hearts below. This is your judgement, that *instead of sweet spices there shall be rottenness, and instead of a girdle a rope, and instead of well-set hair baldness, and instead of a stomacher a girding of sackcloth, and branding instead of beauty. Thy men shall fall by the sword, and thy mighty in the war. And her gates shall lament and mourn, and she shall be desolate and sit upon the ground!*

This was the climax of the prophet's judgement. If the salt have lost its savour, wherewith shall it be salted? It is thenceforth good for nothing but to be cast out and trodden under foot. If the women are corrupt the state is moribund.

III. THE PROPHET OF THE LORD (iv. 2—6).

Is there, then, no hope for Jerusalem? Yes, but not where the prophet sought it at first, in herself, and not in the way he offered it—by the mere presentation of an ideal. There is hope, there is more—there is certain salvation in the Lord, but it only comes after judgement. Contrast that opening picture of the new Jerusalem with this closing one, and we shall find their difference to lie in two things. There the city is more prominent than the Lord, here the Lord is more prominent than the city; there no word of judgement, here judgement sternly emphasized as the indispensable way towards the blessed future. A more vivid sense of the Person of Jehovah Himself, a deep conviction of the necessity of chastisement: these are what Isaiah has gained during his early ministry, without losing hope or heart for the future. The bliss shall come only when the Lord shall *have washed away the filth of the daughters of Zion, and shall have purged the blood of Jerusalem from the midst thereof by the spirit of judgement and the spirit of burning.* It is a corollary of all this that the participants of that future shall be many fewer than in the first vision of the prophet. The process of judgement must weed men out, and in place of all nations coming to Jerusalem, to share its peace and glory, the prophet can speak now only of Israel—and only of a remnant of Israel. *The escaped of Israel, the left in Zion, and he that remaineth in Jerusalem.* This is a great change in Isaiah's ideal, from the supremacy of Israel over all nations to the bare survival of a remnant of his people.

Is there not in this threefold vision a parallel and example for our own civilisation and our thoughts about it? All work and wisdom begin in dreams. We must see our Utopias before we start to build our stone and lime cities.

> "It takes a soul
> To move a body; it takes a high-souled man
> To move the masses even to a cleaner stye;
> It takes the ideal to blow an inch inside
> The dust of the actual."

But the light of our ideals dawns upon us only to show how poor by nature are the mortals who are called to accomplish them. The ideal rises still as to Isaiah only to exhibit the poverty of the real. When we lift our eyes from the hills of vision, and rest them on our fellow-men, hope and enthusiasm die out of us. Isaiah's disappointment is that of every one who brings down his gaze from the clouds to the streets. Be our ideal ever so desirable, be we ever so persuaded of its facility, the moment we attempt to apply it we shall be undeceived. Society cannot be regenerated all at once. There is an expression which Isaiah emphasizes in his motive of cynicism : *The show of their countenance doth witness against them.* It tells us that when he called his countrymen to turn to the light he lifted upon them he saw nothing but the exhibition of their sin made plain. When we bring light to a cavern whose inhabitants have lost their eyes by the darkness, the light does not make them see ; we have to give them eyes again. Even so no vision or theory of a perfect state — the mistake which all young reformers make — can regenerate society. It will only reveal social corruption, and sicken the heart of the reformer himself. For the possession of a great ideal does not mean, as so many fondly imagine, work accomplished; it means work revealed — work revealed so vast, often so impossible, that faith and hope die down, and the enthusiast of yesterday becomes the cynic of to-morrow. *Cease ye from man, whose breath is in his nostrils, for wherein is he to be accounted ?* In this despair, through which every worker for God and man must pass, many a warm heart has grown cold, many an intellect become paralyzed. There is but one way of escape, and that is Isaiah's. It is to believe in God Himself ; it is to believe that He is at work, that His purposes to man are saving purposes, and that with Him there is an inexhaustible source of mercy and virtue. So from the blackest pessimism shall arise new hope and faith, as from beneath Isaiah's darkest verses that glorious passage suddenly bursts like uncontrollable spring from the very feet of winter. *For that day shall the spring of the* LORD *be beautiful and glorious, and the fruit of the land shall be excellent and comely for them that are escaped of Israel.* This is all it is possible to say. There must be a future for man, because God loves him, and God reigns. That future can be reached only through judgement, because God is righteous.

To put it another way: All of us who live to work for our fellow-men or who hope to lift them higher by our word begin with our own visions of a great future. These visions, though our youth lends to them an original generosity and enthusiasm, are, like Isaiah's, largely borrowed. The progressive instincts of the age into which we are born and the mellow skies of prosperity combine with our own ardour to make our ideal one of splendour. Persuaded of its facility, we turn to real life to apply it. A few years pass. We not only find mankind too stubborn to be forced into our moulds, but we gradually become aware of Another Moulder at work upon our subject, and we stand aside in awe to watch His operations. Human desires and national ideals are not always fulfilled; philosophic theories are discredited by the evolution of fact. Uzziah does not reign for ever; the sceptre falls to Ahaz: progress is checked, and the summer of prosperity draws to an end. Under duller skies ungilded judgement comes to view, cruel and inexorable, crushing even the peaks on which we built our future, yet purifying men and giving earnest of a better future, too. And so life, that mocked the control of our puny fingers, bends groaning to the weight of an Almighty Hand. God also, we perceive as we face facts honestly, has His ideal for men; and though He works so slowly towards His end that our restless eyes are too impatient to follow His order, He yet reveals all that shall be to the humbled heart and the soul emptied of its own visions. Awed and chastened, we look back from His Presence to our old ideals. We are still able to recognize their grandeur and generous hope for men. But we see now how utterly unconnected they are with the present—castles in the air, with no ladders to them from the earth. And even if they were accessible, still to our eyes, purged by gazing on God's own ways, they would no more appear desirable. Look back on Isaiah's early ideal from the light of his second vision of the future. For all its grandeur, that picture of Jerusalem is not wholly attractive. Is there not much national arrogance in it? Is it not just the imperfectly idealized reflection of an age of material prosperity such as that of Uzziah's was? Pride is in it, a false optimism, the highest good to be reached without moral conflict. But here is the language of pity, rescue with difficulty, rest only after sore struggle and stripping, salvation by the bare arm of God. So do our imaginations for our own future or for that of the race always contrast with what He Himself has in store for us, promised freely out of His great grace to our unworthy hearts, yet granted in the end only to those who pass towards it through discipline, tribulation and fire.

This, then, was Isaiah's apprenticeship, and its net result was to leave him with the remnant for his ideal: the remnant and Jerusalem secured as its rallying-point.

CHAPTER III.

THE VINEYARD OF THE LORD, OR TRUE PATRIOTISM THE CONSCIENCE OF OUR COUNTRY'S SINS.

Isaiah v.; ix. 8—x. 4 (735 B.C.).

THE prophecy contained in these chapters belongs, as we have seen, to the same early period of Isaiah's career as chapters ii.—iv., about the time when Ahaz ascended the throne after the long and successful reigns of his father and grandfather, when the kingdom of Judah seemed girt with strength and filled with wealth, but the men were corrupt and the women careless, and the earnest of approaching judgement was already given in the incapacity of the weak and woman-ridden king. Yet although this new prophecy issues from the same circumstances as its predecessors, it implies these circumstances a little more developed. The same social evils are treated, but by a hand with a firmer grasp of them. The same principles are emphasized — the righteousness of Jehovah and His activity in judgement—but the form of judgement of which Isaiah had spoken before in general terms looms nearer, and before the end of the prophecy we get a view at close quarters of the Assyrian ranks.

Besides, opposition has arisen to the prophet's teaching. We saw that the obscurities and inconsistencies of chapters ii.—iv. are due to the fact that that prophecy represents several stages of experience through which Isaiah passed before he gained his final convictions. But his countrymen, it appears, have now had time to turn on these convictions and call them in question: it is necessary for Isaiah to vindicate them. The difference, then, between these two sets of prophecies, dealing with the same things, is that in the former (chapters ii.—iv.), we have the obscure and tortuous path of a conviction struggling to light in the prophet's own experience; here, in chapter v., we have its careful array in the light and before the people.

The point of Isaiah's teaching against which opposition was directed was of course its main point, that God was about to abandon Judah. This must have appeared to the popular religion of the day as the rankest heresy. To the Jews the honour of Jehovah was bound up with the inviolability of Jerusalem and the prosperity of Judah. But Isaiah knew Jehovah to be infinitely more concerned for the purity of His people than for their prosperity. He had seen the LORD *exalted in righteousness* above those national and earthly interests, with which vulgar men exclusively identified His will. Did the people appeal to the long time Jehovah had graciously led them for proof that He would not abandon them now? To Isaiah that gracious leading was but for righteousness' sake, and that God might make His own a holy people. Their history, so full of the favours of the Almighty, did not teach Isaiah, as it did the common prophets of his time, the lesson of Israel's political security, but the far different one of their religious responsibility. To him it only meant what Amos had already put in those startting words, *You only have I known of all the families of the earth: therefore I will visit upon you all your iniquities.* Now Isaiah delivered this doctrine at a time when it brought him the hostility of men's passions as well as of their opinions. Judah was arming for war. Syria and Ephraim were marching upon her. To threaten his country with ruin in such an hour was to run the risk of suffering from popular fury as a traitor as well as from priestly prejudice as a heretic. The strain of the moment is felt in the strenuousness of the prophecy. Chapter v., with its appendix, exhibits more grasp and method than its predecessors. Its literary form is finished, its feeling clear. There is a tenderness in the beginning of it, an inexorableness in the end and an eagerness all through, which stamp the chapter as Isaiah's final appeal to his countrymen at this period of his career.

The chapter is a noble piece of patriotism—one of the noblest of a race who, although for the greater part of their history without a fatherland, have contributed more brilliantly than perhaps any other to the literature of patriotism, and that simply because, as Isaiah here illustrates, patriotism was to their prophets identical with religious privilege and responsibility. Isaiah carries this to its bitter end. Other patriots have wept to sing their country's woes; Isaiah's burden is his people's guilt. To others an invasion of their fatherland by its enemies has been the motive to rouse by song or speech their countrymen to repel it. Isaiah also hears the tramp of the invader; but to him is permitted no ardour of defence, and his message to his countrymen is that they must succumb, for the invasion is irresistible and of the very judgement of God. How much it cost the prophet to deliver such a message we may see from those few verses of it in which his heart is not altogether silenced by his conscience. The sweet description of Judah as a vineyard, and the touching accents that break through the roll of denunciation with such phrases as *My people are gone away into captivity unawares*, tell us how the prophet's love of country is struggling with his duty to a righteous God. The course of feeling throughout the prophecy is very striking. The tenderness of the opening lyric seems ready to flow into gentle pleading with the whole people. But as the prophet turns to particular classes and their sins his mood changes to indignation, the voice settles down to judgement; till when it issues upon that clear statement of the coming of the Northern hosts every trace of emotion has left it, and the sentences ring out as unfaltering as the tramp of the armies they describe.

I. THE PARABLE OF THE VINEYARD (v. 1—7).

Isaiah adopts the resource of every misunderstood and unpopular teacher, and seeks to turn the flank of his people's prejudices by an attack in parable on their sympathies. Did they stubbornly believe it impossible for God to abandon a State He had so long and so carefully fostered? Let them judge from an analogous case in which they were all experts. In a picture of great beauty Isaiah describes a vineyard upon one of the sunny promontories visible from Jerusalem. Every care had been given it of which an experienced vine-dresser could think, but it brought forth only wild grapes. The vine-dresser himself is introduced, and appeals to the men of Judah and Jerusalem to judge between him and his vineyard. He gets their assent that all had been done which could be done, and fortified with that resolves to abandon the vineyard. *I will lay it waste; it shall not be pruned nor digged, but there shall come up briers and thorns.* Then the stratagem comes out, the speaker drops the tones of a human cultivator, and in the omnipotence of the Lord of heaven he is heard to say, *I will also command the clouds that they rain no rain upon it.* This diversion upon their sympathies having succeeded, the prophet scarcely needs to charge the people's prejudices in face. His point has been evidently carried. *For the vineyard of Jehovah of hosts is the house of Israel, and the men of Judah his pleasant plant; and He looked for judgement, but behold oppression, for righteousness, but behold a cry.*

The lesson enforced by Isaiah is just this, that in a people's civilization there lie the deepest responsibilities, for that is neither more nor less than their cultivation by God ; and the question for a people is not how secure does this render them, nor what does it count for glory, but how far is it rising towards the intentions of its Author? Does it produce those fruits of righteousness for which alone God cares to set apart and cultivate the peoples ? On this depends the question whether the civilization is secure, as well as the right of the people to enjoy and feel proud of it. There cannot be true patriotism without sensitiveness to this, for however rich be the elements that compose the patriot's temper, as piety towards the past, ardour of service for the present, love of liberty, delight in natural beauty and gratitude for Divine favour, so rich a temper will grow rancid without the salt of conscience; and the richer the temper is, the greater must be the proportion of that salt. All prophets and poets of patriotism have been moralists and satirists as well. From Demosthenes to Tourgenieff, from Dante to Mazzini, from Milton to Russell Lowell, from Burns to Heine, one cannot recall any great patriot who has not known how to use the scourge as well as the trumpet. Many opportunities will present themselves to us of illustrating Isaiah's orations by the letters and speeches of Cromwell, who of moderns most resembles the statesman-prophet of Judah; but nowhere does the resemblance become so close as when we lay a prophecy like this of Jehovah's vineyard by the side of the speeches in which the Lord Protector exhorted the Commons of England, although it was the hour of his and their triumph, to address themselves to their sins.

So, then, the patriotism of all great men has carried a conscience for their country's sins. But while this is always more or less a burden to the true patriot, there are certain periods in which his care for his country ought to be this predominantly, and need be little else. In a period like our own, for instance, of political security and fashionable religion, what need is there in patriotic displays of any other kind? but how much for patriotism of this kind—of men who will uncover the secret sins, however loathsome, and declare the hypocrisies, however powerful, of the social life of the people! These are the patriots we need in times of peace; and as it is more difficult to rouse a torpid people to their sins than to lead a roused one against their enemies, and harder to face a whole people with the support only of conscience than to defy many nations if you but have your own at your back, so these patriots of peace are more to be honoured than those of war. But there is one kind of patriotism more arduous and honourable still. It is that which Isaiah displays here, who cannot add to his conscience hope or even pity, who must hail his country's enemies for his country's good, and recite the long roll of God's favours to his nation only to emphasize the justice of His abandonment of them.

II. The Wild Grapes of Judah (v. 8—24).

The *wild grapes* which Isaiah saw in the vineyard of the Lord he catalogues in a series of Woes (vv. 8—24), fruits all of them of love of money and love of wine. They are abuse of the soil (8—10, 17*), a giddy luxury which has taken to drink (11—16), a moral blindness and headlong audacity of sin which habitual avarice and drunkenness soon develop (18—21), and, again, a greed of drink and money — men's perversion of their strength to wine, and of their opportunities of justice to the taking of bribes (22—24). These are the features of corrupt civilization not only in Judah, and the voice that deplores them cannot speak without rousing others very clamant to the modern conscience. It is with remarkable persistence that in every civilization the two main passions of the human heart, love of wealth and love of pleasure, the instinct to gather and the instinct to squander, have sought precisely these two forms denounced by Isaiah in which to work their social havoc—appropriation of the soil and indulgence in strong drink. Every civilized community develops sooner or later its land-question and its liquor-question. "Questions" they are called by the superficial opinion that all difficulties may be overcome by the cleverness of men; yet problems through which there cries for remedy so vast a proportion of our poverty, crime and madness, are something worse than "questions." They are huge sins, and require not merely the statesman's wit, but all the penitence and zeal of

---

* Ewald happily suggests that verse 17 has dropped out of, and should be restored to, its proper position at the end of the first "woe," where it contributes to the development of the meaning far more than from where it stands in the text.

which a nation's conscience is capable. It is in this that the force of Isaiah's treatment lies. We feel he is not facing questions of State, but sins of men. He has nothing to tell us of what he considers the best system of land tenure, but he enforces the principle that in the ease with which land may be absorbed by one person the natural covetousness of the human heart has a terrible opportunity for working ruin upon society. *Woe unto them that join house to house, that lay field to field, till there be no room, and ye be made to dwell alone in the midst of the land.* We know from Micah that the actual process which Isaiah condemns was carried out with the most cruel evictions and disinheritances. Isaiah does not touch on its methods, but exposes its effects on the country—depopulation and barrenness,—and emphasizes its religious significance. *Of a truth many houses shall be desolate, even great and fair, without an inhabitant. For ten acres of vineyard shall yield one bath, and a homer of seed shall yield but an ephah. . . . Then shall lambs feed as in their pasture, and strangers shall devour the ruins of the fat ones*—*i.e.,* of the luxurious landowners (9, 10, 17. See note on previous page). And in one of those elliptic statements by which he often startles us with the sudden sense that God Himself is acquainted with all our affairs, and takes His own interest in them, Isaiah adds, " All this was whispered to me by Jehovah : *In mine ears—the* LORD *of hosts* " (ver. 9).

During recent agitations in our own country one has often seen the " land laws of the Bible " held forth by some thoughtless demagogue as models for land tenure among ourselves ; as if a system which worked well with a small tribe in a land they had all entered on equal footing, and where there was no opportunity for the industry of the people except in pasture and tillage, could possibly be applicable to a vastly larger and more complex population, with different traditions and very different social circumstances. Isaiah says nothing about the peculiar land *laws* of his people. He lays down principles, and these are principles valid in every civilization. God has made the land, not to feed the pride of the few, but the natural hunger of the many, and it is His will that the most be got out of a country's soil for the people of the country. Whatever be the system of land-tenure—and while all are more or less liable to abuse, it is the duty of a people to agitate for that which will be least liable—if it is taken advantage of by individuals to satisfy their own cupidity, then God will take account of them. There is a responsibility which the State cannot enforce, and the neglect of which cannot be punished by any earthly law, but all the more will God see to it. A nation's treatment of their land is not always prominent as a question which demands the attention of public reformers; but it ceaselessly has interest for God, who ever holds individuals to answer for it. The land-question is ultimately a religious question. For the management of their land the whole nation is responsible to God, but especially those who own or manage estates. This is a sacred office. When one not only remembers the nature of land—how it is an element of life, so that if a man abuse the soil it is as if he poisoned the air or darkened the heavens—but appreciates also the multitude of personal relations which the landowner or factor holds in his hand—the peace of homes, the continuity of local traditions, the physical health, the social fearlessness and frankness, and the thousand delicate associations which their habitations entwine about the hearts of men—one feels that to all who possess or manage land is granted an opportunity of patriotism and piety open to few, a ministry less honourable and sacred than none other committed by God to man for his fellow-men.

After the land-sin Isaiah hurls his second Woe upon the drink-sin, and it is a heavier woe than the first. With fatal persistence the luxury of every civilization has taken to drink; and of all the indictments brought by moralists against nations, that which they reserve for drunkenness is, as here, the most heavily weighted. The crusade against drink is not the novel thing that many imagine who observe only its late revival among ourselves. In ancient times there was scarcely a State in which prohibitive legislation of the most stringent kind was not attempted, and generally carried out with a thoroughness more possible under despots than where, as with us, the slow consent of public opinion is necessary. A horror of strong drink has in every age possessed those who from their position as magistrates or prophets have been able to follow for any distance the drifts of social life. Isaiah exposes as powerfully as ever any of them did in what the peculiar fatality of drinking lies. Wine is a mocker by nothing more than by the moral incredulity which it produces, enabling men to hide from themselves the spiritual and material effects of over-indulgence in it. No one who has had to do with persons slowly falling from moderate to immoderate drinking can mistake Isaiah's meaning when he says, *They regard not the work of the* LORD; *neither have they considered the operation of His hands.* Nothing kills the conscience like steady drinking to a little excess; and religion, even while the conscience is alive, acts on it only as an opiate. It is not, however, with the symptoms of drink in individuals so much as with its aggregate effects on the nation that Isaiah is concerned. So prevalent is excessive drinking, so entwined with the social customs of the country and many powerful interests, that it is extremely difficult to rouse public opinion to its effects. And *so they go into captivity for lack of knowledge.* Temperance reformers are often blamed for the strength of their language, but they may shelter themselves behind Isaiah. As he pictures it, the national destruction caused by drink is complete. It is nothing less than the people's *captivity*, and we know what that meant to an Israelite. It affects all classes: *Their honourable men are famished, and their multitude parched with thirst. . . . The mean man is bowed down, and the great man is humbled.* But the want and ruin of this earth are not enough to describe it. The appetite of hell itself has to be enlarged to suffice for the consumption of the spoils of strong drink. *Therefore hell hath enlarged her desire and opened her mouth without measure; and their glory, and their multitude, and their pomp, and he that rejoiceth among them, descend into it.* The very appetite of hell has to be enlarged! Does it not truly seem as if the wild and wanton waste of drink were preventable, as if it were not, as many are ready to sneer, the inevitable evil of men's hearts choosing this form of issue, but a superfluous audacity of sin, which the devil himself did not desire or tempt men to? It is this feeling of the infernal gratuitousness of most of the drink-evil—the conviction that here hell would be quiet if only she were not stirred up by the extraordinarily wanton provocatives that society and the State offer to excessive drinking—which compels temperance reformers at the present day to isolate drunkenness and make it the object of a special crusade. Isaiah's strong figure has lost none of its strength to-day. When our judges tell us from the bench that nine-tenths of pauperism and crime are caused by drink, and our physicians that if only irregular tippling were abolished half the current sickness of the land would cease, and our statesmen that the ravages of strong drink are equal to those of the historical scourges of war, famine and pestilence combined, surely to swallow such a glut of spoil *the appetite of hell must have been* still more enlarged, *and the mouth of hell made* yet *wider.*

The next three Woes are upon different aggravations of that moral perversity which the prophet has already traced to strong drink. In the first of these it is better to read, *draw punishment near with cords of vanity*, than *draw iniquity*. Then we have a striking antithesis— the drunkards mocking Isaiah over their cups with the challenge, as if it would not be taken up, *Let Jehovah make speed, and hasten His work of judgement, that we may see it,* while all the time they themselves were dragging that judgement near, *as with cart-ropes,* by their persistent diligence in evil. This figure of sinners jeering at the approach of a calamity while they actually wear the harness of its carriage is very striking. But the Jews are not only unconscious of judgement, they are confused as to the very principles of morality: *Who call evil good, and good evil; that put darkness for light, and light for darkness; that put bitter for sweet, and sweet for bitter!*

In his fifth Woe the prophet attacks a disposition to which his scorn gives no peace throughout his ministry. If these sensualists had only confined themselves to their sensuality they might have been left alone; but with that intellectual bravado which is equally born with " Dutch courage " of drink, they interfered in the conduct of the State, and prepared arrogant policies of alliance and war that were the distress of the soberminded prophet all his days. *Woe unto them that are wise in their own eyes and prudent in their own sight.*

In his last Woe Isaiah returns to the drinking habits of the upper classes, from which it would appear that among the judges even of Judah there were "sixbottle men." They sustained their extravagance by subsidies, which we trust were unknown to the mighty men of wine who once filled the seats of justice in our own country. *They justify the wicked for a bribe, and take away the righteousness of the righteous from him.* All these sinners, dead through their rejection of the law of Jehovah of hosts and the word of the Holy One of Israel, shall be like to the stubble, fit only for burning, and their blossom as the dust of the rotten tree.

III. THE ANGER OF THE LORD (v. 25 ; ix. 8—x. 4 ; v. 26—30).

This indictment of the various sins of the people occupies the whole of the second part of the oration. But a third part is now added, in which the prophet catalogues the judgements of the Lord upon them, each of these closing with the weird refrain, *For all this His anger is not turned away, but His hand is stretched out still.* The complete catalogue is usually obtained by inserting between the 25th and 26th verses of chapter v. the long passage from chapter ix., ver. 8, to chapter x., ver. 4. It is quite true that as far as chapter v. itself is concerned it does not need this insertion; but ix. 8— x. 4 is decidedly out of place where it now lies. Its paragraphs end with the same refrain as closes v. 25, which forms, besides, a natural introduction to them, while v. 26—30 form as natural a conclusion. The latter verses describe an Assyrian invasion, and it was always in an Assyrian invasion that Isaiah foresaw the final calamity of Judah. We may, then, subject to further light on the exceedingly obscure subject of the arrangement of Isaiah's prophecies, follow some of the leading critics, and place ix. 8—x. 4 between verses 25—26 of chapter v.; and the more we examine them the more we shall be satisfied with our arrangement, for strung together in this order they form one of the most impressive series of scenes which even an Isaiah has given us.

From these scenes Isaiah has spared nothing that is terrible in history or nature, and it is not one of the least of the arguments for putting them together that their intensity increases to a climax. Earthquakes, armed raids, a great battle and the slaughter of a people; prairie and forest fires, civil strife and the famine fever, that feeds upon itself; another battle-field, with its cringing groups of captives and heaps of slain; the resistless tide of a great invasion; and then, for final prospect, a desolate land by the sound of a hungry sea, and the light is darkened in the clouds thereof. The elements of nature and the elemental passions of man have been let loose together; and we follow the violent floods, remembering that it is sin which has burst the gates of the universe, and given the tides of hell full course through it. Over the storm and battle there comes booming like the storm-bell the awful refrain, *For all this His anger is not turned away, but His hand is stretched out still.* It is poetry of the highest order, but in him who reads it with a conscience mere literary sensations are sobered by the awe of some of the most profound moral phenomena of life. The persistence of Divine wrath, the long-lingering effects of sin in a nation's history, man's abuse of sorrow and his defiance of an angry Providence, are the elements of this great drama. Those who are familiar with *King Lear*, will recognize these elements, and observe how similarly the ways of Providence and the conduct of men are represented there and here.

What Isaiah unfolds, then, is a series of calamities that have overtaken the people of Israel. It is impossible for us to identify every one of them with a particular event in Israel's history otherwise known to us. Some it is not difficult to recognize; but the prophet passes in a perplexing way from Judah to Ephraim and Ephraim to Judah, and in one case, where he represents Samaria as attacked by Syria and the Philistines, he goes back to a period at some distance from his own. There are also passages, as for instance x. 1—4, in which we are unable to decide whether he describes a present punishment or threatens a future one. But his moral purpose, at least, is plain. He will show how often Jehovah has already spoken to His people by calamity, and because they have remained hardened under these warnings, how there now remains possible only the last, worst blow of an Assyrian invasion. Isaiah is justifying his threat of so unprecedented and extreme a punishment for God's people as overthrow by this Northern people, who had just appeared upon Judah's political horizon. God, he tells Israel, has tried everything short of this, and it has failed; now only this remains, and this shall not fail. The prophet's purpose, therefore, being not an accurate historical recital, but moral impressiveness, he gives us a more or less ideal description of former calamities, mentioning only so much as to allow us to recognize here and there that it is actual facts which he uses for his purpose of condemning Israel to captivity, and vindicating Israel's God in bringing that captivity near. The passage thus forms a parallel to that in Amos, with its similar refrain: *Yet ye have not returned unto Me, saith the Lord* (Amos iv. 6—12), and only goes farther than that earlier prophecy in indicating that the instruments of the Lord's final judgement are to be the Assyrians.

Five great calamities, says Isaiah, have fallen on Israel and left them hardened: 1st, earthquake (v. 25); 2nd, loss of territory (ix. 8—12); 3rd, war and a decisive defeat (ix. 13—17); 4th, internal anarchy (ix. 18—21); 5th, the near prospect of captivity (x. 1—4).

1. THE EARTHQUAKE (v. 25).—Amos closes his series with an earthquake; Isaiah begins with one. It may be the same convulsion they describe, or may not. Although the skirts of Palestine both to the east and west frequently tremble to these disturbances, an earthquake in Palestine itself, up on the high central ridge of the land, is very rare. Isaiah vividly describes its awful simplicity and suddenness. *The Lord stretched forth His hand and smote, and the hills shook, and their carcases were like offal in the midst of the streets.* More words are not needed, because there was nothing more to describe. The Lord lifted His hand; the hills seemed for a moment to topple over, and when the living recovered from the shock there lay the dead, flung like refuse about the streets.

2. THE LOSS OF TERRITORY (ix. 8—21).—So awful a calamity, in which the dying did not die out of sight nor fall huddled together on some far off battle-field, but

the whole land was strewn with her slain, ought to have left indelible impression on the people. But it did not. The Lord's own word had been in it for Jacob and Israel (ix. 8), *that the people might know, even Ephraim and the inhabitants of Samaria.* But unhumbled they turned in the stoutness of their hearts, saying, when the earthquake had passed : * *The bricks are fallen, but we will build with hewn stones;* † the *sycomores are cut down, but we will change them into cedars.* Calamity did not make this people thoughtful ; they felt God only to endeavour to forget Him. Therefore He visited them the second time. They did not feel the Lord shaking their land, so He sent their enemies to steal it from them : *the Syrians before and the Philistines behind; and they devour Israel with open mouth.* What that had been for appalling suddenness this was for lingering and harassing—guerilla warfare, armed raids, the land eaten away bit by bit. *Yet the people do not return unto Him that smote them, neither seek they the* LORD *of hosts.*

3. WAR AND DEFEAT (ix. 13—17).—The next consequent calamity passed from the land to the people themselves. A great battle is described, in which the nation is dismembered in one day. War and its horrors are told, and the apparent want of Divine pity and discrimination which they imply is explained. Israel has been led into these disasters by the folly of their leaders, whom Isaiah therefore singles out for blame. *For they that lead these people cause them to err, and they that are led of them are destroyed.* But the real horror

---

* Read past tenses, as in the margin of Revised Version, for all the future tenses, or better, the historical present, down to the end of the chapter.

† It is part of the argument for connecting ix. 8 with v. 25 that this phrase would be very natural after the earthquake described in v. 25.

of war is that it falls not upon its authors, that its
victims are not statesmen, but the beauty of a country's
youth, the helplessness of the widow and orphan.
Some question seems to have been stirred by this in
Isaiah's heart. He asks, Why does the Lord not
rejoice in the young men of His people? Why has He
no pity for widow and orphan, that He thus sacrifices
them to the sin of the rulers? It is because the
whole nation shares the ruler's guilt; *every one is an
hypocrite and an evil-doer, and every mouth speaketh
folly.* As ruler so people, is a truth Isaiah frequently
asserts, but never with such grimness as here. War
brings out, as nothing else does, the solidarity of a
people in guilt.

4. INTERNAL ANARCHY (ix. 18—21).—Even yet the
people did not repent; their calamities only drove them
to further wickedness. The prophet's eyes are opened
to the awful fact that God's wrath is but the blast that
fans men's hot sins to flame. This is one of those two
or three awful scenes in history, in the conflagration
of which we cannot tell what is human sin and what
Divine judgement. There is a panic wickedness,
sin spreading like mania, as if men were possessed
by supernatural powers. The physical metaphors
of the prophet are evident: a forest or prairie fire,
and the consequent famine, whose fevered victims
feed upon themselves. And no less evident are the
political facts which the prophet employs these metaphors to describe. It is the anarchy which has beset
more than one corrupt and unfortunate people, when their
misleaders have been overthrown: the anarchy in which
each faction seeks to slaughter out the rest. Jealousy
and distrust awake the lust for blood, rage seizes the
people as fire the forest, *and no man spareth his*

brother. We have had modern instances of all this; these scenes form a true description of some days of the French Revolution, and are even a truer description of the civil war that broke out in Paris after her late siege.

> " If that the heavens do not their visible spirits
> Send quickly down to tame these vile offences,
> 'T will come,
> Humanity must perforce prey on itself
> Like monsters of the deep." *

5. THE THREAT OF CAPTIVITY (x. 1—4).—Turning now from the past, and from the fate of Samaria, with which it would appear he has been more particularly engaged, the prophet addresses his own countrymen in Judah, and paints the future for them. It is not a future in which there is any hope. The day of their visitation also will surely come, and the prophet sees it close in the darkest night of which a Jewish heart could think—the night of captivity. Where, he asks his unjust countrymen—where *will ye then flee for help? and where will you leave your glory?* Cringing among the captives, lying dead beneath heaps of dead—that is to be your fate, who will have turned so often and then so finally from God. When exactly the prophet thus warned his countrymen of captivity we do not know, but the warning, though so real, produced neither penitence in men nor pity in God. *For all this His anger is not turned away, but His hand is stretched out still.*

6. THE ASSYRIAN INVASION (v. 26—30).—The prophet is, therefore, free to explain that cloud which has appeared far away on the northern horizon. God's hand of judgement is still uplifted over Judah, and it is that

---

* *King Lear,* act iv., sc. 2.

hand which summons the cloud. The Assyrians are coming in answer to God's signal, and they are coming as a flood, to leave nothing but ruin and distress behind them. No description by Isaiah is more majestic than this one, in which Jehovah, who has exhausted every nearer means of converting His people, lifts His undrooping arm with a *flag to the nations that are far off, and hisses* or whistles *for them from the end of the earth. And, behold, they come with speed, swiftly: there is no weary one nor straggler among them; none slumbers nor sleeps; nor loosed is the girdle of his loins, nor broken the latchet of his shoes; whose arrows are sharpened, and all their bows bent; their horses' hoofs are like the flint, and their wheels like the whirlwind; a roar have they like the lion's, and they roar like young lions; yea, they growl and grasp the prey, and carry it off, and there is none to deliver. And they growl upon him that day like the growling of the sea; and if one looks to the land, behold, dark and distress, and the light is darkened in the cloudy heaven.*

Thus Isaiah leaves Judah to await her doom. But the tones of his weird refrain awaken in our hearts some thoughts which will not let his message go from us just yet.

It will ever be a question, whether men abuse more their sorrows or their joys; but no earnest soul can doubt, which of these abuses is the more fatal. To sin in the one case is to yield to a temptation; to sin in the other is to resist a Divine grace. Sorrow is God's last message to man; it is God speaking in emphasis. He who abuses it shows that he can shut his ears when God speaks loudest. Therefore heartlessness or impenitence after sorrow is more dangerous than intemperance in joy; its results are always more tragic. Now Isaiah points out that men's abuse of sorrow is twofold. Men abuse sorrow by mistaking it, and they abuse sorrow by defying it.

Men abuse sorrow by mistaking it, when they see in it nothing but a penal or expiatory force. To many men sorrow is what his devotions were to Louis XI., which having religiously performed, he felt the more brave to sin. So with the Samaritans, who said in the stoutness of their hearts, *The bricks are fallen down, but we will build with hewn stones; the sycomores are cut down, but we will change them into cedars.* To speak in this way is happy, but heathenish. It is to call sorrow " bad luck ; " it is to hear no voice of God in it, saying, " Be pure; be humble ; lean upon Me." This disposition springs from a vulgar conception of God, as of a Being of no permanence in character, easily irritated but relieved by a burst of passion, smartly punishing His people and then leaving them to themselves. It is a temper which says, "God is angry, let us wait a little; God is appeased, let us go ahead again." Over against such vulgar views of a Deity with a temper Isaiah unveils the awful majesty of God in holy wrath: *For all this His anger is not turned away, but His hand is stretched out still.* How grim and savage does it appear to our eyes till we understand the thoughts of the sinners to whom it was revealed! God cannot dispel the cowardly thought, that He is anxious only to punish, except by letting His heavy hand abide till it purify also. The permanence of God's wrath is thus an ennobling, not a stupefying doctrine.

Men also abuse sorrow by defying it, but the end of this is madness. "It forms the greater part of the tragedy of *King Lear,* that the aged monarch, though he has given his throne away, retains his imperiousness of heart, and continues to exhibit a senseless, if sometimes picturesque, pride and selfishness in face of misfortune. Even when he is overthrown he must still command; he fights against the very elements; he is determined to be at least the master of his own sufferings and destiny. But for this the necessary powers fail him; his life thus disordered terminates in madness. It was only by such an affliction that a character like his could be brought to repentance, . . . to humility, which is the parent of true love, and that love in him could be purified. Hence the melancholy close of that tragedy."* As Shakespeare has dealt with the king, so Isaiah with the people; he also shows us sorrow when it is defied bringing forth madness. On so impious a height man's brain grows dizzy, and he falls into that terrible abyss which is not, as some imagine, hell, but God's last purgatory. Shakespeare brings shattered Lear out of it, and Isaiah has a remnant of the people to save.

---

* Ulrici: *Shakespeare's Dramatic Art.*

CHAPTER IV.

ISAIAH'S CALL AND CONSECRATION.

Isaiah vi. (740 B.C.; written 735 ? or 725 ?).

IT has been already remarked that in chapter vi. we should find no other truths than those which have been unfolded in chapters ii.—v.: the Lord exalted in righteousness, the coming of a terrible judgement from Him upon Judah, and the survival of a bare remnant of the people. But chapter vi. treats the same subjects with a difference. In chapters ii.—iv. they gradually appear and grow to clearness in connection with the circumstances of Judah's history; in chapter v. they are formally and rhetorically vindicated; in chapter vi. we are led back to the secret and solemn moments of their first inspiration in the prophet's own soul. It may be asked why chapter vi. comes last and not first in this series, and why in an exposition, attempting to deal, as far as possible, chronologically with Isaiah's prophecies, his call should not form the subject of the first chapter. The answer is simple, and throws a flood of light upon the chapter. In all probability chapter vi. was written after its predecessors, and what Isaiah has put into it is not only what happened in the earliest moments of his prophetic life, but that spelt out and emphasized by his experience since. The ideal character of the narrative, and its date some years after the events which it relates, are now generally admitted. Of course the narrative is all fact. No one will believe that he, whose glance penetrated with such keenness the character of men and movements, looked with dimmer eye into his own heart. It is the spiritual process which the prophet actually passed through before the opening of his ministry. But it is that, developed by subsequent experience, and presented to us in the language of outward vision. Isaiah had been some years a prophet, long enough to make clear that prophecy was not to be for him what it had been for his predecessors in Israel, a series of detached inspirations and occasional missions, with short responsibilities, but a work for life, a profession and a career, with all that this means of postponement, failure, and fluctuation of popular feeling. Success had not come so rapidly as the prophet in his original enthusiasm had looked for, and his preaching had effected little upon the people. Therefore he would go back to the beginning, remind himself of that to which God had really called him, and vindicate the results of his ministry, at which people scoffed and his own heart grew sometimes sick. In chapter vi. Isaiah acts as his own remembrancer. If we keep in mind, that this chapter, describing Isaiah's call and consecration to the prophetic office, was written by a man who felt that office to be the burden of a lifetime, and who had to explain its nature and vindicate its results to his own soul—grown somewhat uncertain, it may be, of her original inspiration—we shall find light upon features of the chapter that are otherwise most obscure.

I. The Vision (vv. 1—4).

Several years, then, Isaiah looks back and says, *In*

the year King Uzziah died. There is more than a date given here; there is a great contrast suggested. Prophecy does not chronicle by time, but by experiences, and we have here, as it seems, the cardinal experience of a prophet's life.

All men knew of that glorious reign with the ghastly end—fifty years of royalty, and then a lazar-house. There had been no king like this one since Solomon; never, since the son of David brought the Queen of Sheba to his feet, had the national pride stood so high or the nation's dream of sovereignty touched such remote borders. The people's admiration invested Uzziah with all the graces of the ideal monarch. The chronicler of Judah tells us *that God helped him and made him to prosper, and his name spread far abroad, and he was marvellously helped till he was strong;* he with the double name—Azariah, Jehovah-his-Helper; Uzziah, Jehovah-his-Strength. How this glory fell upon the fancy of the future prophet, and dyed it deep, we may imagine from those marvellous colours, with which in later years he painted the king in his beauty. Think of the boy, the boy that was to be an Isaiah, the boy with the germs of this great prophecy in his heart— think of him and such a hero as this to shine upon him, and we may conceive how his whole nature opened out beneath that sun of royalty and absorbed its light.

Suddenly the glory was eclipsed, and Jerusalem learned that she had seen her king for the last time: *The Lord smote the king so that he was a leper unto the day of his death, and dwelt in a several house, and he was cut off from the house of the Lord.* Uzziah had gone into the temple, and attempted with his own hands to burn incense. Under a later dispensation of liberty he would have been applauded as a brave Protestant, vindicating the right of every worshipper of God to approach Him without the intervention of a special priesthood. Under the earlier dispensation of law his act could be regarded only as one of presumption, the expression of a worldly and irreverent temper, which ignored the infinite distance between God and man. It was followed, as sins of wilfulness in religion were always followed under the old covenant, by swift disaster. Uzziah suffered as Saul, Uzzah, Nadab and Abihu did. The wrath, with which he burst out on the opposing priests, brought on, or made evident as it is believed to have done in other cases, an attack of leprosy. The white spot stood out unmistakeably from the flushed forehead, and he was thrust from the temple—*yea, himself also hasted to go out.*

We can imagine how such a judgement, the moral of which must have been plain to all, affected the most sensitive heart in Jerusalem. Isaiah's imagination was darkened, but he tells us that the crisis was the enfranchisement of his faith. *In the year King Uzziah died*—it is as if a veil had dropped, and the prophet *saw* beyond what it had hidden, *the Lord sitting on a throne high and lifted up.* That it is no mere date Isaiah means, but a spiritual contrast which he is anxious to impress upon us, is made clear by his emphasis of the rank and not the name of God. It is *the Lord sitting upon a throne—the Lord* absolutely, set over against the human prince. The simple antithesis seems to speak of the passing away of the young man's hero-worship and the dawn of his faith; and so interpreted, this first verse of chapter vi. is only a concise summary of that development of religious experience which we have traced through chapters ii.—iv. Had Isaiah ever been subject to the religious temper of his time, the careless optimism of a prosperous and proud people, who entered upon their religious services without awe, *trampling the courts of the Lord*, and used them like Uzziah, for their *own honour*, who felt religion to be an easy thing, and dismissed from it all thoughts of judgement and feelings of penitence—if ever Isaiah had been subject to that temper, then once for all he was redeemed by this stroke upon Uzziah. And, as we have seen, there is every reason to believe that Isaiah did at first share the too easy public religion of his youth. That early vision of his (ii. 2—5), the establishment of Israel at the head of the nations, to be immediately attained at his own word (v. 5) and without preliminary purification, was it not simply a less gross form of the king's own religious presumption? Uzziah's fatal act was the expression of the besetting sin of his people, and in that sin Isaiah himself had been a partaker. *I am a man of unclean lips, and I dwell in the midst of a people of unclean lips.* In the person of their monarch the temper of the whole Jewish nation had come to judgement. Seeking the ends of religion by his own way, and ignoring the way God had appointed, Uzziah at the very moment of his insistence was hurled back and stamped unclean. The prophet's eyes were opened. The king sank into a leper's grave, but before Isaiah's vision the Divine majesty arose in all its loftiness. *I saw the Lord high and lifted up.* We already know what Isaiah means by these terms. He has used them of God's supremacy in righteousness above the low moral standards of men, of God's occupation of a far higher throne than that of the national deity of Judah, of God's infinite superiority to Israel's vulgar identification of His purposes with her material prosperity or His honour with the compromises of her politics, and especially of God's seat as their Judge over a people, who sought in their religion only satisfaction for their pride and love of ease.

From this contrast the whole vision expands as follows.

Under the mistaken idea that what Isaiah describes is the temple in Jerusalem, it has been remarked, that the place of his vision is wonderful in the case of one who set so little store by ceremonial worship. This, however, to which our prophet looks is no house built with hands, but Jehovah's own heavenly *palace* (ver. 1—not *temple*); only Isaiah describes it in terms of the Jerusalem temple which was its symbol. It was natural that the temple should furnish Isaiah not only with the framework of his vision, but also with the platform from which he saw it. For it was in the temple that Uzziah's sin was sinned and God's holiness vindicated upon him. It was in the temple that, when Isaiah beheld the scrupulous religiousness of the people, the contrast of that with their evil lives struck him, and he summed it up in the epigram *wickedness and worship* (i. 13). It was in the temple, in short, that the prophet's conscience had been most roused, and just where the conscience is most roused there is the vision of God to be expected. Very probably it was while brooding over Uzziah's judgement on the scene of its occurrence that Isaiah beheld his vision. Yet for all the vision contained the temple itself was too narrow. The truth which was to be revealed to Isaiah, the holiness of God, demanded a wider stage and the breaking down of those partitions, which, while they had been designed to impress God's presence on the worshipper, had only succeeded in veiling Him. So while the seer keeps his station on the threshold of the earthly building, soon to feel it rock beneath his feet, as heaven's praise bursts like thunder on the earth, and while his immediate neighbourhood remains the same familiar *house*, all beyond is glorified. The veil of the temple falls away, and everything behind it. No ark nor mercy-seat is visible, but a throne and a court— the palace of God in heaven, as we have it also pictured in the eleventh and twenty-ninth Psalms. The Royal Presence is everywhere. Isaiah describes no face, only a Presence and a Session : *the Lord sitting on a throne, and His skirts filled the palace.*

> "No face ; only the sight
> Of a sweepy garment vast and white
> With a hem that I could recognize." *

Around (not *above*, as in the English version) were ranged the hovering courtiers, of what shape and appearance we know not, except that they veiled their faces and their feet before the awful Holiness,—all wings and voice, perfect readinesses of praise and service. The prophet heard them chant in antiphon, like the temple choirs of priests. And the one choir cried out, *Holy, holy, holy is Jehovah of hosts ;* and the other responded, *The whole earth is full of His glory.*

It is by the familiar name Jehovah of hosts—the proper name of Israel's national God—that the prophet hears the choirs of heaven address the Divine Presence. But what they ascribe to the Deity is exactly what Israel will not ascribe, and the revelation they make of His nature is the contradiction of Israel's thoughts concerning Him.

What, in the first place, is HOLINESS ? We attach this term to a definite standard of morality or an un-

---

* Browning's "Christmas Eve."

usually impressive fulness of character. To our minds it is associated with very positive forces, as of comfort and conviction—perhaps because we take our ideas of it from the active operations of the Holy Ghost. The original force of the term *holiness*, however, was not positive but negative, and throughout the Old Testament, whatever modifications its meaning undergoes, it retains a negative flavour. The Hebrew word for holiness springs from a root which means *to set apart, make distinct, put at a distance from*. When God is described as the Holy One in the Old Testament it is generally with the purpose of withdrawing Him from some presumption of men upon His majesty or of negativing their unworthy thoughts of Him. The Holy One is the Incomparable: *To whom, then, will ye liken Me, that I should be equal to him? saith the Holy One* (xl. 25). He is the Unapproachable: *Who is able to stand before Jehovah, this holy God?* (1 Sam. vi. 20). He is the Utter Contrast of man: *I am God, and not man, the Holy One in the midst of thee* (Hosea xi. 9). He is the Exalted and Sublime: *Thus saith the high and lofty One that inhabiteth eternity, whose name is Holy: I dwell in the high and holy place* (lvii. 15). Generally speaking, then, holiness is equivalent to separateness, sublimity—in fact, just to that loftiness or exaltation which Isaiah has already so often reiterated as the principal attribute of God. In their thrice-repeated *Holy* the seraphs are only telling more emphatically to the prophet's ears what his eyes have already seen, *the Lord high and lifted up*. Better expression could not be found for the full idea of Godhead. This little word *Holy* radiates heaven's own breadth of meaning. Within its fundamental idea—distance or difference from man—what spaces are there not for every attribute of Godhead to flash? If the Holy One be originally He who is distinct from man and man's thoughts, and who impresses man from the beginning with the awful sublimity of the contrast in which He stands to him, how naturally may holiness come to cover not only that moral purity and intolerance of sin to which we now more strictly apply the term, but those metaphysical conceptions as well, which we gather up under the name " supernatural," and so finally, by lifting the Divine nature away from the change and vanity of this world, and emphasizing God's independence of all beside Himself, become the fittest expression we have for Him as the Infinite and Self-existent. Thus the word *holy* appeals in turn to each of the three great faculties of man's nature, by which he can be religiously exercised—his conscience, his affections, his reason; it covers the impressions which God makes on man as a sinner, on man as a worshipper, on man as a thinker. The Holy One is not only the Sinless and Sin-abhorring, but the Sublime and the Absolute too.

But while we recognize the exhaustiveness of the series of ideas about the Divine Nature, which develop from the root meaning of holiness, and to express which the word *holy* is variously used throughout the Scriptures, we must not, if we are to appreciate the use of the word on this occasion, miss the motive of recoil which starts them all. If we would hear what Isaiah heard in the seraphs' song, we must distinguish in the three-fold ascription of holiness the intensity of recoil from the confused religious views and low moral temper of the prophet's generation. It is no scholastic definition of Deity which the seraphim are giving. Not for a moment is it to be supposed, that to that age, whose representative is listening to them, they are attempting to convey an idea of the Trinity. Their thrice-uttered *Holy* is not theological accuracy, but religious emphasis. This angelic revelation of the holiness of God was intended for a generation, some of whom were idol-worshippers, confounding the Godhead with the work of their own hands or with natural objects, and none of whom were free from a confusion in principle of the Divine with the human and worldly, for which now sheer mental slovenliness, now a dull moral sense, and now positive pride was to blame. To worshippers who *trampled* the courts of the Lord with the careless feet, and looked up the temple with the unabashed faces, of routine, the cry of the seraphs, as they veiled their faces and their feet, travailed to restore that shuddering sense of the sublimity of the Divine Presence, which in the impressible youth of the race first impelled man, bowing low beneath the awful heavens, to name God by the name of the Holy. To men, again, careful of the legal forms of worship, but lawless and careless in their lives, the song of the seraphs revealed not the hard truth, against which they had already rubbed conscience trite, that God's law was inexorable, but the fiery fact that His whole nature burned with wrath towards sin. To men, once more, proud of their prestige and material prosperity, and presuming in their pride to take their own way with God, and to employ like Uzziah the exercises of religion for their own honour, this vision presented the real sovereignty of God: the Lord Himself seated on a throne *there*—just where they felt only a theatre for the display of their pride, or machinery for the attainment of their private ends. Thus did the three-fold cry of the angels meet the three-fold sinfulness of that generation of men.

But the first line of the seraph's song serves more than a temporary end. The Trisagion rings, and has need to ring, for ever down the Church. Everywhere and at all times these are the three besetting sins of religious people—callousness in worship, carelessness in life, and the temper which employs the forms of religion simply for self-indulgence or self-aggrandisement. These sins are induced by the same habit of contentment with mere form; they can be corrected only by the vision of the Personal Presence who is behind all form. Our organization, ritual, law and sacrament—we must be able to see them fall away, as Isaiah saw the sanctuary itself disappear, before God Himself, if we are to remain heartily moral and fervently religious. The Church of God has to learn that no mere multiplication of forms, nor a more æsthetic arrangement of them, will redeem her worshippers from callousness. Callousness is but the shell which the feelings develop in self-defence when left by the sluggish and impenetrative soul to beat upon the hard outsides of form. And nothing will fuse this shell of callousness but that ardent flame, which is kindled at the touching of the Divine and human spirits, when forms have fallen away and the soul beholds with open face the Eternal Himself. As with worship, so with morality. Holiness is secured not by ceremonial, but by a reverence for a holy Being. We shall rub our consciences trite against moral maxims or religious rites. It is the effluence of a Presence, which alone can create in us, and keep in us, a clean heart. And if any object that we thus make light of ritual and religious law, of Church and sacrament, the reply is obvious. Ritual and sacrament are to the living God but as the wick of a candle to the light thereof. They are given to reveal Him, and the process is not perfect unless they themselves perish from the thoughts to which they convey Him. If God is not felt to be present, as Isaiah felt Him to be, to the exclusion of all forms, then these will be certain to be employed, as Uzziah employed them, for the sake of the only other spiritual being of whom the worshipper is conscious—himself. Unless we are able to forget our ritual in spiritual communion with the very God, and to become unconscious of our organization in devout consciousness of our personal relation to Him, then ritual will be only a means of sensuous indulgence, organization only a machinery for selfish or sectarian ends. The vision of God—this is the one thing needful for worship and for conduct.

But while the one verse of the antiphon reiterates what Jehovah of hosts is in Himself, the other describes what He is in revelation. *The whole earth is full of His glory.* Glory is the correlative of holiness. Glory is that in which holiness comes to expression. Glory is the expression of holiness, as beauty is the expression of health. If holiness be as deep as we have seen, so varied then will glory be. There is nothing in the earth but it is the glory of God. *The fulness of the whole earth is His glory,* is the proper grammatical rendering of the song. For Jehovah of hosts is not the God only of Israel, but the Maker of heaven and earth, and not the victory of Israel alone, but the wealth and the beauty of all the world is His glory. So universal an ascription of glory is the proper parallel to that of absolute Godhead, which is implied in holiness.

II. THE CALL (vv. 4—8).

Thus, then, Isaiah, standing on earth, on the place of a great sin, with the conscience of his people's evil in his heart, and himself not without the feeling of guilt, looked into heaven, and beholding the glory of God, heard also with what pure praise and readiness of service the heavenly hosts surround His throne. No wonder the prophet felt the polluted threshold rock beneath him, or that as where fire and water mingle there should be the rising of a great smoke. For the smoke described is not, as some have imagined, that of acceptable incense, thick billows swelling through the temple to express the completion and satisfaction of the seraphs' worship; but it is the mist which ever arises where holiness and sin touch each other. It has been described both as the obscurity that envelops a weak mind in presence of a truth too great for it, and the darkness that falls upon a diseased eye when exposed to the mid-day sun. These are only analogies, and may mislead us. What Isaiah actually felt was the dim-eyed shame, the distraction, the embarrassment, the blinding shock of a personal encounter with One whom he was utterly unfit to meet. For this was a personal encounter. We have spelt out the revelation sentence by sentence in gradual argument; but Isaiah did not reach it through argument or brooding. It was not to the prophet what it is to his expositors, a pregnant thought, that his intellect might gradually unfold, but a Personal Presence, which apprehended and overwhelmed him. God and he were there face to face. *Then said I, Woe is me, for I am undone, because a man unclean of lips am I, and in the midst of a people unclean of lips do I dwell; for the King, Jehovah of hosts, mine eyes have beheld.*

The form of the prophet's confession, *uncleanness of lips*, will not surprise us as far as he makes it for himself. As with the disease of the body, so with the sin of the soul; each often gathers to one point of pain. Every man, though wholly sinful by nature, has his own particular consciousness of guilt. Isaiah being a prophet felt his mortal weakness most upon his lips. The inclusion of the people, however, along with himself under this form of guilt, suggests a wider interpretation of it. The lips are, as it were, the blossom of a man. *Grace is poured upon thy lips, therefore God hath blessed thee for ever. If any man offend not in word, the same is a perfect man, able to bridle the whole body also.* It is in the blossom of a plant that the plant's defects become conspicuous; it is when all a man's faculties combine for the complex and delicate office of expression that any fault which is in him will come to the surface. Isaiah had been listening to the perfect praise of sinless beings, and it brought into startling relief the defects of his own people's worship. Unclean of lips these were indeed when brought against that heavenly choir. Their social and political sin—sin of heart and home and market—came to a head in their worship, and what should have been the blossom of their life fell to the ground like a rotten leaf beneath the stainless beauty of the seraphs' praise.

While the prophet thus passionately gathered his guilt upon his lips, a sacrament was preparing on which God concentrated His mercy to meet it. Sacrament and lips, applied mercy and presented sin, now come together. *Then flew unto me one of the seraphim, and in his hand a glowing stone —with tongs had he taken it off the altar—and he touched my mouth and said, Lo, this hath touched thy lips, and so thy iniquity passeth away and thy sin is atoned for.*

The idea of this function is very evident, and a scholar who has said that it "would perhaps be quite intelligible to the contemporaries of the prophet, but is undoubtedly obscure to us," appears to have said just the reverse of what is right; for so simple a process of atonement leaves out the most characteristic details of the Jewish ritual of sacrifice, while it anticipates in an unmistakeable manner the essence of the Christian sacrament. In a scene of expiation laid under the old covenant, we are struck by the absence of oblation or sacrificial act on the part of the sinner himself. There is here no victim slain, no blood sprinkled; an altar is only parenthetically suggested, and even then in its simplest form, of a hearth on which the Divine fire is continually burning. The *glowing stone*, not *live coal* as in the English version, was no part of the temple furniture, but the ordinary means of conveying heat or applying fire in the various purposes of household life. There was, it is true, a carrying of fire in some of the temple services, as, for example, on the great Day of Atonement, but then it was effected by a small grate filled with living embers. In the household, on the other hand, when cakes had to be baked, or milk boiled, or water warmed, or in fifty similar applications of fire, a glowing stone taken from off the hearth was the invariable instrument. It is this swift and simple domestic process which Isaiah now sees substituted for the slow and intricate ceremonial of the temple —a seraph with a glowing stone in his hand, *with tongs had he taken it off the altar.* And yet the prophet feels this only as a more direct expression of the very same idea, with which the elaborate ritual was inspired—for which the victim was slain, and the flesh consumed in fire, and the blood sprinkled. Isaiah desires nothing else, and receives no more, than the ceremonial law was intended to assure to the sinner— pardon of his sin and reconciliation to God. But our prophet will have conviction of these immediately, and with a force which the ordinary ritual is incapable of expressing. The feelings of this Jew are too intense and spiritual to be satisfied with the slow pageant of the earthly temple, whose performances to a man in his horror could only have appeared so indifferent and far away from himself as not to be really his own nor to effect what he passionately desired. Instead therefore of laying his guilt in the shape of some victim on the altar, Isaiah, with a keener sense of its inseparableness from himself, presents it to God upon his own lips. Instead of being satisfied with beholding the fire of God consume it on another body than his own, at a distance from himself, he feels that fire visit the very threshold of his nature, where he has gathered the guilt, and consume it there. The whole secret of this startling nonconformity to the law, on the very floor of the temple, is that for a man who has penetrated to the presence of God the legal forms are left far behind, and he stands face to face with the truth by which they are inspired. In that Divine Presence Isaiah is his own altar; he acts his guilt in his own person, and so he feels the expiatory fire come to his very self directly from the heavenly hearth. It is a replica of the fifty-first Psalm: *For Thou delightest not in sacrifice, else would I give it; Thou hast no pleasure in burnt offering. The sacrifices of God are a broken spirit.* This is my sacrifice, my sense of guilt gathered here upon my lips: my *broken and contrite heart*, who feel myself undone before Thee, *Lord, Thou wilt not despise.*

It has always been remarked as one of the most powerful proofs of the originality and Divine force of Christianity, that from man's worship of God, and especially from those parts in which the forgiveness of sin is sought and assured, it did away with the necessity of a physical rite of sacrifice; that it broke the universal and immemorial habit by which man presented to God a material offering for the guilt of his soul. By remembering this fact we may measure the religious significance of the scene we now contemplate. Nearly eight centuries before there was accomplished upon Calvary that Divine Sacrifice for sin, which abrogated a rite of expiation, hitherto universally adopted by the conscience of humanity, we find a Jew, in the dispensation where such a rite was most religiously enforced, trembling under the conviction of sin, and upon a floor crowded with suggestions of physical sacrifice; yet the only sacrifice he offers is the purely spiritual one of confession. It is most notable. Look at it from a human point of view, and we can estimate Isaiah's immense spiritual originality; look at it from a Divine, and we cannot help perceiving a distinct foreshadow of what was to take place by the blood of Jesus under the new covenant. To this man, as to some others of his dispensation, whose experience our Christian sympathy recognizes so readily in the Psalms, there was granted aforetime boldness to enter into the holiest. For this is the explanation of Isaiah's marvellous disregard of the temple ritual. It is all behind him. This man has passed within the veil. Forms are all behind him, and he is face to face with God. But between two beings in that position, intercourse by the far off and uncertain signals of sacrifice is inconceivable. It can only take place by the simple unfolding of the heart. It must be rational, intelligent and by speech. When man is at such close quarters with God what sacrifice is possible but the sacrifice of the lips? Form for the Divine reply there must be some, for even Christianity has its sacraments, but like them this sacrament is of the very simplest form, and like them it is accompanied by the explanatory word. As Christ under the new covenant took bread and wine, and made the homely action of feeding upon them the sign and seal to His disciples of the forgiveness of their sins, so His angel under the old and sterner covenant took the more severe, but as simple and domestic form of fire to express the same to His prophet. And we do well to emphasize that the experimental value of this sacrament of fire is bestowed by the word attached to it. It is not a dumb sacrament, with a magical efficacy. But the prophet's mind is persuaded and his conscience set at peace by the intelligible words of the minister of the sacrament.

Isaiah's sin being taken away, he is able to discern the voice of God Himself. It is in the most beautiful accordance with what has already happened that he hears this not as command, but request, and answers not of compulsion, but of freedom. *And I heard the voice of the Lord saying, Whom shall I send? and who will go for us? And I said, Here am I; send me.* What spiritual understanding alike of the will of God and the responsibility of man, what evangelic liberty and boldness, are here! Here we touch the spring of that high flight Isaiah takes both in prophecy and in active service for the State. Here we have the secret of the filial freedom, the life-long sense of responsibility, the regal power of initiative, the sustained and unfaltering career, which distinguish Isaiah among the ministers of the old covenant, and stamp him prophet by the heart and for the life, as many of them are only by the office and for the occasion. Other prophets are the servants of the God of heaven; Isaiah stands next the Son Himself. On others the hand of the Lord is laid in irresistible compulsion; the greatest of them are often ignorant, by turns headstrong and craven, deserving correction, and generally in need of supplementary calls and inspirations. But of such scourges and such doles Isaiah's royal career is absolutely without a trace. His course, begun in freedom, is pursued without hesitation or anxiety; begun in utter self-sacrifice, it knows henceforth no moment of grudging or disobedience. *Esaias is very bold*, because he is so free and so fully devoted. In the presence of mind with which he meets each sudden change of politics during that bewildering half-century of Judah's history, we seem to hear his calm voice repeating its first, *Here am I*. Presence of mind he always had. The kaleidoscope shifts: it is now Egyptian intrigue, now Assyrian force; now a false king requiring threat of displacement by God's own hero, now a true king, but helpless and in need of consolation; now a rebellious people to be condemned, and now an oppressed and penitent one to be encouraged:—different dangers, with different sorts of salvation possible, obliging the prophet to promise different futures, and to say things inconsistent with what he had already said. Yet Isaiah never hesitates; he can always say, *Here am I*. We hear that voice again in the spontaneousness and versatility of his style. Isaiah is one of the great kings of literature, with every variety of style under his sway, passing with perfect readiness, as subject or occasion calls, from one to another of the tones of a superbly endowed nature. Everywhere this man impresses us with his personality, with the wealth of his nature and the perfection of his control of it. But the personality is consecrated. The *Here am I* is followed by the *send me*. And its health, harmony and boldness, are derived, Isaiah being his own witness, from this early sense of pardon and purification at the Divine hands. Isaiah is indeed a king and a priest unto God—a king with all his powers at his own command, a priest with them all consecrated to the service of Heaven.

One cannot pass away from these verses without observing the plain answer which they give to the question, What is a call to the ministry of God? In these days of dust and distraction, full of party cries, with so many side issues of doctrine and duty presenting themselves, and the solid attractions of so many other services insensibly leading men to look for the same sort of attractiveness in the ministry, it may prove a relief to some to ponder the simple elements of Isaiah's call to be a professional and life-long prophet. Isaiah got no "call" in our conventional sense of the word, no compulsion that he must go, no articulate voice describing him as the sort of man needed for the work, nor any of those similar "calls" which sluggish and craven spirits so often desire to relieve them of the responsibility or the strenuous effort needed in deciding for a profession which their conscience will not permit them to refuse. Isaiah got no such call. After passing through the fundamental religious experiences of forgiveness and cleansing, which are in every case the indispensable premises of life with God, Isaiah was left to himself. No direct summons was addressed to him, no compulsion was laid on him; but he heard the voice of God asking generally for messengers, and he on his own responsibility answered it for himself in particular. He heard from the Divine lips of the Divine need for messengers, and he was immediately full of the mind that he was the man for the mission, and of the heart to give himself to it. So great an example cannot be too closely studied by candidates for the ministry in our own day. Sacrifice is not the half-sleepy, half-reluctant submission to the force of circumstance or opinion, in which shape it is so often travestied among us, but the resolute self-surrender and willing resignation of a free and reasonable soul. There are many in our day who look for an irresistible compulsion into the ministry of the Church; sensitive as they are to the material bias by which men roll off into other professions, they pray for something of a similar kind to prevail with them in this direction also. There are men who pass into the ministry by social pressure or the opinion of the circles they belong to, and there are men who adopt the profession simply because it is on the line of least resistance. From which false beginnings rise the spent force, the premature stoppages, the stagnancy, the aimlessness and heartlessness, which are the scandals of the professional ministry and the weakness of the Christian Church in our day. Men who drift into the ministry, as it is certain so many do, become mere ecclesiastical flotsam and jetsam, incapable of giving carriage to any soul across the waters of this life, uncertain of their own arrival anywhere, and of all the waste of their generation, the most patent and disgraceful. God will have no drift-wood for His sacrifices, no drift-men for His ministers. Self-consecration is the beginning of His service, and a sense of our own freedom and our own responsibility is an indispensable element in the act of self-consecration. *We*—not God—have to make the decision. We are not to be dead, but living, sacrifices, and everything which renders us less than fully alive both mars at the time the sincerity of our surrender and reacts for evil upon the whole of our subsequent ministry.

III. The Commission (vv. 9—13).

A heart so resolutely devoted as we have seen Isaiah's to be was surely prepared against any degree of discouragement, but probably never did man receive so awful a commission as he describes himself to have done. Not that we are to suppose that this fell upon Isaiah all at once, in the suddenness and distinctness with which he here records it. Our sense of its awfulness will only be increased when we realize that Isaiah became aware of it, not in the shock of a single discovery, sufficiently great to have carried its own anæsthetic along with it, but through a prolonged process of disillusion, and at the pain of those repeated disappointments, which are all the more painful that none singly is great enough to stupefy. It is just at this point of our chapter, that we feel most the need of supposing it to have been written some years after the consecration of Isaiah, when his experience had grown long enough to articulate the dim forebodings of that solemn moment. *Go and say to this people, Hearing, hear ye, but understand not; seeing, see ye, but know not. Make fat the heart of this people, and its ears make heavy, and its eyes smear, lest it see with its eyes, and hear with its ears, and its heart understand, and it turn again and* *be healed.* No prophet, we may be sure, would be asked by God to go and tell his audiences that in so many words, at the beginning of his career. It is only by experience that a man understands that kind of a commission,* and for the required experience Isaiah had not long to wait after entering on his ministry. Ahaz himself, in whose death-year it is supposed by many that Isaiah wrote this account of his consecration—the conduct of Ahaz himself was sufficient to have brought out the convictions of the prophet's heart in this startling form, in which he has stated his commission. By the word of the Lord and an offer of a sign from Him, Isaiah did make fat that monarch's heart and smear his eyes. And perverse as the rulers of Judah were in the examples and policies they set, the people were as blindly bent on following them to destruction. *Every one,* said Isaiah, when he must have been for some time a prophet—*every one is a hypocrite and an evildoer, and every mouth speaketh folly.*

But if that clear, bitter way of putting the matter can have come to Isaiah only with the experience of some years, why does he place it upon the lips of God, as they give him his commission? Because Isaiah is stating not merely his own singular experience, but a truth always true of the preaching of the word of God, and of which no prophet at the time of his consecration to that ministry can be without at least a foreboding. We have not exhausted the meaning of this awful commission when we say that it is only

---

* Even Calvin, though in order to prove that Isaiah had been prophesying for some time before his inaugural vision, says that his commission implies some years' actual experience of the obstinacy of the people.

a forcible anticipation of the prophet's actual experience. There is more here than one man's experience. Over and over again are these words quoted in the New Testament, till we learn to find them true always and everywhere that the Word of God is preached to men,—the description of what would seem to be its necessary effect upon many souls. Both Jesus and Paul use Isaiah's commission of themselves. They do so like Isaiah at an advanced stage in their ministry, when the shock of misunderstanding and rejection has been repeatedly felt, but then not solely as an apt description of their own experience. They quote God's words to Isaiah as a prophecy fulfilled in their own case—that is to say, as the statement of a great principle or truth of which their own ministry is only another instance. Their own disappointments have roused them to the fact, that this is always an effect of the word of God upon numbers of men—to deaden their spiritual faculties. While Matthew and the book of Acts adopt the milder Greek version of Isaiah's commission, John gives a rendering that is even stronger than the original. *He hath blinded,* he says of God Himself, *their eyes and hardened their hearts, lest they should see with their eyes and perceive with their hearts.* In Mark's narrative Christ says that He speaks to them that are outside in parables, *for the purpose that seeing they may see, and not perceive, and hearing they may hear, and not understand, lest haply they should turn again and it should be forgiven them.* We may suspect, in an utterance so strange to the lips of the Lord of salvation, merely the irony of His baffled love. But it is rather the statement of what He believed to be the necessary effect of a ministry like His own. It marks the direction, not of His desire, but of natural sequence.

With these instances we can go back to Isaiah and understand why he should have described the bitter fruits of experience as an imperative laid upon him by God. *Make fat the heart of this people, and its ears make heavy, and its eyes do thou smear.* It is the fashion of the prophet's grammar, when it would state a principle or necessary effect, to put it in the form of a command. What God expresses to Isaiah so imperatively as almost to take our breath away; what Christ uttered with such abruptness that we ask, Does He speak in irony? what Paul laid down as the conviction of a long and patient ministry, is the great truth that the Word of God has not only a saving power, but that even in its gentlest pleadings and its purest Gospel, even by the mouth of Him who came, not to condemn, but to save the world, it has a power that is judicial and condemnatory.

It is frequently remarked by us as perhaps the most deplorable fact of our experience, that there exists in human nature an accursed facility for turning God's gifts to precisely the opposite ends from those for which He gave them. So common is man's misunderstanding of the plainest signs, and so frequent his abuse of the most evident favours of Heaven, that a spectator of the drama of human history might imagine its Author to have been a Cynic or Comedian, portraying for His own amusement the loss of the erring at the very moment of what might have been their recovery, the frustration of love at the point of its greatest warmth and expectancy. Let him look closer, however, and he will perceive, not a comedy, but a tragedy, for neither chance nor cruel sport is here at work, but free will and the laws of habit, with retribution and penalty. These actors are not puppets in the hand of a Power that moves them at will; each of them plays his own part, and the abuse and contradiction, of which he is guilty, are but the prerogative of his freedom. They are free beings who thus reject the gift of Divine assistance, and so piteously misunderstand Divine truth. Look closer still, and you will see that the way they talk, the impression they accept of God's goodness, the effect of His judgements upon them, is determined not at the moment of their choice, and not by a single act of their will, but by the whole tenor of their previous life. In the sudden flash of some gift or opportunity, men reveal the stuff of which they are made, the disposition they have bred in themselves. Opportunity in human life is as often judgement as it is salvation. When we perceive these things, we understand that life is not a comedy, where chance governs or incongruous situations are invented by an Almighty Satirist for his own sport, but a tragedy, with all tragedy's pathetic elements of royal wills contending in freedom with each other, of men's wills clashing with God's: men the makers of their own destinies, and Nemesis not directing, but following their actions. We go back to the very fundamentals of our nature on this dread question. To understand what has been called "a great law in human degeneracy," that "the evil heart can assimilate good to itself and convert it to its nature," we must understand what free will means, and take into account the terrible influence of habit.

Now there is no more conspicuous instance of this law, than that which is afforded by the preaching of the Gospel of God. God's Word, as Christ reminds us, does not fall on virgin soil; it falls on soil already holding other seed. When a preacher stands up with the Word of God in a great congregation, vast as Scripture warrants us for believing his power to be, his is not the only power that is operative. Each man present has a life behind that hour and place, lying away in the darkness, silent and dead as far as the congregation are concerned, but in his own heart as vivid and loud as the voice of the preacher, though he be preaching never so forcibly. The prophet is not the only power in the delivery of God's Word, nor is the Holy Spirit the only power. That would make all preaching of the Word a mere display. But the Bible represents it as a strife. And now it is said of men themselves that they harden their hearts against the Word, and now— because such hardening is the result of previous sinning, and has therefore a judicial character—that God hardens their hearts. *Simon, Simon,* said Christ to a face that spread out to His own all the ardour of worship, *Satan is desiring to have you, but I have prayed that your faith fail not.* God sends His Word into our hearts; the Mediator stands by, and prays that it make us His own. But there are other factors in the operation, and the result depends on our own will; it depends on our own will, and it is dreadfully determined by our habits.

Now this is one of the first facts to which a young reformer or prophet awakes. Such an awakening is a necessary element in his education and apprenticeship. He has seen the Lord high and lifted up. His lips have been touched by the coal from off the altar. His first feeling is that nothing can withstand that power, nothing gainsay this inspiration. Is he a Nehemiah, and the hand of the Lord has been mighty upon him? Then he feels that he has but to tell his fellows of it to make them as enthusiastic in the Lord's work as himself. Is he a Mazzini, aflame from his boyhood with aspirations for his country, consecrated from his birth to the cause of duty? Then he leaps with joy upon his mission; he has but to show himself, to speak, to lead the way, and his country is free. Is he—to descend to a lower degree of prophecy—a Fourier, sensitive more than most to how anarchic society is, and righteously eager to settle it upon stable foundations? Then he draws his plans for reconstruction, he projects his phalanges and phalansteres, and believes that he has solved the social problem. Is he—to come back to the heights—an Isaiah, with the Word of God in him like fire? Then he sees his vision of the perfect state; he thinks to lift his people to it by a word. *O house of Jacob,* he says, *come ye, and let us walk in the light of the Lord!*

For all of whom the next necessary stage of experience is one of disappointment, with the hard commission, *Make the heart of this people fat.* They must learn that, if God has caught themselves young, and when it was possible to make them entirely His own, the human race to whom He sends them is old, too old for them to effect much upon the mass of it beyond the hardening and perpetuation of evil. Fourier finds that to produce his perfect State he would need to re-create mankind, to cut down the tree to the very roots, and begin again. After the first rush of patriotic fervour, which carried so many of his countrymen with him, Mazzini discovers himself in " a moral desert," confesses that the struggle to liberate his fatherland, which has only quickened him to further devotion in so great a cause, has been productive of scepticism in his followers, and has left them withered and hardened of heart, whom it had found so capable of heroic impulses. He tells us how they upbraided and scorned him, left him in exile, and returned to their homes, from which they had set out with vows to die for their country, doubting now whether there was anything at all worth living or dying for outside themselves. Mazzini's description of the first passage of his career is invaluable for the light which it throws upon this commission of Isaiah. History does not contain a more dramatic representation of the entirely opposite effects of the same Divine movement upon different natures. While the first efforts for the liberty of Italy materialized the greater number of his countrymen, whom Mazzini had persuaded to embark upon it, the failure and their consequent defection only served to strip this heroic soul of the last rags of selfishness, and consecrate it more utterly to the will of God and the duty that lay before it.

A few sentences from the confessions of the Italian patriot may be quoted, with benefit to our appreciation of what the Hebrew prophet must have passed through.

"It was the tempest of doubt, which I believe all who devote their lives to a great enterprise, yet have not dried and withered up their soul—like Robespierre—beneath some barren intellectual formula, but have retained a loving heart, are doomed, once at least, to battle through. My heart was overflowing with and greedy of affection, as fresh and eager to unfold to joy as in the days when sustained by my mother's smile, as full of fervid hope for others, at least, if not for myself. But during these fatal months there darkened round me such a hurricane of sorrow, disillusion and deception as to bring before my eyes, in all its ghastly nakedness, a foreshadowing of the old age of my soul, solitary in a desert world, wherein no comfort in the struggle was vouchsafed to me. It was not only the overthrow for an indefinite period of every Italian hope, . . . it was the falling to pieces of that moral edifice of faith and love from which alone I had derived strength for the combat; the scepticism I saw arising round me on every side; the failure of faith in those who had solemnly bound themselves to pursue unshaken the path we had known at the outset to be choked with sorrows; the distrust I detected in those most dear to me, as to the motives and intentions which sustained and urged me onward in the evidently unequal struggle. . . . When I felt that I was indeed alone in the world, I drew back in terror at the void before me. There, in that moral desert, doubt came upon me. Perhaps I was wrong, and the world right? Perhaps my idea was indeed a dream? . . . One morning I awoke to find my mind tranquil and my spirit calmed, as one who has passed through a great danger. The first thought that passed across my spirit was, *Your sufferings are the temptations of egotism, and arise from a misconception of life.* . . . I perceived that although every instinct of my heart rebelled against that fatal and ignoble definition of life which makes it to be a *search after happiness*, yet I had not completely freed myself from the dominating influence exercised by it upon the age. . . . I had been unable to realize the true ideal of love—love without earthly hope. . . . Life is a mission, duty therefore its highest law. From the idea of God I descended to faith in a mission and its logical consequence—duty the supreme rule of life; and having reached that faith, I swore to myself that nothing in this world should again make me doubt or forsake it. It was, as Dante says, passing through martyrdom to peace—'a forced and desperate peace.' I do not deny, for I fraternized with sorrow, and wrapped myself in it as in a mantle; but yet it was peace, for I learned to suffer without rebellion, and to live calmly and in harmony with my own spirit. I reverently bless God the Father for what consolations of affection—I can conceive of no other—He has vouchsafed to me in my later years; and in them I gather strength to struggle with the occasional return of weariness of existence. But even were these consolations denied me, I believe I should still be what I am. Whether the sun shine with the serene splendour of an Italian noon, or the leaden, corpse-like hue of the northern mist be above us, I cannot see that it changes our duty. God dwells above the earthly heaven, and the holy stars of faith and the future still shine within our souls, even though their light consume itself unreflected as the sepulchral lamp."

Such sentences are the best commentary we can offer on our text. The cases of the Hebrew and Italian prophets are wonderfully alike. We who have read Isaiah's fifth chapter know how his heart also was " overflowing with and greedy of affection," and in the second and third chapters we have seen "the hurricane of sorrow, disillusion and deception darken round him." "The falling to pieces of the moral edifice of faith and love," "scepticism rising on every side," "failure of faith in those who had solemnly bound themselves," "distrust detected in those most dear to me"—and all felt by the prophet as the effect of the sacred movement God had inspired him to begin :—how exact a counterpart it is to the cumulative process of brutalizing which Isaiah heard God lay upon him, with the imperative *Make the heart of this people fat!* In such a morally blind, deaf and dead-hearted world Isaiah's faith was indeed "to consume itself unreflected like the sepulchral lamp." The glimpse into his heart given us by Mazzini enables us to realize with what terror Isaiah faced such a void. *O Lord, how long?* This, too, breathes the air of "a forced and desperate peace," the spirit of one who, having realized life as a mission, has made the much more rare recognition that the logical consequence is neither the promise of success nor the assurance of sympathy, but simply the acceptance of duty, with whatever results and under whatever skies it pleases God to bring over him.

> *Until cities fall into ruin without an inhabitant,*
> *And houses without a man,*
> *And the land be left desolately waste,*
> *And Jehovah have removed man far away,*
> *And great be the desert in the midst of the land;*
> *And still if there be a tenth in it,*
> *Even it shall be again for consuming.*
> *Like the terebinth, and like the oak,*
> *Whose stock when they are felled remaineth in them,*
> *The holy seed shall be its stock.*

The meaning of these words is too plain to require exposition, but we can hardly over-emphasize them. This is to be Isaiah's one text throughout his career. "Judgement shall pass through; a remnant shall remain." All the politics of his day, the movement of the world's forces, the devastation of the holy land, the first captivities of the holy people, the reiterated defeats and disappointments of the next fifty years—all shall be clear and tolerable to Isaiah as the fulfilling of the sentence to which he listened in such "forced and desperate peace" on the day of his consecration. He has had the worst branded into him; henceforth no man nor thing may trouble him. He has seen the worst, and knows there is a beginning beyond. So when the wickedness of Judah and the violence of Assyria alike seem most unrestrained—Assyria most bent on destroying Judah, and Judah least worthy to live—Isaiah will yet cling to this, that a remnant must remain. All his prophecies will be variations of this text; it is the key to his apparent paradoxes. He will proclaim the Assyrians to be God's instrument, yet devote them to destruction. He will hail their advance on Judah, and yet as exultingly mark its limit, because of the determination in which he asked the question, *O Lord, how long?* and the clearness with which he understood the *until*, that came in answer to it. Every prediction he makes, every turn he seeks to give to the practical politics of Judah, are simply due to his grasp of these two facts—a withering and repeated devastation, in the end a bare survival. He has, indeed, prophecies which travel farther; occasionally he is permitted to indulge in visions of a new dispensation. Like Moses, he climbs his Pisgah, but he is like Moses also in this, that his lifetime is exhausted with the attainment of the margin of a long period of judgement and struggle, and then he passes from our sight, and no man knoweth his sepulchre unto this day. As abruptly as this vision closes with the announcement of *the remnant*, so abruptly does Isaiah disappear on the fulfilment of the announcement—some forty years subsequent to this vision—in the sudden rescue of the holy seed from the grasp of Sennacherib.

We have now finished the first period of Isaiah's career. Let us catalogue what are his leading doctrines up to this point. High above a very sinful people, and beyond all their conceptions of Him, Jehovah, the national God, rises holy, exalted in righteousness. From such a God to such a people it can only be judgement and affliction that pass; and these shall not be averted by the fact that He is the national God, and they His worshippers. Of this affliction the Assyrians gathering far off upon the horizon are evidently to be the instruments. The affliction shall be very sweeping; again and again shall it come; but the Lord will finally save a remnant of His people. Three elements compose this preaching—a very keen and practical conscience of sin; an overpowering vision of God, in whose immediate intimacy the prophet believes himself to be; and a very sharp perception of the politics of the day.

One question rises. In this part of Isaiah's ministry there is no trace of that Figure whom we chiefly identify with his preaching, the Messiah. Let us have patience; it is not time for him; but the following is his connection with the prophet's present doctrines.

Isaiah's great result at present is the certainty of a remnant. That remnant will require two things—

they will require a rallying-point, and they will require a leader. Henceforth Isaiah's prophesying will be bent to one or other of these. The two grand purposes of his word and work will be, for the sake of the remnant, the inviolateness of Zion, and the coming of the Messiah. The former he has, indeed, already intimated (chap. iv.); the latter is now to share with it his hope and eloquence.

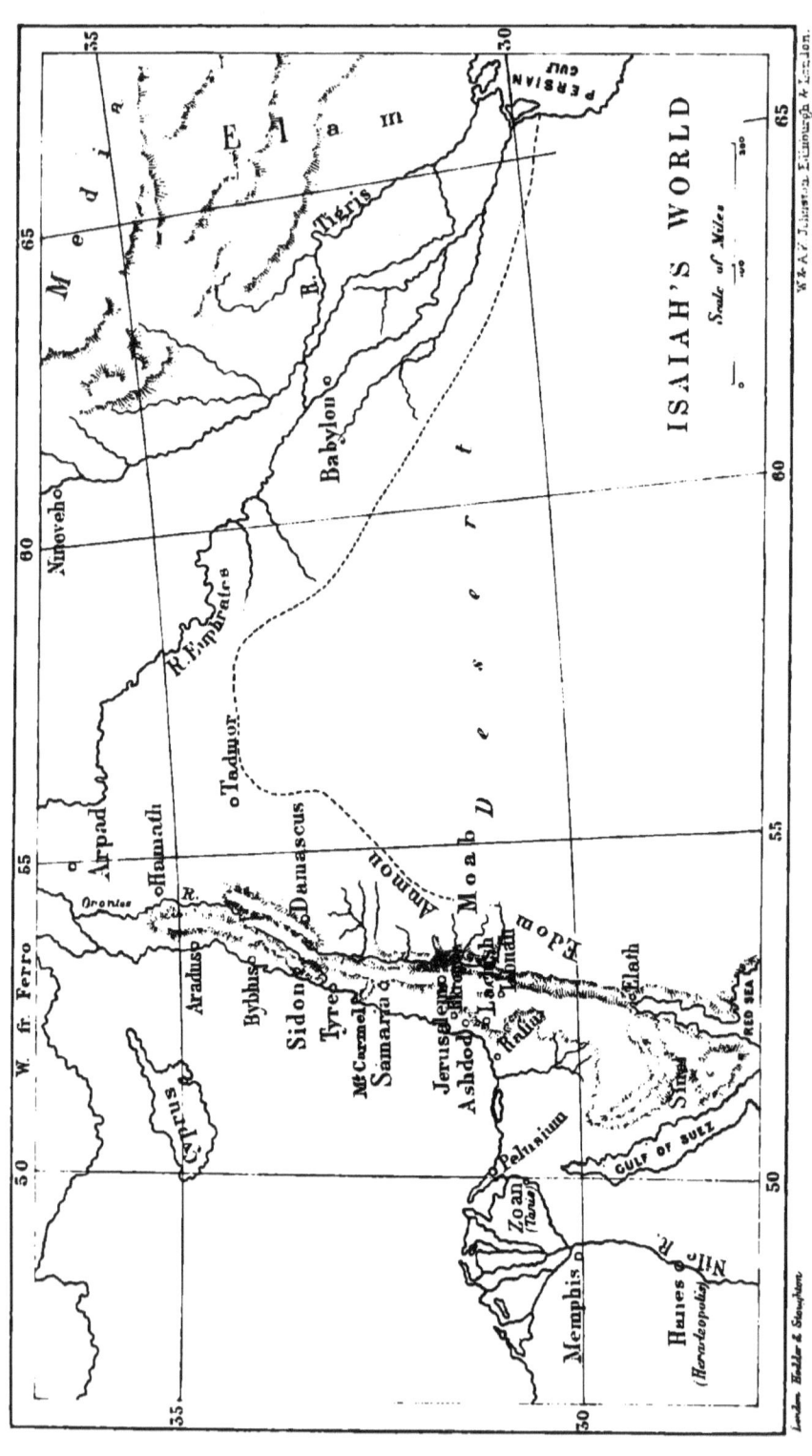

CHAPTER V.

THE WORLD IN ISAIAH'S DAY AND ISRAEL'S GOD.

735-730 B.C.

UP to this point we have been acquainted with Isaiah as a prophet of general principles, preaching to his countrymen the elements of righteousness and judgement, and tracing the main lines of fate along which their evil conduct was rapidly forcing them. We are now to observe him applying these principles to the executive politics of the time, and following Judah's conduct to the issues he had predicted for it in the world outside herself. Hitherto he has been concerned with the inner morals of Jewish society; he is now to engage himself with the effect of these on the fortunes of the Jewish State. In his seventh chapter Isaiah begins that career of practical statesmanship, which not only made him "the greatest political power in Israel since David," but placed him, far above his importance to his own people, upon a position of influence over all ages. To this eminence Isaiah was raised, as we shall see, by two things. First, there was the occasion of his times, for he lived at a juncture at which the vision of the *World*, as distinguished from the *Nation*, opened to his people's eyes. Second, he had the faith which enabled him to realize the government of the World by the One God, whom he has already beheld exalted and sovereign within the Nation. In the Nation we have seen Isaiah led to emphasize very absolutely the righteousness of God ; applying this to the whole World, he is now to speak as the prophet of what we call Providence. He has seen Jehovah ruling in righteousness in Judah ; he is now to take possession of the nations of the World in Jehovah's name. But we mistake Isaiah if we think it is any abstract doctrine of providence which he is about to inculcate. For him God's providence has in the meantime but one end: the preservation of a remnant of the holy people. Afterwards we shall find him expecting besides, the conversion of the whole World to faith in Israel's God.

The World in Isaiah's day was practically Western Asia. History had not long dawned upon Europe ; over Western Asia it was still noon. Draw a line from the Caspian to the mouth of the Persian Gulf; between that line and another crossing the Levant to the west of Cyprus, and continuing along the Libyan border of Egypt, lay the highest forms of religion and civilisation which our race had by that period achieved. This was the World on which Isaiah looked out from Jerusalem, the furthest borders of which he has described in his prophecies, and in the political history of which he illustrated his great principles. How was it composed?

There were, first of all, at either end of it, north-east and south-west, the two great empires of ASSYRIA and EGYPT, in many respects wonderful counterparts of each other. No one will understand the history of Palestine, who has not grasped its geographical position relative to these similar empires. Syria, shut up between the Mediterranean sea and the Arabian desert, has its outlets north and south into two great river-plains, each of them ending in a delta. Territories of that kind exert a double force on the world with which they are connected, now drawing across their boundaries the hungry races of neighbouring highlands and deserts, and again sending them forth, compact and resistless armies. This double action summarises the histories of both Egypt and Assyria from the earliest times to the period which we are now treating, and was the cause of the constant circulation, by which, as the Bible bears witness, the life of Syria was stirred from the Tower of Babel downwards. Mesopotamia and the Nile valley drew races as beggars to their rich pasture grounds, only to send them forth in subsequent centuries as conquerors. The century of Isaiah fell in a period of forward movement. Assyria and Egypt were afraid to leave each other in peace; and the wealth of Phœnicia, grown large enough to excite their cupidity, lay between them. In each of these empires, however, there was something to hamper this aggressive impulse. Neither Assyria nor Egypt was a homogeneous State. The valleys of the Euphrates and the Nile were, each of them the home of two nations. Beside Assyria lay Babylonia, once Assyria's mistress, and now of all the Assyrian provinces by far the hardest to hold in subjection, although it lay the nearest to home. In Isaiah's time, when an Assyrian monarch is unable to come into Palestine, Babylon is generally the reason; and it is by intriguing with Babylon that a king of Judah attempts to keep Assyria away from his own neighbourhood. But Babylon only delayed the Assyrian conquest. In Egypt, on the other hand, power was more equally balanced between the hardier people up the Nile and the wealthier people down the Nile — between the Ethiopians and the Egyptians proper. It was the repeated and undecisive contests between these two during the whole of Isaiah's day, which kept Egypt from being an effective force in the politics of Western Asia. In Isaiah's day no Egyptian army advanced more than a few leagues beyond its own frontier.

Next in this world of Western Asia come the PHŒNICIANS. We may say that they connected Egypt and Assyria, for although Phœnicia proper meant only the hundred and fifty miles of coast between Carmel and the bay of Antioch, the Phœnicians had large colonies on the delta of the Nile and trading posts upon the Euphrates. They were gathered into independent but more or less confederate cities, the chief of them Tyre and Sidon; which, while they attempted the offensive only in trade, were by their wealth and maritime advantages capable of offering at once a stronger attraction and a more stubborn resistance to the Assyrian arms, than any other power of the time. Between Phœnicia proper and the mouths of the Nile, the coast was held by groups of PHILISTINE cities, whose nearness to Egypt rather than their own strength was the source of a frequent audacity against Assyria, and the reason why they appear in the history of this period oftener than any other State as the object of Assyrian campaigns.

Behind Phœnicia and the Philistines lay a number of inland territories: the sister-States of Judah and Northern Israel, with their cousins Edom, Moab, and Aram or Syria. Of which JUDAH and ISRAEL were together about the size of Wales; EDOM a mountain range the size and shape of Cornwall; MOAB, on its north, a broken tableland, about a Devonshire; and ARAM, or SYRIA, a territory round Damascus, of uncertain size, but considerable enough to have resisted Assyria for a hundred and twenty years. Beyond Aram, again, to the north, lay the smaller State of HAMATH, in the mouth of the pass between the Lebanons, with nothing from it to the Euphrates. And then, hovering upon the east of these settled States, were a variety of more or less NOMADIC TRIBES, whose refuges were the vast deserts of which so large a part of Western Asia consists.

Here was a world, with some of its constituents wedged pretty firmly by mutual pressure, but in the main broken and restless—a political surface that was always changing. The whole was subject to the movements of the two empires at its extremes. One of them could not move without sending a thrill through to the borders of the other. The approximate distances were these:—from Egypt's border to Jerusalem, about one hundred miles; from Jerusalem to Samaria, forty-five; from Samaria to Damascus, one hundred and fifteen; from Damascus to Hamath, one hundred and thirty; and from Hamath to the Euphrates, one hundred; in all from the border of Egypt to the border of Assyria four hundred and ninety English statute miles. The main line of war and traffic, coming up from Egypt, kept the coast to the plain of Esdraelon, which it crossed towards Damascus, travelling by the north of the sea of Galilee, *the way of the sea.* Northern Israel was bound to fall an early prey to armies, whose easiest path thus traversed her richest provinces. Judah, on the other hand, occupied a position so elevated and apart, that it was likely to be the last that either Assyria or Egypt would achieve in their subjugation of the States between them.

Thus, then, Western Asia spread itself out in Isaiah's day. Let us take one more rapid glance across it. Assyria to the north, powerful and on the offensive, but hampered by Babylon; Egypt on the south, weakened and in reserve; all the cities and States between turning their faces desperately northwards, but each with an ear bent back for the promises of the laggard southern power, and occasionally supported by its subsidies; Hamath, their advanced guard at the mouth of the pass between the Lebanons, looking out towards the Euphrates; Tyre and Sidon attractive to the Assyrian king, whose policy is ultimately commercial, by their wealth, both they and the Philistine cities obstructing his path by the coast to his great rival of Egypt; Israel bulwarked against Assyria by Hamath and Damascus, but in danger, as soon as they fall, of seeing her richest provinces overrun; Judah unlikely in the general restlessness to retain her hold upon Edom, but within her own borders tolerably secure, neither lying in the Assyrian's path to Egypt, nor wealthy enough to attract him out of it; safe, therefore, in the neutrality which Isaiah ceaselessly urges her to preserve, and in danger of suction into the whirlpool of the approach of the two empires only through the foolish desire of her rulers to secure an utterly unnecessary alliance with the one or the other of them.

For a hundred and twenty years before the advent of Isaiah, the annals of the Assyrian kings record periodical campaigns against the cities of "the land of the west," but these isolated incursions were followed by no permanent results. In 745, however, five years before King Uzziah died, a soldier ascended the throne of Assyria, under the title of Tiglath-pileser II.,* who was determined to achieve the conquest of the whole world and its organization as his empire. Where his armies came, it was not simply to chastise or demand tribute,

---

.* The Pul of 2 Kings xv. 19 and the Tiglath-pileser of 2 Kings xvi. are the same.

but to annex countries, carry away their populations and exploit their resources. It was no longer kings who were threatened; peoples found themselves in danger of extinction. This terrible purpose of the Assyrian was pursued with vast means and the utmost ferocity. He has been called the Roman of the East, and up to a certain degree we may imagine his policy by remembering all that is familiar to us of its execution by Rome: its relentlessness, impetus and mysterious action from one centre; the discipline, the speed, the strange appearance, of his armies. But there was an Oriental savagery about Assyria, from which Rome was free. The Assyrian kings moved in the power of their brutish and stormy gods—gods that were in the shape of bulls and had the wings as of the tempest. The annals of these kings, in which they describe their campaigns, are full of talk about trampling down their enemies; about showering tempests of clubs upon them, and raining a deluge of arrows; about overwhelming them, and sweeping them off the face of the land, and strewing them like chaff on the sea; about chariots with scythes, and wheels clogged with blood; about great baskets stuffed with the salted heads of their foes. It is a mixture of the Roman and Red Indian.

Picture the effect of the onward movement of such a force upon the imaginations and policies of those little States that clustered round Judah and Israel. Settling their own immemorial feuds, they sought alliance with one another against this common foe. Tribes, that for centuries had stained their borders with one another's blood, came together in unions, the only reason for which was that their common fear had grown stronger than their mutual hate. Now and then a king would be found unwilling to enter such an alliance or eager to withdraw from it, in the hope of securing by his exceptional conduct the favour of the Assyrian, whom he sought further to ingratiate by voluntary tribute. The shifting attitudes of the petty kings towards Assyria bewilder the reader of the Assyrian annals. The foes of one year are the tributaries of the next; the State, that has called for help this campaign, appears as the rebel of that. In 742, Uzziah of Judah is cursed by Tiglath-pileser as an arch-enemy; Samaria and Damascus are recorded as faithful tributaries. Seven years later Ahaz of Judah offers tribute to the Assyrian king, and Damascus and Samaria are invaded by the Assyrian armies. What a world it was, and what politics! A world of petty clans, with no idea of a common humanity, and with no motive for union except fear; politics without a noble thought or long purpose in them, the politics of peoples at bay—the last flicker of dying nationalities, —*stumps of smoking firebrands,* as Isaiah described two of them.

When we turn to the little we know of the religions of these tribes, we find nothing to arrest their restlessness or broaden their thoughts. These nations had their religions, and called on their gods, but their gods were made in their own image, their religion was the reflex of their life. Each of them employed, rather than worshipped, its deity. No nation believed in its god except as one among many, with his sovereignty limited to its own territory, and his ability to help it conditioned by the power of the other gods, against whose peoples he was fighting. There was no belief in "Providence," no idea of unity or of progress in history, no place in these religions for the great world-force that was advancing upon their peoples.

From this condemnation we cannot except the people of Jehovah. It is undeniable that the mass of them occupied at this time pretty much the same low religious level as their neighbours. We have already seen (chap. i.) their mean estimate of what God required from themselves; with that corresponded their view of His position towards the world. To the majority of the Israelites their God was but one out of many, with His own battles to fight and have fought for Him, a Patron sometimes to be ashamed of, and by no means a Saviour in whom to place an absolute trust. When Ahaz is beaten by Syria, he says: *Because the gods of the kings of Syria helped them, therefore will I sacrifice to them, that they may help me* (2 Chron. xxviii. 23). Religion to Ahaz was only another kind of diplomacy. He was not a fanatic, but a diplomat, who made his son to pass through the fire to Moloch, and burnt incense in the high places and on the hills, and under every green tree. He was more a political than a religious eclectic, who brought back the pattern of the Damascus altar to Jerusalem. The Temple, in which Isaiah saw the Lord high and lifted up, became under Ahaz, and by the help of the priesthood, the shelter of various idols; in every corner of Jerusalem altars were erected to other gods. This religious hospitality was the outcome neither of imagination nor of liberal thought; it was prompted only by political fear. Ahaz has been mistaken in the same way as Charles I. was—for a bigot, and one who subjected the welfare of his kingdom to a superstitious regard for religion. But beneath the cloak of religious scrupulousness and false reverence,* there was in Ahaz the same selfish fear for the safety of his crown and his

---

* Isa. vii. 12.

dynasty, as those who best knew the English monarch tell us, was the real cause of his ceaseless intrigue and stupid obstinacy.

Now that we have surveyed this world, its politics and its religion, we can estimate the strength and originality of the Hebrew prophets. Where others saw the conflicts of nations, aided by deities as doubtfully matched as themselves, they perceived all things working together by the will of one supreme God and serving His ends of righteousness. It would be wrong to say, that before the eighth century the Hebrew conception of God had been simply that of a national deity, for this would be to ignore the remarkable emphasis placed by the Hebrews from very early times upon Jehovah's righteousness. But till the eighth century the horizon of the Hebrew mind had been the border of their territory; the historical theatre on which it saw God working was the national life. Now, however, the Hebrews were drawn into the world; they felt movements of which their own history was but an eddy; they saw the advance of forces against which their own armies, though inspired by Jehovah, had no chance of material success. The perspective was entirely changed; their native land took to most of them the aspect of a petty and worthless province, their God the rank of a mere provincial deity; they refused the waters of Shiloah, that go softly, and rejoiced in the glory of the king of Assyria, the king of the great River and the hosts that moved with the strength of its floods. It was at this moment that the prophets of Israel performed their supreme religious service. While Ahaz and the mass of the people illustrated the impotence of the popular religion, by admitting to an equal place in the national temple the gods of their victorious foes, the prophets boldly took possession of the whole world in the name of Jehovah of hosts, and exalted Him to the throne of the supreme Providence. Now they could do this only by emphasizing and developing the element of righteousness in the old conception of Him. This attribute of Jehovah took absolute possession of the prophets; and in the strength of its inspiration they were enabled, at a time when it would have been the sheerest folly to promise Israel victory against a foe like Assyria, to asseverate that even that supreme world-power was in the hand of Jehovah, and that He must be trusted to lead up all the movements of which the Assyrians were the main force to the ends He had so plainly revealed to His chosen Israel. Even before Isaiah's time such principles had been proclaimed by Amos and Hosea, but it was Isaiah, who both gave to them their loftiest expression, and applied them with the utmost detail and persistence to the practical politics of Judah. We have seen him, in the preliminary stages of his ministry under Uzziah and Jotham, reaching most exalted convictions of the righteousness of Jehovah, as contrasted with the people's view of their God's "nationalism." But we are now to follow him boldly applying this faith—won within the life of Judah, won, as he tells us, by the personal inspiration of Judah's God—to the problems and movements of the whole world as they bear upon Israel's fate. The God, who is supreme in Judah through righteousness, cannot but be supreme everywhere else, for there is nothing in the world higher than righteousness. Isaiah's faith in a Divine Providence is a close corollary to his faith in Jehovah's righteousness; and of one part of that Providence he had already received conviction—*A remnant shall remain.* Ahaz may crowd Jerusalem with foreign altars and idols, so as to be able to say: "We have with us, on our side, Moloch and Chemosh and Rimmon and the gods of Damascus and Assyria." Isaiah, in the face of this folly, lifts up his simple gospel: "Immanu-El. We have with us, in our own Jehovah of hosts, El, the one supreme God, Ruler of heaven and earth."

CHAPTER VI.

KING AND MESSIAH; PEOPLE AND CHURCH.

Isaiah vii., viii., ix. 1—8.

735—732 B.C.

THIS section of the book of Isaiah (vii.—ix. 7) consists of a number of separate prophecies uttered during a period of at least three years: 735—732 B.C. By 735 Ahaz had ascended the throne; Tiglath-pileser had been occupied in the far east for two years. Taking advantage of the weakness of the former and the distance of the latter, Rezin, king of Damascus, and Pekah, king of Samaria, planned an invasion of Judah. It was a venture they would not have dared had Uzziah been alive. While Rezin marched down the east of the Jordan and overturned the Jewish supremacy in Edom, Pekah threw himself into Judah, defeated the armies of Ahaz in one great battle, and besieged Jerusalem, with the object of deposing Ahaz and setting a Syrian, Ben-Tabeel, in his stead. Simultaneously the Philistines attacked Judah from the south-west. The motive of the confederates was in all probability anger with Ahaz for refusing to enter with them into a Pan-Syrian alliance against Assyria. In his distress Ahaz appealed to Tiglath-pileser, and the Assyrian swiftly responded. In 734—it must have been less than a year since Ahaz was attacked—the hosts of the north had overrun

Samaria and swept as far south as the cities of the Philistines. Then, withdrawing his troops again, Tiglath-pileser left Hoshea as his vassal on Pekah's throne, and sending the population of Israel east of the Jordan into distant captivity, completed a two years' siege of Damascus (734—732) by its capture. At Damascus Ahaz met the conqueror, and having paid him tribute, took out a further policy of insurance in the altar-pattern, which he brought back with him to Jerusalem. Such were the three years, whose rapid changes unfolded themselves in parallel with these prophecies of Isaiah. The details are not given by the prophet, but we must keep in touch with them while we listen to him. Especially must we remember their central point, *the decision of Ahaz to call in the help of Assyria*, a decision which affected the whole course of politics for the next thirty years. Some of the oracles of this section were plainly delivered by Isaiah before that event, and simply seek to inspire Ahaz with a courage which should feel Assyrian help to be needless; others, again, imply that Ahaz has already called in the Assyrian: they taunt him with hankering after foreign strength, and depict the woes which the Assyrian will bring upon the land; while others (for example, the passage ix. 1—7) mean that the Assyrian has already come, and that the Galilean provinces of Israel have been depopulated, and promise a Deliverer. If we do not keep in mind the decision of Ahaz, we shall not understand these seemingly contradictory utterances, which it thoroughly explains. Let us now begin at the beginning of chapter vii. It opens with a bare statement, by way of title, of the invasion of Judah and the futile result; and then proceeds to tell us how Isaiah acted from the first rumour of the confederacy onward.

I. THE KING (chap. vii.).

And it came to pass in the days of Ahaz, the son of Jotham, the son of Uzziah, king of Judah, that Rezin, the king of Syria, and Pekah, the son of Remaliah, king of Israel, went up to Jerusalem to war against it, but could not prevail against it. This is a summary of the whole adventure and issue of the war, given by way of introduction. The narrative proper begins in verse 2, with the effect of the first news of the league upon Ahaz and his people. Their hearts were moved, like the trees of the forest before the wind. The league was aimed so evidently against the two things most essential to the national existence and the honour of Jehovah; the dynasty of David, namely, and the inviolability of Jerusalem. Judah had frequently before suffered the loss of her territory; never till now were the throne and city of David in actual peril. But that, which bent both king and people by its novel terror, was the test Isaiah expected for the prophecies he had already uttered. Taking with him, as a summary of them, his boy with the name Shear-Jashub — *A-remnant-shall-return* — Isaiah faced Ahaz and his court in the midst of their preparation for the siege. They were examining—but more in panic than in prudence—the water supply of the city, when Isaiah delivered to them a message from the Lord, which may be paraphrased as follows: *Take heed and be quiet,* keep your eyes open and your heart still; *fear not, neither be faint-hearted, for the fierce anger of Rezin and Remaliah's son.* They have no power to set you on fire. They are *but stumps of expiring firebrands,* almost burnt out. While you wisely look after your water supply, do so in hope. This purpose of deposing you is vain. *Thus saith the Lord Jehovah: It shall not stand, neither shall it come to pass.* Of whom are you afraid? Look those foes of yours in the face. *The head of Syria is Damascus, and Damascus' head is Rezin:* is he worth fearing? *The head of Ephraim is Samaria, and Samaria's head is Remaliah's son:* is he worth fearing? Within a few years they will certainly be destroyed. But whatever estimate you make of your foes, whatever their future may be, for yourself have faith in God; for you that is the essential thing. *If ye will not believe, surely ye shall not be established.**

This paraphrase seeks to bring out the meaning of a passage confessedly obscure. It seems as if we had only bits of Isaiah's speech to Ahaz and must supply the gaps. No one need hesitate, however, to recognize the conspicuous personal qualities—the combination of political sagacity with religious fear, of common-sense and courage rooted in faith. In a word, this is what Isaiah will say to the king, clever in his alliances, religious and secular, and busy about his material defences: "Take unto you the shield of faith. You have lost your head among all these things. Hold it up like a man behind that shield; take a rational view of affairs. Rate your enemies at their proper value. But for this you must believe in God. Faith in Him is the essential condition of a calm mind and a rational appreciation of affairs."

It is, no doubt, difficult for us to realize that the truth which Isaiah thus enforced on King Ahaz—the government of the world and human history by one supreme God—was ever a truth of which the race stood in ignorance. A generation like ours cannot be expected to put its mind in the attitude of those of Isaiah's

---

* There is a play upon words here, which may be reproduced in English by the help of a North-England term: If ye have not *faith*, ye cannot have *staith*.

contemporaries who believed in the real existence of many gods with limited sovereignties. To us, who are full of the instincts of Divine Providence and of the presence in history of law and progress, it is extremely hard even to admit the fact—far less fully to realize what it means—that our race had ever to receive these truths as fresh additions to their stock of intellectual ideas. Yet, without prejudice to the claims of earlier prophets, this may be confidently affirmed : that Isaiah where we now meet him stood on one side believing in one supreme God, Lord of heaven and earth, and his generation stood on the other side, believing that there were many gods. Isaiah, however, does not pose as the discoverer of the truth he preaches ; he does not present it as a new revelation, nor put it in a formula. He takes it for granted, and proceeds to bring its moral influence to bear. He will infect men with his own utter conviction of it, in order that he may strengthen their character and guide them by paths of safety. His speech to Ahaz is an exhibition of the moral and rational effects of believing in Providence. Ahaz is a sample of the *character* polytheism produced; the state of mind and heart to which Isaiah exhorts him is that induced by belief in one righteous and almighty God. We can make the contrast clear to ourselves by a very definite figure.

The difference, which is made to the character and habits of men if the country they live in has a powerful government or not, is well known. If there be no such central authority, it is a case of every man's hand against his neighbour. Men walk armed to the teeth. A constant attitude of fear and suspicion warps the whole nature. The passions are excited and magnified ; the intelligence and judgement are dwarfed.

Just the same after its kind is life to the man or tribe, who believe, that the world in which they dwell and the life they share with others have no central authority. They walk armed with prejudices, superstitions and selfishnesses. They create, like Ahaz, their own providences, and still, like him, feel insecure. Everything is exaggerated by them; in each evil there lurks to their imagination unlimited hostility. They are without breadth of view or length of patience. But let men believe that life has a central authority, that God is supreme, and they will fling their prejudices and superstitions to the winds, now no more needed than the antiquated fortresses and weapons by which our forefathers, in days when the government was weak, were forced to defend their private interests. When we know that God reigns, how quiet and free it makes us! When things and men are part of His scheme and working out His ends, when we understand that they are not monsters but ministers, how reasonably we can look at them! Were we afraid of Syria and Ephraim? Why, the head of Syria is this fellow Rezin; the head of Ephraim this son of Remaliah! They cannot last long; God's engine stands behind to smite them. By the reasonable government of God, let us be reasonable! Let us take heed and be quiet. Have faith in God, and to faith will come her proper consequent of commonsense.

For the higher a man looks, the farther he sees: to us that is the practical lesson of these first nine verses of the seventh chapter. The very gesture of faith bestows upon the mind a breadth of view. The man, who lifts his face to God in heaven, is he whose eyes sweep simultaneously the farthest prospect of earth, and bring to him a sense of the proportion of things. Ahaz, facing his nearest enemies, does not see over their heads, and in his consternation at their appearance prepares to embark upon any policy that suggests itself, even though it be so rash as the summoning of the Assyrian. Isaiah, on the other hand, with his vision fixed on God as the Governor of the world, is enabled to overlook the dust that darkens Judah's frontier, to see behind it the inevitable advance of the Assyrians, and to be assured that, whether Ahaz calls them to his quarrel or no, they will very soon of their own motion overwhelm both of his enemies. From these *two smoking firebrands* there is then no real danger. But from the Assyrian, if once Judah entangle herself in his toils, there is the most extreme danger. Isaiah's advice is therefore not mere religious quietism; it is prudent policy. It is the best political advice that could have been offered at that crisis, as we have already been able to gather from a survey of the geographical and political dispositions of Western Asia,* apart altogether from religious considerations. But to Isaiah the calmness requisite for this sagacity sprang from his faith. Mr. Bagehot might have appealed to Isaiah's whole policy in illustration of what he has so well described as the military and political benefits of religion. Monotheism is of advantage to men not only by reason of " the high concentration of steady feeling " which it produces, but also for the mental calmness and sagacity, which surely spring from a pure and vivid conviction that the Lord reigneth.†

---

* Page 96.

† *Physics and Politics* (International Scientific Series), pp. 75 ff. One of the finest modern illustrations of the connection between faith and common-sense is found in the *Letters of General Gordon to His Sister.* Gordon's coolness in face of the slave trade, the just survey he makes of it, and the sensible advice which he gives about meeting it stand well in contrast to the haste and rash

One other thing it is well we should emphasize, before we pass from Isaiah's speech to Ahaz. Nothing can be plainer than that Isaiah, though advocating so absolutely a quiescent belief in God, *is no fatalist.* Now other prophets there have been, insisting just as absolutely as Isaiah upon resignation to God the supreme, and the evident practical effect of their doctrine of the Divine sovereignty has been to make their followers, not shrewd political observers, but blind and apathetic fatalists. The difference between them and Isaiah has lain in the kind of character, which they and he have respectively attributed to the Deity, before exalting Him to the throne of absolute power and resigning themselves to His will. Isaiah, though as disciplined a believer in God's sovereignty and man's duty of obedience as any prophet that ever preached these doctrines, was preserved from the fatalism to which they so often lead by the conviction he had previously received of God's righteousness. Fatalism means resignation to fate, and fate means an omnipotence either without character, or (which is the same thing) of whose character we are ignorant. Fate is God *minus* character, and fatalism is the characterless condition to which belief in such a God reduces man. History presents it to our view amid the most

---

proposals of philanthropists at home, and are evidently due to his conviction that the slave trade, like everything else in the world, is in the hands of God, and so may be calmly studied and wisely checkmated. Gordon's letters make very clear how much of his shrewdness in dealing with men was due to the same source. It is instructive to observe throughout, how his complete resignation to the will of God and his perfect obedience delivered him from prejudices and partialities, from distractions and desires, that make sober judgement impossible in other men.

diverse surroundings. The Greek mind, so free and sunny, was bewildered and benumbed by belief in an inscrutable Nemesis. In the East how frequently is a temper of apathy or despair bred in men, to whom God is nothing but a despot! Even within Christianity we have had fanatics, so inordinately possessed with belief in God's sovereignty of election, to the exclusion of all other Divine truths, as to profess themselves, with impious audacity, willing to be damned for His glory. Such instances are enough to prove to us the extreme danger of making the sovereignty of God the *first* article of our creed. It is not safe for men to exalt a deity to the throne of the supreme providence, till they are certified of his character. The vision of mere power intoxicates and brutalizes, no less when it is hallowed by the name of religion, than when, as in modern materialism, it is blindly interpreted as physical force. Only the people who have first learned to know their Deity intimately in the private matters of life, where heart touches heart, and the delicate arguments of conscience are not overborne by the presence of vast natural forces or the intricate movements of the world's history, can be trusted afterwards to enter these larger theatres of religion, without risk of losing their faith, their sensibility or their conscience.

The whole course of revelation has been bent upon this: to render men familiarly and experimentally acquainted with the character of God, before laying upon them the duty of homage to His creative power or submission to His will. In the Old Testament God is the Friend, the Guide, the Redeemer of men, or ever He is their Monarch and Lawgiver.

The Divine name which the Hebrew sees *excellent through all the earth* is the name that he has learned to know at home as *Jehovah, our Lord* (Ps. viii.). Jehovah trains His people to trust His personal troth and loving-kindness within their own courts, before He tests their allegiance and discipline upon the high places of the world. And when, amid the strange terrors of these and the novel magnitudes with which Israel, facing the world, had to reckon, the people lost their presence of mind, His elegy over them was, *My people are destroyed for lack of knowledge.* Even when their temple is full and their sacrifices of homage to His power most frequent, it is still their want of moral acquaintance with Himself of which He complains: *Israel doth not know; My people doth not consider.* What else was the tragedy in which Jewish history closed, than just the failure to perceive this lesson: that to have and to communicate the knowledge of the Almighty's character is of infinitely more value than the attempt to vindicate in any outward fashion Jehovah's supremacy over the world? This latter, this forlorn, hope was what Israel exhausted the evening of their day in attempting. The former—to communicate to the lives and philosophies of mankind a knowledge of the Divine heart and will, gained throughout a history of unique grace and miracle—was the destiny which they resigned to the followers of the crucified Messiah.

For under the New Testament this also is the method of revelation. What our King desires before He ascends the throne of the world is that the world should know Him; and so He comes down among us, to be heard, and seen, and handled of us, that our hearts may learn His heart and know His love, unbewildered by His majesty. And for our part, when we ascribe to our King the glory and the dominion, it is as unto Him that loved us and washed us from our sins in His blood. For the chief thing for individuals, as for nations, is not to believe that God reigneth so much as to know what kind of God He is who reigneth.

But Ahaz would not be persuaded. He had a policy of his own, and was determined to pursue it. He insisted on appealing to Assyria. Before he did so, Isaiah made one more attempt on his obduracy. With a vehemence, which reveals how critical he felt the king's decision to be, the prophet returned as if this time the very voice of Jehovah. *And Jehovah spake to Ahaz, saying, Ask thee a sign of Jehovah thy God; ask it either in Sheol below or in the height above. But Ahaz said, I will not ask, neither will I tempt the Lord.*

Isaiah's offer of a sign was one which the prophets of Israel used to make when some crisis demanded the immediate acceptance of their word by men, and men were more than usually hard to convince—a miracle such as the thunder that Samuel called out of a clear sky to impress Israel with God's opinion of their folly in asking for a king;[*] or as the rending of the altar which the man of God brought to pass to convict the sullen Jeroboam;[†] or as the regress of the shadow on the sun-dial, which Isaiah himself gave in assurance of recovery to the sick Hezekiah.[‡] Such signs are offered only to weak or prejudiced persons. The

---

[*] 1 Sam. xii. 17.   [†] 1 Kings xiii. 3.   [‡] Chap. xxxviii.

most real faith, as Isaiah himself tells us, is unforced, the purest natures those which need no signs and wonders. But there are certain crises at which faith must be immediately forced, and Ahaz stood now at such a crisis; and there are certain characters who, unable to read a writ from the court of conscience and reason, must be served with one from a court—even though it be inferior—whose language they understand; and Ahaz was such a character. Isaiah knew his man, and prepared a pretty dilemma for him. By offering him whatever sign he chose to ask, Isaiah knew that the king would be committed before his own honour and the public conscience to refrain from calling in the Assyrians, and so Judah would be saved; or if the king refused the sign, the refusal would unmask him. Ahaz refused, and at once Isaiah denounced him and all his house. They were mere shufflers, playing fast and loose with God as well as men. *Hear ye now, O house of David. Is it a small thing for you to weary men, that ye must weary my God also?* You have evaded God; therefore God Himself will take you in hand: *the Lord Himself shall give you a sign.*

In order to follow intelligently the rest of Isaiah's address, we must clearly understand how the sign which he now promises differs in nature from the sign he had implored Ahaz to select, of whatever sort he may have expected that selection to be. The king's determination to call in Assyria has come between. Therefore, while the sign Isaiah first offered upon the spot was intended for an immediate pledge that God would establish Ahaz, if only he did not appeal to the foreigner, the sign Isaiah now offers shall come as a future proof of how criminal and disastrous the appeal to the foreigner has been. The first sign would have been an earnest of salvation ; the second is to be an exposure of the fatal evil of Ahaz's choice. The first would have given some assurance of the swift overthrow of Ephraim and Syria ; the second shall be some painful illustration of the fact that not only Syria and Ephraim, but Judah herself, shall be overwhelmed by the advance of the northern power. This second sign is one, therefore, which only time can bring round. Isaiah identifies it with a life not yet born.

A Child, he says, shall shortly be born to whom his mother shall give the name Immanu-El —*God-with-us*. By the time this Child comes to years of discretion, *he shall eat butter and honey*. Isaiah then explains the riddle. He does not, however, explain who the mother is, having described her vaguely as *a* or *the young woman of marriageable age;* for that is not necessary to the sign, which is to consist in the Child's own experience. To this latter he limits his explanation. Butter and honey are the food of privation, the food of a people, whose land, depopulated by the enemy, has been turned into pasture. Before this Child shall arrive at years of discretion not only shall Syria and Ephraim be laid waste, but the Lord Himself will have laid waste Judah. *Jehovah shall bring upon thee, and upon thy people and upon thy father's house days, that have not come, from the day that Ephraim departed from Judah; even the king of Assyria.* Nothing more is said of Immanuel, but the rest of the chapter is taken up with the details of Judah's devastation.

Now this sign and its explanation would have presented little difficulty but for the name of the Child—Immanuel. Erase that, and the passage reads forcibly enough. Before a certain Child, whose birth is vaguely but solemnly intimated in the near future, shall have come to years of discretion, the results of the choice of Ahaz shall be manifest. Judah shall be devastated, and her people have sunk to the most rudimentary means of living. All this is plain. It is a form which Isaiah used more than once to measure the near future. And in other literatures, too, we have felt the pathos of realizing the future results of crime and the length to which disaster lingers, by their effect upon the lives of another generation :—

> "The child that is unborn shall rue
> The hunting of that day!"

But why call the Child Immanuel? The name is evidently part of the sign, and has to be explained in connection with it. Why call a Child *God-with-us* who is not going to act greatly or to be highly honoured, who is only going to suffer, for whom to come to years of intelligence shall only be to come to a sense of his country's disaster and his people's poverty? This Child who is used so pathetically to measure the flow of time and the return of its revenges, about whom we are told neither how he shall behave himself in the period of privation, nor whether he shall survive it—why is he called Immanuel? or why, being called Immanuel, has he so sordid a fate to contrast with so splendid a name?

It seems to the present expositor quite impossible to dissociate so solemn an announcement by Jehovah to the house of David of the birth of a Child, so highly named, from that expectation of the coming of a glorious Prince which was current in this royal family since the days of its founder. Mysterious and abrupt as the intimation of Immanuel's birth may seem to us at this juncture, we cannot forget that it fell from Isaiah's lips on hearts which cherished as their dearest hope the appearance of a glorious descendant of David, and were just now the more sensitive to this hope that both David's city and David's dynasty were in peril. Could Ahaz possibly understand by Immanuel any other child than that Prince whose coming was the inalienable hope of his house ? But if we are right in supposing that Ahaz made this identification, or had even the dimmest presage of it, then we understand the full force of the sign. Ahaz by his unbelief had not only disestablished himself (ver. 9) : he had mortgaged the hope of Israel. In the flood of disaster, which his fatal resolution would bring upon the land, it mattered little what was to happen to himself. Isaiah does not trouble now to mention any penalty for Ahaz. But his resolve's exceeding pregnancy of peril is borne home to the king by the assurance that it will devastate all the golden future, and must disinherit the promised King. The Child, who is Israel's hope, is born ; he receives the Divine name, and that is all of salvation or glory suggested. He grows up not to a throne or the majesty which the seventy-second Psalm pictures—the offerings of Sheba's and Seba's kings, the corn of his land shaking like the fruit of Lebanon, while they of the city flourish like the grass of the earth—but to the food of privation, to the sight of his country razed by his enemies into one vast common fit only for pasture, to loneliness and suffering. Amid the general desolation his figure vanishes from our sight, and only his name remains to haunt, with its infinite melancholy of what might have been, the thorn-choked vineyards and grass-grown courts of Judah.

But even if it were to prove too fine a point, to identify Immanuel with the promised Messiah of David's house, and we had to fall back on some vaguer theory of him, finding him to be a personification,—either a representative of the coming generation of God's people, or a type of the promised to-morrow,—the moral effect of the sign would remain the same; and it is with this alone that we have here to do. Be this an individual, or a generation, or an age,—by the Name bestowed upon it, it was to have been a glorious, God-inhabited age, generation, or individual, and Ahaz has prematurely spoiled everything about it but the Name. The future shall be like a boy cursed by his fathers, brought into the world with glorious rights that are stamped in his title, but only to find his kingdom and estates no longer in existence, and all the circumstances dissipated, in which he might have realized the glorious meaning of his name. Type of innocent suffering, he is born to an empty title, his name the vestige of a great opportunity, the ironical monument of an irreparable crime.

If Ahaz had any conscience left, we can imagine the effect of this upon him. To be punished for sin in one's own body and fortune, this is sore enough; but to see heaven itself blackened and all the gracious future frustrate, this is unspeakably terrible.

Ahaz is thus the Judas of the Old Testament, if that conception of Judas' character be the right one which makes his wilful desire to bring about the kingdom of God in his own violent fashion the motive of his betrayal of Jesus. Of his own obduracy Ahaz has betrayed the Messiah and Deliverer of his people. The assurance of this betrayal is the sign of his obduracy, a signal and terrible proof of his irretrievable sin in calling upon the Assyrians. The king has been found wanting.

II. The People (chap. viii.).

The king has been found wanting; but Isaiah will appeal to the people. Chap. viii. is a collection of addresses to them, as chap. vii. was an expostulation with their sovereign. The two chapters are contemporary. In chap. viii. ver. 1, the narrative goes back upon itself, and returns to the situation as it was before Ahaz made his final resolution of reliance on Assyria. Vv. 1—4 of chap. viii. imply that the Assyrian has not yet been summoned by Ahaz to his assistance, and therefore run parallel to chap. vii. vv. 3—9; but chap. viii. ver. 5 and following verses sketch the evils that are to come upon Judah and Israel, consequent upon the arrival of the Assyrians in Palestine, in answer to the appeal of Ahaz. These evils for land and nation are threatened as absolutely to the people, as they had been to the king. And then the people are thrown over (viii. 14), as the king had been; and Isaiah limits himself to his disciples (ver. 16)—the *remnant* that was foretold in chap. vi.

This appeal from monarch to people is one of the most characteristic features of Isaiah's ministry. Whatever be the matter committed to him, Isaiah is not allowed to rest till he has brought it home to the popular conscience; and however much he may be able to charge national disaster upon the folly of politicians or the obduracy of a king, it is the people whom he holds ultimately responsible. The statesman, according to Isaiah, cannot rise far above the level of his generation; the people set the fashion to their most autocratic rulers. This instinct for the popular conscience, this belief in the moral solidarity of a nation and their governors, was the motive of the most picturesque passages in Isaiah's career, and inspired some of the keenest epigrams in which he conveyed the Divine truth. We have here a case in illustration. Isaiah had met Ahaz and his court *at the conduit of the upper pool, in the highway of the fuller's field*, preparing for the expected siege of the city, and had delivered to them the Lord's message not to fear, for that Syria-Ephraim would certainly be destroyed. But that was not enough. It was now laid upon the prophet to make public and popular advertisement of the same truth.

Isaiah was told to take a large, smooth board, and write thereon in the character used by the common people—*with the pen of a man*—as if it were the title to a prophecy, the compound word " Maher-shalal-hash-baz." This was not only an intelligibly written, but a significantly sonorous, word—one of those popular cries in which the liveliest sensations are struck forth by the crowded, clashing letters, full to the dullest ears of rumours of war : *speed-spoil-hurry-prey*. The interpretation of it was postponed, the prophet meantime taking two faithful witnesses to its publication. In a little a son was born to Isaiah, and to this child he transferred the noisy name. Then its explanation was given. The double word was the alarm of a couple of invasions. *Before the boy shall have knowledge to cry, My father, my mother, the 'riches of Damascus and the spoil of Samaria shall be carried away before the king of Assyria.* So far nothing was told the people that had not been told their king; only the time of the overthrow of their two enemies was fixed with greater precision. At the most in a year, Damascus and Samaria would have fallen. The ground was already vibrating to the footfall of the northern hosts.

The rapid political changes, which ensued in Palestine, are reflected on the broken surface of this eighth chapter.

We shall not understand these abrupt and dislocated oracles, uttered at short intervals during the two years of the Assyrian campaign, unless we realize that northern shadow passing and repassing over Judah and Israel, and the quick alternations of pride and penitence in the peoples beneath it. We need not try to thread the verses on any line of thought. Logical connection among them there is none. Let us at once get down into the currents of popular feeling, in which Isaiah, having left Ahaz, is now labouring, and casting forth these cries.

It is a period of powerful currents, a people wholly in drift, and the strongest man of them arrested only by a firm pressure of the Lord's hand. *For Jehovah spake thus to me with a strong hand, and instructed me, that I should not walk in the way of this people.* The character of the popular movement, *the way of this people*, which nearly lifted Isaiah off his feet, is evident. It is that into which every nation drifts, who have just been loosened from a primitive faith in God, and by fear or ambition have been brought under the fascination of the great world. On the one hand, such a generation is apt to seek the security of its outward life in things materially large and splendid, to despise as paltry its old religious forms, national aspirations and achievements, and be very desirous to follow foreign fashion and rival foreign wealth. On the other hand, the religious spirit of such an age, withdrawn from its legitimate objects, seeks satisfaction in petty and puerile practices, demeaning itself spiritually, in a way that absurdly contrasts with the grandeur of its material ambitions. Such a stage in the life of a people has its analogy in the growth of the individual, when the boy, new to the world, by affecting the grandest companions and models, assumes an ambitious manner, with contempt for his former circumstances, yet inwardly remains credulous, timid and liable to panic. Isaiah reveals that it was such a stage, which both the kingdoms of Israel had now reached. *This people hath refused the waters of Shiloah, that go softly, and rejoice in Rezin and Remaliah's son.*

It was natural, that when the people of Judah contrasted their own estate with that of Assyria, or even of Damascus, they should despise themselves. For what was Judah? A petty principality, no larger than three of our own counties. And what was Jerusalem? A mere mountain village, some sixty or seventy acres of barren rock, cut into tongues by three insignificant valleys, down which there sometimes struggled tiny threads of water, though the beds were oftener dry, giving the town a withered and squalid look—no great river to nourish, ennoble or protect. What were such a country and capital to compare with the empire of Assyria?—the empire of the two rivers, whose powerful streams washed the ramparts, wharves, and palace stairs of mighty cities! What was Jerusalem even to the capital of Rezin? Were not Abana and Pharpar, rivers of Damascus, better than all the waters of Israel, let alone these waterless wâdys, whose bleached beds made the Jewish capital so squalid? It was the Assyrian's vast water system—canals, embankments, sluices, and the wealth of water moving through them—that most impressed the poor Jew, whose streams failed him in summer, and who had to treasure up his scanty stores of rainwater in the cisterns, with which the rocky surface of his territory is still so thickly indented. There had, indeed, been at Jerusalem some attempt to conduct water. It was called *The Shiloah*—*conduit* or *aqueduct*, literally *emissary* in the old sense of the word —a rough, narrow tunnel of some thousand feet in length, hewn through the living rock from the only considerable spring on the east side of Jerusalem, to a reservoir within the walls. To this day *The Shiloah* presents itself as not by any means a first-class piece of engineering. Ahaz had either just made the tunnel or repaired it; but if the water went no faster than it travels now, the results were indeed ridiculous. Well might *this people despise the waters of the Shiloah, that go trickling,* when they thought upon the rivers of Damascus or the broad streams of Mesopotamia. Certainly it was enough to dry up the patriotism of the Judean, if he was capable of appreciating only material value, to look upon this bare, riverless capital, with its bungled aqueduct and trickling water supply. On merely material grounds, Judah was about the last country at that time, in which her inhabitants might be expected to show pride or confidence.

But woe to the people, whose attachment to their land is based upon its material advantages, who have lost their sense for those spiritual presences, from an appreciation of which springs all true love of country, with warrior's courage in her defence and statesman's faith in her destiny! The greatest calamity, which can befall any people, is to forfeit their enthusiasm for the soil, on which their history has been achieved and their hearths and altars lie, by suffering their faith in the presence of God, of which these are but the tokens, to pass away. With this loss Isaiah now reproaches Judah. The people are utterly materialized; their delights have been in gold and silver, chariots and horses, fenced cities and broad streams, and their faith has now followed their delights. But these things to which they flee will only prove their destruction. The great foreign river, whose waters they covet, will overflow them: *even the king of Assyria and all his glory, and he shall come up over all his channels and go over all his banks; and he shall sweep onward into Judah; he shall overflow and pass through; he shall reach even to the neck; and the stretching out of his wings shall fill the breadth of thy land, O Immanuel,* thou who art *God-with-us.* At the sound of the Name, which floats in upon the floods of invasion like the Ark on the waters of old, Isaiah pulls together his distraught faith in his country, and forgetting her faults, flings defiance at her foes. *Associate yourselves, ye peoples, and ye shall be broken in pieces; and give ear, all ye of far-off countries, gird yourselves, and ye shall be broken in pieces. Take counsel together, and it shall be brought to nought; speak the word, and it shall not stand: for Immanu-El*—"With us is God." The challenge was made good. The prophet's faith prevailed over the people's materialism, and Jerusalem remained inviolable till Isaiah's death.

Meantime the Assyrian came on. But the infatuated people of Judah continued to tremble rather before the doomed conspirators, Rezin and Pekah. It must have been a time of huge excitement. The prophet tells us how he was steadied by the pressure of the Lord's hand, and how, being steadied, the meaning of the word "Immanuel" was opened out to him. *God-with-us* is the one great fact of life. Amid all the possible alliances and all the possible fears of a complex political situation, He remains the one certain alliance, the one real fear. *Say ye not, A conspiracy, concerning all whereof this people say, A conspiracy; neither fear ye their fear, nor be in dread thereof. Jehovah of hosts, Him shall ye sanctify; and let Him be your fear, and let Him be your dread.* God is the one great fact of life, but what a double-edged fact—*a sanctuary to all who put their trust in Him, but a rock of offence to both houses of Israel!* The figure is very picturesque. An altar, a common stone on steps, one of those which covered the land in large numbers—it is easy to see what a double purpose that might serve. What a joy the sight would be to the weary wanderer or refugee who sought it, what a comfort as he leant his weariness upon it, and knew he was safe! But those who were flying over the land, not seeking Jehovah, not knowing indeed what they sought, blind and panic-stricken—for them what could that altar do but trip them up like any other common rock in their way? " In fact, Divine justice is something which is either observed, desired, or attained, and is then man's weal, or, on the other hand, is overlooked, rejected, or sought after in a wild, unintelligent spirit, and only in the hour of need, and is then their lasting ruin." *

The Assyrian came on, and the temper of the Jews grew worse. Samaria was indeed doomed from the first, but for some time Isaiah had been excepting Judah from a judgement for which the guilt of Northern Israel was certainly riper. He foresaw, of course, that the impetus of invasion might sweep the Assyrians into Judah, but he had triumphed in this: that Judah was Immanuel's land, and that all who arrayed themselves against her must certainly come to nought. But now his ideas have changed, as Judah has

---

Ewald.

persisted in evil. He knows now that God is for a stumbling-block to *both* houses of Israel; nay, that upon Jerusalem herself He will fall as a gin and a snare. Only for a little group of individuals, separate from both States, and gathered round the prophet and the word of God given to him, is salvation certain. People, as well as king, have been found wanting. There remains only this *remnant*.

Isaiah then at last sees his *remnant*. But the point we have reached is significant for more than the fulfilment of his expectations. This is the first appearance in history of a religious community, apart from the forms of domestic or national life. " Till then no one had dreamed of a fellowship of faith dissociated from all national forms, bound together by faith in the Divine word alone. It was the birth of a new era in religion, for it was the birth of the conception of the Church, the first step in the emancipation of spiritual religion from the forms of political life." *

The plan of the seventh and eighth chapters is now fully disclosed. As the king for his unworthiness has to give place to the Messiah, so the nation for theirs have to give place to the Church. In the seventh chapter the king was found wanting, and the Messiah promised. In the eighth chapter the people are found wanting; and the prophet, turning from them, proceeds to form the Church among those who accept the Word, which king and people have refused. *Bind thou up the testimony, and seal the teaching*† *among my disciples. And I will wait on Jehovah, who hideth His face from*

---

* Robertson Smith, *Prophets of Israel,* p. 275.

† English Version, " law," but not the law of Moses. Isaiah refers to the word that has come by himself.

the house of Jacob, and I will look for Him. Behold, I and the children Jehovah hath given me are for signs and wonders in Israel from Jehovah of hosts, Him that dwelleth in Mount Zion.

This, then, is the situation: revelation concluded, the Church formed upon it, and the nation abandoned. But is that situation final? The words just quoted betray the prophet's hope that it is not. He says: *I will wait.* He says again: The LORD is only *hiding His face from the house of Jacob.* I will expect again the shining of His countenance. I will hope for Divine grace and the nation being once more conterminous. The rest of the section (to ix. 7) is the development of this hope, which stirs in the prophet's heart after he has closed the record of revelation.

The darkness deepened across Israel. The Assyrian had come. The northern floods kept surging among the little States of Palestine, and none knew what might be left standing. We can well understand Isaiah pausing, as he did, in face of such rapid and incontrollable movements. When Tiglath-pileser swept over the plain of Esdraelon, casting down the king of Samaria and the Philistine cities, and then swept back again, carrying off upon his ebb the populations east of the Jordan, it looked very like as if both the houses of Israel should fall. In their panic, the people betook themselves to morbid forms of religion; and at first Isaiah was obliged to quench the hope and pity he had betrayed for them in indignation at the utter contrariety of their religious practices to the word of God. There can be no Divine grace for the people as long as they *seek unto them that have familiar spirits, and unto the wizards that chirp and that mutter.* For such a disposition the prophet has nothing but scorn, *Should not a people seek unto their God? On behalf of the living should they seek unto the dead?* They must come back to the prophet's own word before hope may dawn. *To the revelation and the testimony! If they speak not according to this word, surely there is no morning for them.*

The night, however, grew too awful for scorn. There had been no part of the land so given to the idolatrous practices, which the prophet scathed, as *the land of Zebulon and the land of Naphtali, by the sea beyond Jordan, Galilee of the Gentiles.* But all the horrors of captivity had now fallen upon it, and it had received at the Lord's hand double for all its sins. The night had been torn enough by lightning; was there no dawn? The darkness of these provinces fills the prophet's silenced thoughts. He sees a people *hardly bestead and hungry, fretting themselves, cursing their king*, who had betrayed them, *and their God*, who had abandoned them, *turning their faces upwards* to heaven and *downwards* to the sacred soil from which they were being dragged, *but, behold, distress and darkness, the gloom of anguish; and into thick darkness they are driven away.* It is a murky picture, yet through the smoke of it we are able to discern a weird procession of Israelites departing into captivity. We date it, therefore, about 732 B.C., the night of Israel's first great captivity. The shock and the pity of this rouse the prophet's great heart. He cannot continue to say that there is no morning for those benighted provinces. He will venture a great hope for their people.

Over how many months the crowded verses, viii. 21—ix. 7, must be spread, it is useless now to inquire—whether the revulsion they mark arose all at once in the prophet's mind, or hope grew gradually brighter as the smoke of war died away on Israel's northern frontier during 731 B.C. It is enough that we can mark the change. The prophet's tones pass from sarcasm to pity (viii. 20, 21); from pity to hope (viii. 22—ix. 1); from hope to triumph in the vision of salvation actually achieved (ix. 2). *The people that walked in darkness have seen a great light; they that dwelt in the land of the shadow of death, on them hath the light shined.* For a mutilated, we see a multiplied, nation; for the fret of hunger and the curses of defeat, we hear the joy of harvest and of spoil after victory. *For the yoke of his burden, and the staff of his shoulder, the rod of his oppressor, Thou hast broken as in the day of Midian.* War has rolled away for ever over that northern horizon, and all the relics of war in the land are swept together into the fire. *For all the armour of the armed man in the tumult, and the garments rolled in blood, shall even be for burning, and for fuel of fire.* In the midday splendour of this peace, which, after the fashion of Hebrew prophecy, is described as already realized, Isaiah hails the Author of it all in that gracious and marvellous Child whose birth he had already intimated, Heir to the throne of David, but entitled by a fourfold name, too generous, perhaps, for a mere mortal, *Wonderful-Counsellor, Hero-God, Father-Everlasting, Prince-of-peace,* who shall redeem the realms of his great forerunner and maintain *Israel with justice and righteousness from henceforth, even for ever.*

When, finally, the prophet inquires what has led his thoughts through this rapid change from satisfaction (chap. viii. 16) with the salvation of a small *remnant* of believers in the word of God—a little kernel of patience in the midst of a godless and abandoned people—to the daring vision of a whole nation redeemed and established in peace under a Godlike King, he says: *The zeal of the Lord of hosts hath performed this.*

The zeal, translates our English version, but no one English word will give it. It is that mixture of hot honour and affection to which "jealousy" in its good sense comes near. It is that overflow of the love that cannot keep still, which, when men think God has surely done all He will or can do for an ungrateful race, visits them in their distress, and carries them forward into unconceived dispensations of grace and glory. It is the Spirit of God, which yearns after the lost, speaks to the self-despairing of hope, and surprises rebel and prophet alike with new revelations of love. We have our systems representing God's work up to the limits of our experience, and we settle upon them; but the Almighty is ever greater than His promise or than His revelation of Himself.

CHAPTER VII.

THE MESSIAH.

WE have now reached that point of Isaiah's prophesying at which the Messiah becomes the most conspicuous figure on his horizon. Let us take advantage of it, to gather into one statement all that the prophet told his generation concerning that exalted and mysterious Person.*

When Isaiah began to prophesy, there was current among the people of Judah the expectation of a glorious King. How far the expectation was defined it is impossible to ascertain; but this at least is historically certain. A promise had been made to David (2 Sam. vii. 4—17) by which the permanence of his dynasty was assured. His offspring, it was said, should succeed him, yet eternity was promised not to any individual descendant, but to the dynasty. Prophets earlier than Isaiah emphasized this establishment of the house of David, even in the days of Israel's greatest distress; but they said nothing of a single monarch with whom the fortunes of the house were to be identified. It is

---

* The Messiah, or *Anointed*, is used in the Old Testament of many agents of God: high-priest (Lev. iv. 3); ministers of the Word (Ps. cv. 15); Cyrus (Isa. xlv. 1); but mostly of God's king, actual (1 Sam. xxiv. 7), or expected (Dan. ix. 25). So it became in Jewish theology the technical term for the coming King and the Captain of salvation.

clear, however, even without the evidence of the Messianic Psalms, that the hope of such a hero was quick in Israel. Besides the documentary proof of David's own last words (2 Sam. xxiii.), there is the manifest impossibility of dreaming of an ideal kingdom apart from the ideal king. Orientals, and especially Orientals of that period, were incapable of realizing the triumph of an idea or an institution without connecting it with a personality. So that we may be perfectly sure, that when Isaiah began to prophesy the people not only counted upon the continuance of David's dynasty, as they counted upon the presence of Jehovah Himself, but were familiar with the ideal of a monarch, and lived in hope of its realization.

In the first stage of his prophecy, it is remarkable, Isaiah makes no use of this tradition, although he gives more than one representation of Israel's future in which it might naturally have appeared. No word is spoken of a Messiah even in the awful conversation, in which Isaiah received from the Eternal the fundamentals of his teaching. The only hope there permitted to him is the survival of a bare, leaderless few of the people, or, to use his own word, *a stump*, with no sign of a prominent sprout upon it. In connection, however, with the survival of a remnant, as we have said on chap. vi. (p. 89), it is plain that there were two indispensable conditions, which the prophet could not help having to state sooner or later. Indeed, one of them he had mentioned already. It was indispensable that the people should have a leader, and that they should have a rallying-point. They must have their King, and they must have their City. Every reader of Isaiah knows that it is on these two themes the prophet rises to the height of his eloquence—Jerusalem shall remain inviolable; a glorious King shall be given unto her. But it has not been so generally remarked, that Isaiah is far more concerned and consistent about the secure city than about the ideal monarch. From first to last the establishment and peace of Jerusalem are never out of his thoughts, but he speaks only now and then of the King to come. Through long periods of his ministry, though frequently describing the blessed future, he is silent about the Messiah, and even sometimes so groups the inhabitants of that future, as to leave no room for Him among them. Indeed, the silences of Isaiah upon this Person are as remarkable as the brilliant passages, in which he paints His endowments and His work.

If we consider the moment, chosen by Isaiah for announcing the Messiah and adding his seal to the national belief in the advent of a glorious Son of David, we find some significance in the fact that it was a moment, when the throne of David was unworthily filled and David's dynasty was for the first time seriously threatened. It is impossible to dissociate the birth of a boy called *Immanuel*, and afterwards so closely identified with the fortunes of the whole land (vii. 8), from the public expectation of a King of glory; and critics are almost unanimous in recognizing Immanuel again in the Prince-of-the-Four-Names in chap. ix. Immanuel, therefore, is the Messiah, the promised King of Israel. But Isaiah makes his own first intimation of Him, not when the throne was worthily filled by an Uzziah or a Jotham, but when a fool and traitor to God abused its power, and the foreign conspiracy to set up a Syrian prince in Jerusalem imperilled the whole dynasty. Perhaps we ought not to overlook the fact, that Isaiah does not here designate Immanuel as a descendant of David. The vagueness with which the mother is described has given rise to a vast amount of speculation as to what particular person the prophet meant by her. But may not Isaiah's vagueness be the only intention he had in mentioning a mother at all? The whole house of David shared at that moment the sin of the king (vii. 13); and it is not presuming too much upon the freedom of our prophet to suppose, that he shook himself loose from the tradition, which entailed the Messiah upon the royal family of Judah, and at least left it an open question, whether Immanuel might not, in consequence of their sin, spring from some other stock.

It is, however, far less with the origin, than with the experience, of Immanuel that Isaiah is concerned; and those who embark upon curious inquiries, as to who exactly the mother might be, are busying themselves with what the prophet had no interest in, while neglecting that in which really lay the significance of the sign that he offered.

Ahaz by his wilfulness has made a Substitute necessary. But Isaiah is far more taken up with this: that he has actually mortgaged the prospects of that Substitute. The Messiah comes, but the wilfulness of Ahaz has rendered His reign impossible. He, whose advent has hitherto not been foretold except as the beginning of an era of prosperity, and whose person has not been painted but with honour and power, is represented as a helpless and innocent Sufferer—His prospects dissipated by the sins of others, and Himself born only to share His people's indigence (p. 115). Such a representation of the Hero's fate is of the very highest interest. We are accustomed to associate the conception of a suffering Messiah only with a much later development of prophecy, when Israel went into exile; but the conception meets us already here. It is another proof that *Esaias is very bold*. He calls his Messiah Immanuel, and yet dares to present Him as nothing but a Sufferer—a Sufferer for the sins of others. Born only to suffer with His people, who should have inherited their throne—that is Isaiah's first doctrine of the Messiah.

Through the rest of the prophecies published during the Syro-Ephraitic troubles the Sufferer is slowly transformed into a Deliverer. The stages of this transformation are obscure. In chap. viii. Immanuel is no more defined than in chap. vii. He is still only a Name of hope upon an unbroken prospect of devastation. *The stretching out of his wings—i.e.*, the floods of the Assyrian—*shall fill the breadth of Thy land, O Immanuel*. But this time that the prophet utters the Name, he feels inspired by new courage. He grasps at Immanuel as the pledge of ultimate salvation. Let the enemies of Judah work their worst; it shall be in vain, *for Immanuel, God is with us*. And then, to our astonishment, while Isaiah is telling us how he arrived at the convictions embodied in this Name, the personality of Immanuel fades away altogether, and Jehovah of hosts Himself is set forth as the sole sanctuary of those who fear Him. There is indeed a double displacement here. Immanuel dissolves in two directions. As a Refuge, He is displaced by Jehovah; as a Sufferer and a Symbol of the sufferings of the land, by a little community of disciples, the first embodiment of the Church, who now, with Isaiah, can do nothing except wait for the Lord (pp. 124—126).

Then, when the prophet's yearning thoughts, that will not rest upon so dark a closure, struggle once more, and struggling pass from despair to pity, and from pity to hope, and from hope to triumph in a salvation actually achieved, they hail all at once as the Hero of it the Son whose birth was promised. With an emphasis, which vividly reveals the sense of exhaustion in the living generation and the conviction that only something fresh, and sent straight from God Himself, can now avail Israel, the prophet cries: *Unto us a Child is born; unto us a Son is given.* The Messiah appears in a glory that floods His origin out of sight. We cannot see whether He springs from the house of David; but *the government is to be upon His shoulder,* and He shall reign *on David's throne with righteousness for ever.* His title shall be fourfold: *Wonderful-Counsellor, God-Hero, Father-Everlasting, Prince-of-Peace.*

These Four Names do certainly not invite us to grudge them meaning, and they have been claimed as incontrovertible proofs, that the prophet had an absolutely Divine Person in view. One of the most distinguished and deliberate of Old Testament scholars declares that "the Deliverer whom Isaiah promises is nothing less than a God in the metaphysical sense of the word. The names as a whole correspond to the predicate θεος."* There are serious reasons, however, which make us doubt this conclusion, and, though we firmly hold that Jesus Christ was God, prevent us from recognizing these names as prophecies of His Divinity. Two of the names are capable of being used of an earthly monarch: *Wonderful-Counsellor* and *Prince-of-Peace,* which are, within the range of human virtue, in evident contrast to Ahaz, at once foolish in the conception of his policy and warlike in its results. It will be more difficult to get Western minds to see how *Father-Everlasting* may be applied to a mere man, but the ascription of eternity is not unusual in Oriental

---

* Schultz, *A. T. Theologie,* pp. 726, 727.

titles, and in the Old Testament is sometimes rendered to things that perish. When Hebrews speak of any one as everlasting, that does not necessarily imply Divinity. The second name, which we render *God-Hero*, is, it is true, used of Jehovah Himself in the very next chapter to this, but in the plural it is also used of men by Ezekiel (xxxii. 21). The part of it translated *God* is a frequent name of the Divine Being in the Old Testament, but literally means only *mighty*, and is by Ezekiel (xxxi. 11) applied to Nebuchadnezzar. We should hesitate, therefore, to understand by these names "a God in the metaphysical sense of the word."

We fall back with greater confidence on other arguments of a more general kind, which apply to all Isaiah's prophecies of the Messiah. If Isaiah had one revelation rather than another to make, it was the revelation of the unity of God. Against king and people, who crowded their temple with the shrines of many deities, Isaiah presented Jehovah as the one only God. It would simply have nullified the force of his message, and confused the generation to which he brought it, if either he or they had conceived of the Messiah, with the conceiving of Christian theology, as a separate Divine personality.

Again, as Mr. Robertson Smith has very clearly explained,[*] the functions assigned by Isaiah to the King of the future are simply the ordinary duties of the monarchy, for which He is equipped by the indwelling of that Spirit of God, that makes all wise men wise and valorous men valorous. "We believe in a Divine and eternal Saviour, because the work of salvation as we understand it in the light of the

---

[*] *Prophets of Israel*, p. 306.

New Testament is essentially different from the work of the wisest and best earthly king." But such an earthly king's work is all Isaiah looks for. So that, so far from its being derogatory to Christ to grudge the sense of Divinity to these names, it is a fact that the more spiritual our notions are of the saving work of Jesus, the less inclined shall we be to claim the prophecies of Isaiah in proof of His Deity.

There is a third argument in the same direction, the force of which we appreciate only when we come to discover how very little from this point onwards Isaiah had to say about the promised king. In chaps. i.—xxxix. only three other passages are interpreted as describing the Messiah. The first of these, xi. 1—5, dating perhaps from about 720, when Hezekiah was king, tells us, for the first and only time by Isaiah's lips, that the Messiah is to be a scion of David's house, and confirms what we have said: that His duties, however perfectly they were to be discharged, were the usual duties of Judah's monarchy.* The second passage, xxxii. 1ff., which dates probably from after 705, when Hezekiah was still king, is, if indeed it refers at all to the Messiah, a still fainter, though sweeter, echo of previous descriptions. While the third passage, xxxiii. 17: *Thou shalt see thy king in his beauty*, does not refer to the Messiah at all, but to Hezekiah, then prostrate and in sackcloth, with Assyria thundering at the gate of Jerusalem (701). The mass of Isaiah's predictions of the Messiah thus fall within the reign of Ahaz, and just at the point at which Ahaz proved an unworthy representative of

---

* See further on this passage pp. 180—183. As is there pointed out, while these passages on the Messiah are indeed infrequent and unconnected, there is a very evident progress through them of Isaiah's conception of his Hero's character.

Jehovah, and Judah and Israel were threatened with complete devastation. There is a repetition when Hezekiah has come to the throne. But in the remaining seventeen years, except perhaps for one allusion, Isaiah is silent on the ideal king, although he continued throughout that time to unfold pictures of the blessed future which contained every other Messianic feature, and the realization of which he placed where he had placed his Prince-of-the-Four-Names—in connection, that is, with the approaching defeat of the Assyrians. Ignoring the Messiah, during these years Isaiah lays all the stress of his prophecy on the inviolability of Jerusalem; and while he promises the recovery of the actually reigning monarch from the distress of the Assyrian invasion,—as if that were what the people chiefly desired to see, and not a brighter, stronger substitute,—he hails Jehovah Himself, in solitary and undeputed sovereignty, as Judge, Lawgiver, Monarch and Saviour (xxxiii. 22). Between Hezekiah, thus restored to his beauty, and Jehovah's own presence, there is surely no room left for another royal personage. But these very facts—that Isaiah felt most compelled to predict an ideal king when the actual king was unworthy, and that, on the contrary, when the reigning king proved worthy, approximating to the ideal, Isaiah felt no need for another, and indeed in his prophecies left no room for another—form surely a powerful proof that the king he expected was not a supernatural being, but a human personality, extraordinarily endowed by God, one of the descendants of David by ordinary succession, but fulfilling the ideal which his forerunners had missed. Even if we allow that the four names contain among them the predicate of Divinity, we must not overlook the fact that the

Prince is only called by them. It is not that *He is*, but that *He shall be called, Wonderful-Counsellor, God-Hero, Father-Everlasting, Prince-of-Peace*. Nowhere is there a dogmatic statement that He is Divine. Besides, it is inconceivable that if Isaiah, the prophet of the unity of God, had at any time a second Divine Person in his hope, he should have afterwards remained so silent about Him. To interpret the ascription of the Four Names as a conscious definition of Divinity, at all like the Christian conception of Jesus Christ, is to render the silence of Isaiah's later life and the silence of subsequent prophets utterly inexplicable.

On these grounds, then, we decline to believe that Isaiah saw in the king of the future "a God in the metaphysical sense of the word." Just because we know the proofs of the Divinity of Jesus to be so spiritual, do we feel the uselessness of looking for them to prophecies, that manifestly describe purely earthly and civil functions.

But such a conclusion by no means shuts us out from tracing a relation between these prophecies and the appearance of Jesus. The fact, that Isaiah allowed them to go down to posterity, proves that he himself did not count them to have been exhausted in Hezekiah. And this fact of their preservation is ever so much the more significant, that their literal truth was discredited by events. Isaiah had evidently foretold the birth and bitter youth of Immanuel for the *near* future. Immanuel's childhood was to begin with the devastation of Ephraim and Syria, and to be passed in circumstances consequent on the devastation of Judah, which was to follow close upon that of her two enemies. But although Ephraim and Syria were immediately spoiled, as Isaiah foresaw, Judah lay in peace all the reign of Ahaz and many years after his death. So that had Immanuel been born in the next twenty-five years after the announcement of His birth, He would not have found in His own land the circumstances which Isaiah foretold as the discipline of His boyhood. Isaiah's forecast of Judah's fate was, therefore, falsified by events. That the prophet or his disciples should have allowed it to remain, is proof that they believed it to have contents, which the history they had lived through neither exhausted nor discredited. In the prophecies of the Messiah there was something ideal, which was as permanent and valid for the future as the prophecy of the Remnant or that of the visible majesty of Jehovah. If the attachment, at which the prophet aimed when he launched these prophecies on the stream of time, was denied them by their own age, that did not mean their submersion, but only their freedom to float further down the future and seek attachment there.

This boldness, to entrust to future ages a prophecy discredited by contemporary history, argues a profound belief in its moral meaning and eternal significance; and it is this boldness, in face of disappointment continued from generation to generation in Israel, that constitutes the uniqueness of the Messianic hope among that people. To sublimate this permanent meaning of the prophecies from the contemporary material, with which it is mixed, is not difficult. Isaiah foretells his Prince on the supposition that certain things are fulfilled. When the people are reduced to the last extreme, when there is no more a king to rally or to rule them, when the land is in captivity, when revelation is closed, when, in despair of the darkness of the Lord's face, men have taken to them that have familiar spirits and wizards that peep and mutter, then, in that last sinful, hopeless estate of man, a Deliverer shall appear. *The zeal of the Lord of hosts will perform it.* This is the first article of Isaiah's Messianic creed, and stands back behind the Messiah and all Messianic blessings, their exhaustless origin. Whatsoever man's sin and darkness be, the Almighty lives, and His zeal is infinite. Therefore it is a fact eternally true, that whatsoever Deliverer His people need and can receive shall be sent to them, and shall be styled by whatsoever names their hearts can best appreciate. Titles shall be given Him to attract their hope and their homage, and not a definition of His nature, of which their theological vocabulary would be incapable. This is the vital kernel of Messianic prophecy in Isaiah. The *zeal of the Lord*, kindling the dark thoughts of the prophet as he broods over his people's need of salvation, suddenly makes a Saviour visible—visible just as He is needed there and then. Isaiah hears Him hailed by titles that satisfy the particular wants of the age, and express men's thoughts as far up the idea of salvation and majesty as they of that age can rise. But the prophet has also perceived that sin and disaster will so accumulate before the Messiah comes, that, though innocent, He shall have to bear tribulation and pass to His prime through suffering. No one with open mind can deny, that in this moderate estimate of the prophet's meaning there is a very great deal of the essence of the Gospel as it has been fulfilled in the personal consciousness and saving work of Jesus Christ,—as much of that essence, indeed, as it was possible to communicate to so early a generation, and one whose religious needs were so largely what we call temporal. But if we grant this, and if at the same time we appreciate the uniqueness of such a hope as this of Israel, then surely it must be allowed to have the appearance of a special preparation for Christ's life and work ; and so, to use very moderate words which have been applied to Messianic prophecy in general, it may be taken " as a proof of its true connection with the Gospel dispensation as part of one grand scheme in the counsels of Providence." *

Men do not ask when they drink of a streamlet high up on the hills, " Is this going to be a great river ? " They are satisfied if it is water enough to quench their thirst. And so it was enough for Old Testament believers if they found in Isaiah's prophecy of a Deliverer—as they did find—what satisfied their own religious needs, without convincing them to what volumes it should swell. But this does not mean that in using these Old Testament prophecies we Christians should limit our enjoyment of them to the measure of the generation to whom they were addressed. To have known Christ must make the predictions of the Messiah different to a man. You cannot bring so infinite an ocean of blessing into historic connection with these generous, expansive intimations of the Old Testament without its passing into them. If we may use a rough figure, the Messianic prophecies of the Old Testament are tidal rivers. They not only run, as we have seen, to their sea, which is Christ; they feel His reflex influence. It is not enough for a Christian to have followed the historical direction of the prophecies, or to have proved their connection with the New Testament as parts of one Divine harmony. Forced back by the fulness of meaning to which he has found

---

* Stanton : *The Jewish and Christian Messiah.*

their courses open, he returns to find the savour of the New Testament upon them, and that where he descended shallow and tortuous channels, with all the difficulties of historical exploration, he is borne back on full tides of worship. To use the appropriate words of Isaiah, *the Lord is with him there, a place of broad rivers and streams.*

With all this, however, we must not forget that, beside these prophecies of a great earthly ruler, there runs another stream of desire and promise, in which we see a much stronger premonition of the fact that a Divine Being shall some day dwell among men. We mean the Scriptures in which it is foretold that Jehovah Himself shall visibly visit Jerusalem. This line of prophecy, taken along with the powerful anthropomorphic representations of God,—astonishing in a people like the Jews, who so abhorred the making of an image of the Deity upon the likeness of anything in heaven and earth,—we hold to be the proper Old Testament instinct that the Divine should take human form and tabernacle amongst men. But this side of our subject—the relation of the anthropomorphism of the Old Testament to the Incarnation—we postpone till we come to the second part of the book of Isaiah, in which the anthropomorphic figures are more frequent and daring than they are here.

BOOK II.

PROPHECIES FROM THE ACCESSION OF HEZEKIAH TO THE DEATH OF SARGON, 727—705 B.C.

ISAIAH :—
    xxviii.   725 B.C.
    x. 5—34.   721 B.C.
    xi., xii.   About 720 B.C. ?
    xx.   711 B.C.
    xxi. 1—10.   710 B.C.
    xxxviii., xxxix.   Between 712 and 705 B.C.

BOOK II.

THE prophecies with which we have been engaged (chaps. ii.—x. 4) fall either before or during the great Assyrian invasion of Syria, undertaken in 734—732 by Tiglath-pileser II., at the invitation of King Ahaz. Nobody has any doubt about that. But when we ask what prophecies of Isaiah come next in chronological order, we raise a storm of answers. We are no longer on the sure ground we have been enjoying.

Under the canonical arrangement the next prophecy is "The Woe upon the Assyrian" (x. 5—34). In the course of this the Assyrian is made to boast of having overthrown Samaria (vv. 9—11): *Is not Samaria as Damascus? . . . Shall I not, as I have done unto Samaria and her idols, so do to Jerusalem and her idols?* If *Samaria* mean the capital city of Northern Israel— and the name is never used in these parts of Scripture for anything else—and if the prophet be quoting a boast which the Assyrian was actually in a position to make, and not merely imagining a boast, which he would be likely to make some years afterwards (an entirely improbable view, though held by one great scholar*), then an event is here described as past and over which

---

* Delitzsch, who fancies that the fall of Samaria is a completed affair only in the vision of the prophet, not in reality.

did not happen during Tiglath-pileser's campaign, nor indeed till twelve years after it. Tiglath-pileser did not require to besiege Samaria in the campaign of 734—732. The king, Pekah, was slain by a conspiracy of his own subjects; and Hoshea, the ringleader, who succeeded, willingly purchased the stability of a usurped throne by homage and tribute to the king of kings. So Tiglath-pileser went home again, satisfied to have punished Israel by carrying away with him the population of Galilee. During his reign there was no further appearance of the Assyrians in Palestine, but at his death in 727 Hoshea, after the fashion of Assyrian vassals when the throne at Nineveh changed occupants, attempted to throw off the yoke of the new king, Salmanassar IV. Along with the Phœnician and Philistine cities, Hoshea negotiated an alliance with So, or Seve, the Ethiopian, a usurper who had just succeeded in establishing his supremacy over the land of the Pharaohs. In a year Salmanassar marched south upon the rebels. He took Hoshea prisoner on the borders of his territory (725), but, not content, as his predecessor had been, with the submission of the king, *he came up throughout all the land, and went up to Samaria, and besieged it three years.** He did not live to see the end of the siege, and Samaria was taken in 722 by Sargon, his successor. Sargon overthrew the kingdom and uprooted the people. The northern tribes were carried away into a captivity, from which as tribes they never returned.

It was evidently this complete overthrow of Samaria by Sargon in 722—721, which Isaiah had behind him when he wrote x. 9—11. We must, therefore, date the

---

* 2 Kings xvii. 5.

prophecy after 721, when nothing was left as a bulwark between Judah and the Assyrian. We do so with reluctance. There is much in x. 5—34 which suits the circumstances of Tiglath-pileser's invasion. There are phrases and catch-words coinciding with those in vii.—ix. 7; and the whole oration is simply a more elaborate expression of that defiance of Assyria, which inspires such of the previous prophecies as viii. 9, 10. Besides, with the exception of Samaria, all the names in the Assyrian's boastful catalogue—Carchemish, Calno, Arpad, Hamath and Damascus—might as justly have been vaunted by the lips of Tiglath-pileser as by those of Sargon. But in spite of these things, which seem to vindicate the close relation of x. 5—34 to the prophecies which precede it in the canon, the mention of Samaria as being already destroyed justifies us in divorcing it from them. While they remain dated from before 732, we place it subsequent to 722.

Was Isaiah, then, silent these ten years? Is there no prophecy lying farther on in his book that treats of Samaria as still standing? Besides an address to the fallen Damascus in xvii. 1—11, which we shall take later with the rest of Isaiah's oracles on foreign states, there is one large prophecy, chap. xxviii., which opens with a description of the magnates of Samaria lolling in drunken security on their vine-crowned hill, but God's storms are ready to break. Samaria has not yet fallen, but is threatened and shall fall soon. The first part of chap. xxviii. can only refer to the year, in which Salmanassar advanced upon Samaria—726 or 725. There is nothing in the rest of it to corroborate this date; but the fact, that there are several turns of thought and speech very similar to turns of thought and speech in x. 5—34, makes us the bolder to take away xxviii. from its present connection with xxix.—xxxii., and place it just before x. 5—34.

Here then is our next group of prophecies, all dating from the first seven years of the reign of Hezekiah: xxviii., a warning addressed to the politicians of Jerusalem from the impending fate of those of Samaria (date 725); x. 5—34, a woe upon the Assyrian (date about 720), describing his boasts and his progress in conquest till his sudden crash by the walls of Jerusalem; xi., of date uncertain, for it reflects no historical circumstance, but standing in such artistic contrast to x. that the two must be treated together; and xii., a hymn of salvation, which forms a fitting conclusion to xi. With these we shall take the few fragments of the book of Isaiah which belong to the fifteen years 720—705, and are as straws to show how Judah all that time was drifting down to alliance with Egypt—xx., xxi. 1—10, and xxxviii.—xxxix. This will bring us to 705, and the beginning of a new series of prophecies, the richest of Isaiah's life, and the subject of our third book.

CHAPTER VIII.

GOD'S COMMONPLACE.

Isaiah xxviii. (about 725 b.c.)

THE twenty-eighth chapter of the Book of Isaiah is one of the greatest of his prophecies. It is distinguished by that regal versatility of style, which places its author at the head of Hebrew writers. Keen analyses of character, realistic contrasts between sin and judgement, clever retorts and epigrams, rapids of scorn, and "a spate" of judgement, but for final issue a placid stream of argument banked by sweet parable—such are the literary charms of the chapter, which derives its moral grandeur from the force with which its currents set towards faith and reason, as together the salvation of states, politicians and private men. The style mirrors life about ourselves, and still tastes fresh to thirsty men. The truths are relevant to every day in which luxury and intemperance abound, in which there are eyes too fevered by sin to see beauty in simple purity, and minds so surfeited with knowledge or intoxicated with their own cleverness, that they call the maxims of moral reason commonplace and scorn religious instruction as food for babes.

Some time when the big, black cloud was gathering again on the north, Isaiah raised his voice to the magnates of Jerusalem: "Lift your heads from your wine-bowls; look north. The sunshine is still on Samaria, and your fellow-drinkers there are revelling in security. But the storm creeps up behind. They shall certainly perish soon; even you cannot help seeing that. Let it scare you, for their sin is yours, and that storm will not exhaust itself on Samaria. Do not think that your clever policies, alliance with Egypt or the treaty with Assyria herself, shall save you. Men are never saved from death and hell by making covenants with them. Scorners of religion and righteousness, except ye cease being sceptical and drunken, and come back from your diplomacy to faith and reason, ye shall not be saved! This destruction that looms is going to cover the whole earth. So stop your running to and fro across it in search of alliances. *He that believeth shall not make haste.* Stay at home and trust in the God of Zion, for Zion is the one thing that shall survive." In the parable, which closes the prophecy, Isaiah offers some relief to this dark prospect: "Do not think of God as a mere disaster-monger, maker of terrors for men. He has a plan, even in catastrophe, and this deluge, which looks like destruction for all of us, has its method, term and fruits, just as much as the husbandman's harrowing of the earth or threshing of the corn."

The chapter with this argument falls into four divisions.

I. THE WARNING FROM SAMARIA (vv. 1—6).

They had always been hard drinkers in North Israel. Fifty years before, Amos flashed judgement on those who trusted in the mount of Samaria, *lolling upon their couches and gulping their wine out of basons*, women as well as men. Upon these same drunkards of Ephraim, now soaked and *stunned with wine,* Isaiah fastens his Woe. Sunny the sky and balmy the air in which they lie, stretched upon flowers by the heads of their fat valleys—a land that tempts its inhabitants with the security of perpetual summer. But God's swift storm drives up the valley—hail, rain and violent streams from every gorge. Flowers, wreaths and pampered bodies are trampled in the mire. The glory of sunny Ephraim is as the first ripe fig a man findeth, and *while it is yet in his hand, he eateth it up.* But while drunken magnates and the flowers of a rich land are swept away, there is a residue who can and do abide even that storm, to whom the Lord Himself shall be for a crown, *a spirit of justice to him that sitteth for justice, and for strength to them that turn back the battle at the gate.*

Isaiah's intention is manifest, and his effort a great one. It is to rob passion of its magic and change men's temptations to their disgusts, by exhibiting how squalid passion shows beneath disaster, and how gloriously purity shines surviving it. It is to strip luxury and indulgence of their attractiveness by drenching them with the storm of judgement, and then not to leave them stunned, but to rouse in them a moral admiration and envy by the presentation of certain grand survivals of the storm—unstained justice and victorious valour. Isaiah first sweeps the atmosphere, hot from infective passion, with the cold tempest from the north. Then in the clear shining after rain he points to two figures, which have preserved through temptation and disaster, and now lift against a smiling sky, the ideal that those corrupt judges and drunken warriors have dragged into the mire—*him that sitteth for justice and him that turneth back the battle at the gate.* The escape from sensuality, this passage suggests, is twofold. There is the exposure to nature where God's judgements sweep their irresistible way; and then from the despair, which the unrelieved spectacle of judgement produces, there is the recovery to moral effort through the admiration of those purities and heroisms, that by God's Spirit have survived.

When God has put a conscience into the art or literature of any generation, they have followed this method of Isaiah, but not always to the healthy end which he reaches. To show the slaves of Circe the physical disaster impending—which you must begin by doing if you are to impress their brutalized minds—is not enough. The lesson of Tennyson's "Vision of Sin" and of Arnold's "New Sirens," that night and frost, decay and death, come down at last on pampered sense, is necessary, but not enough. Who stops there remains a defective and morbid moralist. When you have made the sensual shiver before the disease that inevitably awaits them, you must go on to show that there are men who have the secret of surviving the most terrible judgements of God, and lift their figures calm and victorious against the storm-washed sky. Preach the depravity of men, but never apart from the possibilities that remain in them. It is Isaiah's health as a moralist that he combines the two. No prophet ever threatened judgement more inexorable and complete than he. Yet he never failed to tell the sinner, how possible it was for him to be different. If it were necessary to crush men in the mud, Isaiah would not leave them there with the hearts of swine. But he put conscience in them, and the envy of what was pure, and the admiration of what was victorious. Even as they wallowed, he pointed them to the figures of men like themselves, who had survived and overcome by the Spirit of God. Here we perceive the ethical possibilities, that lay in his fundamental doctrine of a remnant. Isaiah never crushed men beneath the fear of judgement, without revealing to them the possibility and beauty of victorious virtue. Had we lived in those great days, what a help he had been to us—what a help he may be still!—not only firm to declare that the wages of sin is death, but careful to effect that our humiliation shall not be despair, and that even when we feel our shame and irretrievableness the most, we shall have the opportunity to behold our humanity crowned and seated on the throne from which we had fallen, our humanity driving back the battle from the gate against which we had been hopelessly driven! That seventh verse sounds like a trumpet in the ears of enervated and despairing men.

II. God's Commonplace (vv. 7—13).

But Isaiah has cast his pearls before swine. The men of Jerusalem, whom he addresses, are too deep in sensuality to be roused by his noble words. *Even priest and prophet stagger through strong drink;* and the class that should have been the conscience of the city, responding immediately to the word of God, *reel in vision and stumble in judgement.* They turn upon Isaiah's earnest message with tipsy men's insolence. Verses 9 and 10 should be within inverted commas, for they are the mocking reply of drunkards over their cups. *Whom is he going to teach knowledge, and upon whom is he trying to force "the Message,"* as he calls it? *Them that are weaned from the milk and drawn from the breasts?* Are we school-children, that he treats us with his endless platitudes and repetitions—*precept upon* *precept and precept upon precept, line upon line and line upon line, here a little and there a little?* So did these bibulous prophets, priests and politicians mock Isaiah's messages of judgement, wagging their heads in mimicry of his simple, earnest tones. "We must conceive the abrupt, intentionally short, reiterated and almost childish words of verse 10 as spoken in mimicry, with a mocking motion of the head, and in a childish, stammering, taunting tone."*

But Isaiah turns upon them with their own words: "You call me, Stammerer! I tell you that God, Who speaks through me, and Whom in me you mock, will one day speak again to you in a tongue that shall indeed sound stammering to you. When those far-off barbarians have reached your walls, and over them taunt you in uncouth tones, then shall you hear how God can stammer. For these shall be the very voice of Him, and as He threatens you with captivity it shall be your bitterness to remember how by me He once offered you *a rest and refreshing*, which you refused. I tell you more. God will not only speak in words, but in deeds, and then truly your nickname for His message shall be fulfilled to you. Then shall the word of the Lord be unto you *precept upon precept, precept upon precept, line upon line, line upon line, here a little and there a little*. For God shall speak with the terrible simplicity and slowness of deeds, with the gradual growth of fate, with the monotonous stages of decay, till step by step you *go, and stumble backward, and be broken, and snared, and taken*. You have scorned my instruction as monosyllables fit for children! By

---

* Ewald. The original runs thus: "Ki tsav la-tsav, tsav la-tsav, qav la-qav, qav la-qav; z'eir sham z'eir sham."

irritating monosyllables of gradual penalty shall God instruct you the second time."

This is not only a very clever and cynical retort, but the statement of a moral principle. We gather from Isaiah that God speaks twice to men, first in words and then by deeds, but both times very simply and plainly. And if men deride and abuse the simplicity of the former, if they ignore moral and religious truths because they are elementary, and rebel against the quiet reiteration of simple voices, with which God sees it most healthy to conduct their education, then they shall be stunned by the commonplace pertinacity, with which the effects of their insolence work themselves out in life. God's ways with men are mostly commonplace; that is the hardest lesson we have to learn. The tongue of conscience speaks like the tongue of time, prevailingly by ticks and moments; not in undue excitement of soul and body, not in the stirring up of our passions nor by enlisting our ambitions, not in thunder nor in startling visions, but by everyday precepts of faithfulness, honour and purity, to which conscience has to rise unwinged by fancy or ambition, and dreadfully weighted with the dreariness of life. If we, carried away upon the rushing interests of the world, and with our appetite spoiled by the wealth and piquancy of intellectual knowledge, despise the simple monitions of conscience and Scripture, as uninteresting and childish, this is the risk we run,—that God will speak to us in another, and this time unshirkable, kind of commonplace. What that is we shall understand, when a career of dissipation or unscrupulous ambition has bereft life of all interest and joy, when one enthusiasm after another grows dull, and one pleasure after another tasteless, when all the little things of life preach to us of judgement, and *the grass-*

hopper becometh a burden, and we, slowly descending through the drab and monotony of decay, suffer the last great commonplace, death. There can be no greater irony than for the soul, which has sinned by too greedily seeking for sensation, to find sensation absent even from the judgements she has brought upon herself. Poor Heine's *Confessions* acknowledge, at once with the appreciation of an artist and the pain of a victim, the satire, with which the Almighty inflicts, in the way that Isaiah describes, His penalties upon sins of sense.

III. Covenants with Death and Hell (vv. 14—22).

To Isaiah's threats of destruction, the politicians of Jerusalem replied, We have bought destruction off! They meant some treaty with a foreign power. Diplomacy is always obscure, and at that distance its details are buried for us in impenetrable darkness. But we may safely conclude that it was either the treaty of Ahaz with Assyria, or some counter-treaty executed with Egypt since this power began again to rise into pretentiousness, or more probably still it was a secret agreement with the southern power, while the open treaty with the northern was yet in force. Isaiah, from the way in which he speaks, seems to have been in ignorance of all, except that the politician's boast was an unhallowed, underhand intrigue, accomplished by much swindling and false conceit of cleverness. This wretched subterfuge Isaiah exposes in some of the most powerful sentences he ever uttered. A faithless diplomacy was never more thoroughly laid bare, in its miserable mixture of political pedantry and falsehood.

Therefore hear the word of Jehovah, ye men of scorn, rulers of this people, which is in Jerusalem!
Because ye have said, We have entered into a covenant

with Death, and with Hell have we made a bargain; the "Overflowing Scourge," a current phrase of Isaiah's which they fling back in his teeth, *when it passeth along, shall not come unto us, for we have set lies as our refuge, and in falsehood have we hidden ourselves* [the prophet's penetrating scorn drags up into their boast the secret conscience of their hearts, that after all lies did form the basis of this political arrangement], *therefore thus saith the Lord Jehovah: Behold, I lay in Zion for foundation a stone, a tried stone, a precious corner-stone of sure foundation: he that believeth shall not make haste.* No need of swift couriers to Egypt, and fret and fever of poor political brains in Jerusalem! The word *make haste* is onomatopoetic, like our *fuss*, and, if fuss may be applied to the conduct of high affairs of state, its exact equivalent in meaning.

And I will set justice for a line, and righteousness for a plummet, and hail shall sweep away the subterfuge of lies, and the secrecy shall waters overflow. And cancelled shall be your covenant with Death, and your bargain with Hell shall not stand.

" The Overflowing Scourge," indeed! *When it passeth over, then ye shall be unto it for trampling. As often as it passeth over, it shall take you away, for morning by morning shall it pass over, by day and by night. Then shall it be sheer terror to realize " the Message" !* Too late then for anything else. Had you realized "the Message" now, what rest and refreshing! But then only terror.

For the bed is shorter than that a man can stretch himself upon it, and the covering narrower than that he can wrap himself in it. This proverb seems to be struck out of the prophet by the belief of the politicians, that they are creating a stable and restful policy for

Judah. It flashes an aspect of hopeless uneasiness over the whole political situation. However they make their bed, with Egypt's or Assyria's help, they shall not find it comfortable. No cleverness of theirs can create a satisfactory condition of affairs, no political arrangement, nothing short of faith, of absolute reliance on that bare foundation-stone laid in Zion,—God's assurance that Jerusalem is inviolable.

For Jehovah shall arise as on Mount Peratsim; He shall be stirred as in the valley of Gibeon, to do His deed —strange is this deed of His, and to bring to pass His act—strange is His act.

Now, therefore, play no more the scorner, lest your bands be made tight, for a consumption, and that determined, have I heard from the Lord, Jehovah of hosts, upon the whole earth. This finishes the matter. Possibility of alliance there is for sane men nowhere in this world of Western Asia, so evidently near convulsion. Only the foundation-stone in Zion shall be left. Cling to that!

When the pedantic members of the General Assembly of the Kirk of Scotland, in the year 1650, were clinging with all the grip of their hard logic, but with very little heart, to the " Divine right of kings," and attempting an impossible state, whose statute-book was to be the Westminster Confession, and its chief executive officer King Charles II., Cromwell, then encamped at Musselburgh, sent them that letter in which the famous sentence occurs : " I beseech you in the bowels of Christ, think it possible you may be mistaken. Precept may be upon precept, line may be upon line," he goes on to say, "and yet the Word of the Lord may be to some a word of Judgement; that they may fall backward, and be broken, and be snared, and be taken! There may be a spiritual fulness, which the world may call drunkenness; as in the second Chapter of the *Acts*. There may be, as well, a carnal confidence upon misunderstood and misapplied precepts, which may be called spiritual drunkenness. There may be a *Covenant made with Death and Hell!* I will not say yours was so. But judge if such things have a politic aim: To avoid the overflowing scourge; or, To accomplish worldly interests? And if therein you have confederated with wicked and carnal men, and have respect for them, or otherwise have drawn them in to associate with us, Whether this be a covenant of God and spiritual? Bethink yourselves; we hope we do.

"I pray you read the Twenty-eighth of Isaiah, from the fifth to the fifteenth verse. And do not scorn to know that it is the Spirit that quickens and giveth life." *

Cromwell, as we have said, is the best commentator Isaiah has ever had, and that by an instinct born, not only of the same faith, but of experience in tackling similar sorts of character. In this letter he is dealing, like Isaiah, with stubborn pedants, who are endeavouring to fasten the national fortunes upon a Procrustean policy. The diplomacy of Jerusalem was very clever; the Covenanting ecclesiasticism of Edinburgh was logical and consistent. But a Jewish alliance with Assyria and the attempt of Scotsmen to force their covenant upon the whole United Kingdom were equally sheer impossibilities. In either case *the bed was shorter than that a man could stretch himself on it, and the covering narrower than that he could wrap himself in it.* Both, too, were *covenants with Death and Hell;* for if the attempt of the Scots to secure Charles II.

---

* *Cromwell's Letters and Speeches,* Letter cxxxvi.

by the Covenant was free from the falsehood of Jewish diplomacy, it was fatally certain if successful to have led to the subversion of their highest religious interests; and history has proved that Cromwell was no more than just in applying to it the strong expressions, which Isaiah uses of Judah's ominous treaties with the unscrupulous heathen. Over against so pedantic an idea, as that of forcing the life of the three nations into the mould of the one Covenant, and so fatal a folly as the attempt to commit the interests of religion to the keeping of the dissolute and perjured king, Cromwell stands in his great toleration of everything but unrighteousness and his strong conviction of three truths:—that the religious life of Great Britain and Ireland was too rich and varied for the Covenant: that national and religious interests so complicated and precious could be decided only upon the plainest principles of faith and justice: and that, tested by these principles, Charles II. and his crew were as utterly without worth to the nation and as pregnant with destruction, as Isaiah felt Assyria and Egypt to be to Judah. The battle-cries of the two parties at Dunbar are significant of the spiritual difference between them. That of the Scots was "The Covenant!" Cromwell's was Isaiah's own, "The Lord of hosts!" However logical, religious and sincere theirs might be, it was at the best a scheme of men too narrow for events, and fatally compromised by its association with Charles II. But Cromwell's battle-cry required only a moderately sincere faith from those who adopted it, to ensure their victory. For to them it meant just what it had meant to Isaiah, loyalty to a Divine providence, supreme in righteousness, the willingness to be guided by events, interpreting them by no tradition or scheme, but only by conscience. He who understands this will be able to see which side was right in that strange civil war, where both so sincerely claimed to be Scriptural.

It may be wondered why we spend so much argument on comparing the attempt to force Charles II. into the Solemn League and Covenant with the impious treaty of Judah with the heathen. But the argument has not been wasted, if it have shown how even sincere and religious men may make covenants with death, and even Church creeds and constitutions become beds too short that a man may lie upon them, coverings narrower than that he can wrap himself in them. Not once or twice has it happened that an old and hallowed constitution has become, in the providence of God, unfit for the larger life of a people or of a Church, and yet is clung to by parties in that Church or people from motives of theological pedantry or ecclesiastical cowardice. Sooner or later a crisis is sure to arrive, in which the defective creed has to match itself against some interest of justice; and then endless compromises have to be entertained, that discover themselves perilously like *bargains with hell*. If we of this generation have to make a public application of the twenty-eighth chapter of Isaiah, it lies in this direction. There are few things, to which his famous proverb of the short bed can be applied more aptly, than to the attempt to fasten down the religious life and thought of the present age too rigorously upon a creed of the fashion of two or three hundred years ago.

But Isaiah's words have wider application. Short of faith as he exemplified it, there is no possibility for the spirit of man to be free from uneasiness. It is so all along the scale of human endeavour. No power of patience or of hope is his, who cannot imagine possibilities of truth outside his own opinions, nor trust a justice larger than his private rights. It is here very often that the real test of our faith meets us. If we seek to fit life solely to the conception of our privileges, if in the preaching of our opinions no mystery of higher truth awe us at least into reverence and caution ; then, whatever religious creeds we profess, we are not men of faith, but shall surely inherit the bitterness and turmoil that are the portion of unbelievers. If we make it the chief aim of our politics to drive cheap bargains for our trade or to be consistent to party or class interests; if we trim our conscience to popular opinion ; if we sell our honesty in business or our love in marriage, that we may be comfortable in the world ; then, however firmly we be established in reputation or in welfare, we have given our spiritual nature a support utterly inadequate to its needs, and we shall never find rest. Sooner or later, a man must feel the pinch of having cut his life short of the demands of conscience. Only a generous loyalty to her decrees will leave him freedom of heart and room for his arm to swing. Nor will any philosophy, however comprehensive, nor poetic fancy, however elastic, be able without the complement of faith to arrange, to account for, or to console us for, the actual facts of experience. It is only belief in the God of Isaiah, a true and loving God, omnipotent Ruler of our life, that can bring us peace. There was never a sorrow, that did not find explanation in that, never a tired thought, that would not cling to it. There are no interests so scattered nor energies so far-reaching that there is not return and rest for them under the shadow of His wings. *He that believeth shall not make haste. Be still*, says a psalm of the same date as Isaiah—*Be still, and know that I am God.*

IV. The Almighty the All-methodical (vv. 23—29).

The patience of faith, which Isaiah has so nobly preached, he now proceeds to vindicate by reason. But the vindication implies that his audience are already in another mood. From confidence in their clever diplomacy, heedless of the fact that God has His own purposes concerning them, they have swung round to despair before His judgements. Their despair, however, is due to the same fault as their careless confidence—the forgetfulness that God works by counsel and method. Even a calamity, so universal and extreme as that, of whose certainty the prophet has now convinced them, has its measure and its term. To persuade the crushed and superstitious Jews of this, Isaiah employs a parable. "You know," he says, "the husbandman. Have you ever seen him keep on *harrowing and breaking the clods of his land* for mere sport, and without farther intention? Does not the harrowing time lead to the sowing time? Or again, when he threshes his crops, does he thresh for ever? Is threshing the end he has in view? Look, how he varies the rigour of his instrument by the kind of plant he threshes. For delicate plants, like fitches and cummin, he does not use the *threshing sledge* with the sharp teeth, or the lumbering *roller, but the fitches are beaten out with a staff and the cummin with a rod.* And in the case of *bread corn*, which needs *his roller and horses*, he does not use these upon it till it is all *crushed to dust.*" The application of this parable is very evident. If the husbandman be so methodical and careful, shall the God who taught him not also be so? If the violent treatment of land and fruits be so measured and adapted for their greater fruitfulness and purity, ought we not to trust God to have the same intentions in His violent treatment of His people? Isaiah here returns to his fundamental gospel: that the Almighty is the All-methodical, too. Men forget this. In their times of activity they think God indifferent; they are too occupied with their own schemes for shaping life, to imagine that He has any. In days of suffering, again, when disaster bursts, they conceive of God only as force and vengeance. Yet, says Isaiah, *Jehovah of hosts is wonderful in counsel, and excellent in that sort of wisdom which causes things to succeed.* This last word of the chapter is very expressive. It literally means *furtherance, help, salvation,* and then *the true wisdom or insight which ensures these: the wisdom which carries things through.* It splendidly sums up Isaiah's gospel to the Jews, cowering like dogs before the coming calamity: God is not mere force or vengeance. His judgements are not chaos. But *He is wonderful in counsel,* and all His ways have *furtherance* or *salvation* for their end.

We have said this is one of the finest prophecies of Isaiah. His political foresight was admirable, when he alone of his countrymen predicted the visitation of Assyria upon Judah. But now, when all are convinced of it, how still more wonderful does he seem facing that novel disaster, with the whole world's force behind it, and declaring its limit. He has not the temptation, so strong in prophets of judgement, to be a mere disaster-monger, and leave judgement on the horizon unrelieved. Nor is he afraid, as other predicters of evil have been, of the monster he has summoned to the land. The secret of this is that from the first he predicted the Assyrian invasion, not out of any private malice nor merely by superior political foresight, but because he knew—and knew, as he tells us, by the inspiration of God's own Spirit—that God required such an instrument to punish the unrighteousness of Judah. If the enemy was summoned by God at the first, surely till the last the enemy shall be in God's hand.

To this enemy we are now to see Isaiah turn with the same message he has delivered to the men of Jerusalem.

CHAPTER IX.

ATHEISM OF FORCE AND ATHEISM OF FEAR.

Isaiah x. 5—34 (about 721 b.c.).

IN chap. xxviii. Isaiah, speaking in the year 725 when Salmanassar IV. was marching on Samaria, had explained to the politicians of Jerusalem how entirely the Assyrian host was in the hand of Jehovah for the punishment of Samaria and the punishment and purification of Judah. The invasion which in that year loomed so awful was not unbridled force of destruction, implying the utter annihilation of God's people, as Damascus, Arpad and Hamath had been annihilated. It was Jehovah's instrument for purifying His people, with its appointed term and its glorious intentions of fruitfulness and peace.

In the tenth chapter Isaiah turns with this truth to defy the Assyrian himself. It is four years later. Samaria has fallen. The judgement, which the prophet spoke upon the luxurious capital, has been fulfilled. All Ephraim is an Assyrian province. Judah stands for the first time face to face with Assyria. From Samaria to the borders of Judah is not quite two days' march, to the walls of Jerusalem a little over two. Now shall the Jews be able to put to the test their prophet's promise! What can possibly prevent Sargon from making Zion as Samaria, and carrying her people away in the track of the northern tribes to captivity?

There was a very fallacious human reason, and there was a very sound Divine one.

The fallacious human reason was the alliance which Ahaz had made with Assyria. In what state that alliance now was, does not clearly appear, but the most optimist of the Assyrian party at Jerusalem could not, after all that had happened, be feeling quite comfortable about it. The Assyrian was as unscrupulous as themselves. There was too much impetus in the rush of his northern floods to respect a tiny province like Judah, treaty or no treaty. Besides, Sargon had as good reason to suspect Jerusalem of intriguing with Egypt, as he had against Samaria or the Philistine cities; and the Assyrian kings had already shown their meaning of the covenant with Ahaz by stripping Judah of enormous tribute.

So Isaiah discounts in this prophecy Judah's treaty with Assyria. He speaks as if nothing was likely to prevent the Assyrian's immediate march upon Jerusalem. He puts into Sargon's mouth the intention of this, and makes him boast of the ease with which it can be accomplished (vv. 7—11). In the end of the prophecy he even describes the probable itinerary of the invader from the borders of Judah to his arrival on the heights, over against the Holy City (vv. 27 last clause to 32).*

Cometh up from the North the Destroyer.

---

* It will be noticed that in the above version a different reading is adopted from the meaningless clause at the end of verse 27 in the English version, out of which a proper heading for the subsequent itinerary has been obtained by Robertson Smith (*Journal of Philology*, 1884, p. 62).

He is come upon Ai; marcheth through Migron; at Michmash musters his baggage.

They have passed through the Pass; " Let Geba be our bivouac."

Terror-struck is Ramah; Gibeah of Saul hath fled.

Make shrill thy voice, O daughter of Gallim! Listen, Laishah! Answer her, Anathoth!

In mad flight is Madmenah; the dwellers in Gebim gather their stuff to flee.

This very day he halteth at Nob; he waveth his hand at the Mount of the Daughter of Zion, the Hill of Jerusalem.

This is not actual fact ; but it is vision of what may take place to-day or to-morrow. For there is nothing —not even that miserable treaty—to prevent such a violation of Jewish territory, within which, it ought to be kept in mind, lie all the places named by the prophet.

But the invasion of Judah and the arrival of the Assyrian on the heights over against Jerusalem does not mean that the Holy City and the shrine of Jehovah of hosts are to be destroyed ; does not mean that all the prophecies of Isaiah about the security of this rallyng-place for the remnant of God's people are to be annulled, and Israel annihilated. For just at the moment of the Assyrian's triumph, when he brandishes his hand over Jerusalem, as if he would harry it like a bird's nest, Isaiah beholds him struck down, and crash like the fall of a whole Lebanon of cedars (vv. 33, 34).

Behold the Lord, Jehovah of hosts, lopping the topmost boughs with a sudden crash,

And the high ones of stature hewn down, and the lofty are brought low!

Yea, He moweth down the thickets of the forest with iron, and Lebanon by a Mighty One falleth.

All this is poetry. We are not to suppose that the prophet actually expected the Assyrian to take the route, which he has laid down for him with so much detail. As a matter of fact, Sargon did not advance across the Jewish frontier, but turned away by the coast-land of Philistia to meet his enemy of Egypt, whom he defeated at Rafia, and then went home to Nineveh, leaving Judah alone. And, although some twenty years later the Assyrian did appear before Jerusalem, as threatening as Isaiah describes, and was cut down in as sudden and miraculous a manner, yet it was not by the itinerary Isaiah here marked for him that he came, but in quite another direction: from the south-west. What Isaiah merely insists upon is that there is nothing in that wretched treaty of Ahaz—that fallacious *human* reason —to keep Sargon from overrunning Judah to the very walls of Jerusalem, but that, even though he does so, there is a most sure *Divine* reason for the Holy City remaining inviolate.

The Assyrian expected to take Jerusalem. But he is not his own master. Though he knows it not, and his only instinct is that of destruction (ver. 7), he is the rod in God's hand. And when God shall have used him for the needed punishment of Judah, then will God visit upon him his arrogance and brutality. This man, who says he will exploit the whole earth as he harries a bird's nest (ver. 14), who believes in nothing but himself, saying, *By the strength of my hand I have done it, and by my wisdom, for I am prudent,* is but the instrument of God, and all his boasting is that of *the axe against him that heweth therewith and of the saw against him that wieldeth it. As if,* says the prophet, with a scorn still fresh for those who make material force the ultimate power in the universe—*As if a rod should shake them that lift it up, or as if a staff should lift up him that is not wood.* By the way, Isaiah has a word for his countrymen. What folly is theirs, who now put all their trust in this world-force, and at another time cower in abject fear before it! Must he again bid them look higher, and see that Assyria is only the agent in God's work of first punishing the whole land, but afterwards redeeming His people! In the midst of denunciation the prophet's stern voice breaks into the promise of this later hope (vv. 24—27*a*); and at last the crash of the fallen Assyrian is scarcely still, before Isaiah has begun to declare a most glorious future of grace for Israel. But this carries us over into the eleventh chapter, and we had better first of all gather up the lessons of the tenth.

This prophecy of Isaiah contains a great Gospel and two great Protests, which the prophet was enabled to make in the strength of it: one against the Atheism of Force, and one against the Atheism of Fear.

The Gospel of the chapter is just that which we have already emphasized as the gospel *par excellence* of Isaiah: the Lord exalted in righteousness, God supreme over the supremest men and forces of the world. But we now see it carried to a height of daring not reached before. This was the first time that any man faced the sovereign force of the world in the full sweep of victory, and told himself and his fellow-men: "This is not travelling in the greatness of its own strength, but is simply a dead, unconscious instrument in the hand of God." Let us, at the cost of a little repetition, get at the heart of this. We shall find it wonderfully modern.

Belief in God had hitherto been local and circumscribed. Each nation, as Isaiah tells us, had walked in the name of its god, and limited his power and prevision to its own life and territory. We do not blame the peoples for this. Their conception of God was narrow, because their life was narrow, and they confined the power of their deity to their own borders because, in fact, their thoughts seldom strayed beyond. But now the barriers, that had so long enclosed mankind in narrow circles, were being broken down. Men's thoughts travelled through the breaches, and learned that outside their fatherland there lay the world. Their lives thereupon widened immensely, but their theologies stood still. They felt the great forces which shook the world, but their gods remained the same petty, provincial deities. Then came this great Assyrian power, hurtling through the nations, laughing at their gods as idols, boasting that it was by his own strength he overcame them, and to simple eyes making good his boast as he harried the whole earth like a bird's nest. No wonder that men's hearts were drawn from the unseen spiritualities to this very visible brutality! No wonder all real faith in the gods seemed to be dying out, and that men made it the business of their lives to seek peace with this world-force, that was carrying everything, including the gods themselves, before it! Mankind was in danger of practical atheism: of placing, as Isaiah tells us, the ultimate faith which belongs to a righteous God in this brute force: of substituting embassies for prayers, tribute for sacrifice, and the tricks and compromises of diplomacy for the endeavour to live a holy and righteous life. Behold, what questions were at issue: questions that have come up again and again in the history of human thought, and that are tugging at us to-day harder than ever!—whether the visible, sensible forces of the universe, that break so rudely in upon our primitive theologies, are what we men have to make our peace with, or whether there is behind them a Being, who wields them for purposes, far transcending them, of justice and of love; whether, in short, we are to be materialists or believers in God. It is the same old, ever-new debate. The factors of it have only changed a little as we have become more learned. Where Isaiah felt the Assyrians, we are confronted by the evolution of nature and history, and the material forces into which it sometimes looks ominously like as if these could be analysed. Everything that has come forcibly and gloriously to the front of things, every drift that appears to dominate history, all that asserts its claim on our wonder, and offers its own simple and strong solution of our life—is our Assyria. It is precisely now, as then, a rush of new powers across the horizon of our knowledge, which makes the God, who was sufficient for the narrower knowledge of yesterday, seem petty and old-fashioned to-day. This problem no generation can escape, whose vision of the world has become wider than that of its predecessors. But Isaiah's greatness lay in this: that it was given to him to attack the problem the first time it presented itself to humanity with any serious force, and that he applied to it the only sure solution—a more lofty and spiritual view of God than the one which it had found wanting. We may thus paraphrase his argument: "Give me a God who is more than a national patron, give me a God who cares only for righteousness, and I say that every material force the world exhibits is nothing but subordinate to Him. Brute force cannot be anything but an instrument, *an axe, a saw*, something essentially mechanical and in need of an arm to lift it. Postulate a supreme and righteous Ruler of the world, and you not only have all its movements explained, but may rest assured, that it shall only be permitted to execute justice and purify men. The world cannot prevent their salvation, if God have willed this."

Isaiah's problem was thus the fundamental one between faith and atheism; but we must notice that it did not arise theoretically, nor did he meet it by an abstract proposition. This fundamental religious question—whether men are to trust in the visible forces of the world or in the invisible God—came up as a bit of practical politics. It was not to Isaiah a philosophical or theological question. It was an affair in the foreign policy of Judah.

Except to a few thinkers, the question between materialism and faith never does present itself as one of abstract argument. To the mass of men it is always a question of practical life. Statesmen meet it in their policies, private persons in the conduct of their fortunes. Few of us trouble our heads about an intellectual atheism, but the temptations to practical atheism abound unto us all day by day. Materialism never presents itself as a mere *ism;* it always takes some concrete form. Our Assyria may be the world in Christ's sense, that flood of successful, heartless, unscrupulous, scornful forces which burst on our innocence, with their challenge to make terms and pay tribute, or go down straightway in the struggle for existence. Beside their frank and forceful demands, how commonplace and irrelevant do the simple precepts of religion often seem; and how the great brazen laugh of the world seems to bleach the beauty out of purity and honour! According to our temper, we either cower before its insolence, whining that character and energy of struggle and religious peace are impossible against it; and that is the Atheism of Fear, with which Isaiah charged the men of Jerusalem, when they were paralysed before Assyria. Or we seek to ensure ourselves against disaster by alliance with the world. We make ourselves one with it, its subjects and imitators. We absorb the world's temper, get to believe in nothing but success, regard men only as they can be useful to us, and think so exclusively of ourselves as to lose the faculty of imagining about us any other right or need or pity. And all that is the Atheism of Force, with which Isaiah charged the Assyrian. It is useless to think, that we common men cannot possibly sin after the grand manner of this imperial monster. In our measure we fatally can. In this commercial age private persons very easily rise to a position of influence, which gives almost as vast a stage for egotism to display itself as the Assyrian boasted. But after all the human Ego needs very little room to develop the possibilities of atheism that are in it. An idol is an idol, whether you put it on a small or a large pedestal. A little man with a little work may as easily stand between himself and God, as an emperor with the world at his feet. Forgetfulness that he is a servant, a trader on graciously entrusted capital—and then at the best an unprofitable one—is not less sinful in a small egoist than in a great one; it is only very much more ridiculous, than Isaiah, with his scorn, has made it to appear in the Assyrian.

Or our Assyria may be the forces of nature, which have swept upon the knowledge of this generation with the novelty and impetus, with which the northern hosts burst across the horizon of Israel. Men to-day, in the course of their education, become acquainted with laws and forces, which dwarf the simpler theologies of their boyhood, pretty much as the primitive beliefs of Israel dwindled before the arrogant face of Assyria. The alternative confronts them either to retain, with a narrowed and fearful heart, their old conceptions of God, or to find their enthusiasm in studying, and their duty in relating themselves to, the forces of nature alone. If this be the only alternative, there can be no doubt but that most men will take the latter course. We ought as little to wonder at men of to-day abandoning certain theologies and forms of religion for a downright naturalism—for the study of powers that appeal so much to the curiosity and reverence of man—as we wonder at the poor Jews of the eighth century before Christ forsaking their provincial conceptions of God as a tribal Deity for homage to this great Assyrian, who handled the nations and their gods as his playthings. But is such the only alternative? Is there no higher and sovereign conception of God, in which even these natural forces may find their explanation and term? Isaiah found such a conception for his problem, and his problem was very similar to ours. Beneath his idea of God, exalted and spiritual, even the imperial Assyrian, in all his arrogance, fell subordinate and serviceable. The prophet's faith never wavered, and in the end was vindicated by history. Shall we not at least attempt his method of solution? We could not do better than by taking his factors. Isaiah got a God more powerful than Assyria, by simply *exalting* the old God of his nation *in righteousness*. This Hebrew was saved from the terrible conclusion, that the selfish, cruel force which in his day carried all before it was the highest power in life, simply by believing righteousness to be more exalted still. But have twenty-five centuries made any change upon this power, by which Isaiah interpreted history and overcame the world? Is righteousness less sovereign now than then, or was conscience more imperative when it spoke in Hebrew than when it speaks in English? Among the decrees of nature, at last interpreted for us in all their scope and reiterated upon our imaginations by the ablest men of the age, truth, purity and civic justice as confidently assert their ultimate victory, as when they were threatened merely by the arrogance of a human despot. The discipline of science and the glories of the worship of nature are indeed justly vaunted over the childish and narrow-minded ideas of God, that prevail in much of our average Christianity. But more glorious than anything in earth or heaven is character, and the adoration of a holy and loving will makes more for " victory and law" than the discipline or the enthusiasm of science. Therefore, if our conceptions of God are overwhelmed by what we know of nature, let us seek to enlarge and spiritualize them. Let us insist, as Isaiah did, upon His righteousness, until our God once more appear indubitably supreme.

Otherwise we are left with the intolerable paradox, that truth and honesty, patience and the love of man to man, are after all but the playthings and victims of force; that, to adapt the words of Isaiah, the rod really shakes him who lifts it up, and the staff is wielding that which is not wood.

CHAPTER X.

THE SPIRIT OF GOD IN MAN AND THE ANIMALS.

Isaiah xi., xii. (about 720 b.c. ?)

BENEATH the crash of the Assyrian with which the tenth chapter closes, we pass out into the eleventh upon a glorious prospect of Israel's future. The Assyrian when he falls shall fall for ever like the cedars of Lebanon, that send no fresh sprout forth from their broken stumps. But out of the trunk of the Judæan oak, also brought down by these terrible storms, Isaiah sees springing a fair and powerful Branch. Assyria, he would tell us, has no future. Judah has a future, and at first the prophet sees it in a scion of her royal house. The nation shall be almost exterminated, the dynasty of David hewn to a stump; *yet there shall spring a shoot from the stock of Jesse, and a branch from his roots shall bear fruit.*

The picture of this future, which fills the eleventh chapter, is one of the most extensive that Isaiah has drawn. Three great prospects are unfolded in it: a prospect of mind, a prospect of nature and a prospect of history. To begin with, there is (vv. 2—5) the geography of a royal mind in its stretches of character, knowledge and achievement. We have next (vv. 5—9) a vision of the restitution of nature, Paradise regained. And, thirdly (vv. 9—16), there is the geography of Israel's redemption, the coasts and highways along which the hosts of the dispersion sweep up from captivity to a station of supremacy over the world. To this third prospect chapter xii. forms a fitting conclusion, a hymn of praise in the mouth of returning exiles.* The human mind, nature and history are the three dimensions of life, and across them all the prophet tells us that the Spirit of the Lord will fill the future with His marvels of righteousness, wisdom and peace. He presents to us three great ideals: the perfect indwelling of our humanity by the Spirit of God; the peace and communion of all nature, covered with the knowledge of God; the traversing of all history by the Divine purposes of redemption.

I. THE MESSIAH AND THE SPIRIT OF THE LORD (xi. 1-5).

The first form, in which Isaiah sees Israel's longed-for future realised, is that which he so often exalts and makes glistering upon the threshold of the future—the form of a king. It is a peculiarity, which we cannot fail to remark about Isaiah's scattered representations of this brilliant figure, that they have no connecting link. They do not allude to one another, nor employ a common terminology, even the word *king* dropping out of some of them. The earliest of the series bestows a name on the Messiah, which none of the others repeat, nor does Isaiah say in any of them, This is He of whom I have spoken before. Perhaps the disconnectedness of these oracles is as strong a proof as is necessary of the view we have formed that

---

* The authenticity of this hymn has been called in question.

throughout his ministry our prophet had before him no distinct, identical individual, but rather an ideal of virtue and kinghood, whose features varied according to the conditions of the time. In this chapter Isaiah recalls nothing of Immanuel, or of the Prince-of-the-Four-Names. Nevertheless (besides for the first time deriving the Messiah from the house of David), he carries his description forward to a stage which lies beyond and to some extent implies his two previous portraits. Immanuel was only a Sufferer with His people in the day of their oppression. The Prince-of-the-Four-Names was the Redeemer of his people from their captivity, and stepped to his throne not only after victory, but with the promise of a long and just government shining from the titles by which He was proclaimed. But now Isaiah not only speaks at length of this peaceful reign—a chronological advance—but describes his hero so inwardly that we also feel a certain spiritual advance. The Messiah is no more a mere experience, as Immanuel was, nor only outward deed and promise, like the Prince-of-the-Four-Names, but at last, and very strongly, *a character.* The second verse is the definition of this character; the third describes the atmosphere in which it lives. *And there shall rest upon him the Spirit of Jehovah, the spirit of wisdom and understanding, the spirit of counsel and might, the spirit of knowledge and the fear of Jehovah; and he shall draw breath in the fear of Jehovah*—in other words, ripeness but also sharpness of mind; moral decision and heroic energy; piety in its two forms of knowing the will of God and feeling the constraint to perform it. We could not have a more concise summary of the strong elements of a ruling mind. But it is only as Judge and Ruler that Isaiah cares here to think of his hero. Nothing is said of the tender virtues, and we feel that the prophet still stands in the days of the need of inflexible government and purgation in Judah.

Dean Plumptre has plausibly suggested, that these verses may represent the programme which Isaiah set before his pupil Hezekiah on his accession to the charge of a nation, whom his weak predecessor had suffered to lapse into such abuse of justice and laxity of morals.* The acts of government described are all of a punitive and repressive character. The hero speaks only to make the land tremble: *And He shall smite the land*† *with the rod of His mouth* [what need, after the whispering, indecisive Ahaz!], *and with the breath of His lips shall He slay the wicked.*

This, though a fuller and more ethical picture of the Messiah than even the ninth chapter, is evidently wanting in many of the traits of a perfect man. Isaiah has to grow in his conception of his Hero, and will grow as the years go on, in tenderness. His thirty-second chapter is a much richer, a more gracious and humane picture of the Messiah. There the Victor of the ninth and righteous Judge of the eleventh chapters is represented as *a Man*, who shall not only punish but protect, and not only reign but inspire, who shall be life as well as victory and justice to His people—*an hiding-place from the wind and a*

---

* Dean Plumptre notes the identity of the ethical terminology of this passage with that of the book of Proverbs, and conjectures that the additions to the original nucleus, chaps. x.—xxiv., and therefore the whole form, of the book of Proverbs, may be due to the editorship of Isaiah, and perhaps was the manual of ethics, on which he sought to mould the character of Hezekiah (*Expositor*, series ii., v., p. 213).

† Perhaps for *land— àrets*—we ought, with Lagarde, to read *tyrant— ârits.*

covert from the tempest, as rivers of water in a dry place, as the shadow of a great rock in a weary land.

A conception so limited to the qualifications of an earthly monarch, as this of chap. xi., gives us no ground for departing from our previous conclusion, that Isaiah had not a "supernatural" personality in his view. The Christian Church, however, has not confined the application of the passage to earthly kings and magistrates, but has seen its perfect fulfilment in the indwelling of Christ's human nature by the Holy Ghost. But it is remarkable, that for this exegesis she has not made use of the most "supernatural" of the details of character here portrayed. If the Old Testament has a phrase for sinlessness, that phrase occurs here, in the beginning of the third verse. In the authorized English version it is translated, *and shall make him of quick understanding in the fear of the Lord*, and in the Revised Version, *His delight shall be in the fear of the Lord*, and on the margin the literal meaning of *delight* is given as *scent*. But the phrase may as well mean, *He shall draw his breath in the fear of the Lord;* and it is a great pity, that our revisers have not even on the margin given to English readers any suggestion of so picturesque, and probably so correct, a rendering. It is a most expressive definition of sinlessness—sinlessness which was the attribute of Christ alone. We, however purely intentioned we be, are compassed about by an atmosphere of sin. We cannot help breathing what now inflames our passions, now chills our warmest feelings, and makes our throats incapable of honest testimony or glorious praise. As oxygen to a dying fire, so the worldliness we breathe is to the sin within us. We cannot help it; it is the atmosphere into which we are born. But from this Christ alone of men was free. He was His own atmosphere, *drawing breath in the fear of the Lord.* Of Him alone is it recorded, that, though living in the world, He was never infected with the world's sin. The blast of no man's cruelty ever kindled unholy wrath within His breast; nor did men's unbelief carry to His soul its deadly chill. Not even when He was led of the devil into the atmosphere of temptation, did His heart throb with one rebellious ambition. Christ *drew breath in the fear of the Lord.*

But draughts of this atmosphere are possible to us also, to whom the Holy Spirit is granted. We too, who sicken with the tainted breath of society, and see the characters of children about us fall away and the hidden evil within leap to swift flame before the blasts of the world—we too may, by Christ's grace, *draw breath*, like Him, *in the fear of the Lord.* Recall some day when, leaving your close room and the smoky city, you breasted the hills of God, and into opened lungs drew deep draughts of the fresh air of heaven. What strength it gave your body, and with what a glow of happiness your mind was filled! What that is physically, Christ has made possible for us men morally. He has revealed stretches and eminences of life, where, following in His footsteps, we also shall draw for our breath the fear of God. This air is inspired up every steep hill of effort, and upon all summits of worship. In the most passion-haunted air, prayer will immediately bring this atmosphere about a man, and on the wings of praise the poorest soul may rise from the miasma of temptation, and sing forth her song into the azure with as clear a throat as the lark's.

And what else is heaven to be, if not this? God, we are told, shall be its Sun; but its atmosphere shall be

His fear, *which is clean and endureth for ever.* Heaven seems most real as a moral open-air, where every breath is an inspiration, and every pulse a healthy joy, where no thoughts from within us find breath but those of obedience and praise, and all our passions and aspirations are of the will of God. He that lives near to Christ, and by Christ often seeks God in prayer, may create for himself even on earth such a heaven, *perfecting holiness in the fear of God.*

II. THE SEVEN SPIRITS OF GOD (xi. 2, 3).

This passage, which suggests so much of Christ, is also for Christian Theology and Art a classical passage on the Third Person of the Trinity. If the texts in the book of Revelation (chaps. i. 4; iii. 1; iv. 5; v. 6) upon the Seven Spirits of God were not themselves founded on this text of Isaiah, it is certain that the Church immediately began to interpret them by its details. While there are only six spirits of God named here—three pairs—yet, in order to complete the perfect number, the exegesis of early Christianity sometimes added *the Spirit of the Lord* at the beginning of verse 2 as the central branch of a seven-branched candlestick; or sometimes *the quick understanding in the fear of the Lord* in the beginning of verse 3 was attached as the seventh branch. (Compare Zech. iv. 6.)

It is remarkable that there is almost no single text of Scripture, which has more impressed itself upon Christian doctrine and symbol than this second verse of the eleventh chapter, interpreted as a definition of the Seven Spirits of God. In the theology, art and worship of the Middle Ages it dominated the expression of the work of the Holy Ghost. First, and most native to its origin, arose the employment of this text at the coronation of kings and the fencing of tribunals of justice. What Isaiah wrote for Hezekiah of Judah became the official prayer, song or ensample of the earliest Christian kings in Europe. It is evidently the model of that royal hymn—not by Charlemagne, as usually supposed, but by his grandson Charles the Bald—the *Veni Creator Spiritus*. In a Greek miniature of the tenth century, the Holy Spirit, as a dove, is seen hovering over King David, who displays the prayer: *Give the king Thy judgements, O God, and Thy righteousness to the king's son,* while there stand on either side of him the figures of Wisdom and Prophecy.* Henry III.'s order of knighthood, " Du Saint Esprit," was restricted to political men, and particularly to magistrates. But perhaps the most interesting identification of the Holy Spirit with the rigorous virtues of our passage occurs in a story of St. Dunstan, who, just before mass on the day of Pentecost, discovered that three coiners, who had been sentenced to death, were being respited till the Festival of the Holy Ghost should be over. " It shall not be thus," cried the indignant saint, and gave orders for their immediate execution. There was remonstrance, but he, no doubt with the eleventh of Isaiah in mind, insisted, and was obeyed. " I now hope," he said, resuming the mass, " that God will be pleased to accept the sacrifice I am about to offer." " Whereupon," says the veracious *Acts of the Saints*, " a snow-white dove did, in the vision of many, descend from heaven, and until the sacrifice was completed remain above his head in silence, with wings extended and motionless." Which may be as much legend as we have the heart to make it, but nevertheless

---

* Didron, *Christian Iconography*, Engl. trans., i., 432.

remains a sure proof of the association, by discerning mediævals who could read their Scriptures, of the Holy Spirit with the decisiveness and rigorous justice of Isaiah's " mirror for magistrates."*

But the influence of our passage may be followed to that wider definition of the Spirit's work, which made Him the Fountain of all intelligence. The Spirits of the Lord mentioned by Isaiah are prevailingly intellectual ; and the mediæval Church, using the details of this passage to interpret Christ's own intimation of the Paraclete as the Spirit of truth,—remembering also the story of Pentecost, when the Spirit bestowed the gifts of tongues, and the case of Stephen, who, in the triumph of his eloquence and learning, was said to be full of the Holy Ghost,—did regard, as Gregory of Tours expressly declared, the Holy Spirit as the "God of the intellect more than of the heart." All Councils were opened by a mass to the Holy Ghost, and few, who have examined with care the windows of mediæval churches, will have failed to be struck with the frequency with which the Dove is seen descending upon the heads of miraculously learned persons, or presiding at discussions, or hovering over groups of figures representing the sciences.† To the mediæval Church, then, the Holy Spirit was the Author of the intellect, more especially of the governing and political intellect ; and there can be little doubt, after a study of the variations of this doctrine, that the first five verses of the eleventh of Isaiah formed upon it the classical text of appeal. To Christians, who have been accustomed by the use of the word *Comforter* to associate the Spirit only with

---

* Didron, *Christian Iconography*, Engl. trans., i., 426.
† See Didron for numerous interesting instances of this.

the gentle and consoling influences of heaven, it may seem strange to find His energy identified with the stern rigour of the magistrate. But in its practical, intelligent and reasonable uses the mediæval doctrine is greatly to be preferred, on grounds both of Scripture and common-sense, to those two comparatively modern corruptions of it, one of which emphasizes the Spirit's influence in the exclusive operation of the grace of orders, and the other, driving to an opposite extreme, dissipates it into the vaguest religiosity. It is one of the curiosities of Christian theology, that a Divine influence, asserted by Scripture and believed by the early Church to manifest itself in the successful conduct of civil offices and the fulness of intellectual learning, should in these latter days be so often set up in a sort of "supernatural" opposition to practical wisdom and the results of science. But we may go back to Isaiah for the same kind of correction on this doctrine, as he has given us on the doctrine of faith; and while we do not forget the richer meaning the New Testament bestows on the operation of the Divine Spirit, we may learn from the Hebrew prophet to seek the inspiration of the Holy Ghost in all the endeavours of science, and not to forget that it is His guidance alone which enables us to succeed in the conduct of our offices and fortunes.

III. The Redemption of Nature (xi. 6-9).

But Isaiah will not be satisfied with the establishment of a strong government in the 'land and the redemption of human society from chaos. He prophesies the redemption of all nature as well. It is one of those errors, which distort both the poetry and truth of the Bible, to suppose that by the bears, lions and reptiles which the prophet now sees tamed in the time of the regeneration, he intends the violent human characters which he so often attacks. When Isaiah here talks of the beasts, he means the beasts. The passage is not allegorical, but direct, and forms a parallel to the well-known passage in the eighth of Romans. Isaiah and Paul, chief apostles of the two covenants, both interrupt their magnificent odes upon the outpouring of the Spirit, to remind us that the benefits of this will be shared by the brute and unintelligent creation. And, perhaps, there is no finer contrast in the Scriptures than here, where beside so majestic a description of the intellectual faculties of humanity Isaiah places so charming a picture of the docility and sportfulness of wild animals,—*And a little child shall lead them.*

We, who live in countries, from which wild beasts have been exterminated, cannot understand the insecurity and terror, that they cause in regions where they abound. A modern seer of the times of regeneration would leave the wild animals out of his vision. They do not impress any more the human conscience or imagination. But they once did so most terribly. The hostility between man and the beasts not only formed once upon a time the chief material obstacle in the progress of the race, but remains still to the religious thinker the most pathetic portion of that groaning and travailing of all creation, which is so heavy a burden on his heart. Isaiah, from his ancient point of view, is in thorough accord with the order of civilisation, when he represents the subjugation of wild animals as the first problem of man, after he has established a strong government in the land. So far from rhetorizing or allegorizing—above which literary forms it would appear to be impossible for the appreciation of some of his commentators to follow him—Isaiah is earnestly celebrating a very real moment in the laborious progress of mankind. Isaiah stands where Hercules stood, and Theseus, and Arthur when

> " There grew great tracts of wilderness,
> Wherein the beast was ever more and more,
> But man was less and less till Arthur came.
> And he drave
> The heathen, and he slew the beast, and felled
> The forest, and let in the sun, and made
> Broad pathways for the hunter and the knight,
> And so returned."

But Isaiah would solve the grim problem of the warfare between man and his lower fellow-creatures in a very different way from that, of which these heroes have set the example to humanity. Isaiah would not have the wild beasts exterminated, but tamed. There our Western and modern imagination may fail to follow him, especially when he includes reptiles in the regeneration, and prophesies of adders and lizards as the playthings of children. But surely there is no genial man, who has watched the varied forms of life that sport in the Southern sunshine, who will not sympathize with the prophet in his joyous vision. Upon a warm spring day in Palestine, to sit upon the grass, beside some old dyke or ruin with its face to the south, is indeed to obtain a rapturous view of the wealth of life, with which the bountiful God has blessed and made merry man's dwelling-place. How the lizards come and go among the grey stones, and flash like jewels in the dust! And the timid snake rippling quickly past through the grass, and the leisurely tortoise, with his shiny back, and the chameleon, shivering into new colour as he passes from twig to stone and stone to straw,—all the air the while alive with the music of the cricket and the bee ! You feel that the ideal is not to destroy these pretty things as vermin. What a loss of colour the lizards alone would imply ! But, as Isaiah declares,—whom we may imagine walking with his children up the steep vineyard paths, to watch the creatures come and go upon the dry dykes on either hand,—the ideal is to bring them into sympathy with ourselves, make pets of them and playthings for children, who indeed stretch out their hands in joy to the pretty toys. Why should we need to fight with, or destroy, any of the happy life the Lord has created ? Why have we this loathing to it, and need to defend ourselves from it, when there is so much suffering we could cure, and so much childlikeness we could amuse and be amused by, and yet it will not let us near ? To these questions there is not another answer but the answer of the Bible: that this curse of conflict and distrust between man and his fellow-creatures is due to man's sin, and shall only be done away by man's redemption.

Nor is this Bible answer,—of which the book of Genesis gives us the one end, and this text of Isaiah the other,—a mere pious opinion, which the true history of man's dealing with wild beasts by extermination proves to be impracticable. We may take on scientific authority a few facts as hints from nature, that after all man is to blame for the wildness of the beasts, and that through his sanctification they may be restored to sympathy with himself. Charles Darwin says : " It deserves notice, that at an extremely ancient period, when man first entered any country the animals living there would have felt no instinctive or inherited fear of him, and would consequently have been tamed far more easily than at present." And he gives some very instructive facts in proof of this with regard to dogs, antelopes, manatees and hawks. "Quadrupeds and birds which have seldom been disturbed by man dread him no more than do our English birds the cows or horses grazing in the fields."* Darwin's details are peculiarly pathetic in their revelation of the brutes' utter trustfulness in man, before they get to know him. Persons, who have had to do with individual animals of a species that has never been thoroughly tamed, are aware that the difficulty of training them lies in convincing them of our sincerity and good-heartedness, and that when this is got over they will learn almost any trick or habit. The well-known lines of Burns to the field-mouse gather up the cause of all this in a fashion very similar to the Bible's.

> "I'm truly sorry man's dominion
> Has broken nature's social union,
> And justifies that ill opinion,
>   Which makes thee startle
> At me, thy poor earth-born companion
>   And fellow-mortal."

How much the appeal of suffering animals to man—the look of a wounded horse or dog with a meaning which speech would only spoil, the tales of beasts of prey that in pain have turned to man as their physician, the approach of the wildest birds in winter to our feet as their Providence—how much all these prove Paul's saying that the *earnest expectation of the creature waiteth for the manifestation of the sons of God*. And we have other signals, than those afforded by the pain and pressure of the beasts themselves, of the time when they and man shall sympathize. The natural history of many of our breeds of domesticated animals teaches

---

* Darwin, *Variation of Animals and Plants under Domestication*, pp. 20, 21.

us the lesson that their growth in skill and character—no one who has enjoyed the friendship of several dogs will dispute the possibility of character in the lower animals—has been proportionate to man's own. Though savages are fond of keeping and taming animals, they fail to advance them to the stages of cunning and discipline, which animals reach under the influence of civilised man.* " No instance is on record," says Darwin, " of such dogs as bloodhounds, spaniels or true greyhounds having been kept by savages; they are the products of long-continued civilisation."

These facts, if few, certainly bear in the direction of Isaiah's prophecy, that not by extermination of the beasts, but by the influence upon them of man's greater force of character, may that warfare be brought to an end, of which man's sin, according to the Bible, is the original cause.

The practical " uses " of such a passage of Scripture as this are plain. Some of them are the awful responsibility of man's position as the keystone of creation, the material effects of sin, and especially the religiousness of our relation to the lower animals. More than once do the Hebrew prophets liken the Almighty's dealings with man to merciful man's dealings with his beasts.† Both Isaiah and Paul virtually declare that man discharges to the lower creatures a mediatorial office. To say so will of course seem an exaggeration to some people, but not to those who, besides being grateful to remember what help in labour and cheer in dreariness we owe our humble fellow-creatures, have been fortunate enough to enjoy the affection and trust of a dumb friend. Men

---

* Galton, quoted by Darwin.
† Isa. lxiii. 13, 14; Hos. xi. 4.

who abuse the lower animals sin very grievously against God; men who neglect them lose some of the religious possibilities of life. If it is our business in life to have the charge of animals, we should magnify our calling. Every coachman and carter ought to feel something of the priest about him; he should think no amount of skill and patience too heavy if it enables him to gain insight into the nature of creatures of God, all of whose hope, by Scripture and his own experience, is towards himself.

Our relation to the lower animals is one of the three great relations of our nature. For God our worship; for man our service; for the beasts our providence, and according both to Isaiah and Paul, the mediation of our holiness.

IV. THE RETURN AND SOVEREIGNTY OF ISRAEL (xi. 10—16).

In passing from the second to the third part of this prophecy, we cannot but feel that we descend to a lower point of view and a less pure atmosphere of spiritual ambition. Isaiah, who has just declared peace between man and beast, finds that Judah must clear off certain scores against her neighbours before there can be peace between man and man. It is an interesting psychological study. The prophet, who has been able to shake off man's primeval distrust and loathing of wild animals, cannot divest himself of the political tempers of his age. He admits, indeed, the reconciliation of Ephraim and Judah; but the first act of the reconciled brethren, he prophesies with exultation, will be to *swoop down upon* their cousins Edom, Moab and Ammon, and their neighbours the Philistines.

We need not longer dwell on this remarkable limitation of the prophet's spirit, except to point out that while Isaiah clearly saw that Israel's own purity would not be perfected except by her political debasement, he could not as yet perceive any way for the conversion of the rest of the world except through Israel's political supremacy.

The prophet, however, is more occupied with an event preliminary to Israel's sovereignty, namely the return from exile. His large and emphatic assertions remind the not yet captive Judah through how much captivity she has to pass before she can see the margin of the blessed future which he has been describing to her. Isaiah's words imply a much more general captivity than had taken place by the time he spoke them, and we see that he is still keeping steadily in view that thorough reduction of his people, to the prospect of which he was forced in his inaugural vision. Judah has to be dispersed, even as Ephraim has been, before the glories of this chapter shall be realized.

We postpone further treatment of this prophecy, along with the hymn (chap. xii.), which is attached to it, to a separate chapter, dealing with all the representations, which the first half of the book of Isaiah contains, of the return from exile.

CHAPTER XI.

DRIFTING TO EGYPT.

ISAIAH xx.; xxi. 1—10; xxxviii.; xxxix.

(720—705 B.C.).

FROM 720, when chap. xi. may have been published, to 705—or, by rough reckoning, from the fortieth to the fifty-fifth year of Isaiah's life—we cannot be sure that we have more than one prophecy from him; but two narratives have found a place in his book which relate events that must have taken place between 712 and 705. These narratives are chap. xx.: How Isaiah Walked Stripped and Barefoot for a Sign against Egypt, and chaps. xxxviii. and xxxix.: The Sickness of Hezekiah, with the Hymn he wrote, and his Behaviour before the Envoys from Babylon. The single prophecy belonging to this period is chap. xxi. 1—10, *Oracle of the Wilderness of the Sea*, which announces the fall of Babylon. There has been considerable debate about the authorship of this oracle, but Cheyne, mainly following Dr. Kleinert, gives substantial reasons for leaving it with Isaiah. We postpone the full exposition of chaps. xxxviii., xxxix., to a later stage, as here it would only interrupt the history. But we will make use of chaps. xx. and xxi. 1—10 in the course of the following historical sketch, which is intended to connect the first great period of Isaiah's prophesying, 740—720, with the second, 705—701.

All these fifteen years, 720—705, Jerusalem was drifting to the refuge into which she plunged at the end of them—drifting to Egypt. Ahaz had firmly bound his people to Assyria, and in his reign there was no talk of an Egyptian alliance. But in 725, when the *overflowing scourge* of Assyrian invasion threatened to sweep into Judah as well as Samaria, Isaiah's words give us some hint of a recoil in the politics of Jerusalem towards the southern power. The *covenants with death and hell*, which the men of scorn flaunted in his face as he harped on the danger from Assyria, may only have been the old treaties with Assyria herself, but the *falsehood and lies* that went with them were most probably intrigues with Egypt. Any Egyptian policy, however, that may have formed in Jerusalem before 719, was entirely discredited by the crushing defeat, which in that year Sargon inflicted upon the empire of the Nile, almost on her own borders, at Rafia.

Years of quietness for Palestine followed this decisive battle. Sargon, whose annals engraved on the great halls of Khorsabad enable us to read the history of the period year by year, tells us that his next campaigns were to the north of his empire, and till 711 he alludes to Palestine only to say that tribute was coming in regularly, or to mention the deportation to Hamath or Samaria of some tribe he had conquered far away. Egypt, however, was everywhere busy among his feudatories. Intrigue was Egypt's *forte*. She is always represented in Isaiah's pages as the talkative power of many promises. Her fair speech was very sweet to men groaning beneath the military pressure of Assyria. Her splendid past, in conjunction with the largeness of her promise, excited the popular imagination. Centres of her influence gathered in every state. An Egyptian party formed in Jerusalem. Their intrigue pushed mines in all directions, and before the century was out the Assyrian peace in Western Asia was broken by two great Explosions. The first of these, in 711, was local and abortive; the second, in 705, was universal, and for a time entirely destroyed the Assyrian supremacy.

The centre of the Explosion of 711 was Ashdod, a city of the Philistines. The king had suddenly refused to continue the Assyrian tribute, and Sargon had put another king in his place. But the people—in Ashdod, as everywhere else, it was the people who were fascinated by Egypt—pulled down the Assyrian puppet and elevated Iaman, a friend to Pharaoh. The other cities of the Philistines, with Moab, Edom and Judah, were prepared by Egyptian promise to throw in their lot with the rebels. Sargon gave them no time. "In the wrath of my heart, I did not divide my army, and I did not diminish the ranks, but I marched against Asdod with my warriors, who did not separate themselves from the traces of my sandals. I besieged, I took, Asdod and Gunt-Asdodim. . . . I then made again these towns. I placed the people whom my arm had conquered. I put over them my lieutenant as governor. I considered them like Assyrians, and they practised obedience."* It is upon this campaign of Sargon that Mr. Cheyne argues for the invasion of Judah, to which he assigns so many of Isaiah's prophecies, as, *e.g.*, chaps. i. and x. 5—34. Some day Assyriology may give us proof of this supposition. We are without it just now.

---

* *Records of the Past*, vii., 40.

Sargon speaks no word of invading Judah, and the only part of the book of Isaiah that unmistakeably refers to this time is the picturesque narrative of chap. xx.

In this we are told that *in the year* the *Tartan*, the Assyrian commander-in-chief, *came to Ashdod when Sargon king of Assyria sent him* [that is to be supposed the year of the first revolt in Ashdod, to which Sargon himself did not come], *and he fought against Ashdod and took it:—in that time Jehovah had spoken by the hand of Isaiah the son of Amoz, saying, Go and loose the sackcloth*, the prophet's robe, *from off thy loins, and thy sandal strip from off thy foot; and he did so, walking naked*, that is unfrocked, *and barefoot.* For Egyptian intrigue was already busy; the temporary success of the Tartan at Ashdod did not discourage it, and it needed a protest. *And Jehovah said, As My servant Isaiah hath walked unfrocked and barefoot three years for a sign and a portent against Egypt and against Ethiopia* [note the double name, for the country was now divided between two rulers, the secret of her impotence to interfere forcibly in Palestine] *so shall the king of Assyria lead away the captives of Egypt and exiles of Ethiopia, young and old, stripped and barefoot, and with buttocks uncovered, to the shame of Egypt. And they shall be dismayed and ashamed, because of Ethiopia their expectation and because of Egypt their boast. And the inhabitant of this coastland* [that is, all Palestine, and a name for it remarkably similar to the phrase used by Sargon, "the people of Philistia, Judah, Edom and Moab, dwelling by the sea"*] *shall say in that day, Behold, such is our expectation, whither we had*

---

* Cheyne.

fled for help to deliver ourselves from the king of Assyria, and how shall we escape—we?

This parade of Isaiah for three years, unfrocked and barefoot, is another instance of that habit on which we remarked in connection with chap. viii. 1: the habit of finally carrying everything committed to him before the bar of the whole nation. It was to the mass of the people God said, *Come and let us reason together.* Let us not despise Isaiah in his shirt any more than we do Diogenes in his tub, or with a lantern in his hand, seeking for a man by its rays at noonday. He was bent on startling the popular conscience, because he held it true that a people's own morals have greater influence on their destinies than the policies of their statesmen. But especially anxious was Isaiah, as we shall again see from chap. xxxi., to bring this Egyptian policy home to the popular conscience. Egypt was a big-mouthed, blustering power, believed in by the mob; to expose her required public, picturesque and persistent advertisement. So Isaiah continued his walk for three years. The fall of Ashdod, left by Egypt to itself, did not disillusion the Jews, and the rapid disappearance of Sargon to another part of his empire where there was trouble, gave the Egyptians audacity to continue their intrigues against him.*

Sargon's new trouble had broken out in Babylon, and was much more serious than any revolt in Syria. Merodach Baladan, king of Chaldea, was no ordinary vassal, but as dangerous a rival as Egypt. When he rose, it meant a contest between Babylon and Nineveh for the sovereignty of the world. He had long been preparing for war. He had an alliance with Elam, and

---

* W. R. Smith, *Prophets of Israel*, p. 282.

the tribes of Mesopotamia were prepared for his signal of revolt. Among the charges brought against him by Sargon is that, "against the will of the gods of Babylon, he had sent during twelve years ambassadors." One of these embassies may have been that which came to Hezekiah after his great sickness (chap. xxxix.). *And Hezekiah was glad of them, and showed them the house of his spicery, the silver, and the gold, and the spices, and the precious oil, and all the house of his armour and all that was found in his treasures: there was nothing in his house nor in all his dominion that Hezekiah showed them not.* Isaiah was indignant. He had hitherto kept the king from formally closing with Egypt; now he found him eager for an alliance with another of the powers of man. But instead of predicting the captivity of Babylon, as he predicted the captivity of Egypt, by the hand of Assyria, Isaiah declared, according to chap. xxxix., that Babylon would some day take Israel captive; and Hezekiah had to content himself with the prospect that this calamity was not to happen in his time.

Isaiah's prediction of the exile of Israel to Babylon is a matter of difficulty. The difficulty, however, is not that of conceiving how he could have foreseen an event which took place more than a century later. Even in 711 Babylon was not an unlikely competitor for the supremacy of the nations. Sargon himself felt that it was a crisis to meet her. Very little might have transferred the seat of power from the Tigris to the Euphrates. What, therefore, more probable than that when Hezekiah disclosed to these envoys the whole state of his resources, and excused himself by saying *that they were come from a far country, even Babylon,* Isaiah, seized by a strong sense of how near Babylon stood to the throne of the nations, should laugh to scorn the excuse of distance, and tell the king that his anxiety to secure an alliance had only led him to place the temptation to rob him in the face of a power that was certainly on the way to be able to do it? No, the difficulty is not that the prophet foretold a captivity of the Jews in Babylon, but that we cannot reconcile what he says of that captivity with his intimation of the immediate destruction of Babylon, which has come down to us in chap. xxi. 1—10.

In this prophecy Isaiah regards Babylon as he has been regarding Egypt—certain to go down before Assyria, and therefore wholly unprofitable to Judah. If the Jews still thought of returning to Egypt when Sargon hurried back from completing her discomfiture in order to beset Babylon, Isaiah would tell them it was no use. Assyria has brought her full power to bear on the Babylonians; Elam and Media are with her. He travails with pain for the result. Babylon is not expecting a siege; but *preparing the table, eating and drinking*, when suddenly the cry rings through her, "*Arise, ye princes; anoint the shield.* The enemy is upon us." So terrible and so sudden a warrior is this Sargon! At his words nations move; when he saith, *Go up, O Elam! Besiege, O Media!* it is done. And he falls upon his foes before their weapons are ready. Then the prophet shrinks back from the result of his imagination of how it happened—for that is too painful—upon the simple certainty, which God revealed to him, that it must happen. As surely as Sargon's columns went against Babylon, so surely must the message return that Babylon has fallen. Isaiah puts it this way. The Lord bade him get on his watchtower—that is his phrase for observing the signs of the times—and speak whatever he saw. And he saw a military column on the march: *a troop of horsemen by pairs, a troop of asses, a troop of camels.* It passed him out of sight, *and he hearkened very diligently* for news. But none came. It was a long campaign. *And he cried like a lion* for impatience, *O my Lord, I stand continually upon the watchtower by day, and am set in my ward every night.* Till at last, *behold, there came a troop of men, horsemen in pairs, and* now *one answered and said, Fallen, fallen is Babylon, and all the images of her gods he hath broken to the ground.* The meaning of this very elliptical passage is just this: as surely as the prophet saw Sargon's columns go out against Babylon, so sure was he of her fall. Turning to his Jerusalem, he says, *My own threshed one, son of my floor, that which I have heard from Jehovah of hosts, the God of Israel, have I declared unto you.* How gladly would I have told you otherwise! But this is His message and His will. Everything must go down before this Assyrian.

Sargon entered Babylon before the year was out, and with her conquest established his fear once more down to the borders of Egypt. In his lifetime neither Judah nor her neighbours attempted again to revolt. But Egypt's intrigue did not cease. Her mines were once more laid, and the feudatories of Assyria only waited for their favourite opportunity, a change of tyrants on the throne at Nineveh. This came very soon. In the fifteenth year of his reign, having finally established his empire, Sargon inscribed on the palace at Khorsabad the following prayer to Assur: "May it be that I, Sargon, who inhabit this palace, may be preserved by destiny during long years for a long life, for the happiness of my body, for the satisfaction of my heart, and may I arrive to my end! May I accumulate in this palace immense treasures, the booties of all countries, the products of mountains and valleys!" The god did not hear. A few months later, in 705, Sargon was murdered; and before Sennacherib, his successor, sat down on the throne, the whole of Assyrian supremacy in the south-west of Asia went up in the air. It was the second of the great Explosions we spoke of, and the rest of Isaiah's prophecies are concerned with its results.

BOOK III.

*ORATIONS ON THE EGYPTIAN IN-
TRIGUES AND ORACLES ON
FOREIGN NATIONS,* 705—702 B.C.

ISAIAH :—
    xxix.   About 703.
    xxx.   A little later.
    xxxi.   „   „
    xxxii. 1—8.
    xxxii. 9—20.   Date uncertain.

---

    xiv. 28—xxi.   736—702
    xxiii.   About 703.

BOOK III.

WE now enter the prophecies of Isaiah's old age, those which he published after 705, when his ministry had lasted for at least thirty-five years. They cover the years between 705, the date of Sennacherib's accession to the Assyrian throne, and 701, when his army suddenly disappeared from before Jerusalem.

They fall into three groups:—

1. Chaps. xxix.—xxxii., dealing with Jewish politics while Sennacherib is still far from Palestine, 704—702, and having Egypt for their chief interest, Assyria lowering in the background.

2. Chaps. xiv. 28—xxi. and xxiii., a group of oracles on foreign nations, threatened, like Judah, by Assyria.

3. Chaps. i., xxii., and xxxiii., and the historical narrative in xxxvi. and xxxvii., dealing with Sennacherib's invasion of Judah and siege of Jerusalem in 701; Egypt and every foreign nation now fallen out of sight, and the storm about the Holy City too thick for the prophet to see beyond his immediate neighbourhood.

The *first and second* of these groups—orations on the intrigues with Egypt and oracles on the foreign nations—delivered while Sennacherib was still far from Syria, form the subject of this Third Book of our exposition.

The prophecies on the siege of Jerusalem are sufficiently numerous and distinctive to be put by themselves, along with their appendix (**xxxviii., xxxix.**), in our Fourth Book.

CHAPTER XII.

ARIEL, ARIEL.

Isaiah xxix. (About 703 B.C.).

IN 705 Sargon, King of Assyria, was murdered, and Sennacherib, his second son, succeeded him. Before the new ruler mounted the throne, the vast empire, which his father had consolidated, broke into rebellion, and down to the borders of Egypt cities and tribes declared themselves again independent. Sennacherib attacked his problem with Assyrian promptitude. There were two forces, to subdue which at the beginning made the reduction of the rest certain: Assyria's vassal kingdom and future rival for the supremacy of the world, Babylon; and her present rival, Egypt. Sennacherib marched on Babylon first.

While he did so the smaller States prepared to resist him. Too small to rely on their own resources, they looked to Egypt, and among others who sought help in that quarter was Judah. There had always been, as we have seen, an Egyptian party among the politicians of Jerusalem; and Assyria's difficulties now naturally increased its influence. Most of the prophecies in chaps. xxix.—xxxii. are forward to condemn the alliance with Egypt and the irreligious politics of which it was the fruit.

At the beginning, however, other facts claim Isaiah's attention. After the first excitement, consequent on the threats of Sennacherib, the politicians do not seem to have been specially active. Sennacherib found the reduction of Babylon a harder task than he expected, and in the end it turned out to be three years before he was free to march upon Syria. As one winter after another left the work of the Assyrian army in Mesopotamia still unfinished, the political tension in Judah must have relaxed. The Government—for King Hezekiah seems at last to have been brought round to believe in Egypt—pursued their negotiations no longer with that decision and real patriotism, which the sense of near danger rouses in even the most selfish and mistaken of politicians, but rather with the heedlessness of principle, the desire to show their own cleverness and the passion for intrigue which run riot among statesmen, when danger is near enough to give an excuse for doing something, but too far away to oblige anything to be done in earnest. Into this false ease, and the meaningless, faithless politics, which swarmed in it, Isaiah hurled his strong prophecy of chap. xxix. Before he exposes in chaps. xxx., xxxi., the folly of trusting to Egypt in the hour of danger, he has here the prior task of proving that hour to be near and very terrible. It is but one instance of the ignorance and fickleness of the people, that their prophet has first to rouse them to a sense of their peril, and then to restrain their excitement under it from rushing headlong for help to Egypt.

Chap. xxix. is an obscure oracle, but its obscurity is designed. Isaiah was dealing with a people, in whom political security and religious formalism had stifled both reason and conscience. He sought to rouse them by a startling message in a mysterious form. He addressed the city by an enigma :—

Ho! Ari-El, Ari-El! City David beleaguered! Add a year to a year, let the feasts run their round, then will I bring straitness upon Ari-El, and there shall be moaning and bemoaning,* *and yet she shall be unto Me as an Ari-El.*

The general bearing of this enigma became plain enough after the sore siege and sudden deliverance of Jerusalem in 701. But we are unable to make out one or two of its points. *Ari-El* may mean either *The Lion of God* (2 Sam. xxiii. 20), or *The Hearth of God* (Ezek. xliii. 15, 16). If the same sense is to be given to the four utterances of the name, then *God's-Lion* suits better the description of ver. 4; but *God's-Hearth* seems suggested by the feminine pronoun in ver. 1, and is a conception to which Isaiah returns in this same group of prophecies (xxxi. 9). It is possible that this ambiguity was part of the prophet's design; but if he uses the name in both senses, some of the force of his enigma is lost to us. In any case, however, we get a picturesque form for a plain meaning. In a year after the present year is out, says Isaiah, God Himself will straiten the city, whose inhabitants are now so careless, and she shall be full of mourning and lamentation. Nevertheless in the end she shall be a true Ari-El: be it a true *God's-Lion*, victor and hero; or a true *God's-Hearth*, His own inviolate shrine and sanctuary.

The next few verses (3—8) expand this warning. In plain words, Jerusalem is to undergo a siege. God Himself shall *encamp against thee—round about* reads our English version, but more probably, as with the

---

* Cheyne.

change of a letter, the Septuagint reads it—*like David.* If we take this second reading, the reference to David in the enigma itself (ver. 1) becomes clear. The prophet has a very startling message to deliver: that God will besiege His own city, the city of David! Before God can make her in truth His own, make her verify her name, He will have to beleaguer and reduce her. For so novel and startling an intimation the prophet pleads a precedent: "*City which David* himself *beleaguered!* Once before in thy history, ere the first time thou wast made God's own hearth, thou hadst to be besieged. As then, so now. Before thou canst again be a true Ari-El I must *beleaguer thee like David.*" This reading and interpretation gives to the enigma a reason and a force which it does not otherwise possess.

Jerusalem, then, shall be reduced to the very dust, and whine and whimper in it (like a sick *lion,* if this be the figure the prophet is pursuing), when suddenly it is *the surge of* her foes—literally *thy strangers*—whom the prophet sees as *small dust, and as passing chaff shall the surge of tyrants be; yea, it shall be in the twinkling of an eye, suddenly. From Jehovah of hosts shall she be visited with thunder and with earthquake and a great noise,—storm-wind, and tempest and the flame of fire devouring. And it shall be as a dream, a vision of the night, the surge of all the nations that war against Ariel, yea all that war against her and her stronghold, and they that press in upon her. And it shall be as if the hungry had been dreaming, and lo! he was eating; but he hath awaked, and his soul is empty: and as if the thirsty had been dreaming, and lo! he was drinking; but he hath awaked, and lo! he is faint, and his soul is ravenous: thus shall be the surge of all the nations that war against Mount Zion.* Now that is a very definite prediction, and in its essentials was fulfilled. In the end Jerusalem was invested by Sennacherib, and reduced to sore straits, when very suddenly—it would appear from other records, in a single night—the beleaguering force disappeared. This actually happened; and although the main business of a prophet, as we now clearly understand, was not to predict definite events, yet, since the result here predicted was one on which Isaiah staked his prophetic reputation and pledged the honour of Jehovah and the continuance of the true religion among men, it will be profitable for us to look at it for a little.

Isaiah foretells a great event and some details. The event is a double one: the reduction of Jerusalem to the direst straits by siege and her deliverance by the sudden disappearance of the besieging army. The details are that the siege will take place after a year (though the prophet's statement of time is perhaps too vague to be treated as a prediction), and that the deliverance will come as a great natural convulsion—thunder, earthquake and fire—which it certainly did not do. The double event, however, stripped of these details, did essentially happen.

Now it is plain that any one with a considerable knowledge of the world at that day must easily have been able to assert the probability of a siege of Jerusalem by the mixed nations who composed Sennacherib's armies. Isaiah's orations are full of proofs of his close acquaintance with the peoples of the world, and Assyria, who was above them. Moreover, his political advice, given at certain crises of Judah's history, was conspicuous not only for its religiousness, but for what we should call its "worldly-wisdom:" it was vindicated by events. Isaiah, however, would not have understood the distinction we have just made. To him political prudence was part of religion. *The LORD of hosts is for a spirit of judgement to him that sitteth in judgement, and for strength to them that turn back the battle to the gate.* Knowledge of men, experience of nations, the mental strength which never forgets history, and is quick to mark new movements as they rise, Isaiah would have called the direct inspiration of God. And it was certainly these qualities in this Hebrew, which provided him with the materials for his prediction of the siege of Jerusalem.

But it has not been found that such talents by themselves enable statesmen calmly to face the future, or clearly to predict it. Such knowledge of the past, such vigilance for the present, by themselves only embarrass, and often deceive. They are the materials for prediction, but a ruling principle is required to arrange them. A general may have a strong and well-drilled force under him, and a miserably weak foe in front; but if the sun is not going to rise to-morrow, if the laws of nature are not going to hold, his familiarity with his soldiers and expertness in handling them will not give him confidence to offer battle. He takes certain principles for granted, and on these his soldiers become of use to him, and he makes his venture. Even so Isaiah handled his mass of information by the grasp which he had of certain principles, and his facts fell clear into order before his confident eyes. He believed in the real government of God. *I also saw the Lord sitting, high and lifted up.* He felt that God had even this Assyria in His hands. He knew that all God's ends were righteousness, and he was still of the conviction that Judah for her wickedness required punishment at the Lord's hands. Grant these convictions to him in the superhuman strength in which he tells us he was conscious of receiving them from God, and it is easy to see how Isaiah could not help predicting a speedy siege of Jerusalem, how he already beheld the valleys around her bristling with barbarian spears.

The prediction of the sudden raising of this siege was the equally natural corollary to another religious conviction, which held the prophet with as much intensity, as that which possessed him with the need of Judah's punishment. Isaiah never slacked his hold on the truth that in the end God would save Zion, and keep her for Himself. Through whatever destruction, a root and remnant of the Jewish people must survive. Zion is impregnable because God is in her, and because her inviolateness is necessary for the continuance of true religion in the world. Therefore as confident as his prediction of the siege of Jerusalem is Isaiah's prediction of her delivery. And while the prophet wraps the fact in vague circumstance, while he masks, as it were, his ignorance of how in detail it will actually take place by calling up a great natural convulsion, yet he makes it abundantly clear—as, with his religious convictions and his knowledge of the Assyrian power, he cannot help doing—that the deliverance will be unexpected and unexplainable by the natural circumstances of the Jews themselves, that it will be evident as the immediate deed of God.

It is well for us to understand this. We shall get rid of the mechanical idea of prophecy, according to which prophets made exact predictions of fact by some particular and purely official endowment. We shall feel that prediction of this kind was due to the most unmistakeable inspiration, the influence upon the prophet's knowledge of affairs of two powerful religious convictions, for which he himself was strongly sure that he had the warrant of the Spirit of God.

Into the easy, selfish politics of Jerusalem, then, Isaiah sent this thunderbolt, this definite prediction: that in a year or more Jerusalem would be besieged and reduced to the direst straits. He tells us that it simply dazed the people. They were like men suddenly startled from sleep, who are too stupid to read a message pushed into their hands (vv. 9—12).

Then Isaiah gives God's own explanation of this stupidity. The cause of it is simply religious formalism. *This people draw nigh unto Me with their mouth, and with their lips do they honour Me, but their heart is far from Me, and their fear of Me is a mere commandment of men, a thing learned by rote.* This was what Israel called religion—bare ritual and doctrine, a round of sacrifices and prayers in adherence to the tradition of the fathers. But in life they never thought of God. It did not occur to these citizens of Jerusalem that He cared about their politics, their conduct of justice, or their discussions and bargains with one another. Of these they said, taking their own way, *Who seeth us, and who knoweth us?* Only in the Temple did they feel God's fear, and there merely in imitation of one another. None had an original vision of God in real life; they learned other men's thoughts about Him, and took other men's words upon their lips, while their heart was far away. In fact, speaking words and listening to words had wearied the spirit and stifled the conscience of them.

For such a disposition Isaiah says there is only one cure. It is a new edition of his old gospel, that God speaks to us in facts, not forms. Worship and a lifeless doctrine have demoralized this people. God shall make Himself so felt in real life that even their dull senses shall not be able to mistake Him. *Therefore, behold, I am proceeding to work marvellously upon this people, a marvellous work and a wonder! and the wisdom of their wise men shall perish, and the cleverness of their clever ones shall be obscured.* This is not the promise of what we call a miracle. It is a historical event on the same theatre as the politicians are showing their cleverness, but it shall put them all to shame, and by its force make the dullest feel that God's own hand is in it. What the people had ceased to attribute to Jehovah was ordinary intelligence; they had virtually said, *He hath no understanding.* The *marvellous work*, therefore, which He threatens shall be a work of wisdom, not some convulsion of nature to cow their spirits, but a wonderful political result, that shall shame their conceit of cleverness, and teach them reverence for the will and skill of God. Are the politicians trying to change the surface of the world, thinking that they *are turning things upside down*, and supposing that they can keep God out of account: *Who seeth us, and who knoweth us?* God Himself is the real Arranger and Politician. He will turn things upside down! Compared with their attempt, how vast His results shall be! As if the whole surface of the earth were altered, *Lebanon changed into garden-land, and garden-land counted as forest!* But this, of course, is metaphor. The intent of the miracle is to show that God hath understanding; therefore it must be a work, the prudence and intellectual force of which politicians can appreciate, and it shall take place in their politics. But not for mere astonishment's sake is *the wonder* to be done. For blessing and morality shall it be: to cure the deaf and blind; to give to the meek and the poor a new joy; to confound the tyrant and the scorner; to make Israel worthy of God and her own great fathers. *Therefore thus saith Jehovah to the house of Jacob, He that redeemed Abraham: Not now ashamed shall Jacob be, and not now shall his countenance blanch.* So unworthy hitherto have this stupid people been of so great ancestors! *But now when his* (Jacob's) *children behold the work of My hand in the midst of him, they shall hallow My name, yea, they shall hallow the Holy One of Jacob, and the God of Israel shall they make their fear. They also that err in spirit shall know understanding, and they that are unsettled shall learn to accept doctrine.*

Such is the meaning of this strong chapter. It is instructive in two ways.

First, it very clearly declares Isaiah's view of the method of God's revelation. Isaiah says nothing of the Temple, the Shechinah, the Altar, or the Scripture; but he points out how much the exclusive confinement of religion to forms and texts has deadened the hearts of his countrymen towards God. In your real life, he says to them, you are to seek, and you shall find, Him. There He is evident in miracles,—not physical interruptions and convulsions, but social mercies and moral providences. The quickening of conscience, the dispersion of ignorance, poor men awakening to the fact that God is with them, the overthrow of the social tyrant, history's plain refutation of the atheist, the growth of civic justice and charity—In these, said the Hebrew prophet to the Old Testament believer, Behold your God!

Wherefore, *secondly*, we also are to look for God in events and deeds. We are to know that nothing can compensate us for the loss of the open vision of God's working in history and in life about us,—not ecstasy of worship nor orthodoxy of doctrine. To confine our religion to these latter things is to become dull towards God even in them, and to forget Him everywhere else. And this is a fault of our day, just as it was of Isaiah's. So much of our fear of God is conventional, orthodox and not original, a trick caught from men's words or fashions, not a part of ourselves, nor won, like all that is real in us, from contact with real life. In our politics, in our conduct with men, in the struggle of our own hearts for knowledge and for temperance, and in service—there we are to learn to fear God. But there, and wherever else we are busy, self comes too much in the way; we are fascinated with our own cleverness; we ignore God, saying, *Who seeth us? who knoweth us?* We get to expect Him only in the Temple and on the Sabbath, and then only to influence our emotions. But it is in deeds, and where we feel life most real, that we are to look for Him. He makes Himself evident to us by wonderful works.

For these He has given us three theatres—the Bible, our country's history, and for each man his own life.

We have to take the Bible, and especially the life of Christ, and to tell ourselves that these wonderful events did really take place. In Christ God did dwell; by Christ He spoke to man; man was converted, redeemed, sanctified, beyond all doubt. These were real events. To be convinced of their reality were worth a hundred prayers.

Then let us follow the example of the Hebrew prophets, and search the history of our own people for the realities of God. Carlyle says in a note to Cromwell's fourth speech to Parliament, that "the Bible of every nation is its own history." This note is drawn from Carlyle by Cromwell's frequent insistence, that we must ever be turning from forms and rituals to study God's will and ways in history. And that speech of Cromwell is perhaps the best sermon ever delivered on the subject of this chapter. For he said: "What are all our histories but God manifesting Himself, that He hath shaken, and tumbled down and trampled upon everything that He hath not planted!" And again, speaking of our own history, he said to the House of Commons: "We are a people with the stamp of God upon us, . . . whose appearances and providences among us were not to be outmatched by any story." Truly this is national religion :—the reverential acknowledgment of God's hand in history; the admiration and effort of moral progress; the stirring of conscience when we see wrong; the expectation, when evil abounds, that God will bring justice and purity to us if we labour with Him for them.

But for each man there is the final duty of turning to himself.

> "My soul repairs its fault
> When, sharpening sense's hebetude,
> She turns on my own life! So viewed,
> No mere mote's breadth but teems immense
> With witnessings of providence:
> And woe to me if when I look
> Upon that record, the sole book
> Unsealed to me, I take no heed
> Of any warning that I read!" *

---

* Browning's *Christmas Eve*.

CHAPTER XIII.

POLITICS AND FAITH.

Isaiah xxx. (about 702 b.c.).

THIS prophecy of Isaiah rises out of circumstances a little more developed than those in which chap. xxix. was composed. Sennacherib is still engaged with Babylon, and it seems that it will yet be long before he marches his armies upon Syria. But Isaiah's warning has at last roused the politicians of Judah from their carelessness. We need not suppose that they believed all that Isaiah predicted about the dire siege which Jerusalem should shortly undergo and her sudden deliverance at the hand of the Lord. Without the two strong religious convictions, in the strength of which, as we have seen, he made the prediction, it was impossible to believe that this siege and deliverance must certainly happen. But the politicians were at least startled into doing something. They did not betake themselves to God, to whom it had been the purpose of Isaiah's last oration to shut them up. They only flung themselves with more haste into their intrigues with Egypt. But in truth haste and business were all that was in their politics: these were devoid both of intelligence and faith. Where the sole motive of conduct is fear, whether uneasiness or panic, force may be displayed, but neither sagacity nor any moral quality. This was the case with Judah's Egyptian policy, and Isaiah now spends two chapters in denouncing it. His condemnation is twofold. The negotiations with Egypt, he says, are bad politics and bad religion; but the bad religion is the root and source of the other. Yet while he vents all his scorn on the politics, he uses pity and sweet persuasiveness when he comes to speak of the eternal significance of the religion. The two chapters are also instructive, beyond most others of the Old Testament, in the light they cast on revelation—its scope and methods.

Isaiah begins with the bad politics. In order to understand how bad they were, we must turn for a little to this Egypt, with whom Judah was now seeking an alliance.

In our late campaign on the Upper Nile we heard a great deal of the Mudir of Dongola. His province covers part of the ancient kingdom of Ethiopia; and in Meirawi, the village whose name appeared in so many telegrams, we can still discover Meroe, the capital of Ethiopia. Now in Isaiah's day the king of Ethiopia was, what the Mudir of Dongola was at the time of our war, an ambitious person of no small energy; and the ruler of Egypt proper was, what the Khedive was, a person of little influence or resource. Consequently there happened what might have happened a few years ago but for the presence of the British army in Egypt. The Ethiopian came down the Nile, defeated Pharaoh and burned him alive. But he died, and his son died after him; and before their successor could also come down the Nile, the legitimate heir to Pharaoh had regained part of his power. Some years ensued of uncertainty as to who was the real ruler of Egypt.

It was in this time of unsettlement that Judah sought Egypt's help. The ignorance of the policy was manifest to all who were not blinded by fear of Assyria or party feeling. To Isaiah the Egyptian alliance is a folly and fatality that deserve all his scorn (vv. 1—8).

Woe to the rebellious children, saith the Lord, executing a policy, but it is not from Me; and weaving a web, but not of My spirit, that they may heap sin upon sin; who set themselves on the way to go down to Egypt, and at My mouth they have not inquired, to flee to the refuge of Pharaoh, and to hide themselves in the shadow of Egypt. But the refuge of Pharaoh shall be unto you for shame, and the hiding in the shadow of Egypt for confusion! How can a broken Egypt help you? When his princes are at Zoan, and his ambassadors are come to Hanes, they shall all be ashamed of a people that cannot profit them, that are not for help nor for profit, but for shame, and also for reproach.

Then Isaiah pictures the useless caravan which Judah has sent with tribute to Egypt, strings of asses and camels struggling through the desert, *land of trouble and anguish*, amid lions and serpents, and all for *a people that shall not profit them* (ver. 6).

What tempted Judah to this profitless expenditure of time and money? Egypt had a great reputation, and was a mighty promiser. Her brilliant antiquity had given her a habit of generous promise, and dazzled other nations into trusting her. Indeed, so full were Egyptian politics of bluster and big language, that the Hebrews had a nickname for Egypt. They called her Rahab—*Stormy-speech, Blusterer, Braggart*. It was the term also for the crocodile, as being a *monster*, so that there was a picturesqueness as well as moral aptness in the name. Ay, says Isaiah, catching at the old name and putting to it another which describes Egyptian helplessness and inactivity, I call her *Rahab Sit-still, Braggart-that-sitteth-still, Stormy-speech Stay-at-home. Blustering and inactivity, blustering and sitting still,* that is her character; *for Egypt helpeth in vain and to no purpose.*

Knowing how sometimes the fate of a Government is affected by a happy speech or epigram, we can understand the effect of this cry upon the politicians of Jerusalem. But that he might impress it on the popular imagination and memory as well, Isaiah wrote his epigram on a tablet, and put it in a book. We must remind ourselves here of chap. xx., and remember how it tells us that Isaiah had already some years before this endeavoured to impress the popular imagination with the folly of an Egyptian alliance, *walking unfrocked and barefoot three years for a sign and a portent upon Egypt and upon Ethiopia* (see p. 199).

So that already Isaiah had appealed from politicians to people on this Egyptian question, just as he appealed thirty years ago from court to market-place on the question of Ephraim and Damascus.* It is another instance of that prophetic habit of his, on which we remarked in expounding chap. viii.; and we must again emphasize the habit, for chap. xxx. here swings round upon it. Whatever be the matter committed to him, Isaiah is not allowed to rest till he brings it home to the popular conscience; and however much he may be able to charge national disaster upon the folly of politicians or the obduracy of a king, it is the people whom he holds ultimately responsible. To Isaiah a nation's politics are not arbitrary; they are not depen-

---

* Chap. viii. 1 (p. 119).

dent on the will of kings or the management of parties. They are the natural outcome of the nation's character. What the people are, that will their politics be. If you wish to reform the politics, you must first regenerate the people; and it is no use to inveigh against a senseless policy, like this Egyptian one, unless you go farther and expose the national temper which has made it possible. A people's own morals have greater influence on their destinies than their despots or legislators. Statesmen are what the State makes them. No Government will attempt a policy for which the nation behind it has not a conscience; and for the greater number of errors committed by their rulers, the blame must be laid on the people's own want of character or intelligence.

This is what Isaiah now drives home (xxx. 9 ff.). He tracks the bad politics to their source in bad religion, the Egyptian policy to its roots in the prevailing tempers of the people. The Egyptian policy was doubly stamped. It was disobedience to the word of God; it was satisfaction with falsehood. The statesmen of Judah shut their ears to God's spoken word; they allowed themselves to be duped by the Egyptian Pretence. But these, says Isaiah, are precisely the characteristics of the whole Jewish people. *For it is a rebellious people, lying children, children that will not hear the revelation of the* LORD. It was these national failings—the want of virtues which are the very substance of a nation: truth and reverence or obedience—that had culminated in the senseless and suicidal alliance with Egypt. Isaiah fastens on their falsehood first: *Which say to the seers, Ye shall not see, and to the prophets, Ye shall not prophesy unto us right things; speak to us smooth things: prophesy deceits.* No wonder such a character had been fascinated by

"Rahab"! It was a natural Nemesis, that a people who desired from their teachers fair speech rather than true vision should be betrayed by the confidence their statesmen placed in the Blusterer, *that blustered and sat still.* Truth is what this people first require, and therefore the *revelation of the* LORD will in the first instance be the revealing of the truth. Men who will strip pretence off the reality of things; men who will call things by their right names, as Isaiah had set himself to do; honest satirists and epigrammatists—these are the bearers of God's revelation. For it is one of the means of Divine salvation to call things by their right names, and here in God's revelation also epigrams have their place. So much for truth.

But reverence is truth's other self, for reverence is simply loyalty to the supremest truth. And it is against the truth that the Jews have chiefly sinned. They had shut their eyes to Egypt's real character, but that was a small sin beside this: that they turned their backs on the greatest reality of all—God Himself. *Get you out of the way,* they said to the prophets, *turn out of the path; keep quiet in our presence about the Holy One of Israel.* Isaiah's effort rises to its culmination when he seeks to restore the sense of this Reality to his people. His spirit is kindled at the words *the Holy One of Israel,* and to the end of chap. xxxi. leaps up in a series of brilliant and sometimes scorching descriptions of the name, the majesty and the love of God. Isaiah is not content to have used his power of revelation to unveil the political truth about Egypt. He will make God Himself visible to this people. Passionately does he proceed to enforce upon the Jews what God thinks about their own condition (vv. 12—14), then to persuade them to rely upon Him alone, and wait for the working of His reasonable laws (vv. 15—18). Rising higher, he purges with pity their eyes to see God's very presence, their ears to hear His voice, their wounds to feel His touch (vv. 19—26). Then he remembers the cloud of invasion on the horizon, and bids them spell, in its uncouth masses, the articulate name of the Lord (vv. 27—33). And he closes with another series of figures by which God's wisdom, and His jealousy and His tenderness are made very bright to them (chap. xxxi.).

These brilliant prophecies may not have been given all at the same time: each is complete in itself. They do not all mention the negotiations with Egypt, but they are all dark with the shadow of Assyria. Chap. xxx. vv. 19—26 almost seem to have been written in a time of actual siege; but vv. 27—33 represent Assyria still upon the horizon. In this, however, these passages are fitly strung together: that they equally strain to impress a blind and hardened people with the will, the majesty and the love of God their Saviour.

I. THE BULGING WALL (vv. 12—14).

Starting from their unwillingness to listen to the voice of the Lord in their Egyptian policy, Isaiah tells the people that if they refused to hear His word for guidance, they must now listen to it for judgement. *Wherefore thus saith the Holy One of Israel: Because ye look down on this word, and trust in perverseness and crookedness, and lean thereon, therefore this iniquity shall be to you as a breach ready to fall, bulging out in a high wall, whose breaking cometh suddenly at an instant.* This iniquity, of course, is the embassy to Egypt. But that, as we have seen, is only the people's own evil character coming to a head; and by the breaking of the wall, we are therefore to suppose that the prophet means the collapse not only of this Egyptian policy, but of the whole estate and substance of the Jewish people. It will not be your enemy that will cause a breach in the nation, but your teeming iniquity shall cause the breach—to wit, this Egyptian folly. Judah will burst her bulwarks from the inside. You may build the strongest form of government round a people, you may buttress it with foreign alliances, but these shall simply prove occasions for the internal wickedness to break forth. Your supposed buttresses will prove real breaches; and of all your social structure there will not be left as much as will make the fragments of a single home, not *a sherd* big enough *to carry fire from the hearth, or to hold water from the cistern.*

II. Not Alliances, but Reliance (vv. 15—18).

At this point, either Isaiah was stung by the demands of the politicians for an alternative to their restless Egyptian policy which he condemned, or more likely he rose, unaided by external influence, on the prophet's native instinct to find some purely religious ground on which to base his political advice. The result is one of the grandest of all his oracles. *For thus saith the Lord Jehovah, the Holy One of Israel: In returning and rest shall ye be saved; in quietness and in confidence shall be your strength; and ye would not. But ye said, No, for upon horses will we flee; wherefore ye shall flee: and upon the swift will we ride; wherefore swift shall be they that pursue you! One thousand at the rebuke of one—at the rebuke of five shall ye flee: till ye be left as a bare pole on the top of a mountain, and as a standard on an hill.*

And therefore will the LORD *wait that He may be gracious unto you, and therefore will He hold aloof that He may have mercy upon you, for a God of judgement is the* LORD; *blessed are all they that wait for Him.* The words of this passage are their own interpretation and enforcement, all but one; and as this one is obscure in its English guise, and the passage really swings from it, we may devote a paragraph to its meaning.

A God of judgement is the LORD is an unfortunately ambiguous translation. We must not take *judgement* here in our familiar sense of the word. It is not a sudden deed of doom, but a long process of law. It means *manner, method, design, order, system,* the ideas, in short, which we sum up under the word "law." Just as we say of a man, *He is a man of judgement,* and mean thereby not that by office he is a doomster, but that by character he is a man of discernment and prudence, so simply does Isaiah say here that *Jehovah is a God of judgement,* and mean thereby not that He is One, whose habit is sudden and awful deeds of penalty or salvation, but, on the contrary, that, having laid down His lines according to righteousness and established His laws in wisdom, He remains in His dealings with men consistent with these.

Now it is a great truth that the All-mighty and All-merciful is the All-methodical too; and no religion is complete in its creed or healthy in its influence, which does not insist equally on all these. It was just the want of this third article of faith which perverted the souls of the Jews in Isaiah's day, which (as we have seen under Chapter I.) allowed them to make their worship so mechanical and material—for how could they have been satisfied with mere forms if they had but once conceived of God as having even ordinary intelligence?

—and which turned their political life into such a mass of intrigue, conceit and falsehood, for how could they have dared to suppose that they would get their own way, or have been so sure of their own cleverness, if only they had had a glimpse of the perception, that God, the Ruler of the world, had also His policy regarding them? They believed He was the Mighty, they believed He was the Merciful, but because they forgot that He was the Wise and the Worker by law, their faith in His might too often turned into superstitious terror, their faith in His mercy oscillated between the sleepy satisfaction that He was an indulgent God and the fretful impatience that He was an indifferent one. Therefore Isaiah persisted from first to last in this: that God worked by law; that He had His plan for Judah, as well as these politicians; and, as we shall shortly find him reminding them when intoxicated with their own cleverness, *that He also is wise* (xxxi. 2). Here by the same thought he bids them be at peace, and upon the rushing tides of politics, drawing them to that or the other mad venture, to swing by this anchor: that God has His own law and time for everything. No man could bring the charge of fatalism against such a policy of quietness. For it thrilled with intelligent appreciation of the Divine method. When Isaiah said, *In returning and rest shall ye be saved; in quietness and confidence shall be your strength*, he did not ask his restless countrymen to yield sullenly to an infinite force or to bow in stupidity beneath the inscrutable will of an arbitrary despot, but to bring their conduct into harmony with a reasonable and gracious plan, which might be read in the historical events of the time, and was vindicated by the loftiest religious convictions. Isaiah preached no submission to fate, but reverence for an all-wise Ruler, whose method was plain to every clear-sighted observer of the fortunes of the nations of the world, and whose purpose could only be love and peace to His own people (cf. p. 110).

III. GOD'S TABLE IN THE MIDST OF THE ENEMIES (vv. 19—26).

This patient purpose of God Isaiah now proceeds to describe in its details. Every line of his description has its loveliness, and is to be separately appreciated. There is perhaps no fairer prospect from our prophet's many windows. It is not argument nor a programme, but a series of rapid glimpses, struck out by language, which often wants logical connection, but never fails to make us see.

To begin with, one thing is sure : the continuance of the national existence. Isaiah is true to his original vision—the survival of a remnant. *For a people in Zion—there shall be abiding in Jerusalem.* So the brief essential is flashed forth. *Thou shalt surely weep no more; surely He will be gracious unto thee at the voice of thy crying; with His hearing of thee He will answer thee.* Thus much of general promise had been already given. Now upon the vagueness of the Lord's delay Isaiah paints realistic details, only, however, that he may make more vivid the real presence of the Lord. The siege shall surely come, with its sorely concrete privations, but the *Lord* will be there, equally distinct. *And though the Lord give you the bread of penury and the water of tribulation*—perhaps the technical name for siege rations—*yet shall not thy Teacher hide Himself any more, but thine eyes shall ever be seeing thy Teacher; and thine ears shall hear a word behind thee, saying, This is the way: walk ye in it, when ye turn to the right hand or when ye turn to the left.* Real, concrete sorrows, these are they that make the heavenly Teacher real! It is linguistically possible, and more in harmony with the rest of the passage, to turn *teachers*, as the English version has it, into the singular, and to render it by *Revealer*. The word is an active participle, "Moreh," from the same verb as the noun "Torah," which is constantly translated "Law" in our version, but is, in the Prophets at least, more nearly equivalent to "instruction," or to our modern term "revelation" (cf. ver. 9). Looking thus to the One Revealer, and hearkening to the One Voice, *the lying and rebellious children* shall at last be restored to that capacity for truth and obedience the loss of which has been their ruin. Devoted to the Holy One of Israel, they shall scatter their idols as loathsome (ver. 22). But thereupon a wonder is to happen. As the besieged people, conscious of the One Great Presence in the midst of their encompassed city, cast their idols through the gates and over the walls, a marvellous vision of space and light and fulness of fresh food bursts upon their starved and straitened souls (ver. 23). Promise more sympathetic was never uttered to a besieged and famished city. Mark that all down the passage there is no mention of the noise or instruments of battle. The prophet has not spoken of the besiegers, who they may be, how they may come, nor of the fashion of their war, but only of the effects of the siege on those within: confinement, scant and bitter rations. And now he is almost wholly silent about the breaking up of the investing army and the trail of their slaughter. No battle breaks this siege, but a vision of openness and plenty dawns noiselessly over its famine and closeness. It is not vengeance or blood that an exhausted and penitent people thirst after. But as they have been caged in a fortress, narrow, dark and stony, so they thirst for the sight of the sower, and the drop of the rain on the broken, brown earth, and the juicy corn, and the meadow for their cribbed cattle, and the noise of brooks and waterfalls, and above and about it all fulness of light. *And He shall give the rain of thy seed, that thou shalt sow the ground withal, and bread, even the increase of the ground, and it shall be juicy and fat; thy cattle shall feed that day in a broad meadow. And the oxen and the young asses that till the ground shall eat savoury provender, winnowed with the shovel and with the fan. And there shall be upon every lofty mountain and upon every lifted hill rivers, streams of water, in the day of the great slaughter, when the towers fall. And the light of the moon shall be as the light of the sun, and the light of the sun shall be sevenfold, as the light of seven days, in the day that the Lord bindeth up the hurt of His people and healeth the stroke of their wound.* It is one of Isaiah's fairest visions, and he is very much to be blamed who forces its beauty of nature into an allegory of spiritual things. Here literally God spreads His people a table in the midst of their enemies.

IV. The Name of the Lord (vv. 27—33).

But Isaiah lays down "the oaten pipe" and lifts again a brazen trumpet to his lips. Between him and that sunny landscape of the future, of whose pastoral details he has so sweetly sung, roll up now the uncouth masses of the Assyrian invasion, not yet fully gathered, far less broken. We are back in the present again, and the whole horizon is clouded.

The passage does not look like one from which comfort or edification can be derived, but it is of extreme interest. The first two verses, for instance, only require a little analysis to open a most instructive glimpse into the prophet's inner thoughts about the Assyrian progress, and show us how they work towards the expression of its full meaning. *Behold, the Name of Jehovah cometh from afar—burning His anger and awful the uplifting smoke; His lips are full of wrath, and His tongue as fire that devoureth; and His breath is as an overflowing torrent—even unto the neck it reacheth—to shake the nations in a sieve of destruction, and a bridle that leadeth astray on the jaws of the peoples.*

The Name of Jehovah is the phrase the prophets use when they wish to tell us of the personal presence of God. When we hear a name cried out, we understand immediately that a person is there. So when the prophet calls, *Behold, the Name of Jehovah*, in face of the prodigious advance of Assyria, we understand that he has caught some intuition of God's presence in that uplifting of the nations of the north at the word of the great King and their resistless sweep southward upon Palestine. In that movement God is personally present. The Divine presence Isaiah then describes in curiously mingled metaphor, which proves how gradually it was that he struggled to a knowledge of its purpose there. First of all he describes the advance of Assyria as a thunderstorm, heavy clouds and darting, devouring fire. His imagination pictures a great face of wrath. The thick curtains of cloud as they roll over one another suggest the heavy lips, and the lightnings the fiery tongue. Then the figure passes from heaven to earth. The thunderstorm has burst, and becomes the *mountain torrent*, which speedily *reaches the necks* of those who are caught in its bed. But then the prophet's conscience suggests something more than sudden and sheer force in this invasion, and the *tossing* of the torrent naturally leads him to express this new element in the figure of *a sieve*. His thought about the Assyrian flood thus passes from one of simple force and rush to one of judgement and being well kept in hand. He sees its ultimate check at Jerusalem, and so his last figure of it is the figure of *a bridle*, or *lasso*, such as is thrown upon the jaws of a wild animal when you wish to catch and tame him.

This gradual progress from the sense of sheer wild force, through that of personal wrath, to discipline and sparing is very interesting. Vague and chaotic that disaster rolled up the horizon upon Judah. *It cometh from afar.* The politicians fled from it to their refuge behind the Egyptian Pretence. But Isaiah bids them face it. The longer they look, the more will conscience tell them that the unavoidable wrath of God is in it; no blustering Rahab will be able to hide them from the anger of the Face that lowers there. But let them look longer still, and the unrelieved features of destruction will change to a hand that sifts and checks, the torrent will become a sieve, and the disaster show itself well held in by the power of their own God.

So wildly and impersonally still do the storms of sorrow and disaster roll up the horizon on men's eyes, and we fly in vague terror from them to our Egyptian refuges. So still does conscience tell us it is futile to flee from the anger of God, and we crouch hopeless beneath the rush of imaginations of unchecked wrath, blackening the heavens and turning every path of life to a tossing torrent. May it then be granted us to have some prophet at our side to bid us face our disaster once more, and see the discipline and judgement of the Lord, the tossing only of His careful sieve, in the wild and cruel waves! We may not be poets like

Isaiah nor able to put the processes of our faith into such splendid metaphors as he, but faith is given us to follow the same course as his thoughts did, and to struggle till she arrives at the consciousness of God in the most uncouth judgements that darken her horizon—the consciousness of God present not only to smite, but to sift, and in the end to spare.

Of the angel who led Israel to the land of promise, God said, *My Name is in him*. Our faith is not perfect till we can, like Isaiah, feel the same of the blackest angel, the heaviest disaster, God can send us, and be able to spell it out articulately: *The LORD, the LORD, a God merciful and gracious, long-suffering and abundant in goodness and truth.*

For delivery, says Isaiah, shall come to the people of God in the crisis, as sudden and as startling into song as the delivery from Egypt was. *Ye shall have a song as in the night when a holy feast is kept, and gladness of heart, as when one goeth with a pipe to come into the mountain of the LORD, to the Rock of Israel.*

After this interval of solemn gladness, the storm and fire break out afresh, and rage again through the passage. But their direction is reversed, and whereas they had been shown rolling up the horizon as towards Judah, they are now shown rolling down the horizon in pursuit of the baffled Assyrian. The music of the verses is crashing. *And the LORD shall cause the peal* of His voice to be heard, and the lighting down of His arm to be seen in the fury of anger, yea flame of devouring fire— bursting and torrent and hailstones. For from the voice of the LORD shall the Assyrian be scattered when He shall smite with the rod. And every passage of the rod of fate which the LORD bringeth down upon him shall be with*

---

* So Dr. B. Davis, quoted by Cheyne.

tabrets and harps, and in battles of waving shall he be fought against. The meaning is obscure, but palpable. Probably the verse describes the ritual of the sacrifice to Moloch, to which there is no doubt the next verse alludes. To sympathize with the prophet's figure, we need of course an amount of information about the details of that ritual which we are very far from possessing. But Isaiah's meaning is evidently this. The destruction of the Assyrian host will be liker a holocaust than a battle, like one of those fatal sacrifices to Moloch which are directed by the solemn waving of a staff, and accompanied by the music, not of war, but of festival. *Battles of waving* is a very obscure phrase, but the word translated *waving* is the technical term for the waving of the victim before the sacrifice to signify its dedication to the deity; "and these *battles of waving* may perhaps have taken place in the fashion in which single victims were thrown from one spear to another till death ensued."* At all events, it is evident that Isaiah means to suggest that the Assyrian dispersion is a religious act, a solemn holocaust rather than one of this earth's ordinary battles, and directed by Jehovah Himself from heaven. This becomes clear enough in the next verse: *For a Topheth hath been set in order beforehand; yea, for Moloch is it arranged; He hath made it deep and broad; the pile thereof is fire and much wood; the breath of the* LORD, *like a torrent of brimstone, shall kindle it.* So the Assyrian power was in the end to go up in flame.

We postpone remarks on Isaiah's sense of the fierceness of the Divine righteousness till we reach his even finer expression of it in chap. xxxiii.

* So Bredenkamp in his recent commentary on Isaiah.

CHAPTER XIV.

THREE TRUTHS ABOUT GOD.

Isaiah xxxi. (about 702 b.c.).

CHAP. XXXI., which forms an appendage to chaps. xxix. and xxx., can scarcely be reckoned among the more important prophecies of Isaiah. It is a repetition of the principles which the prophet has already proclaimed in connection with the faithless intrigues of Judah for an alliance with Egypt, and it was published at a time when the statesmen of Judah were further involved in these intrigues, when events were moving faster, and the prophet had to speak with more hurried words. Truths now familiar to us are expressed in less powerful language. But the chapter has its own value; it is remarkable for three very unusual descriptions of God, which govern the following exposition of it. They rise in climax, enforcing three truths:—that in the government of life we must take into account God's wisdom; we must be prepared to find many of His providences grim and savage-looking; but we must also believe that He is most tender and jealous for His people.

I. Yet He also is Wise (vv. 1—3).

We must suppose the negotiations with Egypt to have taken for the moment a favourable turn, and the statesmen who advocated them to be congratulating themselves upon some consequent addition to the fighting strength of Judah. They could point to many chariots and a strong body of cavalry in proof of their own wisdom and refutation of the prophet's maxim, *In quietness and in confidence shall be your strength; in returning and rest shall ye be saved.*

Isaiah simply answers their self-congratulation with the utterance of a new Woe, and it is in this that the first of the three extraordinary descriptions of God is placed. *Woe unto them that go down to Egypt for help; upon horses do they stay, and trust in chariots because they are many, and in horsemen because they are very strong: but they look not unto the Holy One of Israel, and Jehovah they do not seek. Yet He also is wise.* You have been clever and successful, but have you forgotten that *God also is wise*, that He too has His policy, and acts reasonably and consistently? You think you have been making history; but God also works in history, and surely, to put it on the lowest ground, with as much cleverness and persistence as you do. *Yet He also is wise, and will bring evil, and will not call back His words, but will arise against the house of the evil-doers, and against the help of them that work iniquity.*

This satire was the shaft best fitted to pierce the folly of the rulers of Judah. Wisdom, a reasonable plan for their aims and prudence in carrying it out, was the last thing they thought of associating with God, whom they relegated to what they called their religion—their temples, worship and poetry. When their emotions were stirred by solemn services, or under great disaster, or in the hour of death, they remembered God, and it seemed natural to them that in these great exceptions of life He should interfere ; but in their politics and their trade, in the common course and conduct of life, they ignored Him and put their trust in their own wisdom. They limited God to the ceremonies and exceptional occasions of life, when they looked for His glory or miraculous assistance, but they never thought that in their ordinary ways He had any interest or design.

The forgetfulness, against which Isaiah directs this shaft of satire, is the besetting sin of very religious people, of very successful people, and of very clever people.

It is the temptation of an ordinary Christian, church-going people, like ourselves, with a religion so full of marvellous mercies, and so blessed with regular opportunities of worship, to think of God only in connection with these, and practically to ignore that along the far greater stretches of life He has any interest or purpose regarding us. Formally-religious people treat God as if He were simply a constitutional sovereign, to step in at emergencies, and for the rest to play a nominal and ceremonial part in the conduct of their lives. Ignoring the Divine wisdom and ceaseless providence of God, and couching their hearts upon easy views of His benevolence, they have no other thought of Him, than as a philanthropic magician, whose power is reserved to extricate men when they have got past helping themselves. From the earliest times that way of regarding God has been prevalent, and religious teachers have never failed to stigmatize it with the hardest name for folly. *Fools,* says the Psalmist, *are afflicted when they draw near unto the gates of death; then,* only then, *do they cry unto the Lord in their trouble.*

Thou fool! says Christ of the man who kept God out of the account of his life. God is not mocked, although we ignore half His being and confine our religion to such facile views of His nature. With this sarcasm, Isaiah reminds us that it is not a Fool who is on the throne of the universe; yet is the Being whom the imaginations of some men place there any better? O wise men, *God also is wise.* Not by fits and starts of a benevolence similar to that of our own foolish and inconsistent hearts does He work. Consistency, reason and law are the methods of His action; and they apply closely, irretrievably, to all of our life. Hath He promised evil? Then evil will proceed. Let us believe that God keeps His word; that He is thoroughly attentive to all we do; that His will concerns the whole of our life.

But the temptation to refuse to God even ordinary wisdom is also the temptation of very successful and very clever people, such as these Jewish politicians fancied themselves to be, or such as the Rich Fool in the parable. They have overcome all they have matched themselves against, and feel as if they were to be masters of their own future. Now the Bible and the testimony of men invariably declare that God has one way of meeting such fools—the way Isaiah suggests here. God meets them with their own weapons; He outmatches them in their own fashion. In the eighteenth Psalm it is written, *With the pure Thou wilt show Thyself pure, and with the perverse Thou wilt show Thyself froward.* The Rich Fool congratulates himself that his soul is his own; says God, *This night thy soul shall be required of thee.* The Jewish politicians pride themselves on their wisdom; *Yet God also is wise,* says Isaiah significantly. After Moscow Napoleon is reported to have exclaimed, "The Almighty is too strong for me." But perhaps the most striking analogy to this satire of Isaiah is to be found in the "Confessions" of that Jew, from whose living sepulchre we are so often startled with weird echoes of the laughter of the ancient prophets of his race. When Heine, Germany's greatest satirist, lay upon a bed to which his evil living had brought him before his time, and the pride of art, which had been, as he says, his god, was at last crushed, he tells us what it was that crushed him. They were singing his songs in every street of his native land, and his fame had gone out through the world, while he lay an exile and paralysed upon his "mattress-grave." "Alas!" he cries, "the irony of Heaven weighs heavily upon me. The great Author of the universe, the celestial Aristophanes, wished to show me, the petty, earthly, German Aristophanes, how my most trenchant satires are only clumsy patchwork compared with His, and how immeasurably He excels me in humour and colossal wit." That is just a soul writing in its own heart's blood this terrible warning of Isaiah: *Yet God also is wise.*

Yea, the Egyptians are men, and not God, and their horses flesh, and not spirit; and when Jehovah shall stretch out His hand, both he that helpeth shall stumble, and he that is holpen shall fall, and they all shall perish together.

II. THE LION AND HIS PREY (ver. 4).

But notwithstanding what he has said about God destroying men who trust in their own cleverness, Isaiah goes on to assert that God is always ready to save what is worth saving. The people, the city, His own city— God will save that. To express God's persistent grace towards Jerusalem, Isaiah uses two figures borrowed from the beasts. Both of them are truly Homeric, and fire the imagination at once; but the first is not one we should have expected to find as a figure of the saving grace of God. Yet Isaiah knows it is not enough for men to remember how wise God always is. They need also to be reminded how grim and cruel He must sometimes appear, even in His saving providences.

For thus saith Jehovah unto me: Like as when the lion growleth, and the young lion over his prey, if a mob of shepherds be called forth against him, from their voice he will not shrink in dismay, nor for their noise abase himself; so shall Jehovah of hosts come down to fight for Mount Zion and the hill thereof. A lion with a lamb in his claws, growling over it, while a crowd of shepherds come up against him; afraid to go near enough to kill him, they try to frighten him away by shouting at him. But he holds his prey unshrinking.

It is a figure that startles at first. To liken God with a saving hold upon His own to a wild lion with his claws in the prey! But horror plays the part of a good emphasis; while if we look into the figure, we shall feel our horror change to appreciation. There is something majestic in that picture of the lion with the shouting shepherds, too afraid to strike him. *He will not be dismayed at their voice, nor abase himself for the noise of them.* Is it, after all, an unworthy figure of the Divine Claimant for this city, who kept unceasing hold upon her after His own manner, mysterious and lionlike to men, undisturbed by the screams, formulas, and prayers of her mob of politicians and treaty-mongers? For these are the *shepherds* Isaiah means —sham shepherds, the shrieking crew of politicians, with their treaties and military display. God will save and carry Jerusalem His own way, paying no heed to such. *He will not be dismayed at their voice, nor abase Himself for the noise of them.*

There is more than the unyielding persistency of Divine grace taught here. There is that to begin with. God will never let go what He has made His own: the souls He has redeemed from sin, the societies He has redeemed from barbarism, the characters He has hold of, the lives He has laid His hand upon. Persistency of saving grace—let us learn that confidently in the parable. But that is only half of what it is meant to teach. Look at the shepherds: shepherds shouting round a lion; why does Isaiah put it that way, and not as David did—lions growling round a brave shepherd, with the lamb in his arms? Because it so appeared then in the life Isaiah was picturing, because it often looks the same in real life still. These politicians—they seemed, they played the part of, shepherds; and Jehovah, who persistently frustrated their plans for the salvation of the State—He looked the lion, delivering Jerusalem to destruction. And very often to men does this arrangement of the parts repeat itself; and while human friends are anxious and energetic about them, God Himself appears in providences more lionlike than shepherdly. He grasps with the savage paw of death some one as dear to us as that city was to Isaiah. He rends our body or soul or estate. And friends and our own thoughts gather round the cruel bereavement or disaster with remonstrance and complaint. Our hearts cry out, doing, like shepherds, their best to scare by prayer and cries the foe they are too weak to kill. We all know the scene, and how shabby and mean that mob of human remonstrances looks in face of the great Foe, majestic though inarticulate, that with sullen persistence carries off its prey. All we can say in such times is that if it is God who is the lion, then it is for the best. For *though He slay me, yet will I trust Him;* and, after all, it is safer to rely on the mercies of God, lionlike though they be, than on the weak benevolences and officious pities of the best of human advisers. "Thy will be done"—let perfect reverence teach us to feel that, even when providence seems as savage as men that day thought God's will towards Jerusalem.

In addition then to remembering, when men seem by their cleverness and success to rule life, that God is wiser and His plans more powerful than theirs, we are not to forget, when men seem more anxious and merciful than His dark providence, that for all their argument and action His will shall not alter. But now we are to hear that this will, so hard and mysterious, is as merciful and tender as a mother's.

III. The Mother-bird and her Nest (ver. 5).

As birds hovering, so will Jehovah of hosts cover Jerusalem; He will cover and deliver it: He will pass over and preserve it. At last we are through dark providence, to the very heart of the Almighty. The meaning is familiar from its natural simplicity and frequent use in Scripture. Two features of it our version has not reproduced. The word *birds* means the smaller kind of feathered creatures, and the word *hovering* is feminine in the original : *As little mother-birds hovering, so will Jehovah of hosts protect Jerusalem.* We have been watching in spring the hedge where we know is a nest. Suddenly the mother-bird, who has been sitting on a branch close by, flutters off her perch, passes backwards and forwards, with flapping wings that droop nervously towards the nest over her young. A hawk is in the sky, and till he disappears she will hover—the incarnation of motherly anxiety. This is Isaiah's figure. His native city, on which he poured so much of his heart in lyrics and parables, was again in danger. Sennacherib was descending upon her; and the pity of Isaiah's own heart for her, evil though she was, suggested to him a motherhood of pity in the breast of God. The suggestion God Himself approved. Centuries after, when He assumed our flesh and spoke our language, when He put His love into parables lowly and familiar to our affections, there were none of them more beautiful than that which He uttered of this same city, weeping as He spake: *O Jerusalem, Jerusalem, how often would I have gathered thy children together, as a hen gathereth her brood under her wings, and ye would not!*

With such fountains in Scripture, we need not, as some have done, exalt the Virgin, or virtually make a fourth person in the Godhead, and that a woman, in order to satisfy those natural longings of the heart which the widespread worship of the mother of Jesus tells us are so peremptory. For all fulness dwelleth in God Himself. Not only may we rejoice in that pity and wise provision for our wants, in that pardon and generosity, which we associate with the name of father, but also in the wakefulness, the patience, the love, lovelier with fear, which make a mother's heart so dear and indispensable. We cannot tell along what wakened nerve the grace of God may reach our hearts; but Scripture has a medicine for every pain. And if any feel their weakness as little children feel it, let them know that the Spirit of God broods over them, as a mother over her babe; and if any are in pain or anxiety, and there is no human heart to suffer with them, let them know that as closely as a mother may come to suffer with her child, and as sensitive as she is to its danger, so sensitive is God Almighty to theirs, and that He gives them proof of their preciousness to Him by suffering with them.

How these three descriptions meet the three failings of our faith! We forget that God is ceaselessly at work in wisdom in our lives. We forget that God must sometimes, even when He is saving us, seem lionlike and cruel. We forget that "the heart of the Eternal is most wonderfully kind."

Having thus made vivid the presence of their Lord to the purged eyes of His people, patient, powerful in order, wise in counsel, persistent in grace, and, last of all, very tender, Isaiah concludes with a cry to the people to turn to this Lord, from whom they have so deeply revolted. Let them cast away their idols, and there shall be no fear of the result of the Assyrian invasion. The Assyrian shall fall, not by the sword of man, but the immediate stroke of God. *And his rock shall pass away by reason of terror, and his princes shall be dismayed at the ensign, saith the Lord, whose fire is in Zion, and His furnace in Jerusalem.* And so Isaiah closes this series of prophecies on the keynote with which it opened in the first verse of chap. xxix.: that Jerusalem is Ariel—*the hearth and altar, the dwelling-place and sanctuary, of God.*

CHAPTER XV.

A MAN: CHARACTER AND THE CAPACITY TO DISCRIMINATE CHARACTER.

Isaiah xxxii. 1—8 (about 702 b.c. ?).

THE Assyrians being thus disposed of, Isaiah turns to a prospect, on which we have scarcely heard him speak these twenty years, since Assyria appeared on the frontier of Judah—the religious future and social progress of his own people. This he paints in a small prophecy of eight verses, the first eight of chap. xxxii.—verses 9—20 of that chapter apparently springing from somewhat different conditions.

The first eight verses of chap. xxxii. belong to a class of prophecies which we may call Isaiah's "escapes." Like St. Paul, Isaiah, when he has finished some exposition of God's dealings with His people or argument with the sinners among them, bursts upon an unencumbered vision of the future, and with roused conscience, and voice resonant from long debate, takes his loftiest flights of eloquence. In Isaiah's book we have several of these visions, and each bears a character of its own according to the sort of sinners from whom the prophet shook himself loose to describe it and the kind of indignation that filled his heart at the time. We have already seen, how in some of Isaiah's visions the Messiah has the chief place, while from others He is altogether absent. But here we come upon another inconsistency. Sometimes, as in chap. xi., Isaiah is content with nothing but a new dispensation—the entire transformation of nature, when there shall be no more desert or storm, but to the wild animals docility shall come, and among men an end to sorrow, fraud and war. But again he limits his prophetic soul and promises less. As if, overcome by the spectacle of the more clamant needs and horrible vices of society, he had said, we must first get rid of these, we must supply those, before we can begin to dream of heaven. Such is Isaiah's feeling here. This prophecy is not a vision of society glorified, but of society established and reformed, with its foundation firmly settled (ver. 1), with its fountain forces in full operation (ver. 2), and with an absolute check laid upon its worst habits, as, for instance, the moral grossness, lying and pretence which the prophet has been denouncing for several chapters (vv. 3—8). This moderation of the prophecy brings it within the range of practical morals; while the humanity of it, its freedom from Jewish or Oriental peculiarities, renders it thoroughly modern. If every unfulfilled prophecy ought to be an accusing conscience in the breast of the Christian Church, there will be none more clamant and practical than this one. Its demands are essential to the social interests of to-day.

In ver. 1 we have the presupposition of the whole prophecy: *Behold, in righteousness shall a king reign, and princes—according to justice shall they rule.* A just government is always the basis of Isaiah's vision of the future. Here he defines it with greater abstractness than he has been wont to do. It is remarkable, that a writer, whose pen has already described the figure of the coming King so concretely and with so much detail, should here content himself with a general promise of a righteous government, regarding, as he seems to do, rather the office of kinghood, than any single eminent occupier of it. That the prophet of Immanuel, and still more the prophet of the Prince-of-the-Four-Names (chap. ix. 7), and of the Son of Jesse (chap. xi. 1), should be able to paint the ideal future, and speak of the just government that was to prevail in it, without at the same time referring to his previous very explicit promises of a royal Individual, is a fact which we cannot overlook in support of the opinion we have expressed on pp. 180 and 181 concerning the object of Isaiah's Messianic hopes.

Nor is the vagueness of the first verse corrected by the terms of the second: *And a man shall be as an hiding-place from the wind*, etc. We have already spoken of this verse as an ethical advance upon Isaiah's previous picture of the Messiah (see p. 182). But while, of course, the Messiah was to Isaiah the ideal of human character, and therefore shared whatsoever features he might foresee in its perfect developmnt, it is evident that in this verse Isaiah is not thinking of the Messiah alone or particularly. When he says with such simplicity *a* man, he means any man, he means the ideal for every man. Having in ver. 1 laid down the foundation for social life, he tells us in ver. 2 what the shelter and fountain force of society are to be: not science nor material wealth, but personal influence, the strength and freshness of the human personality. *A man shall be as an hiding-place from the wind and a covert from the tempest, as rivers of water in a dry place, as the shadow of a great rock in a weary land.* After just government (ver. 1) great characters are the prophet's first demand (ver. 2), and then (vv. 3—8) he will ask for the capacity to discriminate character. "Character and the capacity to discriminate character" indeed summarizes this prophecy.

I. A Man (ver. 2).

Isaiah has described personal influence on so grand a scale that it is not surprising that the Church has leapt to his words as a direct prophecy of Jesus Christ. They are indeed a description of Him, out of whose shadow advancing time has not been able to carry the children of men, who has been the shelter and fertility of every generation since He was lifted up, and to whom the affections of individual hearts never rise higher than when they sing—

> " Rock of ages, cleft for me,
> Let me hide myself in Thee."

Such a rock was Christ indeed; but, in accordance with what we have said above, the prophet here has no individual specially in his view, but is rather laying down a general description of the influence of individual character, of which Christ Jesus was the highest instance. Taken in this sense, his famous words present us, *first*, with a philosophy of history, at the heart of which there is, *secondly*, a great gospel, and in the application of which there is, *thirdly*, a great ideal and duty for ourselves.

1. Isaiah gives us in this verse a Philosophy of History. Great men are not the whole of life, but they are the condition of all the rest; if it were not for the big men, the little ones could scarcely live. The first requisites of religion and civilisation are outstanding characters.

In the East the following phenomenon is often observed. Where the desert touches a river-valley or oasis, the sand is in a continual state of drift from the wind, and it is this drift which is the real cause of the barrenness of such portions of the desert at least as abut upon the fertile land. For under the rain, or by infiltration of the river, plants often spring up through the sand, and there is sometimes promise of considerable fertility. It never lasts. Down comes the periodic drift, and life is stunted or choked out. But set down a rock on the sand, and see the difference its presence makes. After a few showers, to the leeward side of this some blades will spring up; if you have patience, you will see in time a garden. How has the boulder produced this? Simply by arresting the drift.

Now that is exactly how great men benefit human life. A great man serves his generation, serves the whole race, by arresting the drift. Deadly forces, blind and fatal as the desert wind, sweep down human history. In the beginning it was the dread of Nature, the cold blast which blows from every quarter on the barbarian, and might have stunted men to animals. But into some soul God breathed a great breath of freedom, and the man defied Nature. Nature has had her revenge by burying the rebel in oblivion. On the distant horizon of history we can see, merely in some old legend, the evidence of his audacity. But the drift was arrested; behind the event men took shelter, in the shelter grew free, and learned to think out what the first great resister felt.

When history had left this rock behind, and the drift had again space to grow, the same thing happened; and the hero this time was Abraham. He laid his back to the practice of his forefathers, and lifting his brow to heaven, was the first to worship the One Unseen God. Abraham believed; and in the shadow of his faith, and sheltered by his example, his descendants learned to believe too. To-day from within the three great spiritual religions men look back to him as the father of the faithful.

When Isaiah, while all his countrymen were rushing down the mad, steep ways of politics, carried off by the only powers that were as yet known in these ways, fear of death and greed to be on the side of the strongest —when Isaiah stood still amid that panic rush, and uttered the memorable words, *In quietness and in confidence shall be your strength; in returning and rest shall ye be saved*, he stopped one of the most dangerous drifts in history, and created in its despite a shelter for those spiritual graces, which have always been the beauty of the State, and are now coming to be recognized as its strength.

When, in the early critical days of the Church, that dark drift of Jewish custom, which had overflown the barriers set to the old dispensation, threatened to spread its barrenness upon the fields of the Gentile world, already white to the harvest of Christ, and Peter and Barnabas and all the Apostles were carried away by it, what was it that saved Christianity? Under God, it was this: that Paul got up and, as he tells us, withstood Peter to the face.

And, again, when the powers of the Roman Church and the Roman Empire, checked for a little by the efforts which began the Reformation, gathered themselves together and rose in one awful front of emperor, cardinals, and princes at the Diet of Worms, what was it that stood fast against that drift of centuries, and proved the rock, under whose shelter men dared to read God's pure word again, and preach His Gospel? It was the word of a lonely monk: "Here stand I. I cannot otherwise. So help me, God."

So that Isaiah is right. A single man has been as *an hiding-place from the wind and a covert from the tempest.* History is swept by drifts: superstition, error, poisonous custom, dust-laden controversy. What has saved humanity has been the upraising of some great man to resist those drifts, to set his will, strong through faith, against the prevailing tendency, and be the shelter of the weaker, but not less desirous, souls of his brethren. "The history of what man has accomplished in the world is at bottom the history of the great men who have worked there." Under God, personal human power is the highest force, and God has ever used it as His chief instrument.

2. But in this philosophy of history there is a GOSPEL. Isaiah's words are not only man's ideal; they are God's promise, and that promise has been fulfilled in Jesus Christ. Jesus Christ is the most conspicuous example—none others are near Him—of this personal influence in which Isaiah places all the shelter and revival of society. God has set His seal to the truth, that the greatest power in shaping human destiny is man himself, by becoming one with man, by using a human soul to be the Saviour of the race. *A man,* says Isaiah, *shall be as an hiding-place from the wind, as the shadow of a great rock in a weary land;* and the Rock of ages was a Man. The world indeed knew that personal character could go higher than all else in the world, but they never knew how high till they saw Jesus Christ, or how often till they numbered His followers.

This figure of a rock, a rock resisting drift, gives us some idea, not only of the commanding influence of Christ's person, but of that special office from which all the glory of His person and of His name arises: that *He saves His people from their sins*.

For what is sin? Sin is simply the longest, heaviest drift in human history. It arose in the beginning, and has carried everything before it since. "The oldest custom of the race," it is the most powerful habit of the individual. Men have reared against it government, education, philosophy, system after system of religion. But sin overwhelmed them all.

Only Christ resisted, and His resistance saves the world. Alone among human lives presented to our view, that of Christ is sinless. What is so prevalent in human nature that we cannot think of a human individual without it never stained Christ's life. Sin was about Him; it was not that He belonged to another sphere of things which lay above it. Sin was about Him. He rose from its midst with the same frailty as other men, encompassed by the same temptations; but where they rose to fall, He rose to stand, and standing, became the world's Saviour. The great tradition was broken; the drift was arrested. Sin never could be the same again after the sinless manhood of Christ. The old world's sins and cruel customs were shut out from the world that came after. Some of them ceased so absolutely as scarcely to be afterwards named; and the rest were so curbed that no civilised society suffered them to pass from its constraint, and no public conscience tolerated them as natural or necessary evils.

What the surface of the world's life bears so deeply, that does every individual, who puts his trust in Jesus, feel to the core. Of Jesus the believer can truly say that life on *this* side of Him is very different from life on *that*. Temptations keep far away from the heart that keeps near to Christ. Under the shadow of our Rock, for us the evil of the present loses all its suggestiveness, the evil of the past its awful surge of habit and guilty fear.

3. But there is not only a philosophy of history and a gospel in this promise of *a man*. There is a great DUTY and IDEAL for every one. If this prophecy distinctly reaches forward to Jesus Christ as its only perfect fulfilment, the vagueness of its expression permits of its application to all, and through Him its fulfilment by all becomes a possibility. Now each of us may be a rock, a shelter and a source of fertility to the life around him in three modes of constant influence. We can be like Christ, the Rock, in shutting out from our neighbours the knowledge and infection of sin, in keeping our conversation so unsuggestive and unprovocative of evil, that, though sin drift upon us, it shall never drift through us. And we may be like Christ, the Rock, in shutting out blame from other men; in sheltering them from the east wind of pitiless prejudice, quarrel or controversy; in stopping the unclean and bitter drifts of scandal and gossip. How many lives have lost their fertility for the want of a little silence and a little shadow! Some righteous people have a terribly north-eastern exposure; children do not play about their doors, nor the prodigal stop there. And again, as there are a number of men and women who fall in struggling for virtue simply because they never see it successful in others, and the spectacle of one pure, heroic character would be their salvation, here is another way in which each servant of God may be a rock. Of

the late Clerk Maxwell it was said, "He made faith in goodness easy to other men." *A man shall be as streams of water in a desert place.*

II. CAPACITY TO DISTINGUISH CHARACTER (vv. 3—8).

But after the coming of this ideal, it is not paradise that is regained. Paradise is farther off. We must have truth to begin with: truth and the capacity to discriminate character. The sternness with which Isaiah thus postpones his earlier vision shows us how sore his heart was about the *lying* temper of his people. We have heard him deploring the fascination of their false minds by the Egyptian Pretence. Their falseness, however, had not only shown itself in their foreign politics, but in their treatment of one another, in their social fashions, judgements and worships. In society there prevailed a want of moral insight and of moral courage. At home also the Jews had failed to call things by their right names (cf. p. 226). Therefore next in their future Isaiah desires the cure of moral blindness, haste and cowardice (vv. 3, 4), with the explosion of all social lies (ver. 5). Men shall stand out for what they are, whether they be bad—for the bad shall not be wanting (vv. 6, 7)—or good (ver. 8). On righteous government (ver. 1) and influence of strong men (ver. 2) must follow social truthfulness (vv. 3—8). Such is the line of the prophet's demands. The details of vv. 3—8 are exceedingly interesting.

And not closed shall be the eyes of them that see, and the ears of them that hear shall be pricked up. The context makes it clear that this is spoken, not of intellectual, but of moral, insight and alertness. *And the heart of the hasty shall learn how to know, and the tongue of the stammerer be quick* (the verb is the same as the *hasty* of the previous clause) *to speak plain things.* **Startlingly plain things**—for the word literally means *blinding-white*, and is so used of the sun—*startlingly plain*, like that scorching epigram upon Egypt. The morally rash and the morally timid are equal fathers of lies.

In illustration Isaiah takes the conventional abuse of certain moral terms, exposes it and declares it shall cease : *The vile person shall no more be called liberal, nor the churl said to be bountiful.* *Liberal* and *bountiful* were conventional names. The Hebrew word for *libera* originally meant exactly that—*open-hearted, generous, magnanimous.* In the East it is the character which above all they call princely. So like our words "noble" and "nobility," it became a term of rank, *lord* or *prince*, and was often applied to men who were not at all great-hearted, but the very opposite—even to the *vile person. Vile person* is literally the *faded* or the *exhausted,* whether mentally or morally—the last kind of character that could be princely. The other conventional term used by Isaiah refers to wealth rather than rank. The Hebrew for *bountiful* literally means *abundant,* a man blessed with plenty, and is used in the Old Testament both for the rich and the fortunate. Its nearest English equivalent is perhaps *the successful man.* To this Isaiah fitly opposes a name, wrongly rendered in our version *churl,* but corrected in the margin to *crafty*—*the fraudulent, the knave.* When moral discrimination comes, says Isaiah, men will not apply the term *princely* to *worn-out* characters, nor grant them the social respect implied by the term. They will not call the *fraudulent* the *fortunate,* nor canonise him as successful, who has gotten his wealth by underhand means. *The worthless character shall no more be called princely, nor the knave hailed as the successful.* But men's characters shall stand out true in their actions, and by their fruits ye shall know them. In those magic days the heart shall come to the lips, and its effects be unmistakeable. *For the worthless person, worthlessness shall he speak*—what else can he?— *and his heart shall do iniquity, to practise profaneness and to utter against the* LORD *rank error, to make empty the soul of the hungry, and he will cause the drink of the thirsty to fail. The tools, too, of the knave* (a play upon words here—"Keli Kelâv," *the knave his knives*) *are evil; he! low tricks he deviseth to destroy the poor with words of falsehood, even when the poor speaks justice* (that is, has justice as well as poverty to plead for him). *But the princely princely things deviseth, and he upon princely things shall stand*—not upon conventional titles or rank, or the respect of insincere hearts, but upon actual deeds of generosity and sacrifice.

After great characters, then, what society needs is capacity to discern character, and the chief obstacle in the way of this discernment is the substitution of a conventional morality for a true morality, and of some distinctions of man's making for the eternal difference which God has set between right and wrong.

Human progress consists, according to Isaiah, of getting rid of these conventions; and in this history bears him out. The abolition of slavery, the recognition of the essential nobility of labour, the abolition of infanticide, the emancipation of woman—all these are due to the release of men's minds from purely conventional notions, and the courageous application in their place of the fundamental laws of righteousness and love. If progress is still to continue, it must be by the same method. In many directions it is still a false conventionalism,—sometimes the relic of barbarism, sometimes the fruit of civilisation,—that blocks the way. The savage notions which obstruct the enforcement of masculine purity have to be exposed. Nor shall we ever get true commercial prosperity, or the sense of security which is indispensable to that, till men begin to cease calling transactions all right merely because they are the custom of the trade and the means to which its members look for profits.

But, above all, as Isaiah tells us, we need to look to our use of language. It is one of the standing necessities of pure science to revise the terminology, to reserve for each object a special name, and see that all men understand the same object by the same name. Otherwise confusion comes in, and science is impossible. The necessity, though not so faithfully recognized, is as imperative in morals. If we consider the disgraceful mistakes in popular morals which have been produced by the transference and degradation of names, we shall feel it to be a religious duty to preserve for these their proper meaning. In the interests of morality, we must not be careless in our use of moral terms. As Socrates says in the *Phædo:* "To use words wrongly and indefinitely is not merely an error in itself; it also creates evil in the soul."* What noxious misconceptions, what mistaken ideals of life, are due to the abuse of these four words alone: "noble," "gentleman," "honour" and "Christian"! By applying these, in flattery or deceit, to persons unworthy of them, men have not only deprived them of the virtue which originally the mere utterance of them was enough to instil into the heart, but have sent forth to the world under their attractiveness second-rate types of character and

---

* Cf. further with this passage F. J. Church, *Trial and Death of Socrates*, Introd. xli. ff.

ideals. The word "gentleman"! How the heart sickens as it thinks what a number of people have been satisfied to aim at a shoddy and superficial life because it was labelled with this gracious name. Conventionalism has deprived the English language of some of its most powerful sermons by devoting terms of singular moral expressiveness to do duty as mere labels upon characters that are dead, or on ranks and offices, for the designation of which mere cyphers might have sufficed.

We must not forget, however, Isaiah's chief means for the abolition of this conventionalism and the substitution of a true moral vision and terminology. These results are to follow from the presence of the great character, *A Man*, whom he has already lifted up. Conventionalism is another of the drifts which that *Rock* has to arrest. Setting ourselves to revise our dictionaries or to restore to our words their original meanings out of our memories is never enough. The rising of a conspicuous character alone can dissipate the moral haze; the sense of his influence will alone fill emptied forms with meaning. So Christ Jesus judged and judges the world by His simple presence; men fall to His right hand and to His left. He calls things by their right names, and restores to each term of religion and morals its original ideal, which the vulgar use of the world had worn away.*

* Cf. with the fifth and sixth verses of chap. xxxii. the forcible passage in the introduction to Carlyle's *Cromwell's Letters*, beginning, "Sure enough, in the Heroic Century, as in the Unheroic, knaves and cowards ... were not wanting. But the question always remains, Did they lie chained?" etc.

CHAPTER XVI.

ISAIAH TO WOMEN

Isaiah xxxii. 9—20 (date uncertain).

THE date of this prophecy, which has been appended to those spoken by Isaiah during the Egyptian intrigues (704—702), is not certain. It is addressed to women, and there is no reason why the prophet, when he was upbraiding the men of Judah for their false optimism, should not also have sought to awaken the conscience of their wives and daughters on what is the besetting sin rather of women than of men. The chief evidence for dissociating the prophecy from its immediate predecessors is that it predicts, or apparently predicts (vv. 13—14), the ruin of Jerusalem, whereas in these years Isaiah was careful to exempt the Holy City from the fate which he saw falling on the rest of the land. But otherwise the argument of the prophecy is almost exactly that of chaps. xxix.—xxx. By using the same words when he blames the women for *ease* and *carelessness* in vv. 9—11, as he does when he promises *confidence* and *quiet resting-places* in vv. 17, 18, Isaiah makes clear that his purpose is to contrast the false optimism of society during the postponement of the Assyrian invasion with that confidence and stability upon righteousness which the Spirit of God can alone create. The prophecy, too, has the usual three stages: sin in the present, judgement in the immediate future, and a state of blessedness in the latter days. The near date at which judgement is threatened—*days beyond a year*—ought to be compared with chap. xxix. 1: *Add ye a year to a year; let the feasts come round.*

The new points are—that it is the women who are threatened, that Jerusalem itself is pictured in ruin, and that the pouring out of the Spirit is promised as the cause of the blessed future.

I. The Charge to the Women (vv. 9—12)

is especially interesting, not merely for its own terms, but because it is only part of a treatment of women which runs through the whole of Scripture.

Isaiah had already delivered against the women of Jerusalem a severe diatribe (chap. iii.), the burden of which was their vanity and haughtiness. With the satiric temper, which distinguishes his earlier prophecies, he had mimicked their ogling and mincing gait, and described pin by pin their fashions and ornaments, promising them instead of these things *rottenness* and *baldness*, and *a girdle of sackcloth and branding for beauty*. But he has grown older, and penetrating below their outward fashion and gait, he charges them with thoughtlessness as the besetting sin of their sex. *Ye women that are at ease, rise up, and hear my voice; ye careless daughters, give ear to my speech. For days beyond a year shall ye be troubled, O careless women, for the vintage shall fail; the ingathering shall not come. Tremble, ye women that are at ease; be troubled, ye careless ones.* By a pair of epithets he describes their fault; and almost thrice does he repeat the pair, as if he would emphasize it past all doubt. The besetting sin of women, as he dins into them, is *ease*; an ignorant and unthinking contentment with things as they are; thoughtlessness with regard to the deeper mysteries of life; disbelief in the possibility of change.

But Isaiah more than hints that these besetting sins of women are but the defects of their virtues. The literal meaning of the two adjectives he uses, *at ease* and *careless*, is *restful* and *trustful*. Scripture throughout employs these words both in a good and a bad sense. Isaiah does so himself in this very chapter (compare these verses with vv. 17, 18). In the next chapter he describes the state of Jerusalem after redemption as a state of *ease* or *restfulness*, and we know that he never ceased urging the people to *trustfulness*. For such truly religious conditions he uses exactly the same names as for the shallow optimism with which he now charges his countrywomen. And so doing, he reminds us of an important law of character. The besetting sins of either sex are its virtues prostituted. A man's greatest temptations proceed from his strength; but the glory of the feminine nature is repose, and trust is the strength of the feminine character, in which very things, however, lies all the possibility of woman's degradation. Woman's faith amounts at times to real intuition; but what risks are attached to this prophetic power—of impatience, of contentment with the first glance at things, "the inclination," as a great moralist has put it, "to take too easily the knowledge of the problems of life, and to rest content with what lies nearest her, instead of penetrating to a deeper foundation." Women are full of indulgence and hope; but what possibilities lie there of deception, false optimism, and want of that anxiety which alone makes progress possible. Women are more inclined than men to believe all things; but how certain is such a temper to sacrifice the claims of truth and honour. Women are full of tact, the just favourites of success, with infinite power to plead and please; but if they are aware of this, how certain is such a self-consciousness to produce negligence and the fatal sleep of the foolish virgins.

Scripture insists repeatedly on this truth of Isaiah's about the besetting sin of women. The prophet Amos has engraved it in one of his sharpest epigrams, declaring that thoughtlessness is capable of turning women into very brutes, and their homes into desolate ruins: *Hear this word, ye kine of Bashan, that are in the mountain of Samaria, which oppress the poor, which crush the needy, which say unto their lords, Bring and let us drink. The Lord Jehovah hath sworn by His holiness that, lo, the days shall come upon you that they shall take you away with hooks, and your residue with fish-hooks, and ye shall go out at the breaches, every one straight before her, and ye shall cast yourselves into Harmon, saith Jehovah.* It is a cowherd's picture of women: a troop of cows, heavy, heedless animals, trampling in their anxiety for food upon every frail and lowly object in the way. There is a cowherd's coarseness in it, but a prophet's insight into character. Not of Jezebels, or Messalinas, or Lady-Macbeths is it spoken, but of the ordinary matrons of Samaria. Thoughtlessness is able to make brutes out of women of gentle nurture, with homes and a religion. For thoughtlessness when joined to luxury or beauty plays with cruel weapons. It means greed, arrogance, indifference to suffering, wantonness, pride of conquest, dissimulation in love, and revenge for little slights; and there is no waste, unkind sport, insolence, brutality, or hysterical violence to which it will not lead. Such women are known, as Amos pictured them, through many degrees of this thoughtlessness: interrupters of conversation, an offence to the wise; devourers of many of the little ones of God's creation for the sake of their own ornament; tormentors of servants and subordinates for the sake of their own ease; out of the enjoyment of power or for admiration's sake breakers of hearts. And are not all such victims of thoughtlessness best compared, with Amos, to a cow—an animal that rushes at its grass careless of the many daisies and ferns it tramples, that will destroy the beauty of a whole country lane for a few mouthfuls of herbage? Thoughtlessness, says Amos —*and the Lord GOD hath sworn it by His holiness*— is the very negation of womanhood, the ruin of homes.

But when we turn from the degradation of woman as thus exposed by the prophets to her glory as lifted up in the New Testament, we find that the same note is struck. Woman in the New Testament is gracious according as she is thoughtful; she offends even when otherwise beautiful by her feeling overpowering her thought. Martha spoils a most estimable character by one moment of unthinking passion, in which she accuses the Master of carelessness. Mary chooses the better part in close attention to her Master's words. The Ten Virgins are divided into five wise and five foolish. Paul seems to have been struck, as Isaiah was, with the natural tendency of the female character, for the first duty he lays upon the old women is to *teach the young women to think discreetly*, and he repeats the injunction, putting it before chastity and industry—*Teach them*, he says, *teach them discretion* (Titus ii. 4, 5). In Mary herself, the mother of our Lord, we see two graces of character, to the honour of which Scripture gives equal place—faith and thoughtfulness. The few sentences, which are all that he devotes to Mary's character, the Evangelist divides equally between these two. She was called *blessed* because she believed the word of the Lord. But trustfulness did not mean in her, as in other women, neglect to think. Twice, at an interval of twelve years, we are shown thoughtfulness and carefulness of memory as the habitual grace of this first among women. *Mary kept all these things and pondered them in her heart. His mother kept all these sayings in her heart.** What was Mary's glory was other women's salvation. By her own logic the sufferer of Capernaum, whom many physicians failed to benefit, found her cure; by her persistent argument the Syrophenician woman received her daughter to health again. And when our Lord met that flippant descendant of *the kine of Bashan, that are in the mount of Samaria*, how did He treat her that He might save her but by giving her matter to think about, by speaking to her in riddles, by exploding her superficial knowledge, and scattering her easy optimism?

So does all Scripture declare, in harmony with the oracle of Isaiah, that thoughtlessness and easy contentment with things as they be, are the besetting sins of woman. But her glory is discretion.

II. The next new point in this prophecy is the

Destruction of Jerusalem (vv. 13—15).

Upon the land of my people shall come up thorns and briers; yea, upon all the houses of joy in the joyous city: for the palace shall be forsaken; the populous city shall be deserted; Ophel and the Watch-tower shall be for dens for ever, a joy of wild asses, a pasture of flocks. The attempt has been made to confine this reference to the

---

* Cf. Newman, *Oxford University Sermons*, xv.

outskirts of the sacred city, but it is hardly a just one. The prophet, though he does not name the city, evidently means Jerusalem, and means the whole of it. Some therefore deny the authenticity of the prophecy. Certainly it is almost impossible to suppose, that so definite a sentence of ruin can have been published at the same time as the assurances of Jerusalem's inviolability in the preceding orations. But that does not prevent the hypothesis that it was uttered by Isaiah at an earlier period, when, as in chaps. ii. and iii., he did say extreme things about the destruction of his city. It must be noticed, however, that Isaiah speaks with some vagueness; that at the present moment he is not concerned with any religious truth or will of the Almighty, but simply desires to contrast the careless gaiety of the women of Jerusalem with the fate hanging over them. How could he do this more forcibly than by turning the streets and gardens of their delights into ruins and the haunts of the wild ass, even though it should seem inconsistent with his declaration that Zion was inviolable? Licence for a certain amount of inconsistency is absolutely necessary in the case of a prophet who had so many divers truths to utter to so many opposite interests and tempers. Besides, at this time he had already reduced Jerusalem very low (xxix. 4).

III. THE SPIRIT OUTPOURED (vv. 15—20).

The rest of the prophecy is luminous rather than lucid, full of suffused rather than distinct meanings. The date of the future regeneration is indefinite— another feature more in harmony with Isaiah's earlier prophecies than his later. The cause of the blessing is the outpouring of the Spirit of God (ver. 15). Righteousness and peace are to come to earth by a distinct creative act of God. Isaiah adds his voice to the invariable testimony of prophets and apostles, who, whether they speak of society or the heart of individual man, place their hope in new life from above by the Spirit of the living God. Victor Hugo says, "There are no weeds in society, only bad cultivators;" and places all hope of progress towards perfection in proper methods of social culture. These are needed, as much as the corn, which will not spring from the sunshine alone, requires the hand of the sower, and the harrow. And Isaiah, too, speaks here of human conduct and effort as required to fill up the blessedness of the future: righteousness and labour. But first, and indispensably, he, with all the prophets, places the Spirit of God.

It appears that Isaiah looked for the fruits of the Spirit both as material and moral. He bases the quiet resting-places and regular labours of the future not on righteousness only, but on fertility and righteousness. *The wilderness shall become a fruitful field*, and *what is* to-day *a fruitful field shall be counted as a forest.* That this proverb, used by Isaiah more than once, is not merely a metaphor for the moral revolution he describes in the next verse, is proved by his having already declared the unfruitfulness of their soil as part of his people's punishment. Fertility is promised for itself, and as the accompaniment of moral bountifulness. *And there shall dwell in the wilderness justice, and righteousness shall abide in the fruitful field. And the work of righteousness shall be peace, and the effect*, or *service, of righteousness, quietness and confidence for ever. And my people shall abide in a peaceable habitation, and in sure dwellings, and in quiet resting-places.*

... *Blessed are ye that sow beside all waters, that send forth the feet of the ox and the ass!*

There is not a prophecy more characteristic of Isaiah. It unfolds what for him were the two essential and equal contents of the will of God: a secure land and a righteous people, the fertility of nature and the purity of society. But in those years (705—702) he did not forget that something must come between him and that paradise. Across the very middle of his vision of felicity there dashes a cruel storm. In the gap indicated above Isaiah wrote, *But it shall hail in the downfall of the forest, and the city shall be utterly laid low.* A hailstorm between the promise and fulfilment of summer! Isaiah could only mean the Assyrian invasion, which was now lowering so dark. Before it bursts we must follow him to the survey which he made, during these years before the siege of Jerusalem, of the foreign nations on whom, equally with Jerusalem, that storm was to sweep.

CHAPTER XVII.

ISAIAH TO THE FOREIGN NATIONS.

Isaiah xiv. 24–32, xv.–xxi., and xxiii. (736–702 B.C.).

THE centre of the Book of Isaiah (chaps. xiii. to xxiii.) is occupied by a number of long and short prophecies which are a fertile source of perplexity to the conscientious reader of the Bible. With the exhilaration of one who traverses plain roads and beholds vast prospects, he has passed through the opening chapters of the book as far as the end of the twelfth; and he may look forward to enjoying a similar experience when he reaches those other clear stretches of vision from the twenty-fourth to the twenty-seventh and from the thirtieth to the thirty-second. But here he loses himself among a series of prophecies obscure in themselves and without obvious relation to one another. The subjects of them are the nations, tribes and cities with which in Isaiah's day, by war or treaty or common fear in face of the Assyrian conquest, Judah was being brought into contact. There are none of the familiar names of the land and tribes of Israel which meet the reader in other obscure prophecies and lighten their darkness with the face of a friend. The names and allusions are foreign, some of them the names of tribes long since extinct, and of places which it is no more possible to identify. It is a very jungle of prophecy, in which, without much Gospel or geographical light, we have to grope our way, thankful for an occasional gleam of the picturesque—a sandstorm in the desert, the forsaken ruins of Babylon haunted by wild beasts, a view of Egypt's canals or Phœnicia's harbours, a glimpse of an Arab raid or of a grave Ethiopian embassy.

But in order to understand the Book of Isaiah, in order to understand Isaiah himself in some of the largest of his activities and hopes, we must traverse this thicket. It would be tedious and unprofitable to search every corner of it. We propose, therefore, to give a list of the various oracles, with their dates and titles, for the guidance of Bible-readers, then to take three representative texts and gather the meaning of all the oracles round them.

First, however, two of the prophecies must be put aside. The twenty-second chapter does not refer to a foreign State, but to Jerusalem itself; and the large prophecy which opens the series (chaps. xiii.—xiv. 23) deals with the overthrow of Babylon in circumstances that did not arise till long after Isaiah's time, and so falls to be considered by us along with similar prophecies at the close of this volume. (See Book V.)

All the rest of these chapters—xiv.—xxi. and xxiii.— refer to Isaiah's own day. They were delivered by the prophet at various times throughout his career; but the most of them evidently date from immediately after the year 705, when, on the death of Sargon, there was a general rebellion of the Assyrian vassals.

1. xiv. 24—27. OATH OF JEHOVAH that the Assyrian shall be broken. Probable date, towards 701.

2. xiv. 28—32. ORACLE FOR PHILISTIA. Warning to Philistia not to rejoice because one Assyrian king is

dead, for a worse one shall arise: *Out of the serpent's root shall come forth a basilisk.* Philistia shall be melted away, but Zion shall stand. The inscription to this oracle (ver. 28) is not genuine. The oracle plainly speaks of the death and accession of Assyrian, not Judæan, kings. It may be ascribed to 705, the date of the death of Sargon and accession of Sennacherib. But some hold that it refers to the previous change on the Assyrian throne—the death of Salmanassar and the accession of Sargon.

3. xv.—xvi. 12. ORACLE FOR MOAB. A long prophecy against Moab. This oracle, whether originally by himself at an earlier period of his life, or more probably by an older prophet, Isaiah adopts and ratifies, and intimates its immediate fulfilment, in xvi. 13, 14: *This is the word which Jehovah spake concerning Moab long ago. But now Jehovah hath spoken, saying, Within three years, as the years of an hireling, and the glory of Moab shall be brought into contempt with all the great multitude, and the remnant shall be very small and of no account.* The dates both of the original publication of this prophecy and of its reissue with the appendix are quite uncertain. The latter may fall about 711, when Moab was threatened by Sargon for complicity in the Ashdod conspiracy (p. 198), or in 704, when, with other States, Moab came under the cloud of Sennacherib's invasion. The main prophecy is remarkable for its vivid picture of the disaster that has overtaken Moab and for the sympathy with her which the Jewish prophet expresses; for the mention of a *remnant* of Moab; for the exhortation to her to send tribute in her adversity *to the mount of the daughter of Zion* (xvi. 1); for an appeal to Zion to shelter the outcasts of Moab and to take up her cause: *Bring counsel, make a decision,*

make thy shadow as the night in the midst of the noonday; hide the outcasts, bewray not the wanderer; for a statement of the Messiah similar to those in chaps. ix. and xi.; and for the offer to the oppressed Moabites of the security of Judah in Messianic times (vv. 4, 5). But there is one great obstacle to this prospect of Moab lying down in the shadow of Judah—Moab's arrogance. *We have heard of the pride of Moab, that he is very proud* (ver. 6, cf. Jer. xlviii. 29, 42; Zeph. ii. 10), which pride shall not only keep this country in ruin, but prevent the Moabites prevailing in prayer at their own sanctuary (ver. 12)—a very remarkable admission about the worship of another god than Jehovah.

4. xvii. 1—11. ORACLE FOR DAMASCUS. One of the earliest and most crisp of Isaiah's prophecies. Of the time of Syria's and Ephraim's league against Judah, somewhere between 736 and 732.

5. xvii. 12—14. UNTITLED. The crash of the peoples upon Jerusalem and their dispersion. This magnificent piece of sound, which we analyse below, is usually understood of Sennacherib's rush upon Jerusalem. Verse 14 is an accurate summary of the sudden break-up and "retreat from Moscow" of his army. The Assyrian hosts are described as *nations*, as they are elsewhere more than once by Isaiah (xxii. 6, xxix. 7). But in all this there is no final reason for referring the oracle to Sennacherib's invasion, and it may just as well be interpreted of Isaiah's confidence of the defeat of Syria and Ephraim (734—723). Its proximity to the oracle against Damascus would then be very natural, and it would stand as a parallel prophecy to viii. 9: *Make an uproar, O ye peoples, and ye shall be broken in pieces; and give ear, all ye of the distances of the earth: gird yourselves, and ye shall be*

broken in pieces; gird yourselves, and ye shall be broken in pieces—a prophecy which we know belongs to the period of the Syro-Ephraimitic league.

6. xviii. UNTITLED. An address to Ethiopia, *land of a rustling of wings, land of many sails, whose messengers dart to and fro upon the rivers in their skiffs of reed.* The prophet tells Ethiopia, cast into excitement by the news of the Assyrian advance, how Jehovah is resting quietly till the Assyrian be ripe for destruction. When the Ethiopians shall see His sudden miracle, they shall send their tribute to Jehovah, *to the place of the name of Jehovah of hosts, Mount Zion.* It is difficult to know to which southward march of Assyria to ascribe this prophecy—Sargon's or Sennacherib's? For at the time of both of these an Ethiopian ruled Egypt.

7. xix. ORACLE FOR EGYPT. The first fifteen verses describe judgement as ready to fall on the land of the Pharaohs. The last ten speak of the religious results to Egypt of that judgement, and they form the most universal and "missionary" of all Isaiah's prophecies. Although doubts have been expressed of the Isaian authorship of the second half of this chapter on the score of its universalism, as well as of its literary style, which is judged to be "a pale reflection" of Isaiah's own, there is no final reason for declining the credit of it to Isaiah, while there are insuperable difficulties against relegating it to the late date which is sometimes demanded for it. On the date and authenticity of this prophecy, which are of great importance for the question of Isaiah's "missionary" opinions, see Cheyne's introduction to the chapter and Robertson Smith's notes in *The Prophets of Israel* (p. 433). The latter puts it in 703, during Sennacherib's advance

upon the south. The former suggests that the second half may have been written by the prophet much later than the first, and justly says, "We can hardly imagine a more 'swan-like end' for the dying prophet."

8. xx. UNTITLED. Also upon Egypt, but in narrative and of an earlier date than at least the latter half of xix. Tells how Isaiah walked naked and barefoot in the streets of Jerusalem for a sign against Egypt and against the help Judah hoped to get from her in the years 711—709, when the Tartan, or Assyrian commander-in-chief, came south to subdue Ashdod. See pp. 198—200.

9. xxi. 1—10. ORACLE FOR THE WILDERNESS OF THE SEA, announcing but lamenting the fall of Babylon. Probably 709. See pp. 202, 203.

10. xxi. 11, 12. ORACLE FOR DUMAH. Dumah, or *Silence*— in Ps. xciv. 17, cxv. 17, *the land of the silence of death*, the grave—is probably used as an anagram for Edom and an enigmatic sign to the wise Edomites, in their own fashion, of the kind of silence their land is lying under—the silence of rapid decay. The prophet hears this silence at last broken by a cry. Edom cannot bear the darkness any more. *Unto me one is calling from Seir, Watchman, how much off the night? how much off the night?* * *Said the watchman, Cometh the morning, and also the night: if ye will inquire, inquire, come back again.* What other answer is possible for a land on which the silence of decay seems to have settled down? He may, however,

---

* Our translation, though picturesque, is misleading. The voice does not inquire, "What of the night?" *i.e.*, whether it be fair or foul weather, but "How much of the night is passed?" literally "What from off the night?" This brings out a pathos that our English version has disguised. Edom feels that her night is lasting terribly long.

give them an answer later on, if they will come back. Date uncertain, perhaps between 704 and 701.

11. xxi. 13—17. ORACLE FOR ARABIA. From Edom the prophet passes to their neighbours the Dedanites, travelling merchants. And as he saw night upon Edom, so, by a play upon words, he speaks of evening upon Arabia: *in the forest, in Arabia*, or with the same consonants, *in the evening*. In the time of the insecurity of the Assyrian invasion the travelling merchants have to go aside from their great trading roads *in the evening to lodge in the thickets*. There they entertain fugitives, or (for the sense is not quite clear) are themselves as fugitives entertained. It is a picture of the *grievousness of war*, which was now upon the world, flowing down even those distant, desert roads. But things have not yet reached the worst. The fugitives are but the heralds of armies, that *within a year* shall waste the *children of Kedar*, for Jehovah, the God of Israel, hath spoken it. So did the prophet of little Jerusalem take possession of even the far deserts in the name of his nation's God.

12. xxiii. ORACLE FOR TYRE. Elegy over its fall, probably as Sennacherib came south upon it in 703 or 702. To be further considered by us (pp. 288 ff.).

These then are Isaiah's oracles for the Nations, who tremble, intrigue and go down before the might of Assyria.

We have promised to gather the circumstances and meaning of these prophecies round three representative texts. These are—

1. *Ah! the booming of the peoples, the multitudes, like the booming of the seas they boom; and the rushing of the*

nations, like the rushing of mighty waters they rush; nations, like the rushing of many waters they rush. But He rebuketh it, and it fleeth afar off, and is chased like the chaff on the mountains before the wind and like whirling dust before the whirlwind (xvii. 12, 13).

2. *What then shall one answer the messengers of a nation? That Jehovah hath founded Zion, and in her shall find refuge the afflicted of His people* (xiv. 32).

3. *In that day shall Israel be a third to Egypt and to Assyria, a blessing in the midst of the earth, for that Jehovah of hosts hath blessed them, saying, Blessed be My people Egypt, and the work of My hands Assyria, and Mine inheritance Israel* (xix. 24, 25).

1. The first of these texts shows all the prophet's prospect filled with storm, the second of them the solitary rock and lighthouse in the midst of the storm: Zion, his own watchtower and his people's refuge; while the third of them, looking far into the future, tells us, as it were, of the firm continent which shall rise out of the waters—Israel no longer a solitary lighthouse, *but in that day shall Israel be a third to Egypt and to Assyria, a blessing in the midst of the earth.* These three texts give us a summary of the meaning of all Isaiah's obscure prophecies to the foreign nations—a stormy ocean, a solitary rock in the midst of it, and the new continent that shall rise out of the waters about the rock.

The restlessness of Western Asia beneath the Assyrian rule (from 719, when Sargon's victory at Rafia extended that rule to the borders of Egypt) found vent, as we saw (p. 198), in two great Explosions, for both of which the mine was laid by Egyptian intrigue. The first Explosion happened in 711, and was confined to Ashdod. The second took place on Sargon's death in 705, and was universal. Till

Sennacherib marched south on Palestine in 701, there were all over Western Asia hurryings to and fro, consultations and intrigues, embassies and engineerings from Babylon to Meroe in far Ethiopia, and from the tents of Kedar to the cities of the Philistines. For these Jerusalem, the one inviolate capital from the Euphrates to the river of Egypt, was the natural centre. And the one far-seeing, steady-hearted man in Jerusalem was Isaiah. We have already seen that there was enough within the city to occupy Isaiah's attention, especially from 705 onward; but for Isaiah the walls of Jerusalem, dear as they were and thronged with duty, neither limited his sympathies nor marked the scope of the gospel he had to preach. Jerusalem is simply his watchtower. His field—and this is the peculiar glory of the prophet's later life—his field is the world.

How well fitted Jerusalem then was to be the world's watchtower, the traveller may see to this day. The city lies upon the great central ridge of Palestine, at an elevation of two thousand five hundred feet above the level of the sea. If you ascend the hill behind the city, you stand upon one of the great view-points of the earth. It is a forepost of Asia. To the east rise the red hills of Moab and the uplands of Gilead and Bashan, on to which wandering tribes of the Arabian deserts beyond still push their foremost camps. Just beyond the horizon lie the immemorial paths from Northern Syria into Arabia. Within a few hours' walk along the same central ridge, and still within the territory of Judah, you may see to the north, over a wilderness of blue hills, Hermon's snowy crest; you know that Damascus is lying just beyond, and that through it and round the base of Hermon swings one of the longest of the old world's highways—the main caravan road from the Euphrates to the Nile. Stand at gaze for a little, while down that road there sweep into your mind thoughts of the great empire, whose troops and commerce it used to carry. Then, bearing these thoughts with you, follow the line of the road across the hills to the western coastland, and so out upon the great Egyptian desert, where you may wait till it has brought you imagination of the southern empire to which it travels. Then, lifting your eyes a little further, let them sweep back again from south to north, and you have the whole of the west, the new world, open to you, across the fringe of yellow haze that marks the sands of the Mediterranean. It is even now one of the most comprehensive prospects in the world. But in Isaiah's day, when the world was smaller, the high places of Judah either revealed or suggested the whole of it.

But Isaiah was more than a spectator of this vast theatre. He was an actor upon it. The court of Judah, of which during Hezekiah's reign he was the most prominent member, stood in more or less close connection with the courts of all the kingdoms of Western Asia; and in those days when the nations were busy with intrigue against their common enemy this little highland town and fortress became a gathering place of peoples. From Babylon, from far-off Ethiopia, from Edom, from Philistia, and no doubt from many other places also, embassies came to King Hezekiah, or to inquire of his prophet. The appearance of some of them lives for us still in Isaiah's descriptions: *tall and shiny* figures of Ethiopians (xviii. 2), with whom we are able to identify the lithe, silky-skinned, shining-black bodies of the present tribes of the Upper Nile. Now the prophet must have talked much with these strangers, for he displays a knowledge of their several countries and ways of life that is full and accurate. The agricultural conditions of Egypt; her social ranks and her industries (xix.); the harbours and markets of Tyre (xxiii.); the caravans of the Arab nomads as in times of war they shun the open desert and seek the thickets (xxi. 14)—Isaiah paints these for us with a vivid realism. We see how this statesman of the least of States, this prophet of a religion which was confessed over only a few square miles, was aware of the wide world, and how he loved the life that filled it. They are no mere geographical terms with which Isaiah thickly studs these prophecies. He looks out upon, and paints for us, lands and cities surging with men—their trades, their castes, their religions, their besetting tempers and sins, their social structures and national policies, all quick and bending to the breeze and the shadow of the coming storm from the north.

We have said that in nothing is the regal power of our prophet's style so manifest as in the vast horizons, which, by the use of a few words, he calls up before us. Some of the finest of these revelations are made in this part of his book, so obscure and unknown to most. Who can ever forget those descriptions of Ethiopia in the eighteenth chapter?—"*Ah! the land of the rustling of wings, which borders on the rivers of Cush, which sendeth heralds on the sea, and in vessels of reed on the face of the waters! Travel, fleet messengers, to a people lithe and shining, to a nation feared from ever it began to be, a people strong, strong and trampling, whose land the rivers divide;* or of Tyre in chapter xxiii.?—"*And on great waters the seed of Shihor, the harvest of the Nile, was her revenue; and she was the mart of nations.* What expanses of sea! what fleets of ships! what floating loads of grain! what concourse of merchants moving on stately wharves beneath high warehouses!

Yet these are only segments of horizons, and perhaps the prophet reaches the height of his power of expression in the first of the three texts, which we have given as representative of his prophecies on foreign nations (p. 278). Here three or four lines of marvellous sound repeat the effect of the rage of the restless world as it rises, storms and breaks upon the steadfast will of God. The phonetics of the passage are wonderful. The general impression is that of a stormy ocean booming in to the shore and then crashing itself out into one long hiss of spray and foam upon its barriers. The details are noteworthy. In ver. 12 we have thirteen heavy M-sounds, besides two heavy B's, to five N's, five H's, and four sibilants. But in ver. 13 the sibilants predominate; and before the sharp rebuke of the Lord the great, booming sound of ver. 12 scatters out into a long *yish-shā 'oon*. The occasional use of a prolonged vowel amid so many hurrying consonants produces exactly the effect now of the lift of a storm swell out at sea and now of the pause of a great wave before it crashes on the shore. "*Ah, the booming of the peoples, the multitudes, like the booming of the seas they boom; and the rushing of the nations, like the rushing of the mighty waters they rush: nations, like the rushing of many waters they rush.* But He checketh it—a short, sharp word with a choke and a snort in it—*and it fleeth far away, and is chased like chaff on mountains before wind, and like swirling dust before a whirlwind.*

So did the rage of the world sound to Isaiah as it crashed into pieces upon the steadfast providence of God. To those who can feel the force of such language nothing need be added upon the prophet's view of the politics of the outside world these twenty years, whether portions of it threatened Judah in their own strength, or the whole power of storm that was in it rose with the Assyrian, as in all his flood he rushed upon Zion in the year 701.

2. But amid this storm Zion stands immovable. It is upon Zion that the storm crashes itself into impotence. This becomes explicit in the second of our representative texts: *What then shall one answer the messengers of a nation? That Jehovah hath founded Zion, and in her shall find a refuge the afflicted of His people* (xiv. 32). This oracle was drawn from Isaiah by an embassy of the Philistines. Stricken with panic at the Assyrian advance, they had sent messengers to Jerusalem, as other tribes did, with questions and proposals of defences, escapes and alliances. They got their answer. Alliances are useless. Everything human is going down. Here, here alone, is safety, because the LORD hath decreed it.

With what light and peace do Isaiah's words break out across that unquiet, hungry sea! How they tell the world for the first time, and have been telling it ever since, that, apart from all the struggle and strife of history, there is a refuge and security of men, which God Himself has assured. The troubled surface of life, nations heaving uneasily, kings of Assyria and their armies carrying the world before them—these are not all. The world and her powers are not all. Religion, in the very teeth of life, builds her refuge for the afflicted.

The world seems wholly divided between force and fear. Isaiah says, It is not true. Faith has her abiding citadel in the midst, a house of God, which neither force can harm nor fear enter.

This then was Isaiah's Interim-Answer to the Nations —Zion at least is secure for the people of Jehovah.

3. Isaiah could not remain content, however, with so narrow an interim-answer: Zion at least is secure, whatever happens to the rest of you. The world was there, and had to be dealt with and accounted for—had even to be saved. As we have already seen, this was the problem of Isaiah's generation; and to have shirked it would have meant the failure of his faith to rank as universal.

Isaiah did not shirk it. He said boldly to his people, and to the nations: "The faith we have covers this vaster life. Jehovah is not only God of Israel. He rules the world." These prophecies to the foreign nations are full of revelations of the sovereignty and providence of God. The Assyrian may seem to be growing in glory; but Jehovah is watching from the heavens, till he be ripe for cutting down (xviii. 4). Egypt's statesmen may be perverse and wilful; but Jehovah of hosts swingeth His hand against the land: *they shall tremble and shudder* (xix. 16). Egypt shall obey His purposes (17). Confusion may reign for a time, but a signal and a centre shall be lifted up, and the world gather itself in order round the revealed will of God. The audacity of such a claim for his God becomes more striking when we remember that Isaiah's faith was not the faith of a majestic or a conquering people. When he made his claim, Judah was still tributary to Assyria, a petty highland principality, that could not hope to stand by material means against the forces which had thrown down her more powerful neighbours. It was no experience of success, no mere instinct of being on the side of fate, which led Isaiah so resolutely to pronounce that not only should his people be secure, but that his God would vindicate His purposes upon empires like Egypt and Assyria. It was simply his sense that Jehovah was exalted in righteousness. Therefore, while inside Judah only the remnant that took the side of righteousness would be saved, outside Judah wherever there was unrighteousness, it would be rebuked, and wherever righteousness, it would be vindicated. This is the supremacy which Isaiah proclaimed for Jehovah over the whole world.

How spiritual this faith of Isaiah was, is seen from the next step the prophet took. Looking out on the troubled world, he did not merely assert that his God ruled it, but he emphatically said, what was a far more difficult thing to say, that it would all be consciously and willingly God's. God rules this, not to restrain it only, but to make it His own. The knowledge of Him, which is to-day our privilege, shall be to-morrow the blessing of the whole world.

When we point to the Jewish desire, so often expressed in the Old Testament, of making the whole world subject to Jehovah, we are told that it is simply a proof of religious ambition and jealousy. We are told that this wish to convert the world no more stamps the Jewish religion as being a universal, and therefore presumably a Divine, religion than the Mohammedans' zeal to force their tenets on men at the point of the sword is a proof of the truth of Islam.

Now we need not be concerned to defend the Jewish religion in its every particular, even as propounded by an Isaiah. It is an article of the Christian creed that Judaism was a minor and imperfect dispensation, where truth was only half revealed and virtue half developed. But at least let us do the Jewish religion justice; and we shall never do it justice till we pay attention to what its greatest prophets thought of the outside world, how they sympathized with this, and *in what way* they proposed to make it subject to their own faith.

Firstly then, there is something in the very manner of Isaiah's treatment of foreign nations, which causes the old charges of religious exclusiveness to sink in our throats. Isaiah treats these foreigners at least as men. Take his prophecies on Egypt or on Tyre or on Babylon —nations which were the hereditary enemies of his nation—and you find him speaking of their natural misfortunes, their social decays, their national follies and disasters, with the same pity and with the same purely moral considerations, with which he has treated his own land. When news of those far-away sorrows comes to Jerusalem, it moves this large-hearted prophet to mourning and tears. He breathes out to distant lands elegies as beautiful as he has poured upon Jerusalem. He shows as intelligent an interest in their social evolutions as he does in those of the Jewish State. He gives a picture of the industry and politics of Egypt as careful as his pictures of the fashions and statecraft of Judah. In short, as you read his prophecies upon foreign nations, you perceive that before the eyes of this man humanity, broken and scattered in his days as it was, rose up one great whole, every part of which was subject to the same laws of righteousness, and deserved from the prophet of God the same love and pity. To some few tribes he says decisively that they shall certainly be wiped out, but even them he does not address in contempt or in hatred. The large empire of Egypt, the great commercial power of Tyre, he speaks of in language of respect and admiration; but that does not prevent him from putting the plain issue to them which he put to his own countrymen: If you are unrighteous, intemperate, impure—lying diplomats and dishonest rulers, you shall certainly perish before Assyria. If you are righteous, temperate, pure, if you do trust in truth and God, nothing can move you.

But, *secondly*, he, who thus treated all nations with the same strict measures of justice and the same fulness of pity with which he treated his own, was surely not far from extending to the world the religious privileges, which he has so frequently identified with Jerusalem. In his old age, at least Isaiah looked forward to the time when the particular religious opportunities of the Jew should be the inheritance of humanity. For their old oppressor Egypt, for their new enemy Assyria, he anticipates the same experience and education, which has made Israel the firstborn of God. Speaking to Egypt, Isaiah concludes a missionary sermon, fit to take its place beside that which Paul uttered on the Areopagus to the younger Greek civilisation, with the words, *In that day shall Israel be a third to Egypt and to Assyria, a blessing in the midst of the earth, for that Jehovah of hosts hath blessed them, saying, Blessed be Egypt My people, and Assyria the work of My hands and Israel Mine inheritance.*

CHAPTER XVIII.

TYRE; OR, THE MERCENARY SPIRIT.

Isaiah xxiii. (702 B.C.).

THE task, which was laid upon the religion of Israel while Isaiah was its prophet, was the task, as we have often told ourselves, of facing the world's forces, and of explaining how they were to be led captive and contributory to the religion of the true God. And we have already seen Isaiah accounting for the largest of these forces: the Assyrian. But besides Assyria, that military empire, there was another power in the world, also novel to Israel's experience and also in Isaiah's day grown large enough to demand from Israel's faith explanation and criticism. This was Commerce, represented by the Phœnicians, with their chief seats at Tyre and Sidon, and their colonies across the seas. Not even Egypt exercised such influence on Isaiah's generation as Phœnicia did; and Phœnician influence, though less visible and painful than Assyrian, was just as much more subtle and penetrating as in these respects the influence of trade exceeds that of war. Assyria herself was fascinated by the glories of Phœnician commerce. The ambition of her kings, who had in that century pushed south to the Mediterranean, was to found a commercial empire. The mercenary spirit, as we learn from prophets earlier than Isaiah, had begun also to leaven the life of the agricultural and shepherd tribes of Western Asia. For good or for evil commerce had established itself as a moral force in the world. Isaiah's chapter on Tyre is, therefore, of the greatest interest. It contains the prophet's vision of commerce the first time commerce had grown vast enough to impress his people's imagination, as well as a criticism of the temper of commerce from the standpoint of the religion of the God of righteousness. Whether as a historical study or a message addressed to the mercantile tempers of our own day, the chapter is worthy of close attention.

But we must first impress ourselves with the utter contrast between Phœnicia and Judah in the matter of commercial experience, or we shall not feel the full force of this excursion which the prophet of a high, inland tribe of shepherds makes among the wharves and warehouses of the great merchant city on the sea.

The Phœnician empire, it has often been remarked, presents a very close analogy to that of Great Britain; but even more entirely than in the case of Great Britain the glory of that empire was the wealth of its trade, and the character of the people was the result of their mercantile habits. A little strip of land, one hundred and forty miles long, and never more than fifteen broad, with the sea upon one side and the mountains upon the other, compelled its inhabitants to become miners and seamen. The hills shut off the narrow coast from the continent to which it belongs, and drove the increasing populations to seek their destiny by way of the sea. These took to it kindly, for they had the Semite's born instinct for trading. Planting their colonies all round the Mediterranean, exploiting every mine within reach of the coastland, establishing great trading depôts both on the Nile and the Euphrates, with fleets that passed the Straits of Gibraltar into the Atlantic and the Straits of Bab-el-Mandeb into the Indian Ocean, the Phœnicians constructed a system of trade, which was not exceeded in range or influence till, more than two thousand years later, Portugal made the discovery of America and accomplished the passage of the Cape of Good Hope. From the coasts of Britain to those of Northwest India, and probably to Madagascar, was the extent of Phœnician credit and currency. Their trade tapped river basins so far apart as those of the Indus, the Euphrates, probably the Zambesi, the Nile, the Rhone, the Guadalquivir. They built ships and harbours for the Pharaohs and for Solomon. They carried Egyptian art and Babylonian knowledge to the Grecian archipelago, and brought back the metals of Spain and Britain. No wonder the prophet breaks into enthusiasm as he surveys Phœnician enterprise! *And on great waters the seed of Shihor, the harvest of the Nile, was her revenue; and she was the mart of nations.*

But upon trade the Phœnicians had built an empire. At home their political life enjoyed the freedom, energy and resources which are supplied by long habits of an extended commerce with other peoples. The constitution of the different Phœnician cities was not, as is sometimes supposed, republican, but monarchical; and the land belonged to the king. Yet the large number of wealthy families at once limited the power of the throne, and saved the commonwealth from being dependent upon the fortunes of a single dynasty. The colonies in close relation with the mother country assured an empire with its life in better circulation and with more reserve of power than either Egypt or

Assyria. Tyre and Sidon were frequently overthrown, but they rose again oftener than the other great cities of antiquity, and were still places of importance when Babylon and Nineveh lay in irreparable ruin. Besides their native families of royal wealth and influence and their flourishing colonies, each with its prince, these commercial States kept foreign monarchs in their pay, and sometimes determined the fate of a dynasty. Isaiah entitles Tyre *the giver of crowns, the maker of kings, whose merchants are princes, and her traffickers are the honourable of the earth.*

But trade with political results so splendid had an evil effect upon the character and spiritual temper of the people. By the indiscriminating ancients the Phœnicians were praised as inventors; the rudiments of most of the arts and sciences, of the alphabet and of money have been ascribed to them. But modern research has proved that of none of the many elements of civilisation which they introduced to the West were they the actual authors. The Phœnicians were simply carriers and middlemen. In all time there is no instance of a nation so wholly given over to buying and selling, who frequented even the battlefields of the world that they might strip the dead and purchase the captive. Phœnician history—though we must always do the people the justice to remember that we have their history only in fragments—affords few signs of the consciousness that there are things which a nation may strive after for their own sake, and not for the money they bring in. The world, which other peoples, still in the reverence of the religious youth of the race, regarded as a house of prayer, the Phœnicians had already turned into a den of thieves. They trafficked even with the mysteries and intelligences; and their own religion is largely a mixture of the religions of the other peoples, with whom they came into contact. The national spirit was venal and mercenary—the heart of an hireling, or, as Isaiah by a baser name describes it, the heart of *an harlot*. There is not throughout history a more perfect incarnation of the mercenary spirit than the Phœnician nation.

Now let us turn to the experience of the Jews, whose faith had to face and account for this world-force.

The history of the Jews in Europe has so identified them with trade that it is difficult for us to imagine a Jew free from its spirit or ignorant of its methods. But the fact is that in the time of Isaiah Israel was as little acquainted with commerce as it is possible for a civilised nation to be. Israel's was an inland territory. Till Solomon's reign the people had neither navy nor harbour. Their land was not abundant in materials for trade— it contained almost no minerals, and did not produce a greater supply of food than was necessary for the consumption of its inhabitants. It is true that the ambition of Solomon had brought the people within the temptations of commerce. He established trading cities, annexed harbours and hired a navy. But even then, and again in the reign of Uzziah, which reflects much of Solomon's commercial glory, Israel traded by deputies, and the mass of the people remained innocent of mercantile habits. Perhaps to moderns the most impressive proof of how little Israel had to do with trade is to be found in their laws of money-lending and of interest. The absolute prohibition which Moses placed upon the charging of interest could only have been possible among a people with the most insignificant commerce. To Isaiah himself commerce must have appeared alien. Human life, as he pictures it, is composed of war, politics and agriculture; his ideals for society are those of the shepherd and the farmer. We moderns cannot dissociate the future welfare of humanity from the triumphs of trade.

> " For I dipt into the future, far as human eye could see,
> Saw the vision of the world and all the wonder that would be;
> Saw the heavens fill with commerce, argosies of magic sails,
> Pilots of the purple twilight, dropping down with costly bales."

But all Isaiah's future is full of gardens and busy fields, of irrigating rivers and canals :—

Until the Spirit be poured upon us from on high, and the wilderness become a fruitful field, and the fruitful field be counted for a forest. . . . Blessed are ye, that sow beside all waters, that send forth the feet of the ox and the ass.

And He shall give the rain of thy seed, that thou shalt sow the ground withal, and bread-corn, the increase of the ground; and it shall be juicy and fat: in that day shall thy cattle feed in large pastures.

Conceive how trade looked to eyes which dwelt with enthusiasm upon scenes like these! It must have seemed to blast the future, to disturb the regularity of life with such violence as to shake religion herself! With all our convictions of the benefits of trade, even we feel no greater regret or alarm than when we observe the invasion by the rude forces of trade of some scene of rural felicity: blackening of sky and earth and stream; increasing complexity and entanglement of life; enormous growth of new problems and temptations; strange knowledge, ambitions and passions, that throb through life and strain the tissue of its simple constitution, like novel engines, which shake the ground and the strong walls, accustomed once to re-echo only the simple music of the mill-wheel and the weaver's shuttle. Isaiah did not fear an invasion of Judah by the habits and the machines of trade. There is no foreboding in this chapter of the day when his own people were to take the place of the Phœnicians as the commercial *harlots* of the world, and a Jew was to be synonymous with usurer and *publican*. Yet we may employ our feelings to imagine his, and understand what this prophet—seated in the sanctuary of a pastoral and agricultural tribe, with its simple offerings of doves, and lambs and sheaves of corn, telling how their homes, and fields and whole rustic manner of life were subject to God—thought, and feared, and hoped of the vast commerce of Phœnicia, wondering how it also should be sanctified to Jehovah.

First of all, Isaiah, as we might have expected from his large faith and broad sympathies, accepts and acknowledges this great world-force. His noble spirit shows neither timidity nor jealousy before it. Before his view what an unblemished prospect of it spreads! His descriptions tell more of his appreciation than long laudations would have done. He grows enthusiastic upon the grandeur of Tyre; and even when he prophesies that Assyria shall destroy it, it is with the feeling that such a destruction is really a desecration, and as if there lived essential glory in great commercial enterprise. Certainly from such a spirit we have much to learn. How often has religion, when brought face to face with the new forces of a generation—commerce, democracy or science—shown either a base timidity or baser jealousy, and met the innovations with cries of detraction or despair! Isaiah reads a lesson to the modern Church in the preliminary spirit with which she should meet the novel experiences of Providence. Whatever judgement may afterwards have to be passed, there is the immediate duty of frankly recognising greatness wherever it may occur. This is an essential principle, from the forgetfulness of which modern religion has suffered much. Nothing is gained by attempting to minimise new departures in the world's history; but everything is lost if we sit down in fear of them. It is a duty we owe to ourselves, and a worship which Providence demands from us, that we ungrudgingly appreciate every magnitude of which history brings us the knowledge.

It is almost an unnecessary task to apply Isaiah's meaning to the commerce of our own day. But let us not miss his example in this: that the right to criticise the habits of trade and the ability to criticise them healthily are alone won by a just appreciation of trade's world-wide glory and serviceableness. There is no use preaching against the venal spirit and manifold temptations and degradations of trade, until we have realised the indispensableness of trade and its capacity for disciplining and exalting its ministers. The only way to correct the abuses of "the commercial spirit," against which many in our day are loud with indiscriminate rebuke, is to impress its victims, having first impressed yourself, with the opportunities and the ideals of commerce. A thing is great partly by its traditions and partly by its opportunities—partly by what it has accomplished and partly by the doors of serviceableness of which it holds the key. By either of these standards the magnitude of commerce is simply overwhelming. Having discovered the world-forces, commerce has built thereon the most powerful of our modern empires. Its exigencies compel peace; its resources are the sinews of war. If it has not always preceded religion and science in the conquest of the globe, it has shared with them their triumphs. Commerce has recast the modern world, so that we hardly think of the old national divisions in the greater social classes which have been its direct creation. Commerce determines national policies; its markets are among the schools of statesmen; its merchants *are* still *princes, and its traffickers the honourable of the earth.*

Therefore let all merchants and their apprentices believe, "Here is something worth putting our manhood into, worth living for, not with our brains only or our appetites, but with our conscience, with our imagination, with every curiosity and sympathy of our nature. Here is a calling with a healthy discipline, with a free spirit, with unrivalled opportunities of service, with an ancient and essential dignity." The reproach which is so largely imagined upon trade is the relic of a barbarous age. Do not tolerate it, for under its shadow, as under other artificial and unhealthy contempts of society, there are apt to grow up those sordid and slavish tempers, which soon make men deserve the reproach that was at first unjustly cast upon them. Dissipate the base influence of this reproach by lifting the imagination upon the antiquity and worldwide opportunities of trade—trade, *whose origin,* as Isaiah so finely puts it, *is of ancient days; and her feet carry her afar off to sojourn.*

So generous an appreciation of the grandeur of commerce does not prevent Isaiah from exposing its besetting sin and degradation.

The vocation of a merchant differs from others in this, that there is no inherent nor instinctive obligation in it to ends higher than those of financial profit—emphasized in our days into the more dangerous constraint of *immediate* financial profit. No profession is of course absolutely free from the risk of this servitude; but other professions offer escapes, or at least mitigations, which are not possible to nearly the same extent in trade. Artist, artisan, preacher and statesman have ideals which generally act contrary to the compulsion of profit and tend to create a nobility of mind strong enough to defy it. They have given, so to speak, hostages to heaven—ideals of beauty, of accurate scholarship or of moral influence, which they dare not risk by abandoning themselves to the hunt for gain. But the calling of a merchant is not thus safeguarded. It does not afford those visions, those occasions of being caught away to the heavens, which are the inherent glories of other lives. The habits of trade make this the first thought—not what things of beauty are in themselves, not what men are as brothers, not what life is as God's discipline, but what things of beauty, and men and opportunities are worth to us—and in these times what they are *immediately* worth —as measured by money. In such an absorption art, humanity, morals and religion become matters of growing indifference.

To this spirit, which treats all things and men, high or low, as matters simply of profit, Isaiah gives a very ugly name. We call it the mercenary or venal spirit. Isaiah says it is the spirit of *the harlot*.

The history of Phœnicia justified his words. To-day we remember her by nothing that is great, by nothing that is original. She left no art nor literature, and her once brave and skilful populations degenerated till we know them only as the slave-dealers, panders and prostitutes of the Roman empire. If we desire to find Phœnicia's influence on the religion of the world, we have to seek for it among the most sensual of Greek myths and the abominable practices of Corinthian worship. With such terrible literalness was Isaiah's harlot-curse fulfilled.

What is true of Phœnicia may become true of Britain,

and what has been seen on the large scale of a nation is exemplified every day in individual lives. The man who is entirely eaten up with the zeal of gain is no better than what Isaiah called Tyre. He has prostituted himself to covetousness. If day and night our thoughts are of profit, and the habit, so easily engendered in these times, of asking only, "What can I make of this?" is allowed to grow upon us, it shall surely come to pass that we are found sacrificing, like the poor unfortunate, the most sacred of our endowments and affections for gain, demeaning our natures at the feet of the world for the sake of the world's gold. A woman sacrifices her purity for coin, and the world casts her out. But some who would not touch her have sacrificed honour and love and pity for the same base wage, and in God's sight are no better than she. Ah, how much need is there for these bold, brutal standards of the Hebrew prophet to correct our own social misappreciations!

Now for a very vain delusion upon this subject! It is often imagined in our day that if a man seek atonement for the venal spirit through the study of art, through the practice of philanthropy or through the cultivation of religion, he shall surely find it. This is false—plausible and often practised but utterly false. Unless a man see and reverence beauty in the very workshop and office of his business, unless he feel those whom he meets there, his employés and customers, as his brethren, unless he keep his business methods free from fraud, and honestly recognise his gains as a trust from the Lord, then no amount of devotion elsewhere to the fine arts, nor perseverance in philanthropy, nor fondness for the Church evinced by ever so large subscriptions, will deliver him from the devil of mercenariness. That is a plea of *alibi* that shall not prevail on the judgement day. He is only living a double life, whereof his art, philanthropy or religion is the occasional and dilettante portion, with not nearly so much influence on his character as the other, his calling and business, in which he still sacrifices love to gain. His real world—the world in which God set him, to buy and sell indeed, but also to serve and glorify his God—he is treating only as a big warehouse and exchange. And so much is this the case at the present day, in spite of all the worship of art and religion which is fashionable in mercantile circles, that we do not go too far when we say that if Jesus were now to visit our large markets and manufactories, in which the close intercourse of numbers of human persons renders the opportunities of service and testimony to God so frequent, He would scourge men from them, as He scourged the traffickers of the Temple, for that they had forgotten that *here* was their Father's house, where their brethren had to be owned and helped, and their Father's glory revealed to the world.

A nation with such a spirit was of course foredoomed to destruction. Isaiah predicts the absolute disappearance of Tyre from the attention of the world. *Tyre shall be forgotten seventy years.* *Then*, like some poor unfortunate whose day of beauty is past, she shall in vain practise her old advertisements on men. *After the end of seventy years it shall be unto Tyre as in the song of the harlot: Take an harp, go about the city, thou harlot that hast been forgotten; make sweet melody, sing many songs, that thou mayest be remembered.*

But Commerce is essential to the world. Tyre must revive; and the prophet sees her revive as the minister of Religion, the purveyor of the food of the servants of the Lord, and of the accessories of their worship. It must be confessed, that we are not a little shocked when we find Isaiah continuing to apply to Commerce his metaphor of a harlot, even after Commerce has entered the service of the true religion. He speaks of her wages being devoted to Jehovah, just in the same manner as those of certain notorious women of heathen temples were devoted to the idol of the temple. This is even against the directions of the Mosaic law. Isaiah, however, was a poet; and in his flights we must not expect him to carry the whole Law on his back. He was a poet, and probably no analogy would have more vividly appealed to his Oriental audience. It will be foolish to allow our natural prejudice against what we may feel to be the unhealthiness of the metaphor to blind us to the magnificence of the thought which he clothes in it.

All this is another proof of the sanity and far sight of our prophet. Again we find that his conviction that judgement is coming does not render his spirit morbid, nor disturb his eye for things of beauty and profit in the world. Commerce, with all her faults, is essential, and must endure, nay shall prove in the days to come Religion's most profitable minister. The generosity and wisdom of this passage are the more striking when we remember the extremity of unrelieved denunciation to which other great teachers of religion have allowed themselves to be hurled by their rage against the sins of trade. But Isaiah, in the largest sense of the expression, is a man of the world—a man of the world because God made the world and rules it. Yet even from his far sight was hidden the length to which in the last days Commerce would carry her services to man and God, proving as she has done, under the flag of another Phœnicia, to all the extent of Isaiah's longing, one of Religion's most sincere and profitable handmaids.

BOOK IV.

JERUSALEM AND SENNACHERIB, 701 B.C.

Isaiah:—
  xxxvi. 1.   Early in 701.
  i.   ,,   ,,
  xxii.   ,,   ,,
  xxxiii.   A little later.
  xxxvi. 2—xxxvii.   ,,   ,,
  ——————
  xxxviii.—xxxix. Date uncertain.

BOOK IV.

INTO this fourth book we put all the rest of the prophecies of the Book of Isaiah, that have to do with the prophet's own time: chaps. i., xxii. and xxxiii., with the narrative in xxxvi., xxxvii. All these refer to the only Assyrian invasion of Judah and siege of Jerusalem: that undertaken by Sennacherib in 701.

It is, however, right to remember once more, that many authorities maintain that there were two Assyrian invasions of Judah—one by Sargon in 711, the other by Sennacherib in 701—and that chaps. i. and xxii. (as well as x. 5—34) belong to the former of these. The theory is ingenious and tempting; but, in the silence of the Assyrian annals about any invasion of Judah by Sargon, it is impossible to adopt it. And although chaps. i. and xxii. differ very greatly in tone from chap. xxxiii., yet to account for the difference it is not necessary to suppose two different invasions, with a considerable period between them. Virtually, as will appear in the course of our exposition, Sennacherib's invasion of Judah was a double one.

1. The first time Sennacherib's army invaded Judah they took all the fenced cities, and probably invested Jerusalem, but withdrew on payment of tribute and the surrender of the *casus belli*, the Assyrian vassal Padi, whom the Ekronites had deposed and given over to the

keeping of Hezekiah. To this invasion refer Isa. i., xxii. and the first verse of xxxvi.: *Now it came to pass in the fourteenth* year of King Hezekiah that Sennacherib, King of Assyria, came up against all the fenced cities of Judah and took them.* This verse is the same as 2 Kings xviii. 13, to which, however, there is added in vv. 14—16 an account of the tribute sent by Hezekiah to Sennacherib at Lachish, that is not included in the narrative in Isaiah. Compare 2 Chron. xxxii. 1.

2. But scarcely had the tribute been paid when Sennacherib, himself advancing to meet Egypt, sent back upon Jerusalem a second army of investment, with which was the Rabshakeh; and this was the army that so mysteriously disappeared from the eyes of the besieged. To the treacherous return of the Assyrians and the sudden deliverance of Jerusalem from their grasp refer Isa. xxxiii., xxxvi. 2—xxxvii., with the fuller and evidently original narrative in 2 Kings xviii. 17—xix. Compare 2 Chron. xxxii. 9—23.

To the history of this double attempt upon Jerusalem in 701—xxxvi. and xxxvii.—there has been appended in xxxviii. and xxxix. an account of Hezekiah's illness and of an embassy to him from Babylon. These events probably happened some years before Sennacherib's invasion. But it will be most convenient for us to take

---

* It is confusing to find this date attached to Sennacherib's invasion of 701, unless, with one or two critics, we place Hezekiah's accession in 715. But Hezekiah acceded in 728 or 727, and 701 would therefore be his twenty-sixth or twenty-seventh year. Mr. Cheyne, who takes 727 as the year of Hezekiah's accession, gets out of the difficulty by reading "Sargon" for "Sennacherib" in this verse and in 2 Kings xiii., and thus secures another reference to that invasion of Judah, which he supposes to have taken place under Sargon between 712 and 710. By the change of a letter some would read *twenty-fourth* for *fourteenth*. But in any case this date is confusing.

them in the order in which they stand in the canon. They will naturally lead us up to a question that it is necessary we should discuss before taking leave of Isaiah—whether this great prophet of the endurance of the kingdom of God upon earth had any gospel for the individual who dropped away from it into death.

CHAPTER XIX.

AT THE LOWEST EBB.

ISAIAH i. and xxii. (701 B.C.).

IN the drama of Isaiah's life we have now arrived at the final act—a short and sharp one of a few months. The time is 701 B.C., the fortieth year of Isaiah's ministry, and about the twenty-sixth of Hezekiah's reign. The background is the invasion of Palestine by Sennacherib. The stage itself is the city of Jerusalem. In the clear atmosphere before the bursting of the storm Isaiah has looked round the whole world—his world—uttering oracles on the nations from Tyre to Egypt and from Ethiopia to Babylon. But now the Assyrian storm has burst, and all except the immediate neighbourhood of the prophet is obscured. From Jerusalem Isaiah will not again lift his eyes.

The stage is thus narrow and the time short, but the action one of the most critical in the history of Israel, taking rank with the Exodus from Egypt and the Return from Babylon. To Isaiah himself it marks the summit of his career. For half a century Zion has been preparing for, forgetting and again preparing for, her first and final struggle with the Assyrian. Now she is to meet her foe, face to face across her own walls. For forty years Isaiah has predicted for the Assyrian an uninterrupted path of conquest to the very gates of Jerusalem, but certain check and confusion there. Sennacherib has overrun the world, and leaps upon Zion. The Jewish nation await their fate, Isaiah his vindication, and the credit of Israel's religion, one of the most extraordinary tests to which a spiritual faith was ever subjected.

In the end, by the mysterious disappearance of the Assyrian, Jerusalem was saved, the prophet was left with his remnant and the future still open for Israel. But at the beginning of the end such an issue was by no means probable. Jewish panic and profligacy almost prevented the Divine purpose, and Isaiah went near to breaking his heart over the city, for whose redemption he had travailed for a lifetime. He was as sure as ever that this redemption must come, but a collapse of the people's faith and patriotism at the eleventh hour made its coming seem worthless. Jerusalem appeared bent on forestalling her deliverance by moral suicide. Despair, not of God but of the city, settled on Isaiah's heart; and in such a mood he wrote chap. xxii. We may entitle it therefore, though written at a time when the tide should have been running to the full, "At the Lowest Ebb."

We have thus stated at the outset the motive of this chapter, because it is one of the most unexpected and startling of all Isaiah's prophecies. In it "we can discern precipices." Beneath our eyes, long lifted by the prophet to behold a future *stretching very far forth*, this chapter suddenly yawns, a pit of blackness. For utterness of despair and the absolute sentence which it passes on the citizens of Zion we have had nothing like it from Isaiah since the evil days of Ahaz. The historical portions of the Bible which cover this period are not cleft by such a crevasse, and of course the official Assyrian annals, full as they are of the details of Sennacherib's campaign in Palestine, know nothing of the moral condition of Jerusalem.* Yet if we put the Hebrew and Assyrian narratives together, and compare them with chaps. i. and xxii. of Isaiah, we may be sure that the following was something like the course of events which led down to this woeful depth in Judah's experience.

In a Syrian campaign Sennacherib's path was plain —to begin with the Phœnician cities, march quickly south by the level coastland, subduing the petty chieftains upon it, meet Egypt at its southern end, and then, when he had rid himself of his only formidable foe, turn to the more delicate task of warfare among the hills of Judah—a campaign which he could scarcely undertake with a hostile force like Egypt on his flank. This course, he tells us, he followed. "In my third campaign, to the land of Syria I went. Luliah (Elulæus), King of Sidon—for the fearful splendour of my majesty overwhelmed him—fled to a distant spot in the midst of the sea. His land I entered." City after city fell to the invader. The princes of Aradus, Byblus and Ashdod, by the coast, and even Moab and Edom, far inland, sent him their submission. He attacked Ascalon, and captured its king. He went on, and took the Philistine cities of Beth-dagon, Joppa, Barka and Azor, all of them within forty miles of Jerusalem, and some even visible from her neighbourhood. South of this group, and a little over twenty-five miles from Jerusalem, lay Ekron; and

---

* *Records of the Past*, i. 33 ff. vii.; Schrader's *Cuneiform Inscriptions and the Old Testament* (Whitehouse's translation).

here Sennacherib had so good a reason for anger, that the inhabitants, expecting no mercy at his hands, prepared a stubborn defence.

Ten years before this Sargon had set Padi, a vassal of his own, as king over Ekron; but the Ekronites had risen against Padi, put him in chains, and sent him to their ally Hezekiah, who now held him in Jerusalem. "These men," says Sennacherib, "were now terrified in their hearts; the shadows of death overwhelmed them."* Before Ekron was reduced, however, the Egyptian army arrived in Philistia, and Sennacherib had to abandon the siege for these arch-enemies. He defeated them in the neighbourhood, at Eltekeh, returned to Ekron, and completed its siege. Then, while he himself advanced southwards in pursuit of the Egyptians, he detached a corps, which, marching eastwards through the mountain passes, overran all Judah and threatened Jerusalem. "And Hezekiah, King of Judah, who had not bowed down at my feet, forty-six of his strong cities, his castles and the smaller towns in their neighbourhood beyond number, by casting down ramparts and by open attack, by battle—*zuk*, of the feet; *nisi*, hewing to pieces and casting down (?)—I besieged, I captured.... He himself, like a bird in a cage, inside Jerusalem, his royal city, I shut him up; siege-towers against him I constructed, for he had given command to renew the bulwarks of the great gate of his city."† But Sennacherib does not say that he took Jerusalem, and simply closes the narrative of his campaign with the account of large tribute which Hezekiah sent after him to Nineveh.

---

* *Records of the Past*, i. 38; vii. 62.
† *Ibid.*, i., 40; Schrader, i., 286.

Here, then, we have material for a graphic picture of Jerusalem and her populace, when chaps. i. and xxii. were uttered by Isaiah.

At Jerusalem we are within a day's journey of any part of the territory of Judah. We feel the kingdom throb to its centre at Assyria's first footfall on the border. The nation's life is shuddering in upon its capital, couriers dashing up with the first news; fugitives hard upon them; palace, arsenal, market and temple thrown into commotion; the politicians busy; the engineers hard at work completing the fortifications, leading the suburban wells to a reservoir within the walls, levelling every house and tree outside which could give shelter to the besiegers, and heaping up the material on the ramparts, till there lies nothing but a great, bare, waterless circle round a high-banked fortress. Across this bareness the lines of fugitives streaming to the gates; provincial officials and their retinues; soldiers whom Hezekiah had sent out to meet the foe, returning without even the dignity of defeat upon them; husbandmen, with cattle and remnants of grain in disorder; women and children; the knaves, cowards and helpless of the whole kingdom pouring their fear, dissoluteness and disease into the already-unsettled populace of Jerusalem. Inside the walls opposing political factions and a weak king; idle crowds, swaying to every rumour and intrigue; the ordinary restraints and regularities of life suspended, even patriotism gone with counsel and courage, but in their place fear and shame and greed of life. Such was the state in which Jerusalem faced the hour of her visitation.

Gradually the Visitant came near over the thirty miles which lay between the capital and the border.

Signs of the Assyrian advance were given in the sky, and night after night the watchers on Mount Zion, seeing the glare in the west, must have speculated which of the cities of Judah was being burned. Clouds of smoke across the heavens from prairie and forest fires told how war, even if it passed, would leave a trail of famine ; and men thought with breaking hearts of the villages and fields, heritage of the tribes of old, that were now bare to the foot and the fire of the foreigner. *Your country is desolate; your cities are burned with fire; your land, strangers devour it in your presence, and it is desolate as the overthrow of strangers. And the daughter of Zion is left as a booth in a vineyard, as a lodge in a garden of cucumbers. Except Jehovah of hosts had left unto us a very small remnant, we should have been as Sodom, we should have been like unto Gomorrah.* * Then came touch of the enemy, the appearance of armed bands, vistas down Jerusalem's favourite valleys of chariots, squadrons of horsemen emerging upon the plateaus to north and west of the city, heavy siege-towers and swarms of men innumerable. *And Elam bare the quiver, with troops of men and horsemen; and Kir uncovered the shield.* At last they saw their fears of fifty years face to face ! Far-away names were standing by their gates, actual bowmen and flashing shields ! As Jerusalem gazed upon the terrible Assyrian armaments, how many of her inhabitants remembered Isaiah's words delivered a generation before !—*Behold, they shall come with speed swiftly; none shall be weary or stumble among them; neither shall the string of their loins be lax nor the latchet of their shoes be broken; whose arrows*

---

* Chap. i. 7—9.

are sharp, and all their bows bent; their horses' hoofs shall be counted like flint, and their wheels like a whirlwind; their roaring shall be like a lion: they shall roar like young lions. For all this His anger is not turned away, but His hand is stretched out still.

There were, however, two supports, on which that distracted populace within the walls still steadied themselves. The one was the Temple-worship, the other the Egyptian alliance.

History has many remarkable instances of peoples betaking themselves in the hour of calamity to the energetic discharge of the public rites of religion. But such a resort is seldom, if ever, a real moral conversion. It is merely physical nervousness, apprehension for life, clutching at the one thing within reach that feels solid, which it abandons as soon as panic has passed. When the crowds in Jerusalem betook themselves to the Temple, with unwonted wealth of sacrifice, Isaiah denounced this as hypocrisy and futility. *To what purpose is the multitude of your sacrifices unto Me? saith Jehovah. . . . I am weary to bear them. And when ye spread forth your hands, I will hide Mine eyes from you; yea, when ye make many prayers, I will not hear* (i. 11—15).

Isaiah might have spared his scornful orders to the people to desist from worship. Soon afterwards they abandoned it of their own will, but from motives very different from those urged by him. The second support to which Jerusalem clung was the Egyptian alliance—the pet project of the party then in power. They had carried it to a successful issue, taunting Isaiah with their success.* He had continued to

---

* See p. 238.

denounce it, and now the hour was approaching when their cleverness and confidence were to be put to the test. It was known in Jerusalem that an Egyptian army was advancing to Sennacherib, and politicians and people awaited the encounter with anxiety.

We are aware what happened. Egypt was beaten at Eltekeh; the alliance was stamped a failure; Jerusalem's last worldly hope was taken from her. When the news reached the city, something took place, of which our moral judgement tells us more than any actual record of facts. The Government of Hezekiah gave way; the rulers, whose courage and patriotism had been identified with the Egyptian alliance, lost all hope for their country, and fled, as Isaiah puts it, *en masse* (xxii. 3). There was no battle, no defeat at arms (*id.* 2, 3); but the Jewish State collapsed.

Then, when the last material hope of Judah fell, fell her religion too. The Egyptian disappointment, while it drove the rulers out of their false policies, drove the people out of their unreal worship. What had been a city of devotees became in a moment a city of revellers. Formerly all had been sacrifices and worship, but now feasting and blasphemy. *Behold, joy and gladness, slaying oxen and killing sheep, eating flesh and drinking wine: Let us eat and drink, for to-morrow we die* (*id.* 13. The reference of ver. 12 is probably to chap. i.).

Now all Isaiah's ministry had been directed just against these two things: the Egyptian alliance and the purely formal observance of religion—trust in the world and trust in religiousness. And together both of these had given way, and the Assyrian was at the gates. Truly it was the hour of Isaiah's vindication. Yet— and this is the tragedy—it had come too late. The prophet could not use it. The two things he said would collapse had collapsed, but for the people there seemed now no help to be justified from the thing which he said would remain. What was the use of the city's deliverance, when the people themselves had failed! The feelings of triumph, which the prophet might have expressed, were swallowed up in unselfish grief over the fate of his wayward and abandoned Jerusalem.

What aileth thee now—and in these words we can hear the old man addressing his fickle child, whose changefulness by this time he knew so well—*what aileth thee now that thou art wholly gone up to the house-tops*—we see him standing at his door watching this ghastly holiday—*O thou that art full of shoutings, a tumultuous city, a joyous town?* What are you rejoicing at in such an hour as this, when you have not even the bravery of your soldiers to celebrate, when you are without that pride which has brought songs from the lips of a defeated people as they learned that their sons had fallen with their faces to the foe, and has made even the wounds of the dead borne through the gate lips of triumph, calling to festival! *For thy slain are not slain with the sword, neither are they dead in battle.*

> *All thy chiefs fled in heaps;*
> *Without bow they were taken:*
> *All thine that were found were taken in heaps;*
> *From far had they run.*
> *Wherefore I say, Look away from me;*
> *Let me make bitterness bitterer by weeping.*
> *Press not to comfort me*
> *For the ruin of the daughter of my people.*

Urge not your mad holiday upon me! *For a day of discomfiture and of breaking and of perplexity hath the Lord, Jehovah of hosts, in the valley of vision, a breaking down of the wall and a crying to the mountain.* These few words of prose, which follow the pathetic elegy, have a finer pathos still. The cumulative force of the successive clauses is very impressive: *disappointment* at the eleventh hour; the sense of a being *trampled* and overborne by sheer brute force; the counsels, courage, hope and faith of fifty years crushed to blank *perplexity,* and all this from Himself—*the Lord, Jehovah of hosts*—in the very *valley of vision,* the home of prophecy; as if He had meant of purpose to destroy these long confidences of the past on the floor where they had been wrestled for and asserted, and not by the force of the foe, but by the folly of His own people, to make them ashamed. The last clause crashes out the effect of it all; every spiritual rampart and refuge torn down, there is nothing left but an appeal to the hills to fall and cover us—*a breaking down of the wall and a crying to the mountain.*

On the brink of the precipice, Isaiah draws back for a moment, to describe with some of his old fire the appearance of the besiegers (vv. 6—8*a*). And this suggests what kind of preparation Jerusalem had made for her foe—every kind, says Isaiah, but the supreme one. The arsenal, Solomon's *forest-house,* with its cedar pillars, had been looked to (ver. 8), the fortifications inspected and increased, and the suburban waters brought within them (vv. 9—11*a*). *But ye looked not unto Him that had done this,* who had brought this providence upon you; *neither had ye respect unto Him that fashioned it long ago,* whose own plan it had been. To your alliances and fortifications you fled in the hour of calamity, but not to Him in whose guidance the course of calamity lay. And therefore, when your engineering and diplomacy failed you, your religion vanished with them. *In that day did the Lord, Jehovah of hosts, call to weeping, and to mourning, and to baldness, and to girding with sackcloth; but, behold, joy and gladness, slaying oxen and killing sheep, eating flesh and drinking wine: Let us eat and drink, for to-morrow we shall die.* It was the dropping of the mask. For half a century this people had worshipped God, but they had never trusted Him beyond the limits of their treaties and their bulwarks. And so when their allies were defeated, and their walls began to tremble, their religion, bound up with these things, collapsed also; they ceased even to be men, crying like beasts, *Let us eat and drink, for to-morrow we die.* For such a state of mind Isaiah will hold out no promise; it is the sin against the Holy Ghost, and for it there is no forgiveness. *And Jehovah of hosts revealed Himself in mine ears. Surely this iniquity shall not be purged from you till ye die, saith the Lord, Jehovah of hosts.*

Back forty years the word had been, *Go and tell this people, Hear ye indeed, but understand not; and see ye indeed, but perceive not. Make the heart of this people fat, and make their ears heavy, and shut their eyes, lest they see with their eyes, and hear with their ears, and understand with their heart, and turn again and be healed.* What happened now was only what was foretold then: *And if there be yet a tenth in it, it shall again be for consumption.* That radical revision of judgement was now being literally fulfilled, when Isaiah, sure at last of his remnant within the walls of Jerusalem, was forced for their sin to condemn even them to death.

Nevertheless, Isaiah had still respect to the ultimate survival of a remnant. How firmly he believed in it could not be more clearly illustrated than by the fact that when he had so absolutely devoted his fellow-citizens to destruction he also took the most practical means for securing a better political future. If there is any reason, it can only be this, for putting the second section of chap. xxii., which advocates a change of ministry in the city (vv. 15—22), so close to the first, which sees ahead nothing but destruction for the State (vv. 1—14).

The *mayor of the palace* at this time was one Shebna, also called *minister* or *deputy* (lit. *friend* of the king). That his father is not named implies perhaps that Shebna was a foreigner; his own name betrays a Syrian origin; and he has been justly supposed to be the leader of the party then in power, whose policy was the Egyptian alliance, and whom in these latter years Isaiah had so frequently denounced as the root of Judah's bitterness. To this unfamilied intruder, who had sought to establish himself in Jerusalem, after the manner of those days, by hewing himself a great sepulchre, Isaiah brought sentence of violent banishment: *Behold, Jehovah will be hurling, hurling thee away, thou big man, and crumpling, crumpling thee together. He will roll, roll thee on, thou rolling-stone, like a ball* thrown out *on broad level ground; there shalt thou die, and there shall be the chariots of thy glory, thou shame of the house of thy lord. And I thrust thee from thy post, and from thy station do they pull thee down.* This vagabond was not to die in his bed, nor to be gathered in his big tomb to the people on whom he had foisted himself. He should continue a *rolling-stone*. For him, like Cain, there was a land of Nod; and upon it he was to find a vagabond's death.

To fill this upstart's place, Isaiah solemnly designated a man with a father: Eliakim, the son of Hilkiah. The formulas he uses are perhaps the official ones customary upon induction to an office. But it may be also, that Isaiah has woven into these some expressions of even greater promise than usual. For this change of office-bearers was critical, and the overthrow of the "party of action" meant to Isaiah the beginning of the blessed future. *And it shall come to pass that in that day I will call My servant Eliakim, the son of Hilkiah; and I will clothe him with thy robe, and with thy girdle will I strengthen him, and thine administration will I give into his hand, and he shall be for a father to the inhabitant of Jerusalem and to the house of Judah. And I will set the key of the house of David upon his shoulder; and he shall open, and none shut: and he shall shut, and none open. And I will hammer him in, a nail in a firm place, and he shall be for a throne of glory to his father's house.* Thus to the last Isaiah will not allow Shebna to forget that he is without root among the people of God, that he has neither father nor family.

But a family is a temptation, and the weight of it may drag even the man of the Lord's own hammering out of his place. This very year we find Eliakim in Shebna's post,[*] and Shebna reduced to be secretary; but Eliakim's family seem to have taken advantage of their relative's position, and either at the time he was designated, or more probably later, Isaiah wrote two sentences of warning upon the dangers of nepotism. Catching at the figure, with which his designation of Eliakim closed, that Eliakim would be a peg in a solid wall, a throne on which the glory of his father's house might settle, Isaiah reminds

---

[*] Isa. xxxvi. 3.

the much-encumbered statesman that the firmest peg will give way if you hang too much on it, the strongest man be pulled down by his dependent and indolent family. *They shall hang upon him all the weight of his father's house, the scions and the offspring* (terms contrasted as degrees of worth), *all the little vessels, from the vessels of cups to all the vessels of flagons. In that day, saith Jehovah of hosts, shall the peg that was knocked into a firm place give way, and it shall be knocked out and fall, and down shall be cut the burden that was upon it, for Jehovah hath spoken.*

So we have not one, but a couple of tragedies. Eliakim, the son of Hilkiah, follows Shebna, the son of Nobody. The fate of the overburdened nail is as grievous as that of the rolling stone. It is easy to pass this prophecy over as a trivial incident; but when we have carefully analysed each verse, restored to the words their exact shade of signification, and set them in their proper contrasts, we perceive the outlines of two social dramas, which it requires very little imagination to invest with engrossing moral interest.

CHAPTER XX.

THE TURN OF THE TIDE: MORAL EFFECTS OF FORGIVENESS.

ISAIAH xxii., contrasted with xxxiii. (701 B.C.).

THE collapse of Jewish faith and patriotism in the face of the enemy was complete. Final and absolute did Isaiah's sentence ring out: *Surely this iniquity shall not be purged from you till ye die, saith Jehovah of hosts.* So we learn from chap. xxii., written, as we conceive, in 701, when the Assyrian armies had at last invested Jerusalem. But in chap. xxxiii., which critics unite in placing a few months later in the same year, Isaiah's tone is entirely changed. He hurls the woe of the Lord upon the Assyrians; confidently announces their immediate destruction; turns, while the whole city's faith hangs upon him, in supplication to the Lord; and announces the stability of Jerusalem, her peace, her glory and the forgiveness of all her sins. It is this great moral difference between chaps. xxii. and xxxiii.—prophecies that must have been delivered within a few months of each other —which this chapter seeks to expound.

In spite of her collapse, as pictured in chap. xxii., Jerusalem was not taken. Her rulers fled; her people, as if death were certain, betook themselves to dissipation; and yet the city did not fall into the hands of the Assyrian. Sennacherib himself does not pretend to have taken

Jerusalem. He tells us how closely he invested Jerusalem, but he does not add that he took it, a silence which is the more significant that he records the capture of every other town which his armies attempted. He says that Hezekiah offered him tribute, and details the amount he received. He adds that the tribute was not paid at Jerusalem (as it would have been had Jerusalem been conquered), but that for " the payment of the tribute and the performance of homage " Hezekiah " despatched his envoy"* to him when he was at some distance from Jerusalem. All this agrees with the Bible narrative. In the book of Kings we are told how Hezekiah sent to the King of Assyria at Lachish, saying, *I have offended; return from me; that which thou puttest upon me I will bear. And the King of Assyria appointed unto Hezekiah, King of Judah, three hundred talents of silver and thirty talents of gold. And Hezekiah gave him all the silver that was found in the house of Jehovah and in the treasures of the king's house. At the same time did Hezekiah cut off the gold from the doors of the temple of Jehovah, and from the pillars which Hezekiah, King of Judah, had overlaid, and gave it to the King of Assyria.*† It was indeed a sore submission, when even the Temple of the Lord had to be stripped of its gold. But it purchased the relief of the city; and no price was too high to pay for that at such a moment as the present, when the populace was demoralised. We may even see Isaiah's

---

* Schrader, *Cuneiform Inscriptions, O.T.*, i., p. 286.

† 2 Kings xviii. 13—16. Here closes a paragraph. Ver. 17 begins to describe what Sennacherib did, in spite of Hezekiah's submission. He had withdrawn the army that had invested Jerusalem, for Hezekiah purchased its withdrawal by the tribute he sent. But Sennacherib, in spite of this, sent another corps of war against Jerusalem, which second attack is described in ver. 17 and onwards.

hand in the submission. The integrity of Jerusalem was the one fact on which the word of the Lord had been pledged, on which the promised remnant could be rallied. The Assyrian must not be able to say that he has made Zion's God like the gods of the heathen; and her people must see that even when they have given her up Jehovah can hold her for Himself, though in holding He tear and wound (xxxi. 4). The Temple is greater than the gold of the Temple; let even the latter be stripped off and sold to the heathen if it can purchase the integrity of the former. So Jerusalem remained inviolate; she was still *the virgin, the daughter of Zion.*

And now upon the redeemed city Isaiah could proceed to rebuild the shattered faith and morals of her people. He could say to them, "Everything has turned out as, by the word of the Lord, I said it should. The Assyrian has come down; Egypt has failed you. Your politicians, with their scorn of religion and their confidence in their cleverness, have deserted you. I told you that your numberless sacrifices and pomp of unreal religion would avail you nothing in your day of disaster, and lo! when this came, your religion collapsed. Your abounding wickedness, I said, could only close in your ruin and desertion by God. But one promise I kept steadfast: that Jerusalem would not fall; and to your penitence, whenever it should be real, I assured forgiveness. Jerusalem stands to-day, according to my word; and I repeat my gospel. History has vindicated my word, but *Come now, let us bring our reasoning to a close, saith the Lord; though your sins be as scarlet, they shall be white as snow: though they be red like crimson, they shall be as wool.* I call upon you to build again on your redeemed city, and by the grace of this pardon, the fallen ruins of your life."

Some such sermon—if indeed not actually part of chap. i.—we must conceive Isaiah to have delivered to the people when Hezekiah had bought off Sennacherib, for we find the state of Jerusalem suddenly altered. Instead of the panic, which imagined the daily capture of the city, and rushed in hectic holiday to the housetops, crying, *Let us eat and drink, for to-morrow we die*, we see the citizens back upon the walls, trembling yet trusting. Instead of sweeping past Isaiah in their revelry and leaving him to feel that after forty years of travail he had lost all his influence with them, we see them gathering round about him as their single hope and confidence (xxxvii.). King and people look to Isaiah as their counsellor, and cannot answer the enemy without consulting him. What a change from the days of the Egyptian alliance, embassies sent off against his remonstrance, and intrigues developed without his knowledge; when Ahaz insulted him, and the drunken magnates mimicked him, and, in order to rouse an indolent people, he had to walk about the streets of Jerusalem for three years, stripped like a captive! Truly this was the day of Isaiah's triumph, when God by events vindicated his prophecy, and all the people acknowledged his leadership.

It was the hour of the prophet's triumph, but the nation had as yet only trials before it. God has not done with nations or men when He has forgiven them. This people, whom of His grace, and in spite of themselves, God had saved from destruction, stood on the brink of another trial. God had given them a new lease of life, but it was immediately to pass through the furnace. They had bought off Sennacherib, but Sennacherib came back.

When Sennacherib got the tribute, he repented of

the treaty he had made with Hezekiah. He may have felt that it was a mistake to leave in his rear so powerful a fortress, while he had still to complete the overthrow of the Egyptians. So, in spite of the tribute, he sent a force back to Jerusalem to demand her surrender. We can imagine the moral effect upon King Hezekiah and his people. It was enough to sting the most demoralised into courage. Sennacherib had doubtless expected so pliant a king and so crushed a people to yield at once. But we may confidently picture the joy of Isaiah, as he felt the return of the Assyrians to be the very thing required to restore spirit to his demoralised countrymen. Here was a foe, whom they could face with a sense of justice, and not, as they had met him before, in carnal confidence and the pride of their own cleverness. Now was to be a war not, like former wars, undertaken merely for party glory, but with the purest feelings of patriotism and the firmest sanctions of religion, a campaign to be entered upon, not with Pharaoh's support and the strength of Egyptian chariots, but with God Himself as an ally—of which it could be said to Judah, *Thy righteousness shall go before thee, and the glory of the Lord shall be thy rereward.*

On what free, exultant wings the spirit of Isaiah must have risen to the sublime occasion! We know him as by nature an ardent patriot and passionate lover of his city, but through circumstance her pitiless critic and unsparing judge. In all the literature of patriotism there are no finer odes and orations than those which it owes to him; from no lips came stronger songs of war, and no heart rejoiced more in the valour that turns the battle from the gate. But till now Isaiah's patriotism had been chiefly a conscience of his country's sins, his passionate love for Jerusalem repressed by as stern a loyalty to righteousness, and all his eloquence and courage spent in holding his people from war and persuading them *to returning and rest*. At last this conflict is at an end. The stubbornness of Judah, which has divided like some rock the current of her prophet's energies, and forced it back writhing and eddying upon itself, is removed. Isaiah's faith and his patriotism run free with the force of twin-tides in one channel, and we hear the fulness of their roar as they leap together upon the enemies of God and the fatherland. *Woe to thee, thou spoiler, and thou wast not spoiled, thou treacherous dealer, and they did not deal treacherously with thee! Whenever thou ceasest to spoil, thou shalt be spoiled; and whenever thou hast made an end to deal treacherously, they shall deal treacherously with thee. O Jehovah, be gracious unto us; for Thee have we waited: be Thou their arm every morning, our salvation also in the time of trouble. From the noise of a surging the peoples have fled; from the lifting up of Thyself the nations are scattered. And gathered is your spoil, the gathering of the caterpillar; like the leaping of locusts, they are leaping upon it. Exalted is Jehovah; yea, He dwelleth on high: He hath filled Zion with justice and righteousness. And there shall be stability of thy times, wealth of salvation, wisdom and knowledge; the fear of Jehovah, it shall be his treasure* (xxxiii. 1—6).

Thus, then, do we propose to bridge the gulf which lies between chaps. i. and xxii. on the one hand and chap. xxxiii. on the other. If they are all to be dated from the year 701, some such bridge is necessary. And the one we have traced is both morally sufficient and in harmony with what we know to have been the course of events.

What do we learn from it all? We learn a great deal upon that truth which chap. xxxiii. closes by announcing —the truth of Divine forgiveness.

The forgiveness of God is the foundation of every bridge from a hopeless past to a courageous present. That God can make the past be for guilt as though it had not been is always to Isaiah the assurance of the future. An old Greek miniature * represents him with Night behind him, veiled and sullen and holding a reversed torch. But before him stands Dawn and Innocence, a little child, with bright face and forward step and torch erect and burning. From above a hand pours light upon the face of the prophet, turned upwards. It is the message of a Divine pardon. Never did prophet more wearily feel the moral continuity of the generations, the lingering and ineradicable effects of crime. Only faith in a pardoning God could have enabled him, with such conviction of the inseparableness of yesterday and to-morrow, to make divorce between them, and turning his back on the past, as this miniature represents, hail the future as Immanuel, a child of infinite promise. From exposing and scourging the past, from proving it corrupt and pregnant with poison for all the future, Isaiah will turn on a single verse, and give us a future without war, sorrow or fraud. His pivot is ever the pardon of God. But nowhere is his faith in this so powerful, his turning upon it so swift, as at this period of Jerusalem's collapse, when, having sentenced the people to death for their iniquity— *It was revealed in mine ears by Jehovah of hosts, Surely this iniquity shall not be purged from you till ye*

---

* Didron, *Christian Iconography*, fig. 52.

die, saith the Lord, Jehovah of hosts (xxii. 14)—he swings round on his promise of a little before—*Though your sins be as scarlet, they shall be white as snow* —and to the people's penitence pronounces in the last verse of chap. xxxiii. a final absolution : *The inhabitant shall not say, I am sick; the people that dwell therein are forgiven their iniquity.* If chap. xxxiii. be, as many think, Isaiah's latest oracle, then we have the literal crown of all his prophesying in these two words: *forgiven iniquity.* It is as he put it early that same year: *Come now and let us bring our reasoning to a close; though your sins be as scarlet, they shall be as white as snow: though they be red like crimson, they shall be as wool.* If man is to have a future, this must be the conclusion of all his past.

But the absoluteness of God's pardon, making the past as though it had not been, is not the only lesson which the spiritual experience of Jerusalem in that awful year of 701 has for us. Isaiah's gospel of forgiveness is nothing less than this : that when God gives pardon He gives Himself. The name of the blessed future, which is entered through pardon—as in that miniature, a child—is Immanuel : *God-with-us.* And if it be correct that we owe the forty-sixth Psalm to these months when the Assyrian came back upon Jerusalem, then we see how the city, that had abandoned God, is yet able to sing when she is pardoned, *God is our refuge and our strength, a very present help in the midst of troubles.* And this gospel of forgiveness is not only Isaiah's. According to the whole Bible, there is but one thing which separates man from God —that is sin, and when sin is done away with, God annot be kept from man. In giving pardon to man, God gives back to man Himself. How gloriously evident this truth becomes in the New Testament! Christ, who is set before us as the Lamb of God, who beareth the sins of the world, is also Immanuel—God-with-us. The Sacrament, which most plainly seals to the believer the value of the One Sacrifice for sin, is the Sacrament in which the believer feeds upon Christ and appropriates Him. The sinner, who comes to Christ, not only receives pardon for Christ's sake, but receives Christ. Forgiveness means nothing less than this: that in giving pardon God gives Himself.

But if forgiveness mean all this, then the objections frequently brought against a conveyance of it so unconditioned as that of Isaiah fall to the ground. Forgiveness of such a kind cannot be either unjust or demoralising. On the contrary, we see Jerusalem permoralised by it. At first, it is true, the sense of weakness and fear abounds, as we learn from the narrative in chaps. xxxvi. and xxxvii. But where there was vanity, recklessness and despair, giving way to dissipation, there is now humility, discipline and a leaning upon God, that are led up to confidence and exultation. Jerusalem's experience is just another proof that any moral results are possible to so great a process as the return of God to the soul. Awful is the responsibility of them who receive such a Gift and such a Guest; but the sense of that awfulness is the atmosphere, in which obedience and holiness and the courage that is born of both love best to grow. One can understand men scoffing at messages of pardon so unconditioned as Isaiah's, who think they "mean no more than a clean slate." Taken in this sense, the gospel of forgiveness must prove a savour of death unto death. But just as Jerusalem interpreted the message of her pardon to mean that *God is in the midst of her; she shall not be moved,* and straightway obedience was in all her hearts, and courage upon all her walls, so neither to us can be futile the New Testament form of the same gospel, which makes our pardoned soul the friend of God, accepted in the Beloved, and our body His holy temple.

Upon one other point connected with the forgiveness of sins we get instruction from the experience of Jerusalem. A man has difficulty in squaring his sense of forgiveness with the return on the back of it of his old temptations and trials, with the hostility of fortune and with the inexorableness of nature. Grace has spoken to his heart, but Providence bears more hard upon him than ever. Pardon does not change the outside of life; it does not immediately modify the movements of history, or suspend the laws of nature. Although God has forgiven Jerusalem, Assyria comes back to besiege her. Although the penitent be truly reconciled to God, the constitutional results of his fall remain: the frequency of temptation, the power of habit, the bias and facility downwards, the physical and social consequences. Pardon changes none of these things. It does not keep off the Assyrians.

But if pardon means the return of God to the soul, then in this we have the secret of the return of the foe. Men could not try nor develop a sense of the former except by their experience of the latter. We have seen why Isaiah must have welcomed the perfidious reappearance of the Assyrians after he had helped to buy them off. Nothing could better test the sincerity of Jerusalem's repentance, or rally her dissipated forces. Had the Assyrians not returned, the Jews would have had no experimental proof of God's restored presence, and the great miracle would never have happened that rang through human history for evermore—a trumpet-call to faith in the God of Israel. And so still *the Lord scourgeth every son whom He receiveth*, because He would put our penitence to the test; because He would discipline our disorganised affections, and give conscience and will a chance of wiping out defeat by victory; because He would baptize us with the most powerful baptism possible—the sense of being trusted once more to face the enemy upon the fields of our disgrace.

That is why the Assyrians came back to Jerusalem, and that is why temptations and penalties still pursue the penitent and forgiven.

CHAPTER XXI.

OUR GOD A CONSUMING FIRE.

ISAIAH xxxiii. (701 B.C.).

WE have seen how the sense of forgiveness and the exultant confidence, which fill chap. xxxiii., were brought about within a few months after the sentence of death, that cast so deep a gloom on chap. xxii. We have expounded some of the contents of chap. xxxiii., but have not exhausted the chapter; and in particular we have not touched one of Isaiah's principles, which there finds perhaps its finest expression: the consuming righteousness of God.

There is no doubt that chap. xxxiii. refers to the sudden disappearance of the Assyrian from the walls of Jerusalem. It was written, part perhaps on the eve of that deliverance, part immediately after morning broke upon the vanished host. Before those verses which picture the disappearance of the investing army, we ought in strict chronological order to take the narrative in chaps. xxxvi. and xxxvii.—the return of the besiegers, the insolence of the Rabshakeh, the prostration of Hezekiah, Isaiah's solitary faith, and the sudden disappearance of the Assyrian. It will be more convenient, however, since we have already entered chap. xxxiii., to finish it, and then to take the narrative of the events which led up to it.

The opening verses of chap. xxxiii. fit the very moment of the crisis, as if Isaiah had flung them across the walls in the teeth of the Rabshakeh and the second embassy from Sennacherib, who had returned to demand the surrender of the city in spite of Hezekiah's tribute for her integrity: *Woe to thee, thou spoiler, and thou wast not spoiled, thou treacherous dealer, and they did not deal treacherously with thee! When thou ceasest to spoil, thou shalt be spoiled; and when thou makest an end to deal treacherously, they shall deal treacherously with thee.* Then follows the prayer, as already quoted, and the confidence in the security of Jerusalem (ver. 2). A new paragraph (vv. 7—12) describes Rabshakeh and his company demanding the surrender of the city; the disappointment of the ambassadors who had been sent to treat with Sennacherib (ver. 7); the perfidy of the great king, who had broken the covenant they had made with him and swept his armies back upon Judah (ver. 8); the disheartening of the land under this new shock (ver. 9); and the resolution of the Lord now to rise and scatter the invaders: *Now will I arise, saith Jehovah; now will I lift up Myself; now will I be exalted. Ye shall conceive chaff; ye shall bring forth stubble; your breath is a fire, that shall devour you. And the peoples shall be as the burnings of lime, as thorns cut down that are burned in the fire* (vv. 10—12).

After an application of this same fire of God's righteousness to the sinners *within* Jerusalem, to which we shall presently return, the rest of the chapter pictures the stunned populace awaking to the fact that they are free. Is the Assyrian really gone, or do the Jews dream as they crowd the walls, and see no trace of him? Have they all vanished—the Rabshakeh, *by the conduit of the upper pool, with his loud voice* and insults; the scribes to whom they handed the tribute, and who prolonged the agony by counting it under their eyes; the scouts and engineers insolently walking about Zion and mapping out her walls for the assault; the close investment of barbarian hordes, with their awesome speech and uncouth looks! *Where is he that counted? where is he that weighed the tribute? where is he that counted the towers? Thou shalt not see the fierce people, a people of a deep speech that thou canst not perceive, of a strange tongue that thou canst not understand.* They have vanished. Hezekiah may lift his head again. O people—sore at heart to see thy king in sackcloth and ashes* as the enemy devoured province after province of thy land and cooped thee up within the narrow walls, thou scarcely didst dare to peep across—take courage, the terror is gone! *A king in his beauty thine eyes shall see; they shall behold the land spreading very far forth* (ver. 17). We had thought to die in the restlessness and horror of war, never again to know what stable life and regular worship were, our Temple services interrupted, our home a battlefield. But *look upon Zion; behold again she is the city of our solemn diets; thine eyes shall see Jerusalem a quiet habitation, a tent that shall not be removed, the stakes whereof shall never be plucked up, neither shall the cords thereof be broken.* But there Jehovah, whom we have known only for affliction, *shall be in majesty for us.* Other peoples have their natural defences, Assyria and Egypt their Euphrates and Nile; but God Himself shall be for us *a place of rivers, streams, broad on both hands, on which never a galley shall go, nor gallant ship*

---

* Chap. xxxvii.

shall pass upon it. Without sign of battle, God shall be our refuge and our strength. It was that marvellous deliverance of Jerusalem by the hand of God, with no effort of human war, which caused Isaiah to invest with such majesty the meagre rock, its squalid surroundings and paltry defences. The insignificant and waterless city was glorious to the prophet because God was in her. One of the richest imaginations which patriot ever poured upon his fatherland was inspired by the simplest faith saint ever breathed. Isaiah strikes again the old keynote (chap. viii.) about the waterlessness of Jerusalem. We have to keep in mind the Jews' complaints of this, in order to understand what the forty-sixth Psalm means when it says, *There is a river the streams whereof make glad the city of our God, the holy place of the tabernacles of the Most High*—or what Isaiah means when he says, *Glorious shall Jehovah be unto us, a place of broad rivers and streams.* Yea, he adds, Jehovah is everything to us: *Jehovah is our Judge; Jehovah is our Lawgiver; Jehovah is our King: He will save us.*

Such were the feelings aroused in Jerusalem by the sudden relief of the city. Some of the verses, which we have scarcely touched, we will now consider more fully as the expression of a doctrine which runs throughout Isaiah, and indeed is one of his two or three fundamental truths—that the righteousness of God is an all-pervading atmosphere, an atmosphere that wears and burns.

For forty years the prophet had been preaching to the Jews his gospel, *God-with-us;* but they never awakened to the reality of the Divine presence till they saw it in the dispersion of the Assyrian army. Then

God became real to them (ver. 14). The justice of God, preached so long by Isaiah, had always seemed something abstract. Now they saw how concrete it was. It was not only a doctrine: it was a fact. It was a fact that was a fire. Isaiah had often called it a fire; they thought this was rhetoric. But now they saw the actual burning—*the peoples as the burning of lime, as thorns cut down that are burned in the fire.* And when they felt the fire so near, each sinner of them awoke to the fact that he had something burnable in himself, something which could as little stand the fire as the Assyrians could. There was no difference in this fire outside and inside the walls. What it burned there it would burn here. Nay, was not Jerusalem the dwelling-place of God, and Ariel the very hearth and furnace of the fire which they saw consume the Assyrians? *Who,* they cried in their terror—*Who among us shall dwell with the devouring fire? Who among us shall dwell with everlasting burnings?*

We are familiar with Isaiah's fundamental God-with-us, and how it was spoken not for mercy only, but for judgement (chap. viii.). If *God-with-us* meant love with us, salvation with us, it meant also holiness with us, judgement with us, the jealousy of God breathing upon what is impure, false and proud. Isaiah felt this so hotly, that his sense of it has broken out into some of the fieriest words in all prophecy. In his younger days he told the citizens not *to provoke the eyes of God's glory,* as if Heaven had fastened on their life two gleaming orbs, not only to pierce them with its vision, but to consume them with its wrath. Again, in the lowering cloud of calamity he had seen *lips of indignation, a tongue as a devouring fire,* and in the overflowing stream which finally issued from it the hot *breath of the Almighty.* These are unforgettable descriptions of the ceaseless activity of Divine righteousness in the life of man. They set our imaginations on fire with the prophet's burning belief in this. But they are excelled by another, more frequently used by Isaiah, wherein he likens the holiness of God to an universal and constant fire. To Isaiah life was so penetrated by the active justice of God, that he described it as bathed in fire, as blown through with fire. Righteousness was no mere doctrine to this prophet: it was the most real thing in history; it was the presence which pervaded and explained all phenomena. We shall understand the difference between Isaiah and his people if we have ever for our eyes' sake looked at a great conflagration through a coloured glass which allowed us to see the solid materials—stone, wood and iron—but prevented us from perceiving the flames and shimmering heat. To look thus is to see pillars, lintels and cross-beams twist and fall, crumble and fade; but how inexplicable the process seems! Take away the glass, and everything is clear. The fiery element is filling all the interstices, that were blank to us before, and beating upon the solid material. The heat becomes visible, shimmering even where there is no flame. Just so had it been with the sinners in Judah these forty years. Their society and politics, individual fortunes and careers, personal and national habits—the home, the Church, the State—common outlines and shapes of life—were patent to every eye, but no man could explain the constant decay and diminution, because all were looking at life through a glass darkly. Isaiah alone faced life with open vision, which filled up for him the interstices of experience and gave terrible explanation to fate. It was a vision that nearly scorched the eyes out of him. Life as he saw it was steeped in flame—the glowing righteousness of God. Jerusalem was full *of the spirit of justice, the spirit of burning. The light of Israel is for a fire, and his Holy One for a flame.* The Assyrian empire, that vast erection which the strong hands of kings had reared, was simply their pyre, made ready for the burning. *For a Tophcth is prepared of old; yea, for the king it is made ready; He hath made it deep and large; the pile thereof is fire and much wood; the breath of Jehovah, like a stream of brimstone, doth kindle it.** So Isaiah saw life, and flashed it on his countrymen. At last the glass fell from their eyes also, and they cried aloud, *Who among us shall dwell with the devouring fire? Who among us shall dwell with everlasting burnings?* Isaiah replied that there is one thing which can survive the universal flame, and that is character: *He that walketh righteously and speaketh uprightly; he that despiseth the gain of fraud, that shaketh his hands from the holding of bribes, that stoppeth his ears from the hearing of blood, and shutteth his eyes from looking on evil, he shall dwell on high: his place of defence shall be the munitions of rocks: his bread shall be given him: his water shall be sure.*

Isaiah's Vision of Fire suggests two thoughts to us.

1. Have we done well to confine our horror of the consuming fires of righteousness to the next life ? If we would but use the eyes which Scripture lends us, the rifts of prophetic vision and awakened conscience by which the fogs of this world and of our own hearts are rent, we should see fires as fierce, a consumption as pitiless, about us here as ever the conscience of a startled

---

* Chaps. iv. 4; xxx. 33.

sinner fearfully looked for across the grave. Nay, have not the fires, with which the darkness of eternity has been made lurid, themselves been kindled at the burnings of this life? Is it not because men have felt how hot this world was being made for sin that they have had a *certain fearful expectation of judgement and the fierceness of fire?* We shudder at the horrible pictures of hell which some older theologians and poets have painted for us; but it was not morbid fancy, nor the barbarism of their age nor their own heart's cruelty that inspired these men. It was their hot honour for the Divine holiness; it was their experience of how pitiless to sin Providence is already in this life; it was their own scorched senses and affections—brands, as many honest men among them felt themselves, plucked from the burning. Our God *is* a consuming fire—here as well as yonder. Hell has borrowed her glare from the imagination of men aflame with the real fieriness of life, and may be—more truly than of old—pictured as the dead and hollow cinder left by those fires, of which, as every true man's conscience is aware, this life is full. It was not hell that created conscience; it was conscience that created hell, and conscience was fired by the vision which fired Isaiah—of all life aglow with the righteousness of God—*God with us,* as He was with Jerusalem, *a spirit of burning and a spirit of justice.* This is the pantheism of conscience, and it stands to reason. God is the one power of life. What can exist beside Him except what is like Him? Nothing—sooner or later nothing but what is like Him. The will that is as His will, the heart that is pure, the character that is transparent— only these dwell with the everlasting fire, and burning with God, as the bush which Moses saw, are nevertheless not consumed. Let us lay it to heart—Isaiah has nothing to tell us about hell-fire, but a great deal about the pitiless justice of God in this life.

2. The second thought suggested by Isaiah's Vision of Life is a comparison of it with the theory of life which is fashionable to-day. Isaiah's figure for life was a burning. Ours is a battle, and at first sight ours looks the truer. Seen through a formula which has become everywhere fashionable, life is a fierce and fascinating warfare. Civilised thought, when asked to describe any form of life or to account for a death or survival, most monotonously replies, "The struggle for existence." The sociologist has borrowed the phrase from the biologist, and it is on everybody's lips to describe their idea of human life. It is uttered by the historian when he would explain the disappearance of this national type, the prevalence of that one. The economist traces depression and failures, the fatal fevers of speculation, the cruelties and bad humours of commercial life, to the same source. A merchant with profits lessening and failure before him relieves his despair and apologizes to his pride with the words, "It is all due to competition." Even character and the spiritual graces are sometimes set down as results of the same material process. Some have sought to deduce from it all intelligence, others more audaciously all ethics; and it is certain that in the silence of men's hearts after a moral defeat there is no excuse more frequently offered to conscience by will than that the battle was too hot.

But fascinating as life is when seen through this formula, does not the formula act on our vision precisely as the glass we supposed, which when we look through it on a conflagration shows us the solid matter and the changes through which this passes, but hides from us the real agent? One need not deny the reality of the struggle for existence, or that its results are enormous. We struggle with each other, and affect each other for good and for evil, sometimes past all calculation. But we do not fight in a vacuum. Let Isaiah's vision be the complement of our own feeling. We fight in an atmosphere that affects every one of us far more powerfully than the opposing wits or wills of our fellow-men. Around us and through us, within and without as we fight, is the all-pervading righteousness of God; and it is far oftener the effects of this which we see in the falls and the changes of life than the effects of our struggle with each other, enormous though these may be. On this point there is an exact parallel between our days and the days of Isaiah. Then the politicians of Judah, looking through their darkened glass at life, said, Life is simply a war in which the strongest prevail, a game which the most cunning win. So they made fast their alliances, and were ready to meet the Assyrian, or they fled in panic before him, according as Egypt or he seemed the stronger. Isaiah saw that with Assyrian and Jew another Power was present—the real reason of every change in politics, collapse or crash in either of the empires—the active righteousness of God. Assyrian and Jew had not only to contend with each other. They were at strife with Him. We now see plainly that Isaiah was right. Far more operative than the intrigues of politicians or the pride of Assyria, because it used these simply as its mines and its fuel, was the law of righteousness, the spiritual force which is as impalpable as the atmosphere, yet strong to burn and try as a furnace seven times heated. And Isaiah is equally right for to-day. As we look at life through our fashionable formula it does seem a mass of struggle, in which we catch only now and then a glimpse of the decisions of righteousness, but the prevailing lawlessness of which we do not hesitate to make the reason of all that happens, and in particular the excuse of our own defeats. We are wrong. Righteousness is not an occasional spark; righteousness is the atmosphere. Though our dull eyes see it only now and then strike into flame in the battle of life, and take for granted that it is but the flash of meeting wits or of steel on steel, God's justice is everywhere, pervasive and pitiless, affecting the combatants far more than they have power to affect one another.

We shall best learn the truth of this in the way the sinners in Jerusalem learned it—each man first looking into himself. *Who among us shall dwell with the everlasting burnings?* Can we attribute all our defeats to the opposition that was upon us at the moment they occurred? When our temper failed, when our charity relaxed, when our resoluteness gave way, was it the hotness of debate, was it the pressure of the crowd, was it the sneer of the scorner, that was to blame? We all know that these were only the occasions of our defeats. Conscience tells us that the cause lay in a slothful or self-indulgent heart, which the corrosive atmosphere of Divine righteousness had been consuming, and which, sapped and hollow by its effect, gave way at every material shock.

With the knowledge that conscience gives us, let us now look at a kind of figure which must be within the horizon of all of us. Once it was the most commanding stature among its fellows, the straight back and broad brow of a king of men. But now what is the last sight of him that will remain with us, flung out there against the evening skies of his life? A bent back (we speak of character), a stooping face, the shrinking outlines of a man ready to collapse. It was not the struggle for existence that killed him, for he was born to prevail in it. It was the atmosphere that told on him. He carried in him that on which the atmosphere could not but tell. A low selfishness or passion inhabited him, and became the predominant part of him, so that his outward life was only its shell; and when the fire of God at last pierced this, he was as thorns cut down, that are burned in the fire.

We can explain much with the outward eye, but the most of the explanation lies beyond. Where our knowledge of a man's life ends, the great meaning of it often only begins. All the vacancy beyond the outline we see is full of that meaning. God is there, and *God is a consuming fire.* Let us not seek to explain lives only by what we see of them, the visible strife of man with man and nature. It is the invisible that contains the secret of what is seen. We see the shoulders stoop, but not the burden upon them; the face darken, but look in vain for what casts the shadow; the light sparkle in the eye, but cannot tell what star of hope its glance has caught. And even so when we behold fortune and character go down in the warfare of this world, we ought to remember that it is not always the things we see that are to blame for the fall, but that awful flame which, unseen by common man, has been revealed to the prophets of God.

Righteousness and retribution, then, are an atmosphere —not lines or laws that we may happen to stumble upon, not explosives, that, being touched, burst out on us, but the atmosphere—always about us and always at work, invisible and yet more mighty than aught we see. *God, in whom we live and move and have our being, is a consuming fire.*

CHAPTER XXII.

THE RABSHAKEH; OR, LAST TEMPTATIONS OF FAITH.

Isaiah xxxvi. (701 b.c.).

IT remains for us now to follow in chaps. xxxvi., xxxvii., the historical narrative of the events, the moral results of which we have seen so vivid in chap. xxxiii.—the perfidious return of the Assyrians to Jerusalem after Hezekiah had bought them off and their final disappearance from the Holy Land.

This historical narrative has also its moral. It is not annals, but drama. The whole moral of Isaiah's prophesying is here flung into a duel between champions of the two tempers, which we have seen in perpetual conflict throughout his book. The two tempers are—on Isaiah's side an absolute and unselfish faith in God, Sovereign of the world and Saviour of His people; on the side of the Assyrians a bare, brutal confidence in themselves, in human cleverness and success, a vaunting contempt of righteousness and of pity. The main interest of Isaiah's book has consisted in the way these tempers oppose each other, and alternately influence the feeling of the Jewish community. That interest is now to culminate in the scene which brings near such thorough representatives of the two tempers as Isaiah and the Rabshakeh, with the crowd of wavering Jews between. Most strikingly, Assyria's last assault is not of force, but of speech, delivering upon faith the subtle arguments of the worldly temper; and as strikingly, while all official religion and power of State stand helpless against them, these arguments are met by the bare word of God. In this mere statement of the situation, however, we perceive that much more than the quarrel of a single generation is being decided. This scene is a parable of the everlasting struggle between faith and force, with doubt and despair between them. In the clever, self-confident, persuasive personage with two languages on his tongue and an army at his back; in the fluttered representatives of official religion who meet him and are afraid of the effect of his speech on the common people; in the ranks of dispirited men who hear the dialogue from the wall; in the sensitive king so aware of faith, and yet so helpless to bring faith forth to peace and triumph; and, in the background of the whole situation, the serene prophet of God, grasping only God's word, and by his own steadfastness carrying the city over the crisis and proving that faith indeed can be *the substance of things hoped for*—we have a phase of the struggle ordained unto every generation of men, and which is as fresh to-day as when Rabshakeh played the cynic and the scribes and elders filled the part of nervous defenders of the faith, under the walls of faith's fortress, two thousand five hundred years ago.

THE RABSHAKEH.

This word is a Hebrew transliteration of the Assyrian Rab-sak, *chief of the officers*. Though there is some doubt on the point, we may naturally presume from the duties he here discharges that the Rabshakeh was a civilian—probably the civil commissioner or political officer attached to the Assyrian army, which was commanded, according to 2 Kings xviii. 16, by the Tartan or commander-in-chief himself.

In all the Bible there is not a personage more clever than this Rabshakeh, nor more typical. He was an able deputy of the king who sent him, but he represented still more thoroughly the temper of the civilisation to which he belonged. There is no word of this man which is not characteristic. A clever, fluent diplomatist, with the traveller's knowledge of men and the conqueror's contempt for them, the Rabshakeh is the product of a victorious empire like the Assyrian, or, say, like the British. Our services sometimes turn out the like of him—a creature able to speak to natives in their own language, full and ready of information, mastering the surface of affairs at a glance, but always baffled by the deeper tides which sway nations; a deft player upon party interests and the superficial human passions, but unfit to touch the deep springs of men's religion and patriotism. Let us speak, however, with respect of the Rabshakeh. From his rank (Sayce calls him the Vizier), as well as from the cleverness with which he explains what we know to have been the policy of Sennacherib towards the populations of Syria, he may well have been the inspiring mind at this time of the great Assyrian empire—Sennacherib's Bismarck.

The Rabshakeh had strutted down from the great centre of civilisation, with its temper upon him, and all its great resources at his back, confident to twist these poor provincial tribes round his little finger. How petty he conceived them we infer from his never styling Hezekiah *the king*. This was to be an occasion for the Rabshakeh's own glorification. Jerusalem was to fall to his clever speeches. He had indeed the army behind him, but the work to be done was not the rough work of soldiers. All was to be managed by him, the civilian and orator. This fellow, with his two languages and clever address, was to step out in front of the army and finish the whole business.

The Rabshakeh spoke extremely well. With his first words he touched the sore point of Judah's policy: her trust in Egypt. On this he spoke like a very Isaiah. But he showed a deeper knowledge of Judah's internal affairs, and a subtler deftness in using it, when he referred to the matter of the altars. Hezekiah had abolished the high places in all parts of the land, and gathered the people to the central sanctuary in Jerusalem. The Assyrian knew that a number of Jews must look upon this disestablishment of religion in the provinces as likely to incur Jehovah's displeasure and turn Him against them. Therefore he said, *But if thou say unto me, We trust in Jehovah our God, is not that He whose high places and whose altars Hezekiah hath taken away, and hath said to Judah and to Jerusalem, Ye shall worship before this altar?* And then, having shaken their religious confidence, he made sport of their military strength. And finally he boldly asserted, *Jehovah said unto me, Go up against this land and destroy it.* All this shows a master in diplomacy, a most clever demagogue. The scribes and elders felt the edge, and begged him to sheathe it in a language unknown to the common people. But he, conscious of his power, spoke the more boldly, addressing himself directly to the poorer sort of the garrison, on whom the siege would press most heavily. His second speech to them is a good illustration of the policy pursued by Assyria at this time towards the cities of Palestine. We know from the annals of Sennacherib that his customary policy, to seduce the populations of a hostile State from allegiance to their rulers, had succeeded in other cases; and it was so plausibly uttered in this case, that it seemed likely to succeed again. To the common soldiers on the walls, with the prospect of being reduced to the foul rations of a prolonged siege (ver. 12), Sennacherib's ambassador offers rich and equal property and enjoyment. *Make a treaty with me, and come out to me, and eat every one of his vine and every one of his fig tree, and drink ye every one of the water of his cistern, until I come and take you away to a land like your own land, a land of corn and grapes, a land of bread-corn and orchards. Every one!*—it is a most subtle assault upon the discipline, comradeship and patriotism of the common soldiers by the promises of a selfish, sensuous equality and individualism. But then the speaker's native cynicism gets the better of him—it is not possible for an Assyrian long to play the part of clemency—and, with a flash of scorn, he asks the sad men upon the walls whether they really believe that Jehovah can save them: *Hath any of the gods of the nations delivered his land out of the hand of the King of Assyria, . . . that Jehovah should deliver Jerusalem out of my hand?* All the range of their feelings does he thus run through, seeking with sharp words to snap each cord of faith in God, of honour to the king and love of country. Had the Jews heart to answer him, they might point out the inconsistency between his claim to have been sent by Jehovah and the contempt he now pours upon their God. But the inconsistency is characteristic. The Assyrian has some acquaintance with the Jewish faith; he makes use of its articles when they serve his purpose, but his ultimatum is to tear them to shreds in their believers' faces. He treats the Jews as men of culture still sometimes treat barbarians, first scornfully humouring their faith and then savagely trampling it under foot.

So clever were the speeches of the Rabshakeh. We see why he was appointed to this mission. He was an expert both in the language and religion of this tribe, perched on its rock in the remote Judæan highlands. For a foreigner he showed marvellous familiarity with the temper and internal jealousies of the Jewish religion. He turned these on each other almost as adroitly as Paul himself did in the disputes between Sadducees and Pharisees. How the fellow knew his cleverness, strutting there betwixt army and town! He would show his soldier friends the proper way of dealing with stubborn barbarians. He would astonish those faith-proud highlanders by exhibiting how much he was aware of the life behind their thick walls and silent faces, *for the king's commandment was, Answer him not.*

And yet did the Rabshakeh, with all his raking, know the heart of Judah? No, truly. The whole interest of this man is the incongruity of the expertness and surface-knowledge, which he spattered on Jerusalem's walls, with the deep secret of God, that, as some inexhaustible well, the fortress of the faith carried within her. Ah, Assyrian, there is more in starved Jerusalem than thou canst put in thy speeches! Suppose Heaven were to give those sharp eyes of thine power to look through the next thousand years, and see this race and this religion thou puffest at, the highest-honoured, hottest-hated of the world, centre of mankind's regard and debate, but thou, and thy king and all the glory of your empire wrapped deep in oblivion. To this little fortress of highland men shall the heart of great peoples turn: kings for its nursing-fathers and queens for its nursing-mothers, the forces of the

Gentiles shall come to it, and from it new civilisations take their laws; while thou and all thy paraphernalia disappear into blackness, haunted only by the antiquary, the world taking an interest in thee just in so far as thou didst once hopelessly attempt to understand Jerusalem and capture her faith by thine own interpretation of it. Curious pigmy, very grand thou thinkest thyself, and surely with some right as delegate of the king of kings, parading thy cleverness and thy bribes before these poor barbarians; but the world, called to look upon you both from this eminence of history, grants thee to be a very good head of an intelligence department, with a couple of languages on thy glib tongue's end, but adjudges that with the starved and speechless men before thee lies the secret of all that is worth living and dying for in this world.

The Rabshakeh's plausible futility and Jerusalem's faith, greatly distressed before him, are typical. Still as men hang moodily over the bulwarks of Zion, doubtful whether life is worth living within the narrow limits which religion prescribes, or righteousness worth fighting for with such privations and hope deferred, comes upon them some elegant and plausible temptation, loudly calling to give the whole thing up. Disregarding the official arguments and evidences that push forward to parley, it speaks home in practical tones to men's real selves—their appetites and selfishnesses. "You are foolish fellows," it says, "to confine yourselves to such narrowness of life and self-denial! The fall of your faith is only a matter of time: other creeds have gone; yours must follow. And why fight the world for the sake of an idea, or from the habits of a discipline? Such things only starve the human spirit; and the world is so generous, so free to every one, so tolerant of each enjoying his own, unhampered by authority or religion."

In our day what has the greatest effect on the faith of many men is just this mixture, that pervades the Rabshakeh's address,—of a superior culture pretending to expose religion, with the easy generosity, which offers to the individual a selfish life, unchecked by any discipline or religious fear. That modern Rabshakeh, Ernest Rénan, with the forces of historical criticism at his back, but confident rather in his own skill of address, speaking to us believers as poor picturesque provincials, patronising our Deity, and telling us that he knows His intentions better than we do ourselves, is a very good representative of the enemies of the Faith, who owe their impressiveness upon common men to the familiarity they display with the contents of the Faith, and the independent, easy life they offer to the man who throws his strict faith off. Superior knowledge, with the offer on its lips of a life on good terms with the rich and tolerant world —pretence of science promising selfishness—that is to-day, as then under the walls of Jerusalem, the typical enemy of the Faith. But if faith be held simply as the silent garrison of Jerusalem held it, faith in a Lord God of righteousness, who has given us a conscience to serve Him, and has spoken to us in plain explanation of this by those whom we can see, understand and trust—not only by an Isaiah, but by a Jesus— then neither mere cleverness nor the ability to promise comfort can avail against our faith. A simple conscience of God and of duty may not be able to answer subtle arguments word for word, but she can feel the incongruity of their cleverness with her own precious secret; she can at least expose the fallacy of their sensuous promises of an untroubled life. No man, who tempts us from a good conscience with God in the discipline of our religion and the comradeship of His people, can ensure that there will be no starvation in the pride of life, no captivity in the easy tolerance of the world. To the heart of man there will always be captivity in selfishness; there will always be exile in unbelief. Even where the romance and sentiment of faith are retained, after the manner of Rénan, it is only to mock us with mirage. *As in a dry and thirsty land, where no water is, our heart and flesh shall cry out for the living God, as we have aforetime seen Him in the sanctuary.* The land, in which the tempter promises a life undisturbed by religious restraints, is not our home, neither is it freedom. By the conscience that is in us, God has set us on the walls of faith, with His law to observe, with His people to stand by; and against us are the world and its tempters, with all their wiles to be defied. If we go down from the charge and shelter of so simple a religion, then, whatever enjoyment we have, we shall enjoy it only with the fears of the deserter and the greed of the slave.

In spite of scorn and sensuous promise from Rabshakeh to Rénan, let us lift the hymn which these silent Jews at last lifted from the walls of their delivered city: *Walk about Zion and go round about her; tell ye the towers thereof. Mark ye well her bulwarks, and consider her palaces, that ye may tell it to the generation to come, For this God is our God for ever and ever. He will be our Guide even unto death.*

CHAPTER XXIII.

THIS IS THE VICTORY. ... OUR FAITH.

Isaiah xxxvii. (701 B.C.).

WITHIN the fortress of the faith there is only silence and embarrassment. We pass from the Rabshakeh, posing outside the walls of Zion, to Hezekiah, prostrate within them. We pass with the distracted councillors, by the walls crowded with moody and silent soldiers, many of them—if this be the meaning of the king's command that they should not parley—only too ready to yield to the plausible infidel. We are astonished. Has faith nothing to say for herself? Have this people of so long Divine inspiration no habit of self-possession, no argument in answer to the irrelevant attacks of their enemy? Where are the traditions of Moses and Joshua, the songs of Deborah and David? Can men walk about Zion, and their very footsteps on her walls ring out no defiance?

Hezekiah's complaint reminds us that in this silence and distress we have no occasional perplexity of faith, but her perpetual burden. Faith is inarticulate because of her greatness. Faith is courageous and imaginative; but can she convert her confidence and visions into fact? Said Hezekiah, *This is a day of trouble, and rebuke and contumely, for the children are come to the birth, and there is not strength to bring them forth.* These words are not a mere metaphor for anguish. They are the definition of a real miscarriage. In Isaiah's contemporaries faith has at last engendered courage, zeal for God's house and strong assurance of victory; but she, that has proved fertile to conceive and carry these confidences, is powerless to bring them forth into real life, to transform them to actual fact. Faith, complains Hezekiah, is not the substance of things hoped for. At the moment when her subjective assurances ought to be realized as facts, she is powerless to bring them to the birth.

It is a miscarriage we are always deploring. Wordsworth has said, "Through love, through hope, through faith's transcendent dower, we feel that we are greater than we know." Yes, greater than we can articulate, greater than we can tell to men like the Rabshakeh, even though he talk the language of the Jews; and therefore, on the whole, it is best to be silent in face of his argument. But greater also, we sometimes fear, than we can realise to ourselves in actual character and victory. All life thrills with the pangs of inability to bring the children of faith to the birth of experience. The man, who has lost his faith or who takes his faith easily, never knows, of course, this anguish of Hezekiah. But the more we have fed on the promises of the Bible, the more that the Spirit of God has engendered in our pure hearts assurances of justice and of peace, the more we shall sometimes tremble with the fear that in outward fact there is no life for these beautiful conceptions of the soul. Do we really believe in the Fatherhood of God—believe in it till it has changed us inwardly, and we carry a new sense of destiny, a new conscience of justice, a new disgust of sin, a new pity for pain? Then how full of the anguish of impotence must our souls feel when they consciously survey one day of common life about us, or when we honestly look back on a year of our own conduct! Does it not seem as if upon one or two hideous streets in some centre of our civilisation all Christianity, with its eighteen hundred years of promise and impetus, had gone to wreck? Is God only for the imagination of man? Is there no God outwardly to control and grant victory? Is He only a Voice, and not the Creator? Is Christ only a Prophet, and not the King?

And then over these disappointments there faces us all the great miscarriage itself—black, inevitable death. Hezekiah cried from despair that the Divine assurance of the permanence of God's people in the world was about to be wrecked on fact. But often by a death-bed we utter the same lament about the individual's immortality. There is everything to prove a future life except the fact of it within human experience. This life is big with hopes, instincts, convictions of immortality; and yet where within our sight have these ever passed to the birth of fact?* Death is a great miscarriage. *The children have come to the birth, and there is not strength to bring them forth.*

And yet within the horizon of this life at least—the latter part of the difficulty we postpone to another chapter—*faith is the substance of things hoped for*, as Isaiah did now most brilliantly prove. For the miracle of Jerusalem's deliverance, to which the narrative proceeds, was not that by faith the prophet foretold it, but that by faith he did actually himself succeed in bringing it to pass. The miracle, we say, was not that

---

* Cf. Browning's *La Saisiaz.*

Isaiah made accurate prediction of the city's speedy relief from the Assyrian, but far more that upon his solitary steadfastness, without aid of battle, he did carry her disheartened citizens through this crisis of temptation, and kept them, though silent, to their walls till the futile Assyrian drifted away. The prediction, indeed, was not, although its terms appear exact, so very marvellous for a prophet to make, who had Isaiah's religious conviction that Jerusalem must survive and Isaiah's practical acquaintance with the politics of the day. *Behold, I am setting in him a spirit; and he shall hear a rumour, and shall return into his own land.* We may recall the parallel case of Charlemagne in his campaign against the Moors in Spain, from which he was suddenly and unseasonably hastened north on a disastrous retreat by news of the revolt of the Saxons.* In the vast Assyrian territories rebellions were constantly occurring, that demanded the swift appearance of the king himself; and God's Spirit, to whose inspiration Isaiah traced all political perception, suggested to him the possibility of one of these. In the end, the Bible story implies that it was not a rumour from some far-away quarter so much as a disaster here in

---

* A still more striking analogy may be found in the case of Napoleon I. when in the East in 1799. He had just achieved a small victory which partly masked the previous failure of his campaign, when "Sir Sydney Smith now contrived that he should receive a packet of journals, by which he was informed of all that had passed recently in Europe and the disasters that France had suffered. His resolution was immediately taken. On August 22nd he wrote to Kleber announcing that he transferred to him the command of the expedition, and that he himself would return to Europe.... After carefully spreading false accounts of his intentions, he set sail on the night of the same day" (Professor Seeley, article 'Napoleon" in the *Ency. Brit.*).

Syria, which compelled Sennacherib's "retreat from Moscow." But it is possible that both causes were at work, and that as Napoleon offered the receipt of news from Paris as his reason for hurriedly abandoning the unfortunate Spanish campaign of 1808, so Sennacherib made the rumour of some news from his capital or the north the occasion for turning his troops from a theatre of war, where they had not met with unequivocal success, and had at last been half destroyed by the plague. Isaiah's further prediction of Sennacherib's death must also be taken in a general sense, for it was not till twenty years later that the Assyrian tyrant met this violent end: *I will cause him to fall by the sword in his own land.* But do not let us waste our attention on the altogether minor point of the *prediction* of Jerusalem's deliverance, when the great wonder, of which the prediction is but an episode, lies lengthened and manifest before us—that Isaiah, when all the defenders of Jerusalem were distracted and her king prostrate, did by the single steadfastness of his spirit sustain her inviolate, and procure for her people a safe and glorious future.

The baffled Rabshakeh returned to his master, whom he found at Libnah, *for he had heard that he had broken up from Lachish.* Sennacherib, the narrative would seem to imply, did not trouble himself further about Jerusalem till he learned that Tirhakah, the Ethiopian ruler of Egypt, was marching to meet him with probably a stronger force than that which Sennacherib had defeated at Eltekeh. Then, feeling the danger of leaving so strong a fortress as Jerusalem in his rear, Sennacherib sent to Hezekiah one more demand for surrender. Hezekiah spread his enemy's letter before the Lord. His prayer that follows is remarkable for two features, which enable us to see how pure and elevated a monotheism God's Spirit had at last developed from the national faith of Israel. The Being whom the king now seeks he addresses by the familiar name *Jehovah of hosts, God of Israel,* and describes by the physical figure—*who art enthroned upon the cherubim.* But he conceives of this God with the utmost loftiness and purity, ascribing to Him not only sovereignty and creatorship, but absolute singularity of Godhead. We have but to compare Hezekiah's prayer with the utterances of his predecessor Ahaz, to whom many gods were real, and none absolutely sovereign, or with the utterances of Israelites far purer than Ahaz, to whom the gods of the nations, though inferior to Jehovah, were yet real existences, in order to mark the spiritual advance made by Israel under Isaiah. It is a tribute to the prophet's force, which speaks volumes, when the deputation from Hezekiah talk to him of *thy God* (ver. 4). For Isaiah by his ministry had made Israel's God to be new in Israel's eyes.

Hezekiah's lofty prayer drew forth through the prophet an answer from Jehovah (vv. 21—32). This is one of the most brilliant of Isaiah's oracles. It is full of much, with which we are now familiar: the triumph of the inviolable fortress, *the virgin daughter of Zion,* and her scorn of the arrogant foe; the prophet's appreciation of Asshur's power and impetus, which only heightens his conviction that Asshur is but an instrument in the hand of God; the old figure of the enemy's sudden check as of a wild animal by hook and bridle; his inevitable retreat to the north. But these familiar ideas are flung off with a terseness and vivacity, which bear out the opinion that here we have a prophecy of Isaiah, not revised and elaborated for subsequent publication, like the rest of his book, but in its original form, struck quickly forth to meet the city's sudden and urgent prayer.

The new feature of this prophecy is the sign added to it (ver. 30). This sign reminds us of that which in opposite terms described to Ahaz the devastation of Judah by the approaching Assyrians (chap. vii.). The wave of Assyrian war is about to roll away again, and Judah to resume her neglected agriculture, but not quite immediately. During this year of 701 it has been impossible, with the Assyrians in the land, to sow the seed, and the Jews have been dependent on the precarious crop of what had fallen from the harvest of the previous year and sown itself—*saphiah*, or *aftergrowth*. Next year, it being now too late to sow for next year's harvest, they must be content with the *shahis*—*wild corn, that which springs of itself. But the third year sow ye, and reap, and plant vineyards and eat the fruit thereof*. Perhaps we ought not to interpret these numbers literally. The use of three gives the statement a formal and general aspect, as if the prophet only meant, It may be not quite at once that we get rid of the Assyrians; but when they do go, then they go for good, and you may till your land again without fear of their return. Then rings out the old promise, so soon now to be accomplished, about *the escaped* and *the remnant;* and the great pledge of the promise is once more repeated: *The zeal of Jehovah of hosts will perform this.* With this exclamation, as in ix. 7, the prophecy reaches a natural conclusion; and vv. 33—35 may have been uttered by Isaiah a little later, when he was quite sure that the Assyrian would not even attempt to repeat his abandoned blockade of Jerusalem.

At last in a single night the deliverance miraculously

came. It is implied by the scattered accounts of those days of salvation, that an Assyrian corps continued to sit before Jerusalem even after the Rabshakeh had returned to the headquarters of Sennacherib. The thirty-third of Isaiah, as well as those Psalms which celebrate the Assyrian's disappearance from Judah, describe it as having taken place from under the walls of Jerusalem and the astonished eyes of her guardians. It was not, however, upon this force—perhaps little more than a brigade of observation (xxxiii. 18)—that the calamity fell which drove Sennacherib so suddenly from Syria. *And there went forth* (*that night,* adds the book of Kings) *the angel of Jehovah; and he smote in the camp of Assyria one hundred and eighty-five thousand; and when* the camp *arose in the morning, behold all of them were corpses, dead men. And Sennacherib, King of Assyria, broke up, and returned and dwelt in Nineveh.* Had this pestilence dispersed the camp that lay before Jerusalem, and left beneath the walls so considerable a number of corpses, the exclamations of surprise at the sudden disappearance of Assyria, which occur in Isa. xxxiii. and in Psalms xlviii. and lxxvi., could hardly have failed to betray the fact. But these simply speak of vague *trouble* coming *upon them that were assembled about Zion,* and of their swift decampment. The trouble was the news of the calamity, whose victims were the main body of the Assyrian army, who had been making for the borders of Egypt, but were now scattered northwards like chaff.

For details of this disaster we look in vain, of course, to the Assyrian annals, which only record Sennacherib's abrupt return to Nineveh. But it is remarkable that the histories of both of his chief rivals in this campaign, Judah and Egypt, should contain independent reminiscences of so sudden and miraculous a disaster to his host. From Egyptian sources there has come down through Herodotus (ii. 14), a story that a king of Egypt, being deserted by the military caste, when "Sennacherib King of the Arabs and Assyrians" invaded his country, entered his sanctuary and appealed with weeping to his god; that the god appeared and cheered him; that he raised an army of artisans and marched to meet Sennacherib in Pelusium; that by night a multitude of field-mice ate up the quivers, bow-strings and shield-straps of the Assyrians; and that, as these fled on the morrow, very many of them fell. A stone statue of the king, adds Herodotus, stood in the temple of Hephæstus, having a mouse in the hand. Now, since the mouse was a symbol of sudden destruction, and even of the plague, this story of Herodotus seems to be merely a picturesque form of a tradition that pestilence broke out in the Assyrian camp. The parallel with the Bible narrative is close. In both accounts it is a prayer of the king that prevails. In both the Deity sends His agent—in the grotesque Egyptian an army of mice, in the sublime Jewish His angel. In both the effects are sudden, happening in a single night. From the Assyrian side we have this corroboration: that Sennacherib did abruptly return to Nineveh without taking Jerusalem or meeting with Tirhakah, and that, though he reigned for twenty years more, he never again made a Syrian campaign. Sennacherib's convenient story of his return may be compared to the ambiguous account which Cæsar gives of his first withdrawal from Britain, laying emphasis on the submission of the tribes as his reason for a swift return to France—a return which was rather due to the destruction of his fleet by storm and the consequent uneasiness of his army. Or, as we have already said, Sennacherib's account may be compared to Napoleon's professed reason for his sudden abandonment of his Spanish campaign and his quick return to Paris in 1808.

The neighbourhood in which the Assyrian army suffered this great disaster * was notorious in antiquity for its power of pestilence. Making every allowance for the untutored imagination of the ancients, we must admit the Serbonian bog, between Syria and Egypt, to have been a place terrible for filth and miasma. The noxious vapours travelled far; but the plagues, with which this swamp several times desolated the world, were first engendered among the diseased and demoralised populations, whose villages festered upon its margin. A Persian army was decimated here in the middle of the fourth century before Christ. "The fatal disease which depopulated the earth in the time of Justinian and his successors first appeared in the neighbourhood of Pelusium, between the Serbonian bog and the eastern channel of the Nile."† To the north of the bog the Crusaders also suffered from the infection. It is, therefore, very probable that the moral terror of this notorious neighbourhood, as well as its malaria, acting upon an exhausted and disappointed army in a devastated land, was the secondary cause in the great disaster, by which the Almighty humbled the arrogance of Asshur. The swiftness, with which Sennacherib's retreat is said to have begun, has been

---

* The statement of the Egyptian legend, that it was from a point in the neighbourhood of Pelusium that Sennacherib's army commenced its retreat, is not contradicted by anything in the Jewish records, which leave the locality of the disaster very vague, but, on the contrary, receives some support from what Isaiah expresses as at least the intention of Sennacherib (chap. xxxvii. 25).

† Gibbon, *Decline and Fall*, xliii.

equalled by the turning-points of other historical campaigns. Alexander the Great's decision to withdraw from India was, after victories as many as Sennacherib's, made in three days. Attila vanished out of Italy as suddenly as Sennacherib, and from a motive less evident. In the famous War of the Fosse the Meccan army broke off from their siege of Mohammed in a single stormy night. Napoleon's career went back upon itself with just as sharp a bend no less than thrice— in 1799, on Sennacherib's own ground in Syria; in 1808, in Spain; and in 1812, when he turned from Moscow upon "one memorable night of frost, in which twenty thousand horses perished, and the strength of the French army was utterly broken." *

The amount of the Assyrian loss is enormous, and implies of course a much higher figure for the army which was vast enough to suffer it; but here are some instances for comparison. In the early German invasions of Italy whole armies and camps were swept away by the pestilential climate. The losses of the First Crusade were over three hundred thousand. The soldiers of the Third Crusade, upon the scene of Sennacherib's war, were reckoned at more than half a million, and their losses by disease alone at over one hundred thousand.† The Grand Army of Napoleon entered Russia two hundred and fifty thousand, but came out, having suffered no decisive defeat, only twelve thousand; on the retreat from Moscow alone ninety thousand perished.

What we are concerned with, however, is neither the immediate occasion nor the exact amount of Sennacherib's loss, but the bare fact, so certainly

---

* Arnold, *Lectures on Modern History*, 177, quoted by Stanley.
† Gibbon, xlii., lix.

established, that, having devastated Judah to the very walls of Jerusalem, the Assyrian was compelled by some calamity apart from human war to withdraw before the sacred city itself was taken. For this was the essential part of Isaiah's prediction; upon this he had staked the credit of the pure monotheism, whose prophet he was to the world. If we keep before us these two simple certainties about the great Deliverance: *first*, that it had been foretold by Jehovah's word, and *second*, that it had been now achieved, despite all human probability, by Jehovah's own arm, we shall understand the enormous spiritual impression which it left upon Israel. The religion of the one supreme God, supreme in might because supreme in righteousness, received a most emphatic historical vindication, a signal and glorious triumph. Well might Isaiah exclaim, on the morning of the night during which that Assyrian host had drifted away from Jerusalem, *Jehovah is our Judge; Jehovah is our Lawgiver; Jehovah is our King: He saveth us.* No other god for the present had any chance in Judah. Idolatry was discredited, not by the political victory of a puritan faction, not even by the distinctive genius or valour of a nation, but by an evident act of Providence, to which no human aid had been contributory. It was nothing less than the baptism of Israel in spiritual religion, the grace of which was never wholly undone.

Nevertheless, the story of Jehovah's triumph cannot be justly recounted without including the reaction which followed upon it within the same generation. Before twenty years had passed from the day, on which Jerusalem, with the forty-sixth Psalm on her lips, sought with all her heart the God of Isaiah, she relapsed into an idolatry, that wore only this sign of the uncompromising puritanism it had displaced: that it was gloomy, and filled with a sense of sin unknown to Israel's idolatries previous to the age of Isaiah. The change would be almost incomprehensible to us, who have realized the spiritual effects of Sennacherib's disappearance, if we had not within our own history a somewhat analogous experience. Puritanism was as gloriously accredited by event and seemed to be as generally accepted by England under Cromwell as faith in the spiritual religion of Isaiah was vindicated by the deliverance of Jerusalem and the peace of Judah under Hezekiah. But swiftly as the ruling temper in England changed after Cromwell's death, and Puritanism was laid under the ban, and persecution and licentiousness broke out, so quickly when Hezekiah died did Manasseh his son—no change of dynasty here—*do evil in the sight of Jehovah, and make Judah to sin, building again the high places and rearing up altars for Baal and altars in the house of Jehovah, whereof Jehovah had said, In Jerusalem will I put My name.* Idolatry was never so rampant in Judah. *Moreover, Manasseh shed innocent blood till he filled Jerusalem from one end to another.* It is in this carnage that tradition has placed the death of Isaiah. He, who had been Judah's best counsellor through five reigns, on whom the whole nation had gathered in the day of her distress, and by whose faith her long-hoped-for salvation had at last become substantive, was violently put to death by the son of Hezekiah. It is said that he was *sawn asunder.*[*]

The parallel, which we are pursuing, does not, however, close here. "As soon," says an English historian, "as the wild orgy of the Restoration was over, men began

---

[*] Heb. xi.

to see that nothing that was really worthy in the work of Puritanism had been undone. The whole history of English progress since the Restoration, on its moral and spiritual sides, has been the history of Puritanism."

For the principles of Isaiah and their victory we may make a claim as much larger than this claim, as Israel's influence on the world has been greater than England's. Israel never wholly lost the grace of the baptism wherewith she was baptized in 701. Even in her history there was no event in which the unaided interposition of God was more conspicuous. It is from an appreciation of the meaning of such a Providence that Israel derives her character—that character which marks her off so distinctively from her great rival in the education of the human race, and endows her ministry with its peculiar value to the world. If we are asked for the characteristics of the Hellenic genius, we point to the august temples and images of beauty in which the wealth and art of man have evolved in human features most glorious suggestions of divinity, or we point to Thermopylæ, where human valour and devotion seem grander even in unavailing sacrifice than the almighty Fate, that renders them the prey of the barbarian. In Greece the human is greater than the divine. But if we are asked to define the spirit of Israel, we remember the worship which Isaiah has enjoined in his opening chapter, a worship that dispenses even with temple and with sacrifice, but, from the first strivings of conscience to the most certain enjoyment of peace, ascribes all man's experience to the word of God. In contrast with Thermopylæ, we recall Jerusalem's Deliverance, effected apart from human war by the direct stroke of Heaven. In Judah man is great simply as he rests on God. The rocks of Thermopylæ, how imperishably beautiful do they shine to latest ages with the comradeship, the valour, the sacrificial blood of human heroes! It is another beauty which Isaiah saw upon the bare, dry rocks of Zion, and which has drawn to them the admiration of the world. *There*, he said, *Jehovah is glory for us, a place of broad rivers and streams.*

In returning and rest shall ye be saved; in quietness and in confidence is your strength. How divine Isaiah's message is, may be proved by the length of time mankind is taking to learn it. The remarkable thing is, that he staked so lofty a principle, and the pure religion of which it was the temper, upon a political result, that he staked them upon, and vindicated them by, a purely local and material success—the relief of Jerusalem from the infidel. Centuries passed, and Christ came. He did not—for even He could not—preach a more spiritual religion than that which He had committed to His greatest forerunner, but He released this religion, and the temper of faith which Isaiah had so divinely expressed, from the local associations and merely national victories, with which even Isaiah had been forced to identify them. The destruction of Jerusalem by the heathen formed a large part of Christ's prediction of the immediate future; and He comforted the remnant of faith with these words, to some of which Isaiah's lips had first given their meaning: *Ye shall neither in this mountain nor yet in Jerusalem worship the Father. God is a Spirit, and they that worship Him must worship Him in spirit and in truth.*

Again centuries passed—no less than eighteen from Isaiah—and we find Christendom, though Christ had come between, returning to Isaiah's superseded problem, and, while reviving its material conditions, unable to apply to them the prophet's spiritual temper. The

Christianity of the Crusades fell back upon Isaiah's position without his spirit. Like him, it staked the credit of religion upon the relief of the holy city from the grasp of the infidel; but, in ghastly contrast to that pure faith and serene confidence with which a single Jew maintained the inviolateness of Mount Zion in the face of Assyria, with what pride and fraud, with what blood and cruelty, with what impious invention of miracle and parody of Divine testimony, did countless armies of Christendom, excited by their most fervent prophets and blessed by their high-priest, attempt in vain the recovery of Jerusalem from the Saracen! The Crusades are a gigantic proof of how easy it is to adopt the external forms of heroic ages, how difficult to repeat their inward temper. We could not have more impressive witness borne to the fact that humanity—though obedient to the orthodox Church, though led by the strongest spirits of the age, though hallowed by the presence of its greatest saints, though enduring all trials, though exhibiting an unrivalled power of self-sacrifice and enthusiasm, though beautified by courtesy and chivalry, and though doing and suffering all for Christ's sake—may yet fail to understand the old precept that *in returning and rest men are saved, in quietness and in confidence is their strength.* Nothing could more emphatically prove the loftiness of Isaiah's teaching than this failure of Christendom even to come within sight of it.

Have we learned this lesson yet? O God of Israel, God of Isaiah, in returning to whom and resting upon whom alone we are saved, purge us of self and of the pride of life, of the fever and the falsehood they breed. Teach us that in quietness and in confidence is our strength. Help us to be still and know that Thou art God.

CHAPTER XXIV.

A REVIEW OF ISAIAH'S PREDICTIONS CONCERNING THE DELIVERANCE OF JERUSALEM.

AS we have gathered together all that Isaiah prophesied concerning the Messiah, so it may be useful for closer students of his book if we now summarise (even at the risk of a little repetition) the facts of his marvellous prediction of the siege and delivery of Jerusalem. Such a review, besides being historically interesting, ought to prove of edification in so far as it instructs us in the kind of faith by which the Holy Ghost inspired a prophet to foretell the future.

1. The primary conviction with which Isaiah felt himself inspired by the Spirit of Jehovah was a purely moral one—that a devastation of Judah was necessary for her people's sin, to which he shortly added a religious one: that a remnant would be saved. He had this double conviction as early as 740 B.C. (vi. 11—13).

2. Looking round the horizon for some phenomenon with which to identify this promised judgement, Isaiah described the latter at first without naming any single people as the invaders of Judah (v. 26 ff.). It may have been that for a moment he hesitated between Assyria and Egypt. Once he named them together as equally the Lord's instruments upon Judah (vii. 18),

but only once. When Ahaz resolved to call Assyria into the Syrian quarrels, Isaiah exclusively designated the northern power as the scourge he had predicted; and when in 732 the Assyrian armies had overrun Samaria, he graphically described their necessary overflow into Judah also (viii.). This invasion did not spread to Judah, but Isaiah's combined moral and political conviction, for both elements of which he claimed the inspiration of God's Spirit, seized him with renewed strength in 725, when Salmanassar marched south upon Israel (xxviii.); and in 721, when Sargon captured Samaria, Isaiah uttered a vivid description of his speedy arrival before Jerusalem (x. 28 ff.). This prediction was again disappointed. But Sargon's departure without invading Judah, and her second escape from him on his return to Syria in 711, did not in the least induce Isaiah to relax either of his two convictions. Judah he proclaimed to be as much in need of punishment as ever (xxix.—xxxii.); and, though on Sargon's death all Palestine revolted from Assyria to Egypt, he persisted that this would not save her from Sennacherib (xiv. 29 ff.; xxix.—xxx.). The "dourness" with which his countrymen believed in Egypt naturally caused the prophet to fill his orations at this time with the *political* side of his conviction that Assyria was stronger than Egypt; but because Jerusalem's Egyptian policy springs from a deceitful temper (xxx. 1, 9, 10) he is as earnest as ever with his *moral* conviction that judgement is coming. After 705 his pictures of a siege of Jerusalem grow more definite (xxix.; xxx.). He seems scorched by the nearness of the Assyrian conflagration (xxx. 27 ff.). At last in 701, when Sennacherib comes to Palestine, the siege is pictured as immediate—chaps. i. and xx., which also show at its height the prophet's moral conviction of the necessity of the siege for punishing his people.

3. But over against this *moral* conviction, that Judah must be devastated for her sin, and this *political*, that Assyria is to be the instrument, even to the extreme of a siege of Jerusalem, the prophet still holds strongly to the *religious* assurance that God cannot allow His shrine to be violated or His people to be exterminated. At first it is only of the people that Isaiah speaks—*the remnant* (vi. ; viii. 18). Jerusalem is not mentioned in the verses that describe the overflowing of all Judah by Assyria (viii. 7). It is only when at last, in 721, the prophet realizes how near a siege of Jerusalem may be (x. 11, 28—32), that he also pictures the sudden destruction of the Assyrian on his arrival within sight of her walls (x. 33). In 705, when the siege of the sacred city once more becomes imminent, the prophet again reiterates to the heathen that Zion alone shall stand among the cities of Syria (xiv. 32). To herself he says that, though she shall be besieged and brought very low, she shall finally be delivered (xxix. 1—8; xxx. 19—26; xxxi. 1, 4, 5). It is true, this conviction seems to be broken—once by a prophecy of uncertain date (xxxii. 14), which indicates a desolation of the buildings of Jerusalem, and once by the prophet's sentence of death upon the inhabitants in the hour of their profligacy (xxii.)—but when the city has repented, and the enemy have perfidiously come back to demand her surrender, Isaiah again asseverates, though all are hopeless, that she shall not fall (xxxvii.).

4. Now, with regard to the method of Jerusalem's deliverance, Isaiah has uniformly described this as happening not by human battle. From the beginning he said that Israel should be delivered in the last extremity

of their weakness (vi. 13). On the Assyrian's arrival over against the city, Jehovah is to lop him off (x. 33). When her enemies have invested Jerusalem, Jehovah is to come down in thunder and a hurricane and sweep them away (after 705, xxix. 5—8). They are to be suddenly disappointed, like a hungry man waking from a dream of food. A beautiful promise is given of the raising of the siege without mention of struggle or any weapon (xxx. 20—26). The Assyrian is to be checked as a wild bull is checked *with a lasso*, is to be slain *by the lighting down of the Lord's arm, by the voice of the Lord*, through a judgement that shall be liker a solemn holocaust to God than a human battle (xxx. 30—33). When the Assyrian comes back, and Hezekiah is crushed by the new demand for surrender, Isaiah says that, by a Divinely inspired impulse, Sennacherib, hearing bad news, shall suddenly return to his own land (xxxviii. 7).

It is only in very little details that these predictions differ. The thunderstorm and torrents of fire are, of course, but poetic variations. In 721, however, the prophet hardly anticipates the very close siege, which he pictures after 705; and while from 705 to 702 he identifies the relief of Jerusalem with a great calamity to the Assyrian army about to invade Judah, yet in 701, when the Assyrians are actually on the spot, he suggests that nothing but a rumour shall cause their retreat and so leave Jerusalem free of them.

5. In all this we see a certain FIXITY and a certain FREEDOM. The freedom, the changes and inconsistencies in the prediction, are entirely limited to those of Isaiah's convictions which we have called political, and which the prophet evidently gathered from his observation of political circumstances as these developed

before his eyes from year to year. But what was fixed and unalterable to Isaiah, he drew from the moral and religious convictions to which his political observation was subservient; viz., Judah's very sore punishment for sin, the survival of a people of God in the world, and their deliverance by His own act.

6. This "Bible-reading" in Isaiah's predictive prophecies reveals very clearly the nature of INSPIRATION under the old covenant. To Isaiah inspiration was nothing more nor less than the possession of certain strong moral and religious convictions, which he felt he owed to the communication of the Spirit of God, and according to which he interpreted, and even dared to foretell, the history of his people and the world. Our study completely dispels, on the evidence of the Bible itself, that view of inspiration and prediction, so long held in the Church, which it is difficult to define, but which means something like this: that the prophet beheld a vision of the future in its actual detail and read this off as a man may read the history of the past out of a book or a clear memory. This is a very simple view, but too simple either to meet the facts of the Bible, or to afford to men any of that intellectual and spiritual satisfaction which the discovery of the Divine methods is sure to afford. The literal view of inspiration is too simple to be true, and too simple to be edifying. On the other hand, how profitable, how edifying, is the Bible's own account of its inspiration! To know that men interpreted, predicted and controlled history in the power of the purest moral and religious convictions—in the knowledge of, and the loyalty to, certain fundamental laws of God—is to receive an account of inspiration, which is not only as satisfying to the reason as it is true to the facts

of the Bible, but is spiritually very helpful by the lofty example and reward it sets before our own faith. By faith differing in degree, but not in kind, from ours, *faith which is the substance of things hoped for*, these men became prophets of God, and received the testimony of history that they spoke from Him. Isaiah prophesied and predicted all he did from loyalty to two simple truths, which he tells us he received from God Himself: that sin must be punished, and that the people of God must be saved. This simple faith, acting along with a wonderful knowledge of human nature and ceaseless vigilance of affairs, constituted inspiration for Isaiah.

There is thus, with great modifications, an analogy between the prophet and the scientific observer of the present day. Men of science are able to affirm the certainty of natural phenomena by their knowledge of the laws and principles of nature. Certain forces being present, certain results must come to pass. The Old Testament prophets, working in history, a sphere where the problems were infinitely more complicated by the presence and powerful operation of man's free-will, seized hold of principles as conspicuous and certain to them as the laws of nature are to the scientist; and out of their conviction of these they proclaimed the necessity of certain events. God is inflexibly righteous, He cannot utterly destroy His people or the witness of Himself among men: these were the laws. Judah shall be punished, Israel shall continue to exist: these were the certainties deduced from the laws. But for the exact conditions and forms both of the punishment and its relief the prophets depended upon their knowledge of the world, of which, as these pages testify, they were the keenest and largest-hearted observers that ever appeared.

This account of prophecy may be offered with advantage to those who are prejudiced against prophecy as full of materials, which are inexplicable to minds accustomed to find a law and reason for everything. Grant the truths of the spiritual doctrines, which the prophets made their premises, and you must admit that their predictions are neither arbitrary nor bewildering. Or begin at the other end : verify that these facts took place, and that the prophets actually predicted them ; and if you are true to your own scientific methods, you will not be able to resist the conclusion that the spiritual laws and principles, by which the predictions were made, are as real as those by which in the realm of nature you proclaim the necessity of certain physical phenomena—and all this in spite of there being at work in the prophets' sphere a force, the free-will of man, which cannot interfere with the laws you work by, as it can with those on which they depend.

But, to turn from the apologetic value of this account of prophecy to the experimental, we maintain that it brings out a new sacredness upon common life. If it be true that Isaiah had no magical means for foretelling the future, but simply his own spiritual convictions and his observation of history, that may, of course, deprive some eyes of a light which they fancied they saw bursting from heaven. But, on the other hand, does it not cast a greater glory upon daily life and history, to have seen in Isaiah this close connection between spiritual conviction and political event ? Does it not teach us that life is governed by faith ; that the truths we profess are the things that make history ; that we carry the future in our hearts ; that not an event happens but is to be used by us as meaning the effect of some law of God, and not a fact appears but is the symbol and sacrament of His truth ?

CHAPTER XXV.

AN OLD TESTAMENT BELIEVER'S SICK-BED; OR, THE DIFFERENCE CHRIST HAS MADE.

Isaiah xxxviii.; xxxix. (DATE UNCERTAIN).

TO the great national drama of Jerusalem's deliverance, there have been added two scenes of a personal kind, relating to her king. Chaps. xxxviii. and xxxix. are the narrative of the sore sickness and recovery of King Hezekiah, and of the embassy which Merodach-baladan sent him, and how he received the embassy. The date of these events is difficult to determine. If, with Canon Cheyne, we believe in an invasion of Judah by Sargon in 711, we shall be tempted to refer them, as he does, to that date—the more so that the promise of fifteen additional years made to Hezekiah in 711, the fifteenth year of his reign, would bring it up to the twenty-nine, at which it is set in 2 Kings xviii. 2. That, however, would flatly contradict the statement both of Isaiah xxxviii. 1 and 2 Kings xx. 1 that Hezekiah's sickness fell in the days of the invasion of Judah by Sennacherib; that is, after 705. But to place the promise of fifteen additional years to Hezekiah after 705, when we know he had been reigning for at least twenty years, would be to contradict the verse, just cited, which sums up the years of his reign as twenty-nine. This is, in fact, one of the instances, in which we must admit our present inability to elucidate the chronology of this portion of the book of Isaiah. Mr. Cheyne thinks the editor mistook the siege by Sennacherib for the siege by Sargon. But as the fact of a siege by Sargon has never been satisfactorily established, it seems safer to trust the statement that Hezekiah's sickness occurred in the reign of Sennacherib, and to allow that there has been an error somewhere in the numbering of the years. It is remarkable that the name of Merodach-baladan does not help us to decide between the two dates. There was a Merodach-baladan in rebellion against Sargon in 710, and there was one in rebellion against Sennacherib in 705. It has not yet been put past doubt as to whether these two are the same. The essential is that there was a Merodach-baladan alive, real or only claimant king of Babylon, about 705, and that he was likely at that date to treat with Hezekiah, being himself in revolt against Assyria. Unable to come to any decision about the conflicting numbers, we leave uncertain the date of the events recounted in chaps. xxxviii., xxxix. The original form of the narrative, but wanting Hezekiah's hymn, is given in 2 Kings xx.*

We have given to this chapter the title "An Old Testament Believer's Deathbed; or, The Difference Christ has made," not because this is the only spiritual suggestion of the story, but because it seems to the present expositor as if this were the predominant feeling

---

* Isa. xxxviii., xxxix., has evidently been abridged from 2 Kings xx. and in some points has to be corrected by the latter. Chap. xxxviii 21, 22, of course, must be brought forward before ver. 7.

left in Christian minds after reading for us the story. In Hezekiah's conduct there is much of courage for us to admire, as there are other elements to warn us; but when we have read the whole story, we find ourselves saying, What a difference Christ has made to me! Take Hezekiah from two points of view, and then let the narrative itself bring out this difference.

Here is a man, who, although he lived more than twenty-five centuries ago, is brought quite close to our side. Death, who herds all men into his narrow fold, has crushed this Hebrew king so close to us that we can feel his very heart beat. Hezekiah's hymn gives us entrance into the fellowship of his sufferings. By the figures he so skilfully uses he makes us feel that pain, the shortness of life, the suddenness of death and the utter blackness beyond were to him just what they are to us. And yet this kinship in pain, and fear and ignorance only makes us the more aware of something else which we have and he has not.

Again, here is a man to whom religion gave all it could give without the help of Christ; a believer in the religion out of which Christianity sprang, perhaps the most representative Old Testament believer we could find, for Hezekiah was at once the collector of what was best in its literature and the reformer of what was worst in its worship; a man permeated by the past piety of his Church, and enjoying as his guide and philosopher the boldest prophet who ever preached the future developments of its spirit. Yet when we put Hezekiah and all that Isaiah can give him on one side, we shall again feel for ourselves on the other what a difference Christ has made.

This difference a simple study of the narrative will make clear.

I.

In those days Hezekiah became sick unto death. They were critical days for Judah—no son born to the king (2 Kings xxi. 1), the work of reformation in Judah not yet consolidated, the big world tossing in revolution all around. Under God, everything depended on an experienced ruler; and this one, without a son to succeed him, was drawing near to death. We will therefore judge Hezekiah's strong passion for life to have been patriotic as well as selfish. He stood in the midtime of his days, with a faithfully executed work behind him and so good an example of kinghood that for years Isaiah had not expressed his old longing for the Messiah. The Lord had counted Hezekiah righteous; that twin-sign had been given him which more than any other assured an Israelite of Jehovah's favour—a good conscience and success in his work. Well, therefore, might he cry when Isaiah brought him the sentence of death, *Ah, now, Jehovah, remember, I beseech Thee, how I have walked before Thee in truth and with a perfect heart, and have done that which is good in Thine eyes. And Hezekiah wept with a great weeping.*

There is difficulty in the strange story which follows. The dial was probably a pyramid of steps on the top of which stood a short pillar or obelisk. When the sun rose in the morning, the shadow cast by the pillar would fall right down the western side of the pyramid to the bottom of the lowest step. As the sun ascended the shadow would shorten, and creep up inch by inch to the foot of the pillar. After noon, as the sun began to descend to the west, the shadow would creep down the eastern steps; and the steps were so measured that each one marked a certain degree of time. It was probably afternoon when Isaiah visited the king. The shadow was *going down* according to the regular law; the sign consisted in causing the shadow to shrink up the steps again. Such a reversal of the ordinary progress of the shadow may have been caused in either of two ways: by the whole earth being thrown back on its axis, which we may dismiss as impossible, or by the occurrence of the phenomenon known as refraction. Refraction is a disturbance in the atmosphere by which the rays of the sun are bent or deflected from their natural course into an angular one. In this case, instead of shooting straight over the top of the obelisk, the rays of the sun had been bent down and inward, so that the shadow fled up to the foot of the obelisk. There are many things in the air which might cause this; it is a phenomenon often observed; and the Scriptural narratives imply that on this occasion it was purely local (2 Chron. xxxii. 31). Had we only the narrative in the book of Isaiah, the explanation would have been easy. Isaiah, having given the sentence of death, passed the dial in the palace courtyard, and saw the shadow lying ten degrees farther up than it should have done, the sight of which coincided with the inspiration that the king would not die; and Isaiah went back to announce to Hezekiah his reprieve, and naturally call his attention to this as a sign, to which a weak and desponding man would be glad to cling. But the original narrative in the book of Kings tells us that Isaiah offered Hezekiah a choice of signs: that the shadow should either advance or retreat, and that the king chose the latter. The sign came in answer to Isaiah's prayer, and is narrated to us as a special Divine interposition. But a medicine accompanied it, and

Hezekiah recovered through a poultice of figs laid on the boil from which he suffered.

While recognising for our own faith the uselessness of a discussion on this sign offered to a sick man, let us not miss the moral lessons of so touching a narrative, nor the sympathy with the sick king which it is fitted to produce, and which is our best introduction to the study of his hymn.

Isaiah had performed that most awful duty of doctor or minister the telling of a friend that he must die. Few men have not in their personal experience a key to the prophet's feelings on this occasion. The leaving of a dear friend for the last time; the coming out into the sunlight which he will nevermore share with us; the passing by the dial; the observation of the creeping shadow; the feeling that it is only a question of time; the passion of prayer into which that feeling throws us that God may be pleased to put off the hour and spare our friend; the invention, that is born, like prayer, of necessity: a cure we suddenly remember; the confidence which prayer and invention bring between them; the return with the joyful news; the giving of the order about the remedy—cannot many in their degree rejoice with Isaiah in such an experience? But he has, too, a conscience of God and God's work to which none of us may pretend: he knows how indispensable to that work his royal pupil is, and out of this inspiration he prophesies the will of the Lord that Hezekiah shall recover.

Then the king, with a sick man's sacramental longing, asks a sign. Out through the window the courtyard is visible; there stands the same step-dial of Ahaz, the long pillar on the top of the steps, the shadow creeping down them through the warm afternoon sunshine. To the sick man it must have been like the finger of death coming nearer. *Shall the shadow*, asks the prophet, *go forward ten steps or go back ten steps?* *It is easy*, says the king, alarmed, *for the shadow to go down ten steps.* Easy for it to go down! Has he not been feeling that all the afternoon? " Do not," we can fancy him saying, with the gasp of a man who has been watching its irresistible descent— "do not let that black thing come farther; but *let the shadow go backward ten steps.*"

The shadow returned, and Hezekiah got his sign. But when he was well, he used it for more than a sign. He read a great spiritual lesson in it. The time, which upon the dial had been apparently thrown back, had in his life been really thrown back; and God had given him his years to live over again. The past was to be as if it had never been, its guilt and weakness wiped out. *Thou hast cast behind Thy back all my sins.* As a new-born child Hezekiah felt himself uncommitted by the past, not a sin's-doubt nor a sin's-cowardice in him, with the heart of a little child, but yet with the strength and dignity of a grown man, for it is the magic of tribulation to bring innocence with experience. *I shall go softly*, or literally, *with dignity or caution, as in a procession, all my years because of the bitterness of my soul. O Lord, upon such things do men live; and altogether in them is the life of my spirit.* . . . *Behold, for perfection was it bitter to me*, so *bitter.* And through it all there breaks a new impression of God. *What shall I say? He hath both spoken with me, and Himself hath done it.* As if afraid to impute his profits to the mere experience itself, *In them is the life of my spirit*, he breaks in with *Yea, Thou hast recovered me; yea, Thou hast made me to live.* And then, by a very pregnant construction, he adds, *Thou hast loved my soul out of the pit of destruction;* that is, of course, *loved, and by Thy love lifted,* but he uses the one word *loved,* and gives it the active force of *drawing* or *lifting.* In this lay the head and glory of Hezekiah's experience. He was a religious man, an enthusiast for the Temple services, and had all his days as his friend the prophet whose heart was with the heart of God; but it was not through any of these means God came near him, not till he lay sick and had turned his face to the wall. Then indeed he cried, *What shall I say?* **He hath both spoken with me, and Himself hath done it!**

Forgiveness, a new peace, a new dignity and a visit from the living God! Well might Hezekiah exclaim that it was only through a near sense of death that men rightly learned to live. *Ah, Lord, it is upon these things that men live; and wholly therein is the life of my spirit.* It is by these things men live, and therein I have learned for the first time what life is!

In all this at least we cannot go beyond Hezekiah, and he stands an example to the best Christian among us. Never did a man bring richer harvest from the fields of death. Everything that renders life really life—peace, dignity, a new sense of God and of His forgiveness—these were the spoils which Hezekiah won in his struggle with the grim enemy. He had snatched from death a new meaning for life; he had robbed death of its awful pomp, and bestowed this on careless life. Hereafter he should walk with the step and the mien of a conqueror—*I shall go in solemn procession all my years because of the bitterness of my soul*—or with the carefulness of a worshipper, who sees at the end of his course the throne of the Most High God, and makes all his life an ascent thither.

This is the effect which every great sorrow and struggle has upon a noble soul. Come to the streets of the living. Who are these, whom we can so easily distinguish from the crowd by their firmness of step and look of peace, walking softly where some spurt and some halt, holding, without rest or haste, the tenor of their way, as if they marched to music heard by their ears alone? These are they which have come out of great tribulation. They have brought back into time the sense of eternity. They know how near the invisible worlds lie to this one, and the sense of the vast silences stills all idle laughter in their hearts. The life that is to other men chance or sport, strife or hurried flight, has for them its allotted distance; is for them a measured march, a constant worship. *For the bitterness of their soul they go in procession all their years.* Sorrow's subjects, they are our kings; wrestlers with death, our veterans: and to the rabble armies of society they set the step of a nobler life.

Count especially the young man blessed, who has looked into the grave before he has faced the great temptations of the world, and has not entered the race of life till he has learned his stride in the race with death. They tell us that on the outside of civilisation, where men carry their lives in their hands, a most thorough politeness and dignity are bred, in spite of the want of settled habits, by the sense of danger alone; and we know how battle and a deadly climate, pestilence or the perils of the sea have sent back to us the most careless of our youth with a self-possession and regularity of mind, that it would have been hopeless to expect them to develop amid the trivial trials of village life.

But the greatest duty of us men is not to seek nor to pray for such combats with death. It is when God has found these for us to remain true to our memories of them. The hardest duty of life is to remain true to our psalms of deliverance, as it is certainly life's greatest temptation to fall away from the sanctity of sorrow, and suffer the stately style of one who knows how near death hovers to his line of march to degenerate into the broken step of a wanton life. This was Hezekiah's temptation, and this is why the story of his fall in the thirty-ninth chapter is placed beside his vows in the thirty-eighth—to warn us how easy it is for those who have come conquerors out of a struggle with death to fall a prey to common life. He had said, *I will walk softly all my years*; but how arrogantly and rashly he carried himself when Merodach-baladan sent the embassy to congratulate him on his recovery. It was not with the dignity of the veteran, but with a childish love of display, perhaps also with the too restless desire to secure an alliance, that he showed the envoys *his storehouse, the silver, and the gold, and the spices, and the precious oil, and all the house of his armour and all that was found in his treasures. There was nothing which Hezekiah did not show them in his house nor in all his dominion.* In this behaviour there was neither caution nor sobriety, and we cannot doubt but that Hezekiah felt the shame of it when Isaiah sternly rebuked him and threw upon all his house the dark shadow of captivity.

It is easier to win spoils from death than to keep them untarnished by life. Shame burns warm in a soldier's heart when he sees the arms he risked life to win rusting for want of a little care. Ours will not burn less if we discover that the strength of character we brought with us out of some great tribulation has been slowly weakened by subsequent self-indulgence of vanity. How awful to have fought for character with death only to squander it upon life! It is well to keep praying, "My God, suffer me not to forget my bonds and my bitterness. In my hours of wealth and ease, and health and peace, by the memory of Thy judgements deliver me, good Lord."

II.

So far then Hezekiah is an example and warning to us all. With all our faith in Christ, none of us, in the things mentioned, may hope to excel this Old Testament believer. But notice very particularly that Hezekiah's faith and fortitude are profitable only for this life. It is when we begin to think, What of the life to come? that we perceive the infinite difference Christ has made.

We know what Hezekiah felt when his back was turned on death, and he came up to life again. But what did he feel when he faced the other way, and his back was to life? With his back to life and facing deathwards, Hezekiah saw nothing, that was worth hoping for. To him to die was to leave God behind him, to leave the face of God as surely as he was leaving the face of man. *I said, I shall not see Jah, Jah in the land of the living; I shall gaze upon man no more with the inhabitants of the world.* The beyond was not to Hezekiah absolute nothingness, for he had his conceptions, the popular conceptions of his time, of a sort of existence that was passed by those who had been men upon earth. The imagination of his people figured the gloomy portals of a nether world—*Sheol*, the *Hollow* (Dante's "hollow realm"), or perhaps the *Craving*—into which death herds the shades of men, bloodless, voiceless, without love or hope or aught that makes life worth living. With such an existence beyond, to die to life here was to Hezekiah like as when *a weaver rolls up* the finished web. My life may be a pattern for others to copy, a banner for others to fight under, but for me it is finished. Death has cut it from the loom. Or it was like going into captivity. *Mine age is removed and is carried away from me into exile, like a shepherd's tent*—exile which to a Jew was the extreme of despair, implying as it did absence from God, and salvation and the possibility of worship. *Sheol cannot praise Thee; death cannot celebrate Thee: they that go down into the pit cannot hope for Thy faithfulness.*

Of this then at the best Hezekiah was sure: a respite of fifteen years—nothing beyond. Then the shadow would not return upon the dial; and as the king's eyes closed upon the dear faces of his friends, his sense of the countenance of God would die too, and his soul slip into the abyss, hopeless of God's faithfulness.

It is this awful anticlimax, which makes us feel the difference Christ has made. This saint stood in almost the clearest light that revelation cast before Jesus. He was able to perceive in suffering a meaning and derive from it a strength not to be exceeded by any Christian. Yet his faith is profitable for this life alone. For him character may wrestle with death over and over again, and grow the stronger for every grapple, but death wins the last throw.

It may be said that Hezekiah's despair of the future is simply the morbid thoughts of a sick man or the exaggerated fancies of a poet. "We must not," it is urged, "define a poet's language with the strictness of a theology." True, and we must also make some allowance for a man dying prematurely in the midst of his days. But if this hymn is only poetry, it would have been as easy to poetise on the opposite possibilities across the grave. So quick an imagination as Hezekiah's could not have failed to take advantage of the slightest scintilla of glory that pierced the cloud. It must be that his eye saw none, for all his poetry droops the other way. We seek in heaven for praise in its fulness; there we know God's servants shall see Him face to face. But of this Hezekiah had not the slightest imagination; he anxiously prayed that he might recover *to strike the stringed instruments all the days of his life in the house of Jehovah. The living, the living, he praiseth thee, as I do this day; the father to the children shall make known Thy truth.* But *they that go down into the pit cannot hope for Thy faithfulness.*

Now compare all this with the Psalms of Christian hope; with the faith that fills Paul; with his ardour who says, *To me to depart is far better;* with the glory which John beholds with open face: the hosts of the redeemed praising God and walking in the light of His face, all the geography of that country laid down, and the plan of the new Jerusalem declared to the very fashion of her stones; with the audacity since of Christian art and song: the rapture of Watts' hymns and the exhilaration of Wesley's praise as they contemplate death; and with the joyful and exact anticipations of so many millions of common men as they turn their faces to the wall. In all these, in even the Book of the Revelation, there is of course a great deal of pure fancy. But imagination never bursts in anywhither till fact has preceded. And it is just because there is a great fact standing between us and Hezekiah that the pureness of our faith and the richness of our imagination of immortality differ so much from his. That fact is

Jesus Christ, His resurrection and ascension. It is He who has made all the difference and brought life and immortality to light.

And we shall know the difference if we lose our faith in that fact. For *except Christ be risen from the dead* and gone before to a country which derives all its reality and light for our imagination from that Presence, which once walked with us in the flesh, there remains for us only Hezekiah's courage to make the best of a short reprieve, only Hezekiah's outlook into Hades when at last we turn our faces to the wall. But to be stronger and purer for having met with death, as he was, only that we must afterwards succumb, with our purity and our strength, to death—this is surely to be, as Paul said, *of all men the most miserable.*

Better far to own the power of an endless life, which Christ has sealed to us, and translate Hezekiah's experience into the new calculus of immortality. If to have faced death as he did was to inherit dignity and peace and sense of power, what glory of kingship and queenship must sit upon those faces in the other world who have been at closer quarters still with the King of terrors, and through Christ their strength have spoiled him of his sting and victory! To have felt the worst of death and to have triumphed—this is the secret of the peaceful hearts, unfaltering looks and faces of glory, *which pass in solemn procession of worship* through all eternity before the throne of God.

We shall consider the Old Testament views of a future life and resurrection more fully in chaps. xxvii. and xxx. of this volume.

CHAPTER XXVI.

HAD ISAIAH A GOSPEL FOR THE INDIVIDUAL?

THE two narratives, in which Isaiah's career culminates—that of the Deliverance of Jerusalem (xxxvj.; xxxvii.) and that of the Recovery of Hezekiah (xxxviii.; xxxix.)—cannot fail, coming together as they do, to suggest to thoughtful readers a striking contrast between Isaiah's treatment of the community and his treatment of the individual, between his treatment of the Church and his treatment of single members. For in the first of these narratives we are told how an illimitable future, elsewhere so gloriously described by the prophet, was secured for the Church upon earth; but the whole result of the second is the gain for a representative member of the Church of a respite of fifteen years. Nothing, as we have seen, is promised to the dying Hezekiah of a future life; no scintilla of the light of eternity sparkles either in Isaiah's promise or in Hezekiah's prayer. The net result of the incident is a reprieve of fifteen years: fifteen years of a character strengthened, indeed, by having met with death, but, it would sadly seem, only in order to become again the prey of the vanities of this world (chap. xxxix.). So meagre a result for the individual stands strangely out against the perpetual glory and peace assured to the community. And it suggests this question: Had

Isaiah any real gospel for the individual? If so, what was it?

First of all, we must remember that God in His providence seldom gives to one prophet or generation more than a single main problem for solution. In Isaiah's day undoubtedly the most urgent problem—and Divine problems are ever practical, not philosophical—was the continuance of the Church upon earth. It had really got to be a matter of doubt whether a body of people possessing the knowledge of the true God, and able to transfuse and transmit it, could possibly survive among the political convulsions of the world, and in consequence of its own sin. Isaiah's problem was the reformation and survival of the Church. In accordance with this, we notice how many of his terms are collective, and how he almost never addresses the individual. It is the *people*, upon whom he calls—*the nation, Israel, the house of Jacob My vineyard, the men of Judah His pleasant plantation.* To these we may add the apostrophes to the city of Jerusalem, under many personifications: *Ariel, Ariel, inhabitress of Zion, daughter of Zion.* When Isaiah denounces sin, the sinner is either the whole community or a class in the community, very seldom an individual, though there are some instances of the latter, as Ahaz and Shebna. It is *This people hath rejected,* or *The people would not.* When Jerusalem collapsed, although there must have been many righteous men still within her, Isaiah said, *What aileth thee that all belonging to thee have gone up to the housetops?* (xxii. 1). His language is wholesale. When he is not attacking society, he attacks classes or groups: *the rulers,* the land-grabbers, the drunkards, *the sinners, the judges, the house of David, the priests and the prophets, the women.* And the sins of these he describes in their social effects, or in their results upon the fate of the whole people; but he never, except in two cases, gives us their individual results. He does not make evident, like Jesus or Paul, the eternal damage a man's sin inflicts on his own soul.

Similarly when Isaiah speaks of God's grace and salvation the objects of these are again collective—*the remnant; the escaped* (also a collective noun); a *holy seed;* a *stock* or *stump*. It is a *restored nation* whom he sees under the Messiah, the perpetuity and glory of a *city* and *a State*. What we consider to be a most personal and particularly individual matter—the forgiveness of sin—he promises, with two exceptions, only to the community: *This people that dwelleth therein hath its iniquity forgiven.* We can understand all this social, collective, and wholesale character of his language only if we keep in mind his Divinely appointed work —the substance and perpetuity of a purified and secure Church of God.

Had Isaiah then no gospel for the individual? This will indeed seem impossible to us if we keep in view the following considerations:—

1. ISAIAH HIMSELF had passed through a powerfully individual experience. He had not only felt the solidarity of the people's sin—*I dwell among a people of unclean lips*—he had first felt his own particular guilt: *I am a man of unclean lips*. One who suffered the private experiences which are recounted in chap. vi.; whose *own eyes* had *seen* the *King, Jehovah of hosts;* who had gathered on his own lips his guilt and felt the fire come from heaven's altar by an angelic messenger specially to purify him; who had further devoted himself to God's service with so thrilling a sense of his own responsibility, and had so thereby felt his solitary and individual

mission—he surely was not behind the very greatest of Christian saints in the experience of guilt, of personal obligation to grace and of personal responsibility. Though the record of Isaiah's ministry contains no narratives, such as fill the ministries of Jesus and Paul, of anxious care for individuals, could he who wrote of himself that sixth chapter have failed to deal with men as Jesus dealt with Nicodemus, or Paul with the Philippian gaoler? It is not picturesque fancy, nor merely a reflection of the New Testament temper, if we realize Isaiah's intervals of relief from political labour and religious reform occupied with an attention to individual interests, which necessarily would not obtain the permanent record of his public ministry. But whether this be so or not, the sixth chapter teaches that for Isaiah all public conscience and public labour found its necessary preparation in personal religion.

2. But, again, Isaiah had an INDIVIDUAL FOR HIS IDEAL. To him the future was not only an established State; it was equally, it was first, a glorious king. Isaiah was an Oriental. We moderns of the West place our reliance upon institutions; we go forward upon ideas. In the East it is personal influence that tells, persons who are expected, followed and fought for. The history of the West is the history of the advance of thought, of the rise and decay of institutions, to which the greatest individuals are more or less subordinate. The history of the East is the annals of personalities; justice and energy in a ruler, not political principles, are what impress the Oriental imagination. Isaiah has carried this Oriental hope to a distinct and lofty pitch. The Hero whom he exalts on the margin of the future, as its Author, is not only a person of great majesty, but a character of considerable decision.

At first only the rigorous virtues of the ruler are attributed to Him (chap. xi. 1 ff.), but afterwards the graces and influence of a much broader and sweeter humanity (xxxii. 2). Indeed, in this latter oracle we saw that Isaiah spoke not so much of his great Hero, as of what any individual might become. *A man*, he says, *shall be as an hiding-place from the wind.* Personal influence is the spring of social progress, the shelter and fountain force of the community. In the following verses the effect of so pure and inspiring a presence is traced in the discrimination of individual character—each man standing out for what he is—which Isaiah defines as his second requisite for social progress. In all this there is much for the individual to ponder, much to inspire him with a sense of the value and responsibility of his own character, and with the certainty that by himself he shall be judged and by himself stand or fall. *The worthless person shall be no more called princely, nor the knave said to be bountiful.*

3. If any details of character are wanting in the picture of Isaiah's Hero, they are supplied by HEZEKIAH's SELF-ANALYSIS (chap. xxxviii.). We need not repeat what we have said in the previous chapter of the king's appreciation of what is the strength of a man's character, and particularly of how character grows by grappling with death. In this matter the most experienced of Christian saints may learn from Isaiah's pupil.

Isaiah had then, without doubt, a gospel for the individual; and to this day the individual may plainly read it in his book, may truly, strongly, joyfully live by it—so deeply does it begin, so much does it help to self-knowledge and self-analysis, so lofty are the ideals and responsibilities which it presents. But is it true that Isaiah's gospel is for this life only?

Was Isaiah's silence on the immortality of the individual due wholly to the cause we have suggested in the beginning of this chapter—that God gives to each prophet his single problem, and that the problem of Isaiah was the endurance of the Church upon earth? There is no doubt that this is only partly the explanation.

The Hebrew belonged to a branch of humanity—the Semitic—which, as its history proves, was unable to develop any strong imagination of, or practical interest in, a future life apart from foreign influence or Divine revelation. The pagan Arabs laughed at Mahommed when he preached to them of the Resurrection; and even to-day, after twelve centuries of Moslem influence, their descendants in the centre of Arabia, according to the most recent authority,* fail to form a clear conception of, or indeed to take almost any practical interest in, another world. The northern branch of the race, to which the Hebrews belonged, derived from an older civilisation a prospect of Hades, that their own fancy developed with great elaboration. This prospect, however, which we shall describe fully in connection with chaps. xiv. and xxvi., was one absolutely hostile to the interests of character in this life. It brought all men, whatever their life had been on earth, at last to a dead level of unsubstantial and hopeless existence. Good and evil, strong and weak, pious and infidel, alike became shades, joyless and hopeless, without even the power to praise God. We have seen in Hezekiah's case how such a prospect unnerved the most pious souls, and that revelation, even though represented at his bedside by an Isaiah, offered him no hope of an issue from it. The strength

---

* Doughty's *Arabia Deserta: Travels in Northern Arabia*, 1876—1878.

of character, however, which Hezekiah professes to have won in grappling with death, added to the closeness of communion with God which he enjoyed in this life, only brings out the absurdity of such a conclusion to life as the prospect of Sheol offered to the individual. If he was a pious man, if he was a man who had never felt himself deserted by God in this life, he was bound to revolt from so God-forsaken an existence after death. This was actually the line along which the Hebrew spirit went out to victory over those gloomy conceptions of death, that were yet unbroken by a risen Christ. *Thou wilt not*, the saint triumphantly cried, *leave my soul in Sheol, nor wilt Thou suffer Thine holy one to see corruption.* It was faith in the almightiness and reasonableness of God's ways, it was conviction of personal righteousness, it was the sense that the Lord would not desert His own in death, which sustained the believer in face of that awful shadow through which no light of revelation had yet broken.

If these, then, were the wings by which a believing soul under the Old Testament soared over the grave, Isaiah may be said to have contributed to the hope of personal immortality just in so far as he strengthened them. By enhancing as he did the value and beauty of individual character, by emphasizing the indwelling of God's Spirit, he was bringing life and immortality to light, even though he spoke no word to the dying about the fact of a glorious life beyond the grave. By assisting to create in the individual that character and sense of God, which alone could assure him he would never die, but pass from the praise of the Lord in this life to a nearer enjoyment of His presence beyond, Isaiah was working along the only line by which the Spirit of God seems to have assisted the Hebrew mind to an assurance of heaven.

But further in his favourite gospel of the REASONABLENESS OF GOD—that God does not work fruitlessly, nor create and cultivate with a view to judgement and destruction—Isaiah was furnishing an argument for personal immortality, the force of which has not been exhausted. In a recent work on *The Destiny of Man* * the philosophic author maintains the reasonableness of the Divine methods as a ground of belief both in the continued progress of the race upon earth and in the immortality of the individual. "From the first dawning of life we see all things working together towards one mighty goal—the evolution of the most exalted and spiritual faculties which characterize humanity. Has all this work been done for nothing? Is it all ephemeral, all a bubble that bursts, a vision that fades? On such a view the riddle of the universe becomes a riddle without a meaning. The more thoroughly we comprehend the process of evolution by which things have come to be what they are, the more we are likely to feel that to deny the everlasting persistence of the spiritual element in man is to rob the whole process of its meaning. It goes far towards putting us to permanent intellectual confusion. For my own part, I believe in the immortality of the soul, not in the sense in which I accept demonstrable truths of science, but as a supreme act of faith in the reasonableness of God's work."

From the same argument Isaiah drew only the former of these two conclusions. To him the certainty that God's people would survive the impending deluge

---

* By Professor Fiske.

of Assyria's brute force was based on his faith that the Lord is *a God of judgement*, of reasonable law and method, and could not have created or fostered so spiritual a people only to destroy them. The progress of religion upon earth was certain. But does not Isaiah's method equally make for the immortality of the individual? He did not draw this conclusion, but he laid down its premises with a confidence and richness of illustration that have never been excelled.

We, therefore, answer the question we put at the beginning of the chapter thus:—Isaiah had a gospel for the individual for this life, and all the necessary premises of a gospel for the individual for the life to come.

BOOK V.

PROPHECIES NOT RELATING TO ISAIAH'S TIME.

ISAIAH:—
    xiii.--xiv. 23
    xxiv.—xxvii.
    xxxiv.
    xxxv.

BOOK V.

IN the first thirty-nine chapters of the Book of Isaiah—the half which refers to the prophet's own career and the politics contemporary with that —we find four or five prophecies containing no reference to Isaiah himself nor to any Jewish king under whom he laboured, and painting both Israel and the foreign world in quite a different state from that in which they lay during his lifetime. These prophecies are chap. xiii., an Oracle announcing the Fall of Babylon, with its appendix, chap. xiv. 1—23, the Promise of Israel's Deliverance and an Ode upon the Fall of the Babylonian Tyrant; chaps. xxiv.—xxvii., a series of Visions of the breaking up of the universe, of restoration from exile, and even of resurrection from the dead; chap. xxxiv., the Vengeance of the Lord upon Edom; and chap. xxxv., a Song of Return from Exile.

In these prophecies Assyria is no longer the dominant world-force, nor Jerusalem the inviolate fortress of God and His people. If Assyria or Egypt is mentioned, it is but as one of the three classical enemies of Israel; and Babylon is represented as the head and front of the hostile world. The Jews are no longer in political freedom and possession of their own land; they are either in exile or just returned from it to a depopulated country. With these altered circumstances come another temper and new doctrine. The horizon is different, and the hopes that flush in dawn upon it are not quite the same as those which we have contemplated with Isaiah in his immediate future. It is no longer the repulse of the heathen invader; the inviolateness of the sacred city; the recovery of the people from the shock of attack, and of the land from the trampling of armies. But it is the people in exile, the overthrow of the tyrant in his own home, the opening of prison doors, the laying down of a highway through the wilderness, the triumph of return and the resumption of worship. There is, besides, a promise of the resurrection, which we have not found in the prophecies we have considered.

With such differences, it is not wonderful that many have denied the authorship of these few prophecies to Isaiah. This is a question that can be looked at calmly. It touches no dogma of the Christian faith. Especially it does not involve the other question, so often—and, we venture to say, so unjustly—started on this point, Could not the Spirit of God have inspired Isaiah to foresee all that the prophecies in question foretell, even though he lived more than a century before the people were in circumstances to understand them? Certainly, God is almighty. The question is not, Could He have done this? but one somewhat different: Did He do it? and to this an answer can be had only from the prophecies themselves. If these mark the Babylonian hostility or captivity as already upon Israel, this is a testimony of Scripture itself, which we cannot overlook, and beside which even unquestionable traces of similarity to Isaiah's style or the fact that these oracles are bound up with Isaiah's own undoubted prophecies have little weight. "Facts" of style will be regarded with suspicion by any one who knows how they are employed by both sides in such a question as this; while the certainty that the Book of Isaiah was put into its present form subsequently to his life will permit of, —and the evident purpose of Scripture to secure moral impressiveness rather than historical consecutiveness will account for,—later oracles being bound up with unquestioned utterances of Isaiah.

Only one of the prophecies in question confirms the tradition that it is by Isaiah, viz., chap. xiii., which bears the title *Oracle of Babylon which Isaiah, son of Amoz, did see;* but titles are themselves so much the report of tradition, being of a later date than the rest of the text, that it is best to argue the question apart from them.

On the other hand, Isaiah's authorship of these prophecies, or at least the possibility of his having written them, is usually defended by appealing to his promise of the return from exile in chap. xi. and his threat of a Babylonish captivity in chap. xxxix. This is an argument that has not been fairly met by those who deny the Isaianic authorship of chaps. xiii.—xiv. 23, xxiv.—xxvii., and xxxv. It is a strong argument, for while, as we have seen (p. 201), there are good grounds for believing Isaiah to have been likely to make such a prediction of a Babylonish captivity as is attributed to him in chap. xxxix. 6, almost all the critics agree in leaving chap. xi. to him. But if chap. xi. is Isaiah's, then he undoubtedly spoke of an exile much more extensive than had taken place by his own day. Nevertheless, even this ability in xi. to foretell an exile so vast does not account for passages in xiii.—xiv. 23, xxiv.—xxvii., which represent the Exile either as present or as actually over. No one who reads these chapters without prejudice can fail to feel the force of such passages in leading him to decide for an exilic or post-exilic authorship (see pp. 429 ff.).

Another argument against attributing these prophecies to Isaiah is that their visions of the last things, representing as they do a judgement on the whole world, and even the destruction of the whole material universe, are incompatible with Isaiah's loftiest and final hope of an inviolate Zion at last relieved and secure, of a land freed from invasion and wondrously fertile, with all the converted world, Assyria and Egypt, gathered round it as a centre. This question, however, is seriously complicated by the fact that in his youth Isaiah did undoubtedly prophesy a shaking of the whole world and the destruction of its inhabitants, and by the probability that his old age survived into a period, whose abounding sin would again make natural such wholesale predictions of judgement as we find in chap. xxiv.

Still, let the question of the eschatology be as obscure as we have shown, there remains this clear issue. In some chapters of the Book of Isaiah, which, from our knowledge of the circumstances of his times, we know must have been published while he was alive, we learn that the Jewish people has never left its land, nor lost its independence under Jehovah's anointed, and that the inviolateness of Zion and the retreat of the Assyrian invaders of Judah, without effecting the captivity of the Jews, are absolutely essential to the endurance of God's kingdom on earth. In other chapters we find that the Jews have left their land, have been long in exile (or from other passages have just returned), and that the religious essential is no more the independence of the Jewish State under a theocratic king, but only the resumption of the Temple worship. Is it possible for one man to have written both these sets of chapters? Is it possible for one age to have produced them? That is the whole question.

CHAPTER XXVII.

BABYLON AND LUCIFER.

Isaiah xiii. 2—xiv. 23 (DATE UNCERTAIN).

THIS double oracle is against the City (xiii. 2—xiv. 2) and the Tyrant (xiv. 3—23) of Babylon.

I. THE WICKED CITY (xiii. 2—xiv. 23).

The first part is a series of hurried and vanishing scenes — glimpses of ruin and deliverance caught through the smoke and turmoil of a Divine war. The drama opens with the erection of a gathering *standard upon a bare mountain* (ver. 2). He who gives the order explains it (ver. 3), but is immediately interrupted by *Hark! a tumult on the mountains, like a great people. Hark! the surge of the kingdoms of nations gathering together. Jehovah of hosts is mustering the host of war.* It is *the day of Jehovah* that is *near*, the day of His war and of His judgement upon the world.

This Old Testament expression, *the day of the* LORD, starts so many ideas that it is difficult to seize any one of them and say this is just what is meant. For *day* with a possessive pronoun suggests what has been appointed aforehand, or what must come round in its turn; means also opportunity and triumph, and also swift performance after long delay. All these thoughts are excited when we couple *a day* with any person's name. And therefore as with every dawn some one awakes saying, This is my day; as with every dawn comes some one's chance, some soul gets its wish, some will shows what it can do, some passion or principle issues into fact: so God also shall have His day, on which His justice and power shall find their full scope and triumph. Suddenly and simply, like any dawn that takes its turn on the round of time, the great decision and victory of Divine justice shall at last break out of the long delay of ages. *Howl ye, for the day of Jehovah is near; as destruction from the Destructive does it come.* Very savage and quite universal is its punishment. *Every human heart melteth.* Countless faces, white with terror, light up its darkness like flames. Sinners are *to be exterminated out of the earth; the world is to be punished for its iniquity.* Heaven, the stars, sun and moon aid the horror and the darkness, heaven shivering above, the earth quaking beneath; and between, the peoples like shepherdless sheep drive to and fro through awful carnage.

From ver. 17 the mist lifts a little. The vague turmoil clears up into a siege of Babylon by the Medians, and then settles down into Babylon's ruin and abandonment to wild beasts. Finally (xiv. 1) comes the religious reason of so much convulsion: *For Jehovah will have compassion upon Jacob, and choose again Israel, and settle them upon their own ground; and the foreign sojourner shall join himself to them, and they shall associate themselves to the house of Jacob.*

This prophecy evidently came to a people already in captivity—a very different circumstance of the Church of God from that in which we have seen her under Isaiah. But upon this new stage it is still the same old conquest. Assyria has fallen, but Babylon has taken her place. The old spirit of cruelty and covetousness has entered a new body; the only change is that it has become wealth and luxury instead of brute force and military glory. It is still selfishness and pride and atheism. At this, our first introduction to Babylon, it might have been proper to explain why throughout the Bible from Genesis to Revelation this one city should remain in fact or symbol the enemy of God and the stronghold of darkness. But we postpone what may be said of her singular reputation, till we come to the second part of the Book of Isaiah where Babylon plays a larger and more distinct role. Here her destruction is simply the most striking episode of the Divine judgement upon the whole earth. Babylon represents civilisation; she is the brow of the world's pride and enmity to God. One distinctively Babylonian characteristic, however, must not be passed over. With a ring of irony in his voice, the prophet declares, *Behold, I stir up the Medes against thee, who regard not silver and take no pleasure in gold.* The worst terror that can assail us is the terror of forces, whose character we cannot fathom, who will not stop to parley, who do not understand our language nor our bribes. It was such a power, with which the resourceful and luxurious Babylon was threatened. With money the Babylonians did all they wished to do, and believed everything else to be possible. They had subsidised kings, bought over enemies, seduced the peoples of the earth. The foe whom God now sent them was impervious to this influence. From their pure highlands came down upon corrupt civilisation a simple people, whose banner was a leathern apron, whose goal was not booty nor ease but power and mastery, who came not to rob but to displace.

The lessons of the passage are two: that the

people of God are something distinct from civilisation, though this be universal and absorbent as a very Babylon; and that the resources of civilisation are not even in material strength the highest in the universe, but God has in His armoury weapons heedless of men's cunning, and in His armies agents impervious to men's bribes. Every civilisation needs to be told, according to its temper, one of these two things. Is it hypocritical? Then it needs to be told that civilisation is not one with the people of God. Is it arrogant? Then it needs to be told that the resources of civilisation are not the strongest forces in God's universe. Man talks of the triumph of mind over matter, of the power of culture, of the elasticity of civilisation; but God has natural forces, to which all these are as the worm beneath the hoof of the horse: and if moral need arise, He will call His brute forces into requisition. *Howl ye, for the day of Jehovah is near; as destruction from the Destructive does it come.* There may be periods in man's history when, in opposition to man's unholy art and godless civilisation, God can reveal Himself only as destruction.

II. THE TYRANT (xiv. 3—23).

To the prophecy of the overthrow of Babylon there is annexed, in order to be sung by Israel in the hour of her deliverance, a *satiric ode* or *taunt-song* (Heb. *mashal*, Eng. ver. *parable*) upon the King of Babylon. A translation of this spirited poem in the form of its verse (in which, it is to be regretted, it has not been rendered by the English revisers) will be more instructive than a full commentary. But the following remarks of introduction are necessary. The word *mashal*, by which this ode is entitled, means *comparison, similitude* or *parable*, and was applicable to every sentence composed of at least two members that compared or contrasted their subjects. As the great bulk of Hebrew poetry is sententious, and largely depends for rhythm upon its parallelism, *mashal* received a general application; and while another term—*shîr*—more properly denotes lyric poetry, *mashal* is applied to rhythmical passages in the Old Testament of almost all tempers: to mere predictions, proverbs, orations, satires or taunt-songs, as here, and to didactic pieces. The parallelism of the verses in our ode is too evident to need an index. But the parallel verses are next grouped into strophes. In Hebrew poetry this division is frequently effected by the use of a refrain. In our ode there is no refrain, but the strophes are easily distinguished by difference of subject-matter. Hebrew poetry does not employ rhyme, but makes use of assonance, and to a much less extent of alliteration—a form which is more frequent in Hebrew prose. In our ode there is not much either of assonance or alliteration. But, on the other hand, the ode has but to be read to break into a certain rough and swinging rhythm. This is produced by long verses rising alternate with short ones falling. Hebrew verse at no time relied for a metrical effect upon the modern device of an equal or proportionate number of syllables. The longer verses of this ode are sometimes too short, the shorter too long, variations to which a rude chant could readily adapt itself. But the alternation of long and short is sustained throughout, except for a break at ver. 10 by the introduction of the formula *And they answered and said*, which evidently ought to stand for a long and a short verse if the number of double verses in the second strophe is to be the same as it is —seven—in the first and in the third.

The scene of the poem, the Underworld and abode of the shades of the dead, is one on which some of the most splendid imagination and music of humanity has been expended. But we must not be disappointed if we do not here find the rich detail and glowing fancy of Virgil's or of Dante's vision. This simple and even rude piece of metre, liker ballad than epic, ought to excite our wonder not so much for what it has failed to imagine as for what, being at its disposal, it has resolutely stinted itself in employing. For it is evident that the author of these lines had within his reach the rich, fantastic materials of Semitic mythology, which are familiar to us in the Babylonian remains. With an austerity, that must strike every one who is acquainted with these, he uses only so much of them as to enable him to render with dramatic force his simple theme—the vanity of human arrogance.*

For this purpose he employs the idea of the Underworld which was prevalent among the northern Semitic peoples. Sheol—the *gaping* or *craving* place—which we shall have occasion to describe in detail when we come to speak of belief in the resurrection,† is the state after death that craves and swallows all living. There dwell the shades of men amid some unsubstantial reflection of their earthly state (ver. 9), and with consciousness and passion only sufficient to greet the

---

* "Those principles of natural philosophy which smothered the religions of the East with their rank and injurious growth are almost entirely absent from the religion of the Hebrews. Here the motive-power of development is to be found in ethical ideas, which, though not indeed alien to the life of other nations, were not the source from which their religious notions were derived."—(Lotze's *Microcosmos*, Eng. Transl., ii., 466.)

† P. 447 ff.

arrival of the new-comer and express satiric wonder at his fall (ver. 9). With the arrogance of the Babylonian kings, this tyrant thought to scale the heavens to set his throne in the *mount of assembly* of the immortals, *to match the Most High*.* But his fate is the fate of all mortals—to go down to the weakness and emptiness of Sheol. Here, let us carefully observe, there is no trace of a judgement for reward or punishment. The new victim of death simply passes to his place among his equals. There was enough of contrast between the arrogance of a tyrant claiming Divinity and his fall into the common receptacle of mortality to point the prophet's moral without the addition of infernal torment. Do we wish to know the actual punishment of his pride and cruelty? It is visible above ground (strophe 4); not with his spirit, but with his corpse; not with himself, but with his wretched family. His corpse is unburied, his family exterminated; his name disappears from the earth.†

Thus, by the help of only a few fragments from the popular mythology, the sacred satirist achieves his

---

* It is, however, only just to add that, as Mr. Sayce has pointed out in the Hibbert Lectures for 1887 (p. 365), the claims of Babylonian kings and heroes for a seat on the mountain of the gods were not always mere arrogance, but the first efforts of the Babylonian mind to emancipate itself from the gloomy conceptions of Hades and provide a worthy immortality for virtue. Still most of the kings who pray for an entrance among the gods do so on the plea that they have been successful tyrants—a considerable difference from such an assurance as that of the sixteenth Psalm.

† The popular Semitic conception of Hades contained within it neither grades of condition, according to the merits of men, nor any trace of an infernal torment in aggravation of the unsubstantial state to which all are equally reduced. This statement is true of the Old Testament till at least the Book of Daniel. Sheol is lit by no

purpose. His severe monotheism is remarkable in its contrast to Babylonian poems upon similar subjects. He will know none of the gods of the underworld. In place of the great goddess, whom a Babylonian would certainly have seen presiding, with her minions, over the shades, he personifies—it is a frequent figure of Hebrew poetry—the abyss itself. *Sheol shuddereth at thee.* It is the same when he speaks (ver. 13) of the deep's great opposite, that *mount of assembly* of the gods, which the northern Semites believed to soar to a silver sky *in the recesses of the north* (ver. 14), upon the great range which in that direction bounded the Babylonian plain. This Hebrew knows of no gods there but One, whose are the stars, who is the Most High. Man's arrogance and cruelty are attempts upon His majesty. He inevitably overwhelms them. Death is their penalty: blood and squalor on earth, the concourse of shuddering ghosts below.

> *The kings of the earth set themselves,*
> *And the rulers take counsel together,*
> *Against the Lord and against His Anointed.*
> *He that sitteth in the heavens shall laugh;*
> *The Lord shall have them in derision.*

He who has heard that laughter sees no comedy in aught else. This is the one unfailing subject of

---

lurid fires, such as made the later Christian hell intolerable to the lost. That life is unsubstantial; that darkness and dust abound; above all, that God is not there, and that it is impossible to praise Him, is all the punishment which is given in Sheol. Extraordinary vice is punished above ground, in the name and family of the sinner. Sheol, with its monotony, is for average men; but extraordinary piety can break away from it (Ps. xvi.).

Hebrew satire, and it forms the irony and the rigour of the following ode.*

The only other remarks necessary are these. In ver. 9 the Authorized Version has not attempted to reproduce the humour of the original satire, which styles them that were chief men on earth *chief-goats* of the herd, bell-wethers. The phrase *they that go down to the stones of the pit* should be transferred from ver. 19 to ver. 20.

And thou shalt lift up this proverb upon the King of Babylon, and shalt say,—

I.

Ah! stilled is the tyrant,
 And stilled is the fury!
Broke hath Jehovah the rod of the wicked,
 Sceptre of despots:
Stroke of (the) peoples with passion,
 Stroke unremitting,
Treading in wrath (the) nations,
 Trampling unceasing.
Quiet, at rest, is the whole earth,
 They break into singing;
Even the pines are jubilant for thee,
 Lebanon's cedars!
" Since thou liest low, cometh not up
 Feller against us."

II.

Sheol trom under shuddereth at thee
 To meet thine arrival,

---

* Readers will remember a parallel to this ode in Carlyle's famous chapter on Louis the Unforgotten. No modern has rivalled Carlyle in his inheritance of this satire, except it be he whom Carlyle called "that Jew blackguard Heine."

> Stirring up for thee the shades,
>   All great-goats of earth!
> Lifteth erect from their thrones
>   All kings of peoples.

10. *All of them answer and say to thee,—*

> "Thou, too, made flaccid like us,
>   To us hast been levelled!
> Hurled to Sheol is the pride of thee,
>   Clang of the harps of thee;
> Under thee strewn are (the) maggots
>   Thy coverlet worms."

III.

> How art thou fallen from heaven
>   Daystar, son of the dawn
> (How) art thou hewn down to earth,
>   Hurtler at nations.
> And thou, thou didst say in thine heart,
>   "The heavens will I scale,
> Far up to the stars of God
>   Lift high my throne,
> And sit on the mount of assembly,
>   Far back of the north,
> I will climb on the heights of (the) cloud,
>   I will match the Most High!"
> Ah! to Sheol thou art hurled,
>   Far back of the pit!

IV.

> Who see thee at thee are gazing;
>   Upon thee they muse:
> Is this the man that staggered the earth,
>   Shaker of kingdoms?

Setting the world like the desert,
 Its cities he tore down;
Its prisoners he loosed not
 (Each of them) homeward.
All kings of peoples, yes all,
 Are lying in their state;
But thou! thou art flung from thy grave,
 Like a stick that is loathsome.
Beshrouded with slain, the pierced of the sword,
 Like a corpse that is trampled.
They that go down to the stones of a crypt,
 Shalt not be with them in burial.
For thy land thou hast ruined,
 Thy people hast slaughtered.
Shall not be mentioned for aye
 Seed of the wicked!
Set for his children a shambles,
 For guilt of their fathers!
They shall not rise, nor inherit (the) earth,
 Nor fill the face of the world with cities.

V.

But I will arise upon them,
 Sayeth Jehovah of hosts;
And I will cut off from Babel
 Record and remnant,
And scion and seed,
 Saith Jehovah:
Yea, I will make it the bittern's heritage,
 Marshes of water!
And I will sweep it with sweeps of destruction,
 Sayeth Jehovah of hosts.

CHAPTER XXVIII.

THE EFFECT OF SIN ON OUR MATERIAL CIRCUMSTANCE.

Isaiah xxiv. (date uncertain).

THE twenty-fourth of Isaiah is one of those chapters, which almost convince the most persevering reader of Scripture that a consecutive reading of the Authorized Version is an impossibility. For what does he get from it but a weary and unintelligent impression of destruction, from which he gladly escapes to the nearest clear utterance of gospel or judgement? Criticism affords little help. It cannot clearly identify the chapter with any historical situation. For a moment there is a gleam of a company standing outside the convulsion, and to the west of the prophet, while the prophet himself suffers captivity.* But even this fades before we make it out; and all the rest of the chapter has too universal an application—the language is too imaginative, enigmatic and even paradoxical—to be applied to an actual historical situation, or to its

---

* Vv. 14—16, which are very perplexing. In 14 a company is introduced to us very vaguely as *those* or *yonder ones*, who are represented as seeing the bright side of the convulsion which is the subject of the chapter. *They cry aloud from the sea;* that is, *from the west* of the prophet. He is therefore in the east, and in captivity, in the centre of the convulsion. The problem is to find any actual historical situation, in which part of Israel was in the east in captivity, and part in the west free and full of reasons for praising God for the calamity, out of which their brethren saw no escape for themselves.

development in the immediate future. This is an ideal description, the apocalyptic vision of a last, great day of judgement upon the whole world; and perhaps the moral truths are all the more impressive that the reader is not distracted by temporary or local references.

With the very first verse the prophecy leaps far beyond all particular or national conditions: *Behold, Jehovah shall be emptying the earth and rifling it; and He shall turn it upside down and scatter its inhabitants.* This is expressive and thorough; the words are those which were used for cleaning a dirty dish. To the completeness of this opening verse there is really nothing in the chapter to add. All the rest of the verses only illustrate this upturning and scouring of the material universe. For it is with the material universe that the chapter is concerned. Nothing is said of the spiritual nature of man—little, indeed, about man at all. He is simply called *the inhabitant of the earth*, and the structure of society (ver. 2) is introduced only to make more complete the effect of the convulsion of the earth itself. Man cannot escape those judgements which shatter his material habitation. It is like one of Dante's visions. *Terror, and Pit and Snare upon thee, O inhabitant of the earth! And it shall come to pass that he who fleeth from the noise of the Terror shall fall into the Pit, and he who cometh up out of the midst of the Pit shall be taken in the Snare. For the windows on high are opened, and the foundations of the earth do shake. Broken, utterly broken, is the earth; shattered, utterly shattered, the earth; staggering, very staggering, the earth; reeling, the earth reeleth like a drunken man: she swingeth to and fro like a hammock.* And so through the rest of the chapter it is the material life of man that is cursed: *the new wine, the vine, the tabrets, the harp, the song,* and the merriness in men's hearts which these call forth. Nor does the chapter confine itself to the earth. The closing verses carry the effect of judgement to the heavens and far limits of the material universe. *The host of the high ones on high* (ver. 21) are not spiritual beings, the angels. They are material bodies, the stars. *Then, too, shall the moon be confounded, and the stars ashamed,* when the Lord's kingdom is established and His righteousness made gloriously clear.

What awful truth is this for illustration of which we see not man, but his habitation, the world and all its surroundings, lifted up by the hand of the Lord, broken open, wiped out and shaken, while man himself, as if only to heighten the effect, staggers hopelessly like some broken insect on the quaking ruins? What judgement is this, in which not only one city or one kingdom is concerned, as in the last prophecy of which we treated, but the whole earth is convulsed, and moon and sun confounded?

The judgement is the visitation of man's sins on his material surroundings—*The earth's transgression shall be heavy upon it; and it shall rise, and not fall.* The truth on which this judgement rests is that between man and his material circumstance—the earth he inhabits, the seasons which bear him company through time and the stars to which he looks high up in heaven—there is a moral sympathy. *The earth also is profaned under the inhabitants thereof, because they have transgressed the laws, changed the ordinance, broken the everlasting covenant.*

The Bible gives no support to the theory that matter itself is evil. God created all things; *and God saw everything that He had made; and, behold, it was very good.*

When, therefore, we read in the Bible that the earth is cursed, we read that it is cursed for man's sake; when we read of its desolation, it is as the effect of man's crime. The Flood, the destruction of Sodom and Gomorrah, the plagues of Egypt and other great physical catastrophes happened because men were stubborn or men were foul. We cannot help noticing, however, that matter was thus convulsed or destroyed, not only for the purpose of punishing the moral agent, but because of some poison which had passed from him into the unconscious instruments, stage and circumstance of his crime. According to the Bible, there would appear to be some mysterious sympathy between man and Nature. Man not only governs Nature; he infects and informs her. As the moral life of the soul expresses itself in the physical life of the body for the latter's health or corruption, so the conduct of the human race affects the physical life of the universe to its farthest limits in space. When man is reconciled to God, the wilderness blossoms like a rose; but the guilt of man sullies, infects and corrupts the place he inhabits and the articles he employs; and their destruction becomes necessary, not for his punishment so much as because of the infection and pollution that is in them.

The Old Testament is not contented with a general statement of this great principle, but pursues it to all sorts of particular and private applications. The curses of the Lord fell, not only on the sinner, but on his dwelling, on his property and even on the bit of ground these occupied. This was especially the case with regard to idolatry. When Israel put a pagan population to the sword, they were commanded to raze the city, gather its wealth together, burn all that was burnable and put the rest into the temple of the Lord as a thing *devoted* or *accursed*, which it would harm themselves to share (Deut. vii. 25, 26 ; xiii. 7). The very site of Jericho was cursed, and men were forbidden to build upon its horrid waste. The story of Achan illustrates the same principle.

It is just this principle which chap. xxiv. extends to the whole universe. What happened in Jericho because of its inhabitants' idolatry is now to happen to the whole earth because of man's sin. *The earth also is profane under her inhabitants, because they have transgressed the laws, changed the ordinance, broken the everlasting covenant.* In these words the prophet takes us away back to the covenant with Noah, which he properly emphasizes as a covenant with all mankind. With a noble universalism, for which his race and their literature get too little credit, this Hebrew recognises that once all mankind were holy unto God, who had included them under His grace, that promised the fixedness and fertility of nature. But that covenant, though of grace, had its conditions for man. These had been broken. The race had grown wicked, as it was before the Flood; and therefore, in terms which vividly recall that former judgement of God—*the windows on high are opened*—the prophet foretells a new and more awful catastrophe. One word which he employs betrays how close he feels the moral sympathy to be between man and his world. *The earth*, he says, *is profane*. This is a word, whose root meaning is *that which has fallen away* or *separated itself*, which is *delinquent*. Sometimes, perhaps, it has a purely moral significance, like our word "abandoned" in the common acceptance: he who has fallen far and utterly into sin, *the reckless sinner*. But mostly it has rather the religious meaning of one who has fallen out of the covenant relation with God and the relevant benefits and privileges. Into this covenant not only Israel and their land, but humanity and the whole world, have been brought. Is man under covenant grace? The world is also. Does man fall? So does the world, becoming with him *profane*. The consequence of breaking the covenant oath was expressed in Hebrew by a technical word; and it is this word which, translated *curse*, is applied in ver. 6 to the earth.

The whole earth is to be broken up and dissolved. What then is to become of the people of God—the indestructible remnant? Where are they to settle? In this new deluge is there a new ark? For answer the prophet presents us with an old paradise (ver. 23). He has wrecked the universe; but he says now, *Jehovah of hosts shall dwell in Mount Zion and in Jerusalem.* It would be impossible to find a better instance of the limitations of Old Testament prophecy than this return to the old dispensation after the old dispensation has been committed to the flames. At such a crisis as the conflagration of the universe for the sin of man, the hope of the New Testament looks for the creation of a new heaven and a new earth, but there is no scintilla of such a hope in this prediction. The imagination of the Hebrew seer is beaten back upon the theatre his conscience has abandoned. He knows " the old is out of date," but for him " the new is not yet born ;" and, therefore, convinced as he is that the old must pass away, he is forced to borrow from its ruins a provisional abode for God's people, a figure for the truth which grips him so firmly, that, in spite of the death of all the universe for man's sin, there must be a visibleness and locality of the Divine majesty, a place where the people of God may gather to bless His holy name.

In this contrast of the power of spiritual imagination possessed respectively by the Old and New Testaments we must not, however, lose the ethical interest which the main lesson of this chapter has for the individual conscience. A breaking universe, the great day of judgement, may be too large and too far off to impress our conscience. But each of us has his own world—body, property and environment—which is as much and as evidently affected by his own sins as our chapter represents the universe to be by the sins of the race.

To grant that the moral and physical universes are from the same hand is to affirm a sympathy and mutual reaction between them. This affirmation is confirmed by experience, and this experience is of two kinds. To the guilty man Nature seems aware, and flashes back from her larger surfaces the magnified reflection of his own self-contempt and terror. But, besides, men are also unable to escape attributing to the material instruments or surroundings of their sin a certain infection, a certain power of recommunicating to their imaginations and memories the desire for sin, as well as of inflicting upon them the pain and penalty of the disorder it has produced among themselves. Sin, though born, as Christ said, in the heart, has immediately a material expression; and we may follow this outwards through man's mind, body and estate, not only to find it "hindering, disturbing, complicating all," but reinfecting with the lust and odour of sin the will which gave it birth. As sin is put forth by the will, or is cherished in the heart, so we find error cloud the mind, impurity the imagination, misery the feelings, and pain and weariness infect the flesh and bone. God, who modelled it, alone knows how far man's physical form has been degraded by the sinful thoughts and habits of which for ages it has been the tool and expression; but even our eyes may sometimes trace the despoiler, and that not only in the case of what are preferably named sins of the flesh, but even with lusts that do not require for their gratification the abuse of the body. Pride, as one might think the least fleshly of all the vices, leaves yet in time her damning signature, and will mark the strongest faces with the sad symptoms of that mental break-down, for which unrestrained pride is so often to blame. If sin thus disfigures the body, we know that sin also infects the body. The habituated flesh becomes the suggester of crime to the will which first constrained it to sin, and now wearily, but in vain, rebels against the habits of its instrument. But we recall all this about the body only to say that what is true of the body is true of the soul's greater material surroundings. With the sentence *Thou shalt surely die*, God connects this other: *Cursed is the ground for thy sake.*

When we pass from a man's body, the wrapping we find next nearest to his soul is his property. It has always been an instinct of the race, that there is nothing a man may so infect with the sin of his heart as his handiwork and the gains of his toil. And that is a true instinct, for, in the first place, the making of property perpetuates a man's own habits. If he is successful in business, then every bit of wealth he gathers is a confirmation of the motives and tempers in which he conducted his business. A man deceives himself as to this, saying, Wait till I have made enough; then I will put away the meanness, the harshness and the dishonesty with which I made it. He shall not be able. Just because he has been successful, he will continue in his habit without thinking; just because there has been no break-down to convict of folly and suggest penitence, so he becomes hardened. Property is a bridge on which our passions cross from one part of our life to another. The Germans have an ironical proverb: "The man who has stolen a hundred thousand dollars *can afford* to live honestly." The emphasis of the irony falls on the words in italics: he can afford, but never does. His property hardens his heart, and keeps him from repentance.

But the instinct of humanity has also been quick to this: that the curse of ill-gotten wealth passes like bad blood from father to child. What is the truth in this matter? A glance at history will tell us. The accumulation of property is the result of certain customs, habits and laws. In its own powerful interest property perpetuates these down the ages, and infects the fresh air of each new generation with their temper. How often in the history of mankind has it been property gained under unjust laws or cruel monopolies which has prevented the abolition of these, and carried into gentler, freer times the pride and exclusiveness of the age, by whose rude habits it was gathered. This moral transference, which we see on so large a scale in public history, is repeated to some extent in every private bequest. A curse does not necessarily follow an estate from the sinful producer of it to his heir; but the latter is, *by the bequest itself*, generally brought into so close a contact with his predecessor as to share his conscience and be in sympathy with his temper. And the case is common where an heir, though absolutely up to the date of his succession separate from him who made and has left the property, nevertheless finds himself unable to alter the methods, or to escape the temper, in which the property has been managed. In nine cases out of ten property carries conscience and transfers habit; if the guilt does not descend, the infection does.

When we pass from the effect of sin upon property to its effect upon circumstance, we pass to what we can affirm with even greater conscience. Man has the power of permanently soaking and staining his surroundings with the effect of sins in themselves momentary and transient. Sin increases terribly by the mental law of association. It is not the gin-shop and the face of wanton beauty that alone tempt men to sin. Far more subtle seductions are about every one of us. That we have the power of inflicting our character upon the scenes of our conduct is proved by some of the dreariest experiences of life. A failure in duty renders the place of it distasteful and enervating. Are we irritable and selfish at home? Then home is certain to be depressing, and little helpful to our spiritual growth. Are we selfish and niggardly in the interest we take in others? Then the congregation we go to, the suburb we dwell in, will appear insipid and unprofitable; we shall be past the possibility of gaining character or happiness from the ground where God planted us and meant us to grow. Students have been idle in their studies till every time they enter them a reflex languor comes down like stale smoke, and the room they desecrated takes its revenge on them. We have it in our power to make our workshops, our laboratories and our studies places of magnificent inspiration, to enter which is to receive a baptism of industry and hope; and we have power to make it impossible ever to work in them again at full pitch. The pulpit, the pew, the very communion-table, come under this law. If a minister of God have made up his mind to say nothing from his accustomed place, which has not cost him toil, to feel nothing but a dependence on God and a desire for souls, then he will never set foot there but the power of the Lord shall be upon him. But there are men who would rather set foot anywhere than in their pulpit—men who out of it are full of fellowship, information, and infective health, but there they are paralysed with the curse of their idle past. How history shows us that the most sacred shelters and institutions of man become tainted with sin, and are destroyed in revolution or abandoned to decay by the intolerant conscience of younger generations! How the hidden life of each man feels his past sins possessing his home and hearth, his pew, and even his place at the Sacrament, till it is sometimes better for his soul's health to avoid these!

Such considerations give a great moral force to the doctrine of the Old Testament that man's sin has rendered necessary the destruction of his material circumstances, and that the Divine judgement includes a broken and a rifled universe.

The New Testament has borrowed this vision from the Old, but added, as we have seen, with greater distinctness, the hope of new heavens and a new earth. We have not concluded the subject, however, when we have pointed this out, for the New Testament has another gospel. The grace of God affects even the material results of sin; the Divine pardon that converts the sinner converts his circumstance also; Christ Jesus sanctifies even the flesh, and is the Physician of the body as well as the Saviour of the soul. To Him physical evil abounds only that He may show forth His glory in curing it. *Neither did this man sin nor his parents, but that the works of God should be made manifest in him*. To Paul the *whole creation groaneth and travaileth with* the sinner *till now*, the hour of the sinner's redemption. The Gospel bestows an evangelic liberty which permits the strong Christian to partake of meats offered to idols. And, finally, *all things work together for good to them that love God*, for although to the converted and forgiven sinner the material pains which his sins have brought on him may continue into his new life, they are experienced by him no more as the just penalties of an angry God, but as the loving, sanctifying chastisements of his Father in heaven.

CHAPTER XXIX.

GOD'S POOR.

ISAIAH XXV.—xxvii. (DATE UNCERTAIN).

WE have seen that no more than the faintest gleam of historical reflection brightens the obscurity of chap. xxiv., and that the disaster which lowers there is upon too world-wide a scale to be forced within the conditions of any single period in the fortunes of Israel. In chaps. xxv.—xxvii., which may naturally be held to be a continuation of chap. xxiv., the historical allusions are more numerous. Indeed, it might be said they are too numerous, for they contradict one another to the perplexity of the most acute critics. They imply historical circumstances for the prophecy both before and after the exile. On the one hand, the blame of idolatry in Judah (xxvii. 9), the mention of Assyria and Egypt (xxvii. 12, 13), and the absence of the name of Babylon are indicative of a pre-exilic date.* Arguments from style are always precarious; but it is striking that some critics, who deny that chaps. xxiv.—xxvii. can have come as a whole from Isaiah's time, profess to see his hand in certain passages.† Then, secondly, through these verses

---

* The mention of Moab (xxv. 10, 11) is also consistent with a pre-exilic date, but does not necessarily imply it.
† *E.g.*, xxv. 6—8, 10, 11; xxvii. 10, 11, 9, 12, 13.

which point to a pre-exilic date there are woven, almost inextricably, phrases of .actual exile: expressions of the sense of living on a level and in contact with the heathen (xxvi. 9, 10); a request to God's people to withdraw from the midst of a heathen public to the privacy of their chambers (20, 21); prayers and promises of deliverance from the oppressor (*passim*); hopes of the establishment of Zion, and of the repopulation of the Holy Land. And, thirdly, some verses imply that the speaker has already returned to Zion itself: he says more than once, *in this mountain;* there are hymns celebrating a deliverance actually achieved, as—God *has done a marvel. For Thou hast made a citadel into a heap, a fortified city into a ruin, a castle of strangers to be no city, not to be built again.* Such phrases do not read as if the prophet were creating for the lips of his people a psalm of triumph against a far future deliverance; they have in them the ring of what has already happened.

This bare statement of the allusions of the prophecy will give the ordinary reader some idea of the difficulties of Biblical criticism. What is to be made of a prophecy uttering the catch-words and breathing the experience of three distinct periods? One solution of the difficulty may be that we have here the composition of a Jew already returned from exile to a desecrated sanctuary and depopulated land, who has woven through his original utterances of complaint and hope the experience of earlier oppressions and deliverances, using even the names of earlier tyrants. In his immediate past a great city that oppressed the Jews has fallen, though, if this is Babylon, it is strange that he nowhere names it. But his intention is rather religious than historical; he seeks to give a general representation of the attitude of the world to the people of God, and of the judgement which God brings on the world. This view of the composition is supported by either of two possible interpretations of that difficult verse xxvii. 10: *In that day Jehovah with His sword, the hard and the great and the strong, shall perform visitation upon Leviathan, Serpent Elusive, and upon Leviathan, Serpent Tortuous; and He shall slay the Dragon that is in the sea.* Cheyne treats these monsters as mythic personifications of the clouds, the darkness and the powers of the air, so that the verse means that, just as Jehovah is supreme in the physical world, He shall be in the moral. But it is more probable that the two Leviathans mean Assyria and Babylon—the *Elusive* one, Assyria on the swift-shooting Tigris; the *Tortuous* one, Babylon on the winding Euphrates—while *the Dragon that is in the sea* or *the west* is Egypt. But if the prophet speaks of a victory over Israel's three great enemies all at once, that means that he is talking universally or ideally; and this impression is further heightened by the mythic names he gives them. Such arguments, along with the undoubted post-exilic fragments in the prophecy, point to a late date, so that even a very conservative critic, who is satisfied that Isaiah is the author, admits that "the *possibility* of exilic authorship does not allow itself to be denied."

If this character which we attribute to the prophecy be correct—viz., that it is a summary or ideal account of the attitude of the alien world to Israel, and of the judgement God has ready for the world—then, though itself be exilic, its place in the Book of Isaiah is intelligible. Chaps. xxiv.—xxvii. fitly crown the long list of Isaiah's oracles upon the foreign nations;

they finally formulate the purposes of God towards the nations and towards Israel, whom the nations have oppressed. Our opinions must not be final or dogmatic about this matter of authorship; the obscurities are not nearly cleared up. But if it be ultimately found certain that this prophecy, which lies in the heart of the Book of Isaiah, is not by Isaiah himself, that need neither startle nor unsettle us. No doctrinal question is stirred by such a discovery, not even that of the accuracy of the Scriptures. For that a book is entitled by Isaiah's name does not necessarily mean that it is all by Isaiah; and we shall feel still less compelled to believe that these chapters are his when we find other chapters called by his name while these are not said to be by him. In truth there is a difficulty here, only because it is supposed that a book entitled by Isaiah's name must necessarily contain nothing but what is Isaiah's own. Tradition may have come to say so; but the Scripture itself, bearing as it does unmistakable marks of another age than Isaiah's, tells us that tradition is wrong: and the testimony of Scripture is surely to be preferred, especially when it betrays, as we have seen, sufficient reasons why a prophecy, though not Isaiah's, was attached to his genuine and undoubted oracles. In any case, however, as even the conservative critic whom we have quoted admits, "for the religious value" of the prophecy "the question" of the authorship "is thoroughly irrelevant."

We shall perceive this at once as we now turn to see what is the religious value of our prophecy. Chaps. xxv.—xxvii. stand in the front rank of evangelical prophecy. In their experience of religion, their characterisations of God's people, their expressions of faith, their missionary hopes and hopes of immortality, they are very rich and edifying. Perhaps their most signal feature is their designation of the people of God. In this collection of prayers and hymns the people of God are not regarded as a political body. They are only once called the *nation* and spoken of in connection with a territory (xxvi. 15). Only twice are they named with the national names of Israel and Jacob (xxvii. 6, 9, 12). We miss Isaiah's promised king, his pictures of righteous government, his emphasis upon social justice and purity, his interest in the foreign politics of his State, his hopes of national grandeur and agricultural felicity. In these chapters God's people are described by adjectives signifying spiritual qualities. Their nationality is no more pleaded, only their suffering estate and their hunger and thirst after God. The ideals that are presented for the future are neither political nor social, but ecclesiastical. We saw how closely Isaiah's prophesying was connected with the history of his time. The people of this prophecy seem to have done with history, and to be interested only in worship. And along with the assurance of the continued establishment of Zion as the centre for a secure and holy people, filling a secure and fertile land,—with which, as we have seen, the undoubted visions of Isaiah content themselves, while silent as to the fate of the individuals who drop from this future through death,— we have the most abrupt and thrilling hopes expressed for the resurrection of these latter to share in the glory of the redeemed and restored community.

Among the names applied to God's people there are three which were destined to play an enormous part in the history of religion. In the English version these appear as two: *poor and needy;* but in the original they are three. In chap. xxv. 4: *Thou hast been a stronghold to the poor and a stronghold to the needy, poor* renders a Hebrew word, "dāl," literally *wavering, tottering, infirm,* then *slender* or *lean,* then *poor* in fortune and estate; *needy* literally renders the Hebrew "'ebhyôn," Latin *egenus.* In chap. xxvi. 6: *the foot of the poor and the steps of the needy, needy* renders "dāl," while *poor* renders "'ănî," a passive form—*forced, afflicted, oppressed,* then *wretched,* whether under persecution, poverty, loneliness or exile, and so *tamed, mild, meek.* These three words, in their root ideas of *infirmity, need* and positive *affliction,* cover among them every aspect of physical poverty and distress. Let us see how they came also to be the expression of the highest moral and evangelical virtues.

If there is one thing which distinguishes the people of the revelation from other historical nations, it is the evidence afforded by their dictionaries of the power to transmute the most afflicting experiences of life into virtuous disposition and effectual desire for God. We see this most clearly if we contrast the Hebrews' use of their words for *poor* with that of the first language which was employed to translate these words—the Greek in the Septuagint version of the Old Testament. In the Greek temper there was a noble pity for the unfortunate; the earliest Greeks regarded beggars as the peculiar protegés of Heaven. Greek philosophy developed a capacity for enriching the soul in misfortune; Stoicism gave imperishable proof of how bravely a man could hold poverty and pain to be things indifferent, and how much gain from such indifference he could bring to his soul. But in the vulgar opinion of Greece penury and sickness were always disgraceful; and Greek dictionaries mark the degradation of terms, which at first merely noted physical disadvantage, into epithets of contempt or hopelessness. It is very striking that it was not till they were employed to translate the Old Testament ideas of poverty that the Greek words for "poor" and "lowly" came to bear an honourable significance. And in the case of the Stoic, who endured poverty or pain with such indifference, was it not just this indifference that prevented him from discovering in his tribulations the rich evangelical experience which, as we shall see, fell to the quick conscience and sensitive nerves of the Hebrew?

Let us see how this conscience was developed. In the East poverty scarcely ever means physical disadvantage alone: in its train there follow higher disabilities. A poor Eastern cannot be certain of fair play in the courts of the land. He is very often a wronged man, with a fire of righteous anger burning in his breast. Again, and more important, misfortune is to the quick religious instinct of the Oriental a sign of God's estrangement. With us misfortune is so often only the cruelty, sometimes real sometimes imagined, of the rich; the unemployed vents his wrath at the capitalist, the tramp shakes his fist after the carriage on the highway. In the East they do not forget to curse the rich, but they remember as well to humble themselves beneath the hand of God. With an unfortunate Oriental the conviction is supreme, God is angry with me; I have lost His favour. His soul eagerly longs for God.

A poor man in the East has, therefore, not only a hunger for food: he has the hotter hunger for justice, the deeper hunger for God. Poverty in itself, without extraneous teaching, develops nobler appetites. The physical, becomes the moral, pauper; poor in substance, he grows poor in spirit. It was by developing, with the aid of God's Spirit, this quick conscience and this deep desire for God, which in the East are the very soul of physical poverty, that the Jews advanced to that sense of evangelical poverty of heart, blessed by Jesus in the first of His Beatitudes as the possession of the kingdom of heaven.

Till the Exile, however, the poor were only a portion of the people. In the Exile the whole nation became poor, and henceforth "God's poor" might become synonymous with "God's people." This was the time when the words received their spiritual baptism. Israel felt the physical curse of poverty to its extreme of famine. The pains, privations and terrors, which the glib tongues of our comfortable middle classes, as they sing the psalms of Israel, roll off so easily for symbols of their own spiritual experience, were felt by the captive Hebrews in all their concrete physical effects. The noble and the saintly, the gentle and the cultured, priest, soldier and citizen, woman, youth and child, were torn from home and estate, were deprived of civil standing, were imprisoned, fettered, flogged and starved to death. We learn something of what it must have been from the words which Jeremiah addressed to Baruch, a youth of good family and fine culture: *Seekest thou great things for thyself? Seek them not, for, behold, I will bring evil upon all flesh, saith the* LORD*; only thy life will I give unto thee for a prey in all places whither thou goest.* Imagine a whole nation plunged into poverty of this degree— not born into it having known no better things, nor stunted into it with sensibility and the power of expression sapped out of them, but plunged into it, with the unimpaired culture, conscience and memories of the flower of the people. When God's own hand sent fresh from Himself a poet's soul into "the clay biggin'" of an Ayrshire ploughman, what a revelation we received of the distress, the discipline and the graces of poverty! But in the Jewish nation as it passed into exile there were a score of hearts with as unimpaired an appetite for life as Robert Burns; and, worse than he, they went to feel its pangs away from home. Genius, conscience and pride drank to the dregs in a foreign land the bitter cup of the poor. The Psalms and Lamentations show us how they bore their poison. A Greek Stoic might sneer at the complaint and sobbing, the self-abasement so strangely mixed with fierce cries for vengeance. But the Jew had within him the conscience that will not allow a man to be a Stoic. He never forgot that it was for his sin he suffered, and therefore to him suffering could not be a thing indifferent. With this, his native hunger for justice reached in captivity a famine pitch; his sense of guilt was equalled by as sincere an indignation at the tyrant who held him in his brutal grasp. The feeling of estrangement from God increased to a degree that only the exile of a Jew could excite: the longing for God's house and the worship lawful only there; the longing for the relief which only the sacrifices of the Temple could bestow; the longing for God's own presence and the light of His face. *My soul thirsteth for Thee, my flesh longeth after Thee, in a dry and thirsty land, where no water is, as I have looked upon Thee in the sanctuary, to see Thy power and Thy glory. For Thy lovingkindness is better than life!*

Thy lovingkindness is better than life!—is the secret of it all. There is that which excites a deeper hunger in the soul than the hunger for life, and for the food and money that give life. This spiritual poverty is most richly bred in physical penury, it is strong enough to displace what feeds it. The physical poverty of Israel which had awakened these other hungers of the soul—hunger for forgiveness, hunger for justice, hunger for God—was absorbed by them; and when Israel came out of exile, *to be poor* meant, not so much to be indigent in this world's substance as to feel the need of pardon, the absence of righteousness, the want of God.

It is at this time, as we have seen, that Isa. xxiv.—xxvii. was written; and it is in the temper of this time that the three Hebrew words for "poor" and "needy" are used in chaps. xxv. and xxvi. The returned exiles were still politically dependent and abjectly poor. Their discipline therefore continued, and did not allow them to forget their new lessons. In fact, they developed the results of these further, till in this prophecy we find no fewer than five different aspects of spiritual poverty.

1. We have already seen how strong the sense of sin is in chap. xxiv. This POVERTY of PEACE is not so fully expressed in the following chapters, and indeed seems crowded out by the sense of the *iniquity of the inhabitants of the earth* and the desire for their judgement (xxvi. 21).

2. The feeling of the POVERTY of JUSTICE is very strong in this prophecy. But it is to be satisfied; in part it has been satisfied (xxv. 1—4). *A strong city*, probably Babylon, has fallen. *Moab shall be trodden down in his place, even as straw is trodden down in the water of the dunghill.* The complete judgement is to come when the Lord shall destroy the two *Leviathans* and the great *Dragon of the west* (xxvii. 1). It is followed by the restoration of Israel to the state in which Isaiah (chap v. 1) sang so sweetly of her. *A pleasant vineyard, sing ye of*

her. *I, Jehovah, her Keeper, moment by moment do I water her; lest any make a raid upon her, night and day will I keep her.* The Hebrew text then reads, *Fury is not in Me;* but probably the Septuagint version has preserved the original meaning: *I have no walls.* If this be correct, then Jehovah is describing the present state of Jerusalem, the fulfilment of Isaiah's threat, chap. v. 6: *Walls I have not; let there but be briers and thorns before me! With war will I stride against them; I will burn them together.* But then there breaks the softer alternative of the reconciliation of Judah's enemies: *Or else let him seize hold of My strength; let him make peace with Me—peace let him make with Me.* In such a peace Israel shall spread, and his fulness become the riches of the Gentiles. *In that by-and-bye Jacob shall take root, Israel blossom and bud, and fill the face of the world with fruit.*

Perhaps the wildest cries that rose from Israel's famine of justice were those which found expression in chap. xxxiv. This chapter is so largely a repetition of feelings we have already met with elsewhere in the Book of Isaiah, that it is necessary now only to mention its original features. The subject is, as in chap. xiii., the Lord's judgement upon all the nations; and as chap. xiii. singled out Babylon for special doom, so chap. xxxiv. singles out Edom. The reason of this distinction will be very plain to the reader of the Old Testament. From the day the twins struggled in their mother Rebekah's womb, Israel and Edom were either at open war or burned towards each other with a hate, which was the more intense for wanting opportunities of gratification. It is an Eastern edition of the worst chapters in the history of England and Ireland. No bloodier massacres stained Jewish hands than those which attended their invasions of Edom, and Jewish psalms of vengeance are never more flagrant than when they touch the name of the children of Esau. The only gentle utterance of the Old Testament upon Israel's hereditary foe is a comfortless enigma. Isaiah's *Oracle for Dumah* (xxii. 11 f.), shows that even that large-hearted prophet, in face of his people's age-long resentment at Edom's total want of appreciation of Israel's spiritual superiority, could offer Edom, though for the moment submissive and inquiring, nothing but a sad, ambiguous answer. Edom and Israel, each after his fashion, exulted in the other's misfortunes: Israel by bitter satire when Edom's impregnable mountain-range was treacherously seized and overrun by his allies (Obadiah 4—9); Edom, with the harassing, pillaging habits of a highland tribe, hanging on to the skirts of Judah's great enemies, and cutting off Jewish fugitives, or selling them into slavery, or malignantly completing the ruin of Jerusalem's walls after her overthrow by the Chaldeans (Obadiah 10—14; Ezek. xxxv. 10—15; Ps. cxxxi. 7). In *the quarrel of Zion* with the nations of the world Edom had taken the wrong side,—his profane, earthy nature incapable of understanding his brother's spiritual claims, and therefore envious of him, with the brutal malice of ignorance, and spitefully glad to assist in disappointing such claims. This is what we must remember when we read the indignant verses of chap. xxxiv. Israel, conscious of his spiritual calling in the world, felt bitter resentment that his own brother should be so vulgarly hostile to his attempts to carry it out. It is not our wish to defend the temper of Israel towards Edom. The silence of Christ before the Edomite Herod and his men of war has taught the spiritual servants of God what is their proper attitude towards the malignant and obscene treatment of their claims by vulgar men. But at least let us remember that chap. xxxiv., for all its fierceness, is inspired by Israel's conviction of a spiritual destiny and service for God, and by the natural resentment that his own kith and kin should be doing their best to render these futile. That a famine of bread makes its victims delirious does not tempt us to doubt the genuineness of their need and suffering. As little ought we to doubt or to ignore the reality or the purity of those spiritual convictions, the prolonged starvation of which bred in Israel such feverish hate against his twin-brother Esau. Chap xxxiv., with all its proud prophecy of judgement, is, therefore, also a symptom of that aspect of Israel's poverty of heart, which we have called a hunger for the Divine justice.

3. POVERTY OF THE EXILE. But as fair flowers bloom upon rough stalks, so from Israel's stern challenges of justice there break sweet prayers for home. Chap. xxxiv., the effusion of vengeance on Edom, is followed by chap. xxxv., the going forth of hope to the return from exile and the establishment of the ransomed of the Lord in Zion.* Chap. xxxv. opens with a prospect beyond the return, but after the first two verses addresses itself to the people still in a foreign captivity, speaking of their salvation (vv. 3, 4), of the miracles that will take place in themselves (vv. 5, 6) and in the desert between them and their home (vv. 6, 7), of the

---

* Even at the risk of incurring Canon Cheyne's charge of "ineradicable error," I feel I must keep to the older view of chap. xxxv. which makes it refer to the return from exile. No doubt the chapter covers more than the mere return, and includes "the glorious condition of Israel after the return;" but vv. 4 and 10 are undoubtedly addressed to Jews still in exile and undelivered.

highway which God shall build, evident and secure (vv. 8, 9), and of the final arrival in Zion (ver. 10). In that march the usual disappointments and illusions of desert life shall disappear. The *mirage shall become a pool;* and the clump of vegetation which afar off the hasty traveller hails for a sign of water, but which on his approach he discovers to be the withered grass of a *jackal's lair*, shall indeed be *reeds and rushes*, standing green in fresh water. Out of this exuberant fertility there emerges in the prophet's thoughts a great highway, on which the poetry of the chapter gathers and reaches its climax. Have we of this nineteenth century, with our more rapid means of passage, not forgotten the poetry of the road? Are we able to appreciate either the intrinsic usefulness or the gracious symbolism of the king's highway? How can we know it as the Bible-writers or our forefathers knew it when they made the road the main line of their allegories and parables of life? Let us listen to these verses as they strike the three great notes in the music of the road: *And an highway shall be there, and a way; yea, The Way of Holiness shall it be called, for the unclean shall not pass over it* · that is what is to distinguish this road from all other roads. But here is what it is as being a road. First, it shall be unmistakably plain: *The wayfaring man, yea fools, shall not err therein.* Second, it shall be perfectly secure: *No lion shall be there, nor shall any ravenous beast go up thereon; they shall not be met with there.* Third, it shall bring to a safe arrival and ensure a complete overtaking: *And the ransomed of the Lord shall return and come with singing unto Zion, and everlasting joy shall be upon their heads; they shall overtake gladness and joy, and sorrow and sighing shall flee away.*

4. So Israel was to come home. But to Israel

home meant the Temple, and the Temple meant God. The poverty of the Exile was, in the essence of it, POVERTY OF GOD, POVERTY OF LOVE. The prayers which express this are very beautiful,—that trail like wounded animals to the feet of their master, and look up in His face with large eyes of pain. *And they shall say in that day, Lo, this is our God: we have waited for Him, that He should save us; this is the LORD: we have waited for Him; we will rejoice and be glad in His salvation. . . . Yea, in the way of Thy ordinances, O LORD, have we waited for Thee; to Thy name and to Thy Memorial was the desire of our soul. With my soul have I desired Thee in the night; yea, by my spirit within me do I seek Thee with dawn* (chaps. xxv. 9; xxvi. 8).

An Arctic explorer was once asked, whether during eight months of slow starvation which he and his comrades endured they suffered much from the pangs of hunger. No, he answered, we lost them in the sense of abandonment, in the feeling that our countrymen had forgotten us and were not coming to the rescue. It was not till we were rescued and looked in human faces that we felt how hungry we were. So is it ever with God's poor. They forget all other need, as Israel did, in their need of God. Their outward poverty is only the weeds of their heart's widowhood. *But Jehovah of hosts shall make to all the peoples in this mountain a banquet of fat things, a banquet of wines on the lees, fat things bemarrowed, wines on the lees refined.*

We need only note here—for it will come up for detailed treatment in connection with the second half of Isaiah—that the centre of Israel's restored life is to be the Temple, not, as in Isaiah's day, the king; that her dispersed are to gather from all parts of the world at the sound of the Temple *trumpet;* and that her national life is to consist in worship (cf. xxvii. 13).

These then were four aspects of Israel's poverty of heart: a hunger for pardon, a hunger for justice, a hunger for home, and a hunger for God. For the returning Jews these wants were satisfied only to reveal a deeper poverty still, the complaint and comfort of which we must reserve to another chapter.

CHAPTER XXX.

THE RESURRECTION.

Isaiah xxvi. 14—19; xxv. 6-9.

GRANTED the pardon, the justice, the Temple and the God, which the returning exiles now enjoyed, the possession of these only makes more painful the shortness of life itself. This life is too shallow and too frail a vessel to hold peace and righteousness and worship and the love of God. St. Paul has said, *If in this life only we have hope in Christ, we are of all men most miserable.* What avails it to have been pardoned, to have regained the Holy Land and the face of God, if the dear dead are left behind in graves of exile, and all the living must soon pass into that captivity,[*] from which there is no return?

It must have been thoughts like these, which led to the expression of one of the most abrupt and powerful of the few hopes of the resurrection which the Old Testament contains. This hope, which lightens chap. xxv. 7, 8, bursts through again—without logical connection with the context—in vv. 14—19 of chap. xxvi.

The English version makes ver. 14 to continue the reference to the *lords*, whom in ver. 13 Israel confesses to have served instead of Jehovah. "They are *dead; they shall not live:* they are *deceased; they shall not rise.*"

---

[*] Hezekiah's expression for death, xxxviii. 12.

Our translators have thus intruded into their version the verb " they are," of which the original is without a trace. In the original, *dead* and *deceased* (literally *shades*) are themselves the subject of the sentence—a new subject and without logical connection with what has gone before. The literal translation of ver 14 therefore runs : *Dead men do not live; shades do not rise: wherefore Thou visitest them and destroyest them, and perisheth all memory of them.* The prophet states a fact, and draws an inference. The fact is, that no one has ever returned from the dead ; the inference, that it is God's own *visitation* or *sentence* which has gone forth upon them, and they have really ceased to exist. But how intolerable a thought is this in presence of the other fact that God has here on earth above gloriously enlarged and established His people (ver. 15). *Thou hast increased the nation, Jehovah; Thou hast increased the nation. Thou hast covered Thyself with glory; Thou hast expanded all the boundaries of the land.* To this follows a verse (16), the sense of which is obscure, but palpable. It " feels" to mean that the contrast which the prophet has just painted between the absolute perishing of the dead and the glory of the Church above ground is the cause of great despair and groaning : *O Jehovah, in The Trouble they supplicate Thee; they pour out incantations* when *Thy discipline is upon them.** In face of *The* Trouble

---

* I think this must be the meaning of ver. 16, if we are to allow that it has any sympathy with vv. 14 and 15. Bredenkamp suggests that the persons meant are themselves the dead. Jehovah has glorified the Church on earth ; but the dead below are still in trouble, and *pour out prayers* (Virgil's " preces fundunt," *Æneid*, vi., 55), beneath this *punishment* which God causes to pass on all men (ver. 14). Bredenkamp bases this exegesis chiefly on the word for " prayer," which means *chirping* or *whispering*, a kind of voice imputed to the shades by the

and *The* Discipline *par excellence* of God, what else can man do but betake himself to God? God sent death; in death He is the only resource. Israel's feelings in presence of The Trouble are now expressed in ver. 17: *Like as a woman with child that draweth near the time of her delivery writheth and crieth out in her pangs, so have we been before Thee, O Jehovah.* Thy Church on earth is pregnant with a life, which death does not allow to come to the birth. *We have been with child; we have been in the pangs, as it were; we have brought forth wind; we make not the earth,* in spite of all we have really accomplished upon it in our return, our restoration and our enjoyment of Thy presence—*we make not the earth salvation, neither are the inhabitants of the world born.**

The figures are bold. Israel achieves, through God's grace, everything but the recovery of her dead; this, which alone is worth calling *salvation,* remains wanting to her great record of deliverances. The living Israel is restored, but how meagre a proportion of the people it is! The graves of home and of exile do not give up their dead. These are not born again to be inhabitants of the upper world.

The figures are bold, but bolder is the hope that breaks from them. Like as when the Trumpet shall

---

Hebrews and other ancient peoples. But while this word does originally mean *whispering,* it is never in Scripture applied to the dead, but, on the other hand, is a frequent name for *divining* or *incantation.* I therefore have felt compelled to understand it as used in this passage of the living, whose only resource in face of death—*God's discipline par excellence*—is to pour out incantations. If it be objected that the prophet would scarcely parallel the ordinary incantations on behalf of the dead with supplications to Jehovah, the answer is that he is talking poetically or popularly.

* English version, *fallen; i.e.,* like our expression for the birth of animals, *dropped.*

sound, ver. 19 peals forth the promise of the resurrection—peals the promise forth, in spite of all experience, unsupported by any argument, and upon the strength of its own inherent music. *Thy dead shall live! my dead bodies shall arise!* The change of the personal pronoun is singularly dramatic. Returned Israel is the speaker, first speaking *to* herself: *thy dead*, as if upon the depopulated land, in face of all its homes in ruin, and only the sepulchres of ages standing grim and steadfast, she addressed some despairing double of herself; and secondly speaking *of* herself: *my dead bodies*, as if all the inhabitants of these tombs, though dead, were still her own, still part of her, the living Israel, and able to arise and bless with their numbers their bereaved mother. These she now addresses: *Awake and sing, ye dwellers in the dust, for a dew of lights is Thy dew, and the land bringeth forth the dead.**

If one has seen a place of graves in the East, he will appreciate the elements of this figure, which takes *dust* for death and *dew* for life. With our damp graveyards *mould* has become the traditional trappings of death; but where under the hot Eastern sun things do not rot into lower forms of life, but crumble into sapless powder, that will not keep a worm in life, *dust* is the natural symbol of death. When they die, men go not to feed fat the mould, but *down into the dust;* and there the foot of the living falls silent, and his voice is choked, and the light is thickened and in retreat, as if it were creeping away to die. The only creatures the visitor starts are timid, unclean bats, that flutter and whisper about him like the ghosts of the dead. There are no

---

* Technical Hebrew word for the inhabitants of the underworld— *the shades.*

flowers in an Eastern cemetery; and the withered branches and other ornaments are thickly powdered with the same dust that chokes, and silences and darkens all.

Hence the Semitic conception of the underworld was dominated by dust. It was not water nor fire nor frost nor altogether darkness, which made the infernal prison horrible, but that upon its floor and rafters, hewn from the roots and ribs of the primeval mountains, dust lay deep and choking. Amid all the horrors he imagined for the dead, Dante did not include one more awful than the horror of dust. The picture which the northern Semites had before them when they turned their faces to the wall was of this kind.*

> The house of darkness. . . .
> The house men enter, but cannot depart from.
> The road men go, but cannot return.
> The house from whose dwellers the light is withdrawn.
> The place where dust is their food, their nourishment clay.
> The light they behold not; in darkness they dwell.
> They are clothed like birds, all fluttering wings.
> On the door and the gateposts, the dust lieth deep.

Either, then, an Eastern sepulchre, or this its infernal double, was gaping before the prophet's eyes. What more final and hopeless than the dust and the dark of it?

But for dust there is dew, and even to graveyards the morning comes that brings dew and light together. The wonder of dew is that it is given from a clear heaven, and that it comes to sight with the dawn. If the Oriental looks up when dew is falling, he sees nothing to thank for it between him and the stars. If he sees dew in the morning, it is equal liquid and lustre; it seems to distil from the beams of the sun—*the sun,*

---

* Extracted from the Assyrian *Descent of Istar to Hades* (Dr. Jeremias' German translation, p. 11, and *Records of the Past*, i., 145).

which riseth with healing under his wings. The dew is thus doubly "dew of light." But our prophet ascribes the dew of God, that is to raise the dead, neither to stars nor dawn, but, because of its Divine power, to that higher supernal glory which the Hebrews conceived to have existed before the sun, and which they styled, as they styled their God, by the plural of majesty: *A dew of lights is Thy dew.** As, when the dawn comes, the drooping flowers of yesterday are seen erect and lustrous with the dew, every spike a crown of glory, so also shall be the resurrection of the dead. There is no shadow of a reason for limiting this promise to that to which some other passages of resurrection in the Old Testament have to be limited: a corporate restoration of the holy State or Church. This is the resurrection of its individual members to a community which is already restored, the recovery by Israel of her dead men and women from their separate graves, each with his own freshness and beauty, in that glorious morning when the Sun of righteousness shall arise, with healing under His wings—*Thy dew*, O Jehovah!

Attempts are so often made to trace the hopes of resurrection, which break the prevailing silence of the Old Testament on a future life, to foreign influences experienced in the Exile, that it is well to emphasize the origin and occasion of the hopes that utter themselves so abruptly in this passage. Surely nothing could be more inextricably woven with the national fortunes of Israel, as nothing could be more native and original to Israel's temper, than the verses just expounded. We need not deny that their residence among a people, accustomed as the Babylonians were to belief in the resurrection, may have thawed in the Jews

---

* Cf. James i. 17.

that reserve which the Old Testament clearly shows that they exhibited towards a future life. The Babylonians themselves had received most of their suggestions of the next world from a non-Semitic race; and therefore it would not be to imagine anything alien to the ascertained methods of Providence if we were to suppose that the Hebrews, who showed what we have already called the Semitic want of interest in a future life, were intellectually tempered by their foreign associations to a readiness to receive any suggestions of immortality, which the Spirit of God might offer them through their own religious experience. That it was this last, which was the effective cause of Israel's hopes for the resurrection of her dead, our passage puts beyond doubt. Chap. xxvi. shows us that the occasion of these hopes was what is not often noticed: the returned exiles' disappointment with the meagre repopulation of the holy territory. A restoration of the State or community was not enough: the heart of Israel wanted back in their numbers her dead sons and daughters.

If the occasion of these hopes was thus an event in Israel's own national history, and if the impulse to them was given by so natural an instinct of her own heart, Israel was equally indebted to herself for the convictions that the instinct was not in vain. Nothing is more clear in our passage than that Israel's first ground of hope in a future life was her simple, untaught reflection upon the power of her God. Death was *His chastening.* Death came from Him, and remained in His power. Surely He would deliver from it. This was a very old belief in Israel. *The Lord killeth and maketh alive; He bringeth down to Sheol and bringeth up.* Such words, of course, might be only an extreme figure for recovery from disease, and the silence of so great a saint as

Hezekiah about any other issue into life than by convalescence from mortal sickness staggers us into doubt whether an Israelite ever did think of a resurrection. But still there was Jehovah's almightiness; a man could rest his future on that, even if he had not light to think out what sort of a future it would be. So mark in our passage, how confidence is chiefly derived from the simple utterance of the name of Jehovah, and how He is hailed as *our God.* It seems enough to the prophet to connect life with Him and to say merely, *Thy dew.* As death is God's own discipline, so life, *Thy dew,* is with Him also.

Thus in its foundation the Old Testament doctrine of the resurrection is but the conviction of the sufficiency of God Himself, a conviction which Christ turned upon Himself when He said, *I am the Resurrection and the Life. Because I live, ye shall live also.*

If any object that in this picture of a resurrection we have no real persuasion of immortality, but simply the natural, though impossible, wish of a bereaved people that their dead should to-day rise from their graves to share to-day's return and glory—a revival as special and extraordinary as that appearing of the dead in the streets of Jerusalem when the Atonement was accomplished, but by no means that general resurrection at the last day which is an article of the Christian faith—if any one should bring this objection, then let him be referred to the previous promise of immortality in chap. xxv. The universal and final character of the promise made there is as evident as of that for which Paul borrowed its terms in order to utter the absolute consequences of the resurrection of the Son of God: *Death is swallowed up in victory.* For the prophet, having in ver. 6 described the restoration of the people, whom exile had starved with a famine of ordinances, to *a feast in Zion of fat things and wines on the lees well refined*, intimates that as certainly as exile has been abolished, with its dearth of spiritual intercourse, so certainly shall God Himself destroy death: *And He shall swallow up in this mountain*—perhaps it is imagined, as the sun devours the morning mist on the hills—*the mask of the veil, the veil that is upon all the peoples, and the film spun upon all the nations. He hath swallowed up death for ever, and the Lord Jehovah shall wipe away tears from off all faces, and the reproach of His people shall He remove from off all the earth, for Jehovah hath spoken it. And they shall say in that day, Behold, this is our God: we have waited for Him, and He shall save us; this is Jehovah: we have waited for Him; we will rejoice and be glad in His salvation.* Thus over all doubts, and in spite of universal human experience, the prophet depends for immortality on God Himself. In chap. xxvi. 3 our version beautifully renders, *Thou wilt keep* him *in perfect peace* whose *mind* is *stayed* on Thee, *because he trusteth in Thee.* This is a confidence valid for the next life as well as for this. *Therefore trust ye in the* LORD for ever. Amen.

Almighty God, we praise Thee that, in the weakness of all our love and the darkness of all our knowledge before death, Thou hast placed assurance of eternal life in simple faith upon Thyself. Let this faith be richly ours. By Thine omnipotence, by Thy righteousness, by the love Thou hast vouchsafed, we lift ourselves and rest upon Thy word. *Because I live, ye shall live also.* Oh keep us steadfast in union with Thyself, through Jesus Christ our Lord. Amen.

INDEX TO CHAPS. I.—XXXIX.

Chapters of Isaiah.	Date b.c.	Chapters of the Exposition.
i.	701	I., XIX., p. 311 ff.
ii.-iv.	740-735	II.
v.	735	III.
vi.	740; written 735 or 727	IV., XXVI., 391 f.
vii.-ix. 7	734-732	VI.
vii. 14 ff.	734	VII. 133
viii.	734-733	VII. 135
ix. 1-7	732	VII. 136
ix. 8-x. 4	735	III. 47 ff.
x. 5-34	About 721	IX. 147
xi. [xii.]	About 720 ?	X.
xi. 1-6	.	VII. 138
xiii.-xiv. 23	?	XXVII.
xiv. 24-27	Towards 701	XVII. 272
xiv. 28-32	705	XVII. 272
xv.-xvi. 12	?	XVII. 273
xvi. 13, 14	711 or 704 ?	XVII. 273
xvii. 1-11	Between 736 and 732	XVII. 274
xvii. 12-14	?	XVII. 274, 277, 281 f.
xviii.	711 or towards 701 ?	XVII. 275
xix.	703 or after 700 ?	XVII. 275, 278, 284 ff.
xx.	711-709	XI. 198-200, XVII. 276
xxi. 1-10	Probably 709	XI. 201, XVII. 276
xxi. 11, 12	Between 704 and 701	XVII. 276
xxi. 13, 17	.	XVII. 277
xxii.	701	XIX., XX.
xxiii.	703 or 702	XVII. 277, XVIII.
xxiv.	?	XXVIII.
xxv.-xxvii.	?	XXIX.-XXX.
xxviii.	About 725	VIII. 149
xxix.-xxxii.	.	p. 207

Chapters of Isaiah.	Date B.C.	Chapters of the Exposition.
xxix.	About 703	XII.
xxx.	About 702	XIII.
xxxi.	About 702	XIV.
xxxii. 1-8	About 702?	XV.
xxxii. 9-20	Date uncertain	XVI.
xxxiii.	701	XX., XXI., 207, 304
xxxiv.	?	XXIX. 438 ff.
xxxv.	?	XXIX. 440 f.
xxxvi. 1	701	303 f.
xxxvi. 2-xxxvii.	701	303 f.
xxxvi. 2-22	701	XXII. 303 f.
xxxvii.	701	XXIII.
xxxviii.-xxxix.	Date uncertain	XXV. 304
xxxviii.	.	XXVI. 303
xxxix.	.	XI. 201

SHORT INDEX OF SUBJECTS.

Ahaz, 98; compared with Charles I., 99, 103 ff., 113; Judas of Old Testament, 118.
Animals, the lower, 190 ff.; our mediatorship to, 193.
Anthropomorphism, 144.
Arabia, 277.
Aram, 94, 103 ff.
Ashdod, 198.
Assyria and Assyrians, 53, 92 f., 95, 97, 103 f., 122, and *passim*.
Atheism, two kinds of, 172 ff.

Babylon, 93, 201, 405.
Babylonian captivity, 201, 402.
Bribery, 47.

Captivity of Israel, first, 128; second, 148.
Christ, 80, 142 ff., 254 ff., 328, 426.
Church, origin of idea of, 126.
Commerce, 296.
Conscience, 6; its threefold character, 12; simplicity, 151.
Cromwell, 160 ff., 220.

Damascus, 95, 120, 122, 274.
Drunkenness, 44 f., 152 ff.

Earthquake, 50.
Edom, 94, 276, 438 ff.
Egypt, 92, 96, 197 ff., 222 ff., *passim*.
Ekron, 308 f.
Eliakim, 317.
Ethiopia, 93, 222, 275.

Faith, moral results of, 106 f., 163 f.; power to shape history, 109, 352 ff.

Fatalism, 110.
Forgiveness of sin, 13, 71 ff., 326 ff., 361, 381.
Formalism, 216, 240.
Free-will, 82.

Glory, 68.

Hamath, 94.
Heine, 158, 242, 413.
Hezekiah, 352, 378 ff, *passim*.
Holiness, 63 ff.
Holy Spirit, 185—188.

Immanuel, 102, 115, 124 ff., 133 ff.
Immortality, 385 ff., 394 ff., 410, 444 ff.
Individual, the, and the community, 389 ff.
Inspiration, 23 ff., 213, 372.
Isaiah: apprenticeship, 19; youth, 21, 59; a son of Jerusalem, 22; threefold vision, 23—25; idealist, 25; realist, 27; prophet, 30; patriotism, a conscience of his country's sins, 30 f.; call and consecration, 57 ff.; personality, 75 f., 253; comp. with Mazzini, 85—87; with Moses, 88; contribution to religious development of Israel, 101, 284, 288; no fatalist, 110; habit of appealing to the people, 119; saved from the popular drift, 121; scorn, 127; sanity, 109, 154 f., 166, 300; comp. with Cromwell, 160 ff., 220; self-control, 166; regard for animals, 190; walks stripped for a sign

199; inspiration, 213, 372; working of his imagination, 234; style, 281; humanity, 285, 294; triumph, 323 ff.; imagination and conscience, 335; lesson for all time, 366; contrasted with Crusaders, 367; personal religion, 391; ideal, 392; satire, 29,139,156.
Israel, religious condition, 99; and Greece, 365.

Jerusalem, 22, 25 ff., 169 f., 211 f., 231 f., 243, 267 f., 279, Book IV., *passim*.

"King Lear," 49, 55.

Land question, 41 ff.
Language, abuse of, 260.

Maher-shalal-hash-baz, 120.
Mazzini, 84—86.
Merodach-baladan, 200, 376.
Messiah, 89, 90, 115 ff., 129, 131—144, 180 ff., 249.
Moab, 94, 273.
Monotheism, moral and political advantages,108—110; growth in Israel, 357, 363.

Name of the LORD, 233 ff.
Nature, fourfold use of by the prophets, 16 f.; redemption of, 188; destruction of, 417 ff.

Palestine, 92.
People, the, ultimately responsible, 119, 198, 224 ff.
Philistines, 94, 272.

Phœnicia, 94, 96, 288 ff.
Poetry, Hebrew, 411.
Polytheism, 99, 107.
Preaching the word, 82, 83.
Prophecy, its power of vision, 23—25; its service to religion, 100 f.
Providence, 98.

Rabshakeh, the, 343 ff.
Remnant, the, 31, 87, 101, 126, 129, and *passim*.
Resurrection, 387, 444 ff.
Return from exile, 195, 401 ff., 429, 440 f., 450.
Righteousness, Isaiah's doctrine of, 334 ff.

Sacrament, an Old Testament, 74.
Samaria, 95, 147, 152 ff.
Sargon, 148, 169, 198 ff.
Scepticism, 15.
Sennacherib, 209, 302, 308 ff., 355 ff.
Serbonian bog, 361.
Shebna, 317.
Sheol, 385, 410, 447 ff.
Shiloah, 122.
Sin, 52, 69, *passim;* effect on man's material circumstance, 416.
Sorrow, man's abuse of, 54.

Tiglath-pileser II., 96, 103 f.

Uzziah, 59 f., 98.

War, 51.
Women, Isaiah to, 262.
Wrath of God, 47 f., 55.

THE EXPOSITOR'S BIBLE, 1888-9.

Crown 8vo, Cloth, Price 7s. 6d. each.

I.

THE EPISTLE TO THE GALATIANS. By the Rev. Prof. G. G. FINDLAY, B.A. Second Edition.

"Professor G. G. Findlay discloses a minute acquaintance with his subject, an earnest desire to penetrate its inmost meaning, and a marked capacity of illustrating and enforcing the text."—*Record.*

II.

ISAIAH. I. to XXXIX. By the Rev. GEORGE ADAM SMITH, M.A., Aberdeen. Fifth Edition.

"This is a very attractive book. Mr. George Adam Smith has evidently such a mastery of the scholarship of his subject that it would be a sheer impertinence for most scholars, even though tolerable Hebraists, to criticise his translations; and certainly it is not the intention of the present reviewer to attempt anything of the kind, to do which he is absolutely incompetent."—*Spectator.*

III.

THE PASTORAL EPISTLES. By the Rev. A. PLUMMER, D.D., Master of Univ. Coll., Durham. Second Edition.

"Full of life and vigour. . . . No difficulty in the Epistles is evaded, rather are troublesome passages attacked with keener relish. Dr. Plummer has spared no pains on his task, and has produced what is practically the best commentary we have on these important Epistles."—*British Weekly.*

IV.

THE FIRST EPISTLE TO THE CORINTHIANS. By the Rev. MARCUS DODS, D.D., Professor of New Testament Exegesis, New College, Edinburgh. Second Edition.

"Marked by the author's well-known characteristics of rich Scriptural learning catholicity of tone, deep spiritual insight."—*Academy.*

V.

THE REVELATION OF ST. JOHN. By the Rev. Prof. W. MILLIGAN, D.D., of the University of Aberdeen.

"Clear and scholarly."—*Saturday Review.*

VI.

THE EPISTLES OF ST. JOHN. By the Right Rev. W. ALEXANDER, D.D., Lord Bishop of Derry and Raphoe.

"The discourses are eloquent and impressive, and show a thorough knowledge of the subject."—*Scotsman.*

LONDON: HODDER & STOUGHTON, 27, PATERNOSTER ROW.

THE EXPOSITOR'S BIBLE, 1887-8.
(FIRST YEAR'S ISSUE.)

I.
ST. MARK. By the Rev. G. A. CHADWICK, D.D, Dean of Armagh. Third Edition.

"A valuable, interesting, and delightful work, almost every page of which contains something worthy of quotation."—*English Churchman.*

II.
THE EPISTLES TO THE COLOSSIANS AND PHILEMON. By the Rev. ALEXANDER MACLAREN, D.D. Fourth Edition.

"There will be found in it much that is instructive and much that is practical, many sound views of life and religion as well as considerable insight into the spirit and meaning of the Apostle."—*Scotsman.*

III.
THE BOOK OF GENESIS. By the Rev. MARCUS DODS, D.D., Professor of New Testament Exegesis, New College, Edinburgh. Fourth Edition.

"Dr. Dods sets himself to bring out the great lessons with which the book is pregnant. This he does in a way so lucid, forcible, and practical, that his volume cannot fail to be of great service to those who read it."—*Nonconformist.*

IV.
THE FIRST BOOK OF SAMUEL. By the Rev. Professor W. G. BLAIKIE, D.D., LL.D. Third Edition.

"Fully equal in interest and value with the preceding volumes of the series. . . . Of the utmost value to preachers and teachers, being very full of suggestive thoughts."—*English Churchman.*

V.
THE SECOND BOOK OF SAMUEL. By the same Author. Third Edition.

"Professor Blaikie tells the story of David's royal life with very graphic power, and his language is simple to homeliness."—*Ecclesiastical Gazette.*

VI.
THE EPISTLE TO THE HEBREWS. By the Rev. Principal T. C. EDWARDS, D.D., Author of "A Commentary on the First Epistle to the Corinthians." Third Edition.

"It is a painstaking, substantial, worthy exposition."—*British Weekly.*

LONDON: HODDER & STOUGHTON, 27, PATERNOSTER ROW.

WORKS BY REV. MARCUS DODS, D.D.

I.
ISAAC, JACOB, AND JOSEPH. Fifth Thousand.
3s. 6d.

"The present volume is worthy of the writer's reputation. He deals with the problems of human life and character, which these biographies suggest, in a candid and manly fashion."—*Spectator.*

II.
THE PARABLES OF OUR LORD. FIRST SERIES.
THE PARABLES RECORDED BY ST. MATTHEW. Sixth Thousand. 3s. 6d.

"There is certainly no better volume on the subject in our language."—*Glasgow Mail.*

III.
THE PARABLES OF OUR LORD. SECOND SERIES.
THE PARABLES RECORDED BY ST. LUKE. Fifth Thousand. Crown 8vo, cloth, 3s. 6d.

"An original exposition marked by strong common sense and practical exhortation."—*Literary Churchman.*

IV.
MOHAMMED, BUDDHA, AND CHRIST.
Fifth Thousand. Crown 8vo, cloth, 3s. 6d.

"His materials have been carefully collected from the best sources, have been thoroughly digested in his own mind, and are here given forth to his readers in well-arranged, clear, and precise language."—*Scotsman.*

V.
ISRAEL'S IRON AGE: Sketches from the Period of the Judges.
Fifth Edition. Crown 8vo, cloth, 5s.

"Powerful lectures. This is a noble volume, full of strength. Young men especially will find in it a rich storehouse of prevailing incentive to a godly life. Dr. Dods searches with a masterly hand."—*Nonconformist.*

VI.
THE PRAYER THAT TEACHES TO PRAY.
Sixth Edition. Crown 8vo, 2s. 6d.

"It is highly instructive, singularly lucid, and unmistakably for quiet persona use."—*Clergyman's Magazine.*

LONDON: HODDER & STOUGHTON, 27, PATERNOSTER ROW.

THE FOREIGN BIBLICAL LIBRARY.
Price 7s. 6d. each Volume.

Now Complete in Three Volumes.

PROFESSOR KURTZ'S CHURCH HISTORY.
Authorised Translation from the latest Revised Edition by the Rev. JOHN MACPHERSON, M.A.

"Kurtz's Manual of Church History, which Mr. Macpherson has translated with admirable care and skill, is the one book of the kind adapted for present use. It is not meant for the general reader who needs to be interested, but for the student who desires information, and is glad to have it in the most compressed form, and he who goes to it with this aim will not be disappointed. He will find the chief events of each age, its chief writers, the lists of their works, the changes in doctrine and discipline, the developments of ritual, noted in brief and clear language, and arranged in the form easiest to understand and remember."—*Spectator.*

Now Complete in Two Volumes.

PROFESSOR WEISS' MANUAL OF INTRODUCTION TO THE NEW TESTAMENT.
Translated by A. J. K. DAVIDSON.

"As a thoroughly complete and satisfactory introduction from the point of view of a fairly conservative criticism, no book can compete with Weiss. It is throughout full of knowledge, of sense, and of vigour."—*Expositor.*

"The volume is well worth studying as the result of the labours of one of the best living German commentators."—*Record.*

Now Complete in Three Volumes.

PROFESSOR FRANZ DELITZSCH'S COMMENTARY ON THE BOOK OF PSALMS.
Translated by Rev. DAVID EATON, M.A. From the latest Edition, specially Revised by the Author.

"The translator has been faithful to the ideas as well as to the language of the original. The Supplementary Corrigenda have been incorporated in the text, so that the English reader has probably the best existing commentary on the Psalms in a perfectly reliable form."—*Academy.*

In One Volume.

ROTHE'S STILL HOURS.
With an Introductory Essay by the Rev. JOHN MACPHERSON, M.A. Translated by JANE T. STODDART.

"The book may be heartily recommended to those unable to read the original. Students of German thought will find one of its most important pages mirrored in 'Still Hours.'"—*Academy.*

"It is a book of the first order, full of Rothe himself, and of which one wearies as little as of the face of a friend. It forces its way into our regard, and becomes our constant companion, refusing to be put on the shelf. It has something for every mood. It wins us with a ceaseless attraction to open it, and it never disappoints."—Dr. *Marcus Dods.*

LONDON : HODDER & STOUGHTON, 27, PATERNOSTER ROW.

THE THEOLOGICAL EDUCATOR.
Price 2s. 6d. each.

THE LANGUAGE OF THE NEW TESTAMENT. By Rev. WILLIAM HENRY SIMCOX, M.A., Rector of Harlaxton.

"This is the most living grammar of the New Testament we have."—*Expositor.*
"An excellent little book."—*Scotsman.*

OUTLINES OF CHRISTIAN DOCTRINE. By the Rev. H. C. G. MOULE, M.A., Principal of Ridley Hall, Cambridge. Sixth Thousand.

"It forms an admirable introduction to the subject, and seems in intellectual power to even surpass any other of Mr. Moule's published writings."—*Record.*

AN INTRODUCTION TO THE NEW TESTAMENT. By Rev. Prof. MARCUS DODS, D.D. Fifth Thousand.

"When we compare it with even the best of the extant volumes on the same subject, we are bound to acknowledge that Dr. Dods has compressed into the 247 pages of this little book more than is to be found in much bulkier works."—*Christian Leader.*

A MANUAL OF CHRISTIAN EVIDENCES. By the Rev. C. A. ROW, M.A., Prebendary of St. Paul's. Sixth Thousand.

"A veritable *multum in parvo*, clear, cogent, and concise, without being sketchy or superficial."—*Saturday Review.*

AN INTRODUCTION TO THE TEXTUAL CRITICISM OF THE NEW TESTAMENT. By the Rev. Professor B. B. WARFIELD, D.D. Third Thousand.

"A book so full of information, so well reasoned, so brightly written, has never before been put in the hands of theological students."—*Expositor.*

A HEBREW GRAMMAR. By the Rev. W. H. LOWE, M.A., Joint Author of "A Commentary on the Psalms," etc., etc.; Hebrew Lecturer, Christ's College, Cambridge. Second Thousand.

"A short Hebrew Grammar from a competent scholar is always welcome, since most of those compiled in this country cannot be trusted in every respect. We therefore take pleasure in recommending to beginners the Hebrew Grammar by the Rev. W. H. Lowe."—*Athenæum.*

AN EXPOSITION OF THE APOSTLES' CREED. By the Rev. J. E. YONGE, M.A., late Fellow of King's College, Cambridge, and Assistant Master in Eton College.

A MANUAL OF THE BOOK OF COMMON PRAYER. Showing its History and Contents. By the Rev. CHARLES HOLE, B.A., King's College, London.

A MANUAL OF CHURCH HISTORY. By the Rev. A. C. JENNINGS, M.A. In Two Vols.
    Vol. I.—From the First to the Tenth Century.
    Vol. II.—From the Eleventh to the Nineteenth Century.

LONDON : HODDER & STOUGHTON, 27, PATERNOSTER ROW.

WORKS BY THE REV. PROF. A. B. BRUCE, D.D.

I.
THE LIFE OF WILLIAM DENNY, Shipbuilder,
Dumbarton. With Portrait. Second Edition. 8vo, cloth, 12s.

"A most interesting biography."—*Academy.*

II.
THE GALILEAN GOSPEL. Third Edition.
Crown 8vo, cloth, 3s. 6d.

"We heartily commend this little volume as giving an outline ably drawn of the teachings of Christ."—*Spectator.*

III.
THE MIRACULOUS ELEMENT IN THE GOSPELS. In 8vo, cloth, 12s.

IV.
THE CHIEF END OF REVELATION. Third Thousand. In crown 8vo, cloth, 6s.

"This series of lectures has the conspicuous essence of boldness, vigour, breadth, and moral elevation."—*Professor Salmond.*

V.
THE PARABOLIC TEACHING OF CHRIST.
A Systematic and Critical Study of the Parables of our Lord. Third Edition. 8vo, cloth, 12s.

"Professor Bruce brings to his task the learning and the liberal and finely sympathetic spirit which are the best gifts of an expositor of Scripture. His treatment of his subject is vigorous and original."—*Spectator.*

WORKS BY THE REV. DR. W. M. TAYLOR, of New York.

THE PARABLES OF OUR SAVIOUR EXPOUNDED AND ILLUSTRATED. Second Edition. In crown 8vo, cloth, 7s. 6d.

"A real exposition in eloquent language, such as will be valued by Bible students."—*English Churchman.*

THE LIMITATIONS OF LIFE, and OTHER SERMONS. Second Edition. Crown 8vo, cloth, 7s. 6d.

"Dr. Taylor's sermons are full of spiritual earnestness and power."—*London Quarterly Review.*

CONTRARY WINDS, and OTHER SERMONS.
Crown 8vo, 7s. 6d.

JOHN KNOX. Cheap Edition. Price 1s.

"A short biography, which has two great merits: it presents in short compass, and yet in their true proportions, all the important events of the Reformer's life; and the warm appreciation of Knox's character and achievements by which it is pervaded is never allowed to descend to the level of mere undiscriminating eulogy."—*Scotsman.*

LONDON: HODDER & STOUGHTON, 27, PATERNOSTER ROW.

PROFESSOR LAIDLAW'S NEW WORK.

THE MIRACLES OF OUR LORD. Expository
and Homiletic. By the Rev. JOHN LAIDLAW, D.D., Professor of Theology, New College, Edinburgh; Author of "The Bible Doctrine of Man," etc. Crown 8vo, cloth, 7s. 6d.

REV. JAMES STALKER'S NEW WORK.

IMAGO CHRISTI: The Example of Jesus
Christ. By the Rev. JAMES STALKER. M.A., Author of "The Life of Jesus Christ," "The Life of St. Paul," etc. Third Edition, completing 10,000. 8vo, cloth, 5s.

"Mr. Stalker certainly proves that the subject is a fruitful one. He shows that the activity of Christ was of a more varied kind than perhaps we are apt to imagine."—*Scotsman.*

JOHN G. PATON, Missionary to the New
Hebrides. An Autobiography. Edited by his Brother, the Rev. JAS. PATON, B.A.

PART I.—With Portrait. Twelfth Thousand. Crown 8vo, 6s.

"The most robust and the most fascinating piece of autobiography that I have met with in many a day."—*Dr. T. L. Cuyler.*
"I consider it unsurpassed in missionary biography."—*Rev. Dr. A. T. Pierson.*

PART II.—With Frontispiece. Ninth Thousand. Crown 8vo, 6s.

"This second half is not a whit behind its predecessor in genuine, living, fascinating interest."—*Christian.*

WORKS BY PROF. HENRY DRUMMOND, F.R.S.E., F.G.S.

I.

THE GREATEST THING IN THE WORLD.
An Address on 1 Corinthians xiii. Ninth Edition, completing 120,000. Paper covers, 1s.; cloth elegant, gilt edges, 2s. 6d.

II.

TROPICAL AFRICA. Third Edition, completing
20,000. With Six Maps and Illustrations, 6s.

"Professor Drummond is here at his very best. The article on mimicry especially is worthy to rank with anything ever written by Wallace, Bates, or Darwin himself on this fascinating subject."—*Academy.*

III.

NATURAL LAW IN THE SPIRITUAL
WORLD. Twenty-Fifth Edition, completing 92,000. Crown 8vo, 3s. 6d.

"This is one of the most impressive and suggestive books on religion that we have read for a long time."—*Spectator.*

LONDON: HODDER & STOUGHTON, 27, PATERNOSTER ROW.

COMPLETION OF THE OLD TESTAMENT.

The Sermon Bible.

Each Volume contains upwards of Five Hundred Sermon Outlines and Several Thousand References.

Strongly bound in half buckram, price 7s. 6d. each.

I.
GENESIS TO 2 SAMUEL.

"We do not hesitate to pronounce this the most practically useful work of its kind at present extant. It is not a Commentary but a *Thesaurus* of sermons on texts, arranged consecutively chapter after chapter, and book after book. . . . We are bound to say that the object announced by the compilers is on the way to be realised, and here will be given the essence of the best homiletic literature of this generation."—*Literary Churchman.*

II.
1 KINGS TO PSALM LXXVI.

"Preachers anxious to discover the best books out of which they may collect golden thoughts on any particular text, for use in their sermons, will doubtless be glad of the volume before us, which aims at being a guide-book, pointing out where sermons and articles on those texts may be found. In addition to this, extracts from sermons are given in the book itself."—*English Churchman.*

III.
PSALM LXXVII. TO SONG OF SOLOMON.

"Such admirable epitomes of the best homiletic literature as are contained in this volume cannot fail to be helpful to preachers."—*London Quarterly Review.*

"Like its two predecessors, the third volume is distinguished by the perfect catholicity of the selections, the admirable condensation of the sermons and expositions that are quoted, and the fulness of the references to the best sermon literature on each of the texts. It is beyond question the richest treasury of modern homiletics which has ever issued from the press."—*Christian Leader.*

IV.
ISAIAH TO MALACHI.

"As a guide to the sermon literature of the day, and a mine of homiletic wealth, the 'Sermon Bible' occupies a place of usefulness peculiarly its own."—*Christian.*

"A great number of the best contemporary sermons are here rendered generally available in a very convenient form at a very low price indeed."—*Literary Churchman.*

"There is, as in previous volumes, great diversity of thought, the homiletic matter being the product of minds widely differing in theological views."—*Rock.*

LONDON : HODDER & STOUGHTON, 27, PATERNOSTER ROW.

PLEASE DO NOT REMOVE
CARDS OR SLIPS FROM THIS POCKET

UNIVERSITY OF TORONTO LIBRARY

BS   Smith, (Sir) George Adam
1515   The book of Isaiah
S56
1890
v.1

www.ingramcontent.com/pod-product-compliance
Lightning Source LLC
Chambersburg PA
CBHW051237300426
44114CB00011B/775